# Lecture Notes in Artificial Intelligence    4087

Edited by J. G. Carbonell and J. Siekmann

Subseries of Lecture Notes in Computer Science

Friedhelm Schwenker   Simone Marinai (Eds.)

# Artificial Neural Networks in Pattern Recognition

Second IAPR Workshop, ANNPR 2006
Ulm, Germany, August 31 – September 2, 2006
Proceedings

 Springer

Volume Editors

Friedhelm Schwenker
University of Ulm, Albert-Einstein-Allee 11, 89069 Ulm, Germany
E-mail: friedhelm.schwenker@uni-ulm.de

Simone Marinai
University of Florence, Via di Santa Marta 3, 50139 Florence , Italy
E-mail: simone.marinai@dsi.unifi.it

Library of Congress Control Number: 2006931356

CR Subject Classification (1998): I.2, I.5, I.4, H.3, F.2.2, J.3

LNCS Sublibrary: SL 7 – Artificial Intelligence

ISSN        0302-9743
ISBN-10     3-540-37951-7 Springer Berlin Heidelberg New York
ISBN-13     978-3-540-37951-5 Springer Berlin Heidelberg New York

Typesetting: Camera-ready by author, data conversion by Scientific Publishing Services, Chennai, India
Printed on acid-free paper        SPIN: 11829898        06/3142        5 4 3 2 1 0

# Preface

The second IAPR TC3 Workshop on Artificial Neural Networks in Pattern Recognition, ANNPR 2006, was held at the University of Ulm (Germany), August 31 - September 2, 2006. The Neural Networks and Computational Intelligence (TC3) group is one of the 20 Technical Committees of the International Association for Pattern Regognition (IAPR). The scope of TC3 includes Computational Intelligence approaches, such as fuzzy systems, evolutionary computing and artificial neural networks in various pattern recognition applications. ANNPR 2006 succeeded the outstanding first ANNPR workshop held at the University of Florence in September 2003 and focused on artificial neural networks inspired from pattern recognition tasks.

In recent years, the field of neural networks has matured considerably in both methodology and real-world applications. As reflected in this book, artificial neural networks in pattern recognition combine many ideas from machine learning, advanced statistics, signal and image processing, and statistical pattern recognition for solving complex real-world pattern recognition problems.

High quality across such a diverse field of research can only be achieved through a rigorous and selective review process. For this workshop, 49 papers were submitted out of which 26 were selected for inclusion in the proceedings. ANNPR 2006 featured research work in the areas of neural network learning – unsupervised, semi-supervised and supervised – support vector machines, multiple classifier systems, pattern recognition in image processing, and data mining in bioinformatics.

We would like to thank all authors for the effort they put into their submissions, and the Scientific Committee for taking the time to provide high-quality reviews and selecting the best contributions for the final workshop program.

A number of organizations supported ANNPR 2006 including the IAPR, in particular the TC3 of IAPR, the University of Ulm and the University of Florence. Last, but not least, we are grateful to Springer for publishing the ANNPR 2006 proceedings in their LNCS/LNAI series.


June 2006                                        Friedhelm Schwenker and Simone Marinai

# Organization

## Organization Committee

Simone Marinai, University of Florence (Italy)
Friedhelm Schwenker, University of Ulm (Germany)

## Program Committee

Shigeo Abe
Hervé Bourlard
Monica Bianchini
Horst Bunke
Patrick Gallinari
Neamat El Gayar
Marco Gori
Barbara Hammer

Tom Heskes
José Manuel Inesta
Rudolf Kruse
Cheng-Lin Liu
Marco Maggini
Erkki Oja
Günther Palm
Marcello Pelillo

Raul Rojas
Fabio Roli
Edmondo Trentin
Ad Chung Tsoi
Michel Verleysen
Stefan Wermter

## Sponsoring Institutions

# Table of Contents

## Unsupervised Learning

## Semi-supervised Learning

## Supervised Learning

## Support Vector Learning

## Multiple Classifier Systems

# Simple and Effective Connectionist Nonparametric Estimation of Probability Density Functions

Edmondo Trentin

Dipartimento di Ingegneria dell'Informazione
Università di Siena, V. Roma, 56 - Siena (Italy)

**Abstract.** Estimation of probability density functions (pdf) is one major topic in pattern recognition. Parametric techniques rely on an arbitrary assumption on the form of the underlying, unknown distribution. Nonparametric techniques remove this assumption In particular, the Parzen Window (PW) relies on a combination of local window functions centered in the patterns of a training sample. Although effective, PW suffers from several limitations. Artificial neural networks (ANN) are, in principle, an alternative family of nonparametric models. ANNs are intensively used to estimate probabilities (e.g., class-posterior probabilities), but they have not been exploited so far to estimate pdfs. This paper introduces a simple neural-based algorithm for unsupervised, nonparametric estimation of pdfs, relying on PW. The approach overcomes the limitations of PW, possibly leading to improved pdf models. An experimental demonstration of the behavior of the algorithm w.r.t. PW is presented, using random samples drawn from a standard exponential pdf.

## 1 Introduction

One major topic in pattern recognition is the problem of estimating probability density functions (pdf) [5]. Albeit popular, parametric techniques (e.g. maximum-likelihood for Gaussian mixtures) rely on an arbitrary assumption on the form of the underlying, unknown distribution [8]. Nonparametric techniques (e.g. $k_n$-nearest neighbors [4]) remove this assumption and attempt a direct estimation of the pdf from a data sample. The Parzen Window (PW) is one of the most popular nonparametric approaches to pdf estimation, relying on a combination of local window functions centered in the patterns of the training sample [5]. Although effective, PW suffers from several limitations, including:

(i) the estimate is not expressed in a compact functional form (i.e., a probability law), but it is a sum of as many local windows as the size of the sample;
(ii) the local nature of the window functions tend to yield a fragmented model, which is basically "memory based" and (by definition) is prone to overfitting;

F. Schwenker and S. Marinai (Eds.): ANNPR 2006, LNAI 4087, pp. 1–10, 2006.

(iii) the whole training sample has to be kept always in memory in order to compute the estimate of the pdf over any new (test) patterns, resulting in a high complexity of the technique in space and time;

(iv) the form of the window function chosen has a deep influence on the eventual form of the estimated model, unless an asymptotic case (i.e., infinite sample) is considered;

(v) the PW model heavily depends on the choice of an initial width of the local region of the feature space where the windows are centered.

Artificial neural networks (ANN) are, in principle, an alternative family of nonparametric models [6]. Given the "universal approximation" property [2] of certain ANN families (multilayer perceptrons [10] and radial basis function networks [9]), they might be a suitable model for any given (continuous) form of data distributions. While ANNs are intensively used for estimating probabilities [7] (e.g., posterior probabilities in classification tasks [2]), they have not been exploited so far for estimating pdfs. For instance, Bourlard and Morgan apply ANNs in order to estimate probabilistic quantities within a hidden Markov model (HMM) framework [3], but they use the ANN as a sate-posterior probability model, instead of modeling the emission-likelihoods that are required in the formal definition of standard HMMs. One of the main rationales behind this fact is that connectionist modeling of probabilities is easily (and somewhat heuristically) achieved by standard supervised backpropagation [10], once 0/1 target outputs are defined for the training data [2] (along the line of the Widrow-Hoff algorithm for linear discriminants [4]). Moreover, it is also simple to introduce constraints within the model that ensure the ANN may be interpreted in probabilistic terms, e.g. using sigmoid output activations (that range in the $(0, 1)$ interval), along with a softmax-like mechanism [1] which ensures that all the outputs sum to 1. Learning a pdf, on the contrary, is an unsupervised and far less obvious task.

This paper introduces a neural-based algorithm for unsupervised, nonparametric density estimation. The algorithm is presented in detail in Section 2, along with a concise review of the PW technique which is used within the ANN training scheme. The approach overcomes the limitations of PW, and it may lead to better pdf models than the PW itself. An experimental demonstration of the behavior of the algorithm w.r.t. PW is presented in Section 3, using random samples drawn from a standard exponential pdf.

## 2   The Proposed Estimation Algorithm

The algorithm is introduced by reviewing the basic concepts of PW estimation (refer to [4]). Let us consider a pdf $p(\mathbf{x})$, defined over a real-valued, $d$-dimensional feature space. The probability that a pattern $\mathbf{x}' \in \mathcal{R}^d$, drawn from $p(\mathbf{x})$, falls in a certain region $R$ of the feature space is $P = \int_R p(\mathbf{x})d\mathbf{x}$. Let then $\mathcal{T} = \{\mathbf{x}_1, \dots, \mathbf{x}_n\}$ be an unsupervised sample of $n$ patterns, identically and independently distributed (i.i.d.) according to $p(\mathbf{x})$. If $k_n$ patterns in $\mathcal{T}$ fall within

$R$, an empirical estimate of $P$ can be obtained as $P \simeq k_n/n$. If $p(\mathbf{x})$ is continuous and $R$ is small enough to prevent $p(\mathbf{x})$ from varying its value over $R$ in a significant manner, we are also allowed to write $\int_R p(\mathbf{x})d\mathbf{x} \simeq p(\mathbf{x}')V$, where $\mathbf{x}' \in R$, and $V$ is the volume of region $R$. As a consequence of the discussion, we can obtain an estimated value of the pdf $p(\mathbf{x})$ over pattern $\mathbf{x}'$ as:

$$p(\mathbf{x}') \simeq \frac{k_n/n}{V_n} \tag{1}$$

where $V_n$ denotes the volume of region $R_n$ (i.e., the choice of the region width is explicitly written as a function of $n$), assuming that smaller regions around $\mathbf{x}'$ are considered as the sample size $n$ increases. This is expected to allow Equation (1) to yield improved estimates of $p(\mathbf{x})$, i.e. to converge to the exact value of $p(\mathbf{x}')$ as $n$ (hence, also $k_n$) tends to infinity (a discussion of the asymptotic behavior of nonparametric models of this kind can be found in [4]).

The basic instance of the PW technique assumes that $R_n$ is a hypercube having edge $h_n$, such that $V_n = h_n^d$. The edge $h_n$ is usually defined as a function of $n$ as $h_n = h_1/\sqrt{n}$, in order to ensure a correct asymptotic behavior. The value $h_1$ has to be chosen empirically, and it heavily affects the resulting model. The formalization of the idea requires to define a unit-hypercube window function in the form

$$\varphi(\mathbf{y}) = \begin{cases} 1 & \text{if } \mid y_j \mid \leq 1/2, j = 1, \ldots, d \\ 0 & \text{otherwise} \end{cases} \tag{2}$$

such that $\varphi(\frac{\mathbf{x}'-\mathbf{x}}{h_n})$ has value 1 iff $\mathbf{x}'$ falls within the $d$-dimensional hypercubic region $R_n$ centered in $\mathbf{x}$ and having edge $h_n$. This implies that $k_n = \sum_{i=1}^n \varphi(\frac{\mathbf{x}'-\mathbf{x}_i}{h_n})$. Using this expression, from Equation (1) we can write

$$p(\mathbf{x}') \simeq \frac{1}{n} \sum_{i=1}^n \frac{1}{V_n} \varphi(\frac{\mathbf{x}' - \mathbf{x}_i}{h_n}) \tag{3}$$

which is the PW estimate of $p(\mathbf{x}')$ from the sample $\mathcal{T}$. The model is usually refined by considering smoother window functions $\varphi(.)$, instead of hypercubes, e.g. standard Gaussian kernels with zero mean and unit covariance matrix.

Let us now consider a feedforward ANN that we wish to train in order to learn a model of the probability law $p(\mathbf{x})$ from the unsupervised dataset $\mathcal{T}$. The idea is to use the PW model as a target output for the ANN, and to apply standard backpropagation to learn the ANN connection weights. A unbiased variant of this idea is proposed, according to the following unsupervised algorithm (expressed in pseudo-code):

```
Input: T = {x_1,...,x_n}, h_1.
Output: p̃(.) /*the connectionist estimate of p(.) */

1. Let h_n = h_1/√n
2. Let V_n = h_n^d
3. For i=1 to n do /* loop over T */
```

3.1             Let $\mathcal{T}_i = \mathcal{T} \setminus \{\mathbf{x}_i\}$

3.2             Let $y_i = \frac{1}{n} \sum_{\mathbf{x} \in \mathcal{T}_i} \frac{1}{V_n} \varphi(\frac{\mathbf{x}_i - \mathbf{x}}{h_n})$ /* target output */

4. Let $\mathcal{S} = \{(\mathbf{x}_i, y_i) \mid i = 1, \ldots, n\}$ /* supervised training set */

5. Train the ANN via backpropagation over $\mathcal{S}$

6. Let $\tilde{p}(.)$ be equal to the ANN

7. Return $\tilde{p}(.)$

We call the ANN trained this way the Parzen Neural Network (PNN). Since the PNN output is assumed to be an estimate of a pdf, it must be non-negative. This is granted once standard sigmoids (in the form $y = \frac{1}{1+e^{-x}}$) are used in the output layer. Standard sigmoids range in the $(0, 1)$ interval, while pdfs may take any positive value. For this reason, sigmoids with adaptive amplitude $\lambda$ (i.e., in the form $y = \frac{\lambda}{1+e^{-x}}$), as described in [11], should be taken into consideration. A direct alternative is using linear output activation functions, forcing negative outputs to zero once training is completed. Nevertheless, as in the $k_n$-nearest neighbor technique [4], the PNN is not necessarily a *pdf* (in general, the integral of $\tilde{p}(.)$ over the feature space is not 1).

There are two major aspects of the algorithm that shall be clearly pointed out. First, the PW generation of target outputs (steps 3-3.2) is unbiased. Computation of the target for $i$-th input pattern $\mathbf{x}_i$ does not involve $\mathbf{x}_i$ in the underlying PW model. This is crucial in smoothing the local nature of PW. In practice, the target (estimated pdf value) over $\mathbf{x}_i$ is determined by the concentration of patterns in the sample (different from $\mathbf{x}_i$) that occurs in the surroundings of $\mathbf{x}_i$. In particular, if an isolated pattern (i.e., an outlier) is considered, its exclusion from the PW model turns out to yield a close-to-zero target value. This phenomenon is evident along the possible tails of certain distributions, and it is observed in the experiments described in Section 3.

A second relevant aspect of the algorithm is that it trains the ANN only over the locations (in the feature space) of the patterns belonging to the original sample. At first glance, a different approach could look more promising: once the PW model has been estimated from $\mathcal{T}$, generate a huge supervised training set by covering the input interval in a "uniform" manner, and by evaluating target outputs via the PW model. A more homogeneous and exhaustive coverage of the feature space would be expected, as well as a more precise ANN approximation of the PW. As a matter of fact, training the ANN this way reduces its generalization capabilities, resulting in a more "nervous" surface of the estimated pdf, since the PW model has a natural tendency to yield unreliable estimates over regions of the feature space that are not covered by the training sample (again, refer to the experimental demonstration in Section 3).

It is immediately seen that, in spite of the simplicity of its training algorithm, the PNN is expected to overcome most of the PW limitations listed[1] in Section 1. The following Section highlights that, in addition, the PNN may turn out to be more accurate than the PW estimate.

---

[1] Response of the PNN w.r.t. point (i) in that list depends on the complexity of the ANN architecture that is used.

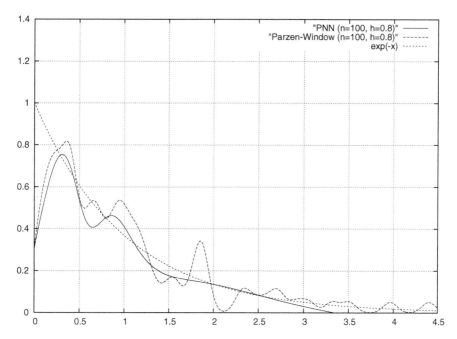

**Fig. 1.** Nonparametric estimates of the pdf from a random sample of 100 points drawn from the standard exponential distribution. Parzen-Window and PNN are estimated using an initial edge $h_1 = 0.8$.


## 3    Experimental Demonstration

A simple, illustrative estimation task is considered. Samples in this Section are randomly drawn from the popular exponential pdf, defined as

$$p(x) = \frac{1}{\beta} e^{-(x-\alpha)/\beta} \quad \text{with} \quad x \geq \alpha, \beta > 0 \tag{4}$$

where $\alpha$ is the location and $\beta$ is the scale. This distribution is unlikely to be modeled under a parametric assumption (e.g., via maximum-likelihood with a mixture of Gaussian densities), unless the form of Equation (4) is known in advance. The application of nonparametric techniques is sought. In the following experiments, a *standard* exponential distribution is used, having $\alpha = 0$ and $\beta = 1.0$.

In the first instance, a random sample of $n = 100$ points was generated according to $p(x)$. Figures 1–4 show the resulting PW and PNN models, estimated from the sample and plotted against the original pdf, for decreasing values of $h_1$. The latter ranged from 0.8 to 0.1. As expected, the PW estimates are heavily affected by the choice for $h_1$, and the shape of the corresponding estimated pdf is unnaturally peaked around the individual points in the training dataset. The overall trend of the original distribution is better fit for small values of $h_1$, but

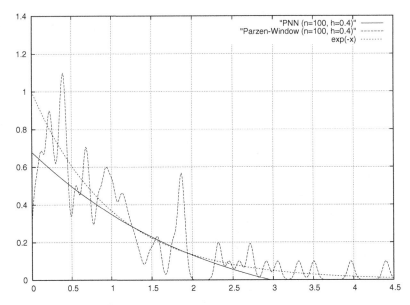

**Fig. 2.** Nonparametric estimates of the pdf from a random sample of 100 points drawn from the standard exponential distribution. Parzen-Window and PNN are estimated using an initial edge $h_1 = 0.4$.

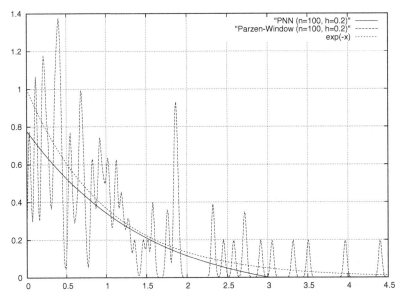

**Fig. 3.** Nonparametric estimates of the pdf from a random sample of 100 points drawn from the standard exponential distribution. Parzen-Window and PNN are estimated using an initial edge $h_1 = 0.2$.

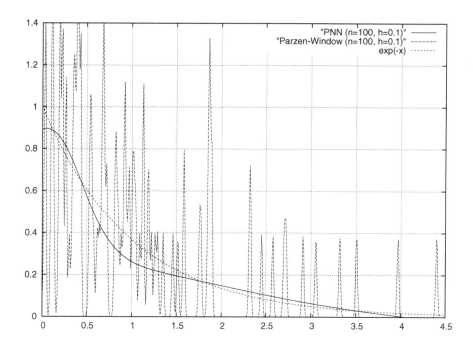

**Fig. 4.** Nonparametric estimates of the pdf from a random sample of 100 points drawn from the standard exponential distribution. Parzen-Window and PNN are estimated using an initial edge $h_1 = 0.1$.

the function obtained turns out to be very sensitive to local sampling irregularities. Moreover, the PW model includes peaks along the tail of the pdf, due to the presence of isolated points (within the sample) belonging to low-probability regions. The presence of local peaks basically violates the natural shape of the underlying pdf. Finally, as far as concerns complexity, the PW model requires the combination of $n = 100$ window functions, i.e. a total of 100 free parameters that had to be determined from the data.

The PNN is trained on the same values of $h_1$ as the corresponding PW. A compact ANN topology was used, namely 6 sigmoids in the hidden layer and a linear output unit. The latter is forced to non-negative values at test time, by converting negative outputs to zero. It is seen from the graphics that the PNN estimate is smoother, much closer to the reference exponential pdf than the PW is. Sensitivity to the choice of $h_1$ is significantly decreased w.r.t. PW. It is worth noticing the difference between the PNN curve and the form of the PW model that, roughly speaking, constitutes the target output for PNN during training. The unbiased nature of the training algorithm (steps 3-3.2) is further exploited in the avoidance of individual peaks, especially along the tail of the distribution. Complexity of the model is reduced in a substantial manner, as well, namely 18 free parameters to be learned from the data: 6 input-to-hidden weights, 6 hidden-to-output weights, and 6 individual bias (i.e. diagonalization) values for

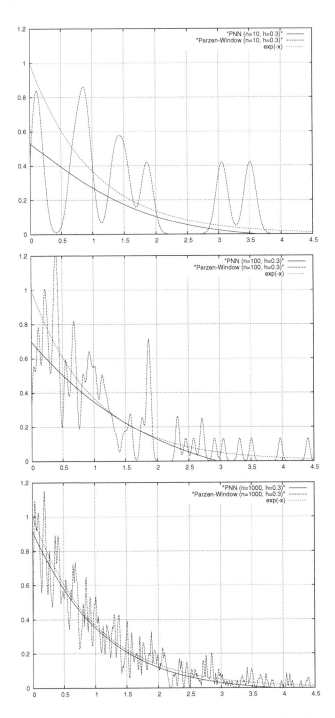

**Fig. 5.** Estimates of the pdf for an increasing sample size: $n = 10$ (top), $n = 100$ (mid), $n = 1000$ (bottom). Initial edge $h_1 = 0.3$.

the sigmoids. Experiments with an increased number of hidden units did not lead to significant improvement in the modeling capabilities of the PNN, and the contour of the estimated pdf remained basically the same.

Figure 5 plots the results obtained for an increasing number $n$ of training data. An intermediate value of $h_1 = 0.3$ was applied. The same PNN architecture described above was used. As expected, both PW and PNN models improve as the size of the sample increases. For $n = 1000$ the PNN (18 free parameters, 6 nonlinear functions to be evaluated and combined at test time) is close to the reference exponential pdf, PW (1000 free parameters, 1000 nonlinear functions to be evaluated and combined at test time), is still sensitive to individual training points and outliers (see, again, the tail of the distribution). In real-world applications, e.g. speech processing, the sample size (e.g., $n >> 1000$) may make the PW approach computationally infeasible at test time (too complex in space and time requirements), while the PNN (once the resource-demanding training process is completed) remains compact and efficient.

## 4    Conclusion

This paper presented a simple and effective neural-based nonparametric technique for the estimation of probability density functions. The estimation method can be seen as an unsupervised learning algorithm for neural networks, since it takes an unlabelled training sample and learns the proper ANN connection weights using the gradient method. A reference, unbiased PW estimate is used to drive the learning process. In this respect, it is worth underlining the strong difference in shape between the PW estimate and the corresponding PNN, i.e. the latter is not limited to approximate the PW closely. The PNN overcomes most of the limitations of classic nonparametric techniques, e.g. PW and $k_n$-nearest neighbor. As in the $k_n$-nearest neighbor case, the PNN is not in general a pdf, but the resulting model is expected to be close to the actual pdf and, eventually, useful. Standard regularization techniques [2] can be used to increase the generalization capabilities of the PNN, yielding even smoother pdf representations. We are currently carrying out experiments on real-world data for pattern classification problems.

## References

1. Y. Bengio. *Neural Networks for Speech and Sequence Recognition*. International Thomson Computer Press, London, UK, 1996.
2. C. M. Bishop. *Neural Networks for Pattern Recognition*. Oxford University Press, Oxford, 1995.
3. H. Bourlard and N. Morgan. *Connectionist Speech Recognition. A Hybrid Approach*, volume 247. Kluwer Academic Publishers, Boston, 1994.
4. R. O. Duda and P. E. Hart. *Pattern Classification and Scene Analysis*. Wiley, New York, 1973.
5. K. Fukunaga. *Statistical Pattern Recognition*. Academic Press, San Diego, second edition, 1990.

6. S. Haykin. *Neural Networks (A Comprehensive Foundation)*. Macmillan, New York, 1994.
7. D. Husmeier. *Neural Networks for Conditional Probability Estimation*. Springer-Verlag, London, 1999.
8. A.M. Mood, F.A. Graybill, and D.C. Boes. *Introduction to the Theory of Statistics*. McGraw-Hill International, Singapore, 3rd edition, 1974.
9. J. Park and I. W. Sandberg. Universal approximation using radial-basis-function networks. *Neural Computation*, 3(2):246–257, 1991.
10. D.E. Rumelhart, G.E. Hinton, and R.J. Williams. Learning internal representations by error propagation. In D.E. Rumelhart and J.L. McClelland, editors, *Parallel Distributed Processing*, volume 1, chapter 8, pages 318–362. MIT Press, Cambridge, 1986.
11. E. Trentin. Networks with trainable amplitude of activation functions. *Neural Networks*, 14(4–5):471–493, May 2001.

# Comparison Between Two Spatio-Temporal Organization Maps for Speech Recognition

Zouhour Neji Ben Salem[1], Laurent Bougrain[2], and Frédéric Alexandre[2]

[1] AI Unit, CRISTAL Laratory, National School of Computer Sciences,
Manouba Campus, Tunisia
zouhourbensalem@hotmail.com
[2] Cortex Team, LORIA Laboratory, Nancy, France
{Laurent.bougrain,Frederic.Alexandre}@loria.fr

**Abstract.** In this paper, we compare two models biologically inspired and gathering spatio-temporal data coding, representation and processing. These models are based on Self-Organizing Map (SOM) yielding to a Spatio-Temporel Organization Map (STOM). More precisely, the map is trained using two different spatio-temporal algorithms taking their roots in biological researches: The ST-Kohonen and the Time-Organized Map (TOM). These algorithms use two kinds of spatio-temporal data coding. The first one is based on the domain of complex numbers, while the second is based on the ISI (Inter Spike Interval). STOM is experimented in the field of speech recognition in order to evaluate its performance for such time variable application and to prove that biological models are capable of giving good results as stochastic and hybrid ones.

## 1 Introduction

Spatio-temporal classical connectionist networks comprise an important class of neural networks that can deal with patterns distributed both in time and space. In the case of Automatic Speech Recognition (ASR), this class of models have been shown to yield good performance (sometimes better than Hidden Markov Models) on short isolated speech units. By their recurrent aspect and their implicit or explicit temporal memory they can perform some kind of integration over time. Yet till now spatio-temporal biologically inspired models are the most less used for ASR. This class of models is very relevant to be exanimate because the advance realized in neurophysiologic researches have yield to the emergence of neuromimetic models especially for explicitly processing of temporal information and we know that in ASR, there is a time dimension or a sequential dimension which is highly variable and difficult to handle directly in ANNs. These models present an alternative approach to ASR which might in the long term help to overcome restrictions of current speech recognition technology with regard to noise tolerance or speaker independence. Some of these biological models have demonstrated good performance for ASR, we can cite the work of Béroule [20 ] concerning dynamic propagation or Durand [19 ] for super units map. In this paper we present STOM map extending the SOM map from the

F. Schwenker and S. Marinai (Eds.): ANNPR 2006, LNAI 4087, pp. 11–20, 2006.

processing of purely spatial signals to the processing of spatio-temporal signals using biologically inspired approaches and algorithms. Moreover, STOM represents the time dimension, depending on the parameters used, either as the level of weight or the map. The use of SOM in this paper is coming from the conviction of universal auto-organization concept covering the major part of human brain [11]. This concept could be able to explain all experimental findings concerning the plasticity of cortical to-pographies. A possible candidate for universal self-organization is the SOM map. STOM map will be trained using two different spatio-temporal algorithms. The first one is the ST-Kohonen algorithm proposed by Mozayyani [13]. It is an algorithm using spatio-temporal inputs which are represented by a spatio-temporal coding ap-proach proposed by Vaucher [12]. The latter uses the domain of complex numbers to encode inputs. The choice of this domain derives from the fact that it is the only do-main supplying two degree of freedom allowing to represent the two correlated data. The second algorithm is TOM (Time Organized Map) [11]. Its main additional idea comparing to SOM is the functionally reasonable transfer of temporal signal distances into spatial signals distances in topographic neural representations. This is achieved by neural dynamics of propagating waves. The inputs processed by this algorithm are encoded using an approach based on the ISI (Inter Spike Interval)[2],[16]. Each input is presented as a pair containing the spatial information of the stimuli, and the tempo-ral distance that separate it from its successor.

STOM is experimented in the domain of speech recognition of isolated digits. Sec-tion two of this paper presents the encoding approach used for STOM inputs, while section three is devoted to describe ST-Kohonen training model and propose also an extension of TOM for two dimensions. In section four, we show the application of the two encoding approaches to the analysis of acoustic signal and we compare experi-mental results between the two models obtained in the domain of speech recognition. Section five concludes the paper and presents some perspectives for the model.

## 2   The Spatio-Temporal Encoding Approaches

### 2.1   The Complex Approach

The spatio-temporal technique takes its roots from the work undertaken by neurobi-ologists to model passive electric properties of the dendrites trees [15], in particular Rall's work [17]. It is based on a particular modeling of the Post-Synaptic Potentials (PSP) and of their mix. According to the formalization made by Agmon-Snir [1], which characterizes one PSP(t) by its moments of order k, only the first two moment are kept, each one of them being respectively associated to the norm and phase of a complex number. The use of complex domain is justified by the fact that it is the only domain offering numbers having two degree of freedom. This property allows encod-ing the two correlated data at the same time. The Spatio-Temporal coding technique (Fig. 1.) is introduced for the aim to provide the classical artificial neurons the capac-ity of processing sequences in asynchronous manner, leading to the emergence of STANN [12] (Spatio-Temporal Artificial Neural Network). It consists on adding the delay; at the level of input; to introduce temporal information. It improves the work of 'Integrate and Fire' neuron [9], [7] using the field of complex numbers. The spatio-temporal coding is done as following: Each input produces a train of impulses, for each impulse or spike I characterized by its amplitude $\mu_I$ and the temporal delay $d_I$ which separates the current instant of time from the time at which the impulse has been occurred, a complex number $z_I$ is assigned. $z_I$ Contains $\mu_I$ as its module and $\varphi_I$ as its phase as following:

$$z_I = \mu_I e^{i\rho}{}_I$$
$$\rho_I = \arctan(\mu_t d_I)$$

(1)

$\mu_t$ is a constant inverse to time. To incorporate the attenuation of amplitude through time, the amplitude of the input could be calculated using the following formula:

$$\mu_I(t + \Delta t) = \mu_I(t)e^{-\mu_s \Delta t}$$

(2)

According to Baig [14], the couple ($\mu_s, \mu_t$) must satisfy the following condition in order to obtain a good complex encoding.

$$\mu_s = \mu_t = \frac{1}{T_w}$$

(3)

$T_W$ represents the temporal window used to encode all the coming inputs.

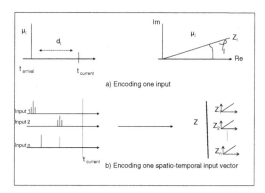

**Fig. 1.** The Spatio-Temporal Complex coding approach

## 2.2 The Temporal Coding Approach

Recent neurobiological findings experimented by Spengler et al [3] have demonstrated the importance of temporal interval between stimuli. In these experiments, tactile stimuli with different relations in space and time were applied to monkey. After months of training, the primary somatosensory cortex was mapped, showing that temporally separated stimuli (with an ISI of about 300ms) were segregated within cortical topography, while stimuli having an ISI under 100ms are integrated. Thus the dynamic of incoming stimuli reflects the stimuli's relatedness with regard to their functional meaning. Stimulus dynamic is therefore important for the learning of topography. Accordingly, many researchers think that the design of incoming flux of $n$ stimuli $S_i$ could be represented as sequence of couple containing the stimulus and $ISI_i$ interval expressing the temporal proximity of consecutive stimuli.

$$(S_i, ISI_i)$$

$$i = 1,..,n$$

(4)

# 3 Spatio-Temporal Training

## 3.1 The ST-Kohonen

ST-Kohonen map [14] is a SOM having complex neurons. These latter have input and weighting vectors defined in the complex domain as described in the above section. The ST-Kohonen algorithm works in the same manner as classical Kohonen one, however, the winner is chosen according to the hermitienne distance instead of the Euclidian one:

$$\delta(X, W_i) = \|X - W_i\| = \sqrt{{}^t(X - W_i)\overline{(X - W_i)}}$$

(5)

$X$ designes the map input and $W_i$ is the weighting vector of the neuron i. Both the input and the weight vectors are defined in the complex domain $C^p$. The adaptation rule for ST-Kohonen is the same as the one presented in Kohonen, yet we manage complex vectors instead of real. With ST-Kohonen we made a spatio-temporal classification which is very relevant in ASR because it allows classifying speech according to its feature extractors and their temporal occurrence or sequences. However, topology obtained by the map is spatial because weights are updated according to the distance of neurons in the map and not in the input space.

## 3.2 The Time Organized Map Algorithm (TOM)

The TOM algorithm was presented by Wiemer [11] for a better understanding of the self-organization and the geometric structure of cortical signal representations. TOM was proposed for one dimension SOM map, reader can refer to [11] for more details about the algorithm. In the present section, we present an extension of TOM for two dimensions.

High-dimensionally coded stimuli are applied to TOM two dimensions (Fig. 2.) at discrete times. They are described by a sequence $(S_n, ISI_n)$. The layer is composed of $N_1^c.N_2^c$ neurons ('c' for cortical). At time $t_n$, a stimulus $s_n = s_A(t_n)$ is presented to the map resulting in a feedforward activation obtained by multiplying the connection matrix with the stimulus: The activity $c_A(t_n)$ builds up from the current feedforward

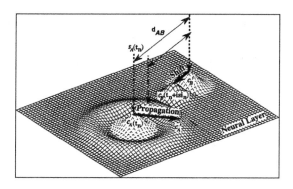

**Fig. 2.** Wave propagation and interaction in a two dimension TOM map

activation $c^{ff}(t_n)$, and the activity state of the map, that has evolved out of the earlier activity $c(t_{n-1})$ from time $t_{n-1}$ to $t_n$. The evolution of map activity between two stimulations is of wave-like type; excitation propagates into its surround. This dynamic may result from local interactions [5],[6],[8] e.g. between excitatory and inhibitory neurons. The dynamic is fundamental in the sense of a general principal of locality. In other words, 'effects propagate from point to neighboring point. In case of a monomodal and rotation symmetric of map activity, an 'elementary wave' propagates as is shown by Fig. 2. Assuming linear superposition, the dynamic corresponding to general activity patterns can be reduced to the superposition of elementary waves. As an analogue, one may think of water waves that a raindrop generates when it falls down. During the $isi_n$, and assuming a constant propagation speed, the wave has propagated along a certain distance reaching neurons having position that verify the following formula:

$$c'_A(n) = k_{ff}(n) \pm v.ISI_n \qquad (6)$$

Where $k_{ff}(n)$ is the neuron activated by the stimulus $s_A(t_n)$. The stimulus $s_B(t_n + isi_n)$ (applied at that time), generates also a feedforwrad activation resulting in the activity $c'_B$. This activity will propagates in the map yielding to an interaction zone between the two waves. Considering this interaction, the activity of the map must be shifted to towards this zone because it consists of neurons that are excited by the two stimuli. In a neural field model, and also in biological model [4] the length of the shift depends on the distances between the wave front of the stimulus $s_A(t_n)$, which is $c'_A(n)$, and $k_{ff}(n + isi_n)$, the neuron activated by $s_B(t_n + isi_n)$. This distance could be determined using the shortest path linking the two neurons $k_{ff}(n)$ and $k_{ff}(n + isi_n)$. Thus the two dimensional interaction could be reduced to one-dimensional interaction along this shortest path. This reduction allows us to apply one dimensional TOM algorithm along this path. The neurons that constitute this shortest path must have a coordinate $(i_k, j_k)$ verifying the following formula:

$j_k = round(A.i_k + b)$ and

$$[i_{k_{ff}(n)} < i_k < i_{k_{ff}(n+isi_n)} \text{ or } i_{k_{ff}(n+isi_n)} < i_k < i_{k_{ff}(n)}] \text{ and} \tag{7}$$

$$[j_{k_{ff}(n)} < j_k < j_{k_{ff}(n+isi_n)} \text{ or } j_{k_{ff}(n+isi_n)} < j_k < j_{k_{ff}(n)}]$$

Where:

$$A = \frac{j_{n+isi_n} - j_n}{i_{n+isi_n} - i_n}, \text{ et } b = j_n - A.i_n \tag{8}$$

$(i_n, j_n)$ and $(i_{n+isi_n}, j_{n+isi_n})$ are the coordinates of the neuron $k_{ff}(n)$ and $k_{ff}(n+isi_n)$. Once the path is determined, the different steps proposed for TOM one dimension algorithm could be applied. These steps are as follows:

## Determination of the Shift Toward the Interaction Zone Due to the Propagation of Waves

The interaction shift is calculated according to the distance that separates the current winner from the border of the propagation waves introduced by the earlier stimulus

$$\Delta_{int}(n) = f(c'_A(n) - k_{ff}(n)) \tag{9}$$

The interaction function $f$ expresses the distance dependency of the shift. Wiermer proposed the following function

$$f(k) = K.\tanh(\frac{k}{K})\exp(-\frac{k^2}{2\sigma_K^2}) \tag{10}$$

$K$ represents the strength of the interaction. The form of the interaction function is shown by (Fig. 3.) for different values of $K$ and $\sigma_K$.

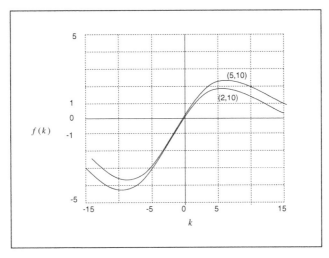

**Fig. 3.** The non linear interaction function for $(K, \sigma_k) = (5,10)$ et $(2,10)$

**Shift Due to Noise**
Noise in the network is expressed by a noise term that is randomly drawn from a normal distribution with zero mean and standard deviation

$$\Delta_{noise} \rightarrow N(0, \sigma_{noise}(n)) \tag{11}$$

The standard deviation decrease monotonically in time from its initial value $\sigma_0$ to its final value $\sigma_f$.

$$\sigma_{noise}(n) = \sigma_0 (\frac{\sigma_f}{\sigma_0})^{n/n'_f} \ \text{si} \ n \le n'_f \tag{12}$$

And remains constant to its final value for the remaining of the steps learning.

**New Winner Position**
The winner $k_{learn}(n)$ is determined as the integer closest to the position of the maximal feedforward activation shifted by interaction and noise.

$$k_{learn}(n) = round(k_{ff} + \Delta_{int} + \Delta_{noise}) \tag{13}$$

**New Winner Adaptation Weights**
Only winner weights are adapted by learning step. They are shifted toward the presented stimulus.

$$\Delta W_{k_{learn}(n)}(n) = \alpha.(S_n - W_{k_{learn}(n)}(n)) \tag{14}$$

$\alpha$ is the learning rate, it is constant during all the training.

## 4   Experimentation

### 4.1   The Data Coding and Model

The map is trained and tested with isolated words of TI-Digit database. The number of speakers contributing to the application is 110 distributed as 55 men and 55 women pronouncing the eleven vocal digits (0, 1, ..,9 and 'oh'). Each speaker pronounces one digit twice: one occurrence is used for the training and the other for the test. We use the Mel Frequency Cesptral Coefficients (MFCC) vectors [18] as feature extractor; it is composed of 12 coefficients. The speech signal were collected in quiet environment and digitized at 16 KHz. The window size for calculating each MFCC contains 512 points. Windows are overlapping and are separated with 10ms (160 points) between two consecutive MFCC. To permit the spatio-temporal coding with complex numbers, we suppose that all coefficients for one MFCC vector have the same time of occurrence. Thus, complex MFCC vectors will have the following form:

$$MFCC_{real} = \left\{ \begin{matrix} c_1 \\ \cdot \\ .. \\ c_{12} \end{matrix} \right\} \Rightarrow MFCC_{complex} = \left\{ \begin{matrix} c_1 e^{i\rho_1} \\ \cdot \\ .. \\ c_{12} e^{i\rho_1} \end{matrix} \right\} \tag{15}$$

The phase is calculated using the following formula:

$$\rho_i = \arctan(1 - 0.01(i-1)) \tag{16}$$

The temporal encoding approach is straight forward. In fact each input is couple of the following form:

$$(S_n, isi_n) = \left( \left\{ \begin{matrix} c_1 \\ ... \\ c_{12} \end{matrix} \right\}, 10ms \right) \tag{17}$$

## 4.2 Experimental Results

STOM is tested by either ST-Kohonen algorithm or TOM in speech recognition. For the TOM algorithm, we have used the same parameters proposed by Wiemer which are as follows: $v = 1, K = 5, \sigma_k = \sigma_0 = 15, \sigma_f = 0.1, \alpha = 0.01, n'_f = 0.1.10^9$.

These parameters are determined empirically and have demonstrated good results comparing to other values.

**Table 1.** Three protocols for digit recognition using ST-Kohonen and TOM models

| Recognition rate | ST-Kohonen | TOM |
|---|---|---|
| Monolocutor | 98,56% | 99,34% |
| Speaker independent | 97,5% | 98,32% |
| Unknown locutor | 96,9% | 98,45% |

In order to evaluate the learning and robustness capacities of the two models, we have tested them for digit recognition using three distinct protocols: the monolocutor recognition, the speaker independent recognition and the unknown locator recognition. For the monolocutor, we take the first occurrence of digits as learning base and the second occurrence as test base. In the Speaker independent protocol, all first occurrences of each digit form the learning base and all second occurrences of digits form the test base. For unknown locator, 28 of women and men first occurrences are taken for learning base and the 27 others for the test base. The results are reported in the above table (Table 1.). For the three protocols TOM model performs better than the spatio-temporal classification made by ST-Kohonen. Indeed, the spatio-temporal interaction between inputs can capture more the fine spatio-temporal structure inherent to speech signal. However, the main drawback of TOM is the time of convergence. In fact, the algorithm has needed $10^9$ loops to converge. This slowness could be interpreted by the fact that TOM update only the winner by each loop yielding to an increasing of time for the map to be organized. ST-Kohonen presents better result compared to other time-based neural networks [10]; this fact is explained by the use of coding approach gathering spatio-temporal data as inputs allowing a spatio-temporal classification.

## 5   Conclusion

The Spatio-temporal Organization Maps presented in this paper are an extension of SOM map to spatio-temporal domain. This extension is based on biologically inspired approaches related to coding or processing data. STOM is trained using two spatio-temporal processing algorithms. The results obtained by applying STOM in speech recognition are good and both algorithms are qualified for processing the fine spatio-temporal structure of speech signal. This might provide an insight into speech recognition using biologically models and could in the long run overcome the limitation of HMM-based speech technology or hybrid models regarding for example noise. Further research could be focused on testing the presented models using corpus collected in real world. It could be also possible to combine biologically model for speech perception, a model of human cochlea for example,  with STOM because we think that it can be a fruitful area that needs to be explored.

## References

1. Agmon-Snir, H. and Segev, I. :Signal Delay and iInput Synchronization in Passive Dendritic Structures. Journal of Neurophysiology, 70(5) (1973).
2. Cariani, P.:As If Time Really Mattered: Temporal Strategies for Neural Coding of Sensory Information'. CC-AI. 12(1-2) (1995).
3. Spengler, F. Hilger, T. Wang, X. and  Merzenich, M:Learning induced formation of cortical populations involved in tactile object recognition. Social Neurosciences. 22. (1999) 105-110.
4. Wilson, H. Cowan, J.:A mathematical theory of the functional dynamics of cortical and thalamic nervous tissue. Biology Cybernetic. 13 (1973) 55-80.
5. Amari,S.:Topographic organization of nerve fields. Bull Math Biology. 42 (1980) 339-364.
6. Szentagothai, J.:The module concept in cerebral cortex architecture. Brain research (1995) 475-496.
7. Vinh ho, H. :Un reseau de neurons a decharge pour la reconnaissance des processus spatio-temporels..PhD thesis,  Genie Electric Department, Monreal University  (1992).
8. Wiemer, J. Spengler, F. Joublin, F. and Wacquant, S.:Learning cortical topography from spatiotemporal stimuli. Biology cybernetic. 82 (2000) 173-187.
9. Casti, A. R. R. Omurtag, A., Sornborger, A., aplan, E.,  Knight, B., Victor, J.,  Sirovich, L.:A population study of integrate and fire or burst neuron,  Neural Computation, Volume 14 Issue 5 (2002).
10. Laurence, S. Tsoi, A. C. Back, A. D. : The gamma MLP for speech phoneme recognition. Advances in Neural Information Processing System, 8  (1996) 785-791.
11. Wiemer, J. C.:The Time-Organized Map (TOM) algorithm: extending the self-organizing map (SOM) to spatiotemporal signals. Neural Networks, 15 (2003).

12. Vaucher, G. :A la recherche d'une algerbre neuronale spatio-temporal. P.hD thesis. Nancy University (1996).
13. Mozayyani, N., Alanou, V., Derfus, J. and Vaucher, G.:A spatio-temporal data coding applied to kohonen maps. Inter conf on Artificial Neural Natwork (1995) 75-79.
14. Baig, A. B. :Une approche methodologique de l'utilisation des STAN applique a la reconnaissance visuelle de la parole. PhD thesis, Suplec, campus universitaire de rennes (2000).
15. Vaucher, G.:A Complex-Valued spiking machine, ICANN (2003) 967-976.
16. Thorpe, S.:Spiking arrival times: Ahighly efficient coding scheme for neural networks. In Parallel Processing in Neural System, Elseiver Press (1990).
17. Rall, W.:Core conductor theory and cable properties. In handbookof physiology:the nervous system, Americain physiology society (1977).
18. Calliope. La parole et son traitement automatique. *Masson*, Paris, Milan , Barcelone, (1989).
19. Durand, S.:Learning speech as acoustic sequences with the unsupervised model TOM. In NEURAP, 8th international conference on neural networks and their applications. Marseille french 1995.
20. Béroulle, D. :Un modèle de mémoire adaptative, dynamique et associative, pour le traitement automatique de la parole. Thèse de l'université de Paris 11 (1985).

# Adaptive Feedback Inhibition Improves Pattern Discrimination Learning

Frank Michler, Thomas Wachtler, and Reinhard Eckhorn

AppliedPhysics/NeuroPhysics Group, Department of Physics,
Philipps-University Marburg, Renthof 7, D-35032 Marburg, Germany
frank.michler@physik.uni-marburg.de
http://www.physik.uni-marburg.de

**Abstract.** Neural network models for unsupervised pattern recognition learning are challenged when the difference between the patterns of the training set is small. The standard neural network architecture for pattern recognition learning consists of adaptive forward connections and lateral inhibition, which provides competition between output neurons. We propose an additional adaptive inhibitory feedback mechanism, to emphasize the difference between training patterns and improve learning. We present an implementation of adaptive feedback inhibition for spiking neural network models, based on spike timing dependent plasticity (STDP). When the inhibitory feedback connections are adjusted using an anti-Hebbian learning rule, feedback inhibition suppresses the redundant activity of input units which code the overlap between similar stimuli. We show, that learning speed and pattern discriminatability can be increased by adding this mechanism to the standard architecture.

## 1 Introduction

### 1.1 Standard Architecture

Standard neural networks for unsupervised pattern recognition learning typically consist of adaptive forward connections and lateral inhibition (e.g. Fukushima 1975; Földiák 1990). Usually, the forward connections are modified using Hebbian learning rules: if pre- and postsynaptic activity is highly correlated, excitatory synapses are strengthened while inhibitory synapses are weakened. For excitatory synapses, Hebbian learning increases the correlation between pre- and postsynaptic activity and the connections grow infinitely. Connection strengths can be limited e.g. by using normalization mechanisms.

Lateral inhibitory connections introduce a *winner-take-all (WTA)* dynamics: if an output neuron is strongly activated, other output neurons receive strong inhibition and generate little or no output activity. WTA prevents the output neurons from being active all at the same time. When the lateral inhibitory connections are learned with an *anti-Hebbian* learning rule, as proposed by Földiák (1990), connections are strengthened if correlation between pre- and postsynaptic activity is high. Thus, strongly correlated output neurons will have strong inhibitory connections, which will reduce their correlation. This decorrelation can lead to a sparse representation of the input stimuli (Földiák,

F. Schwenker and S. Marinai (Eds.): ANNPR 2006, LNAI 4087, pp. 21–32, 2006.

1990). After self-organization, the neurons in the output layer of such networks should respond selectively to a single stimulus pattern or a subset of the training set, depending on the relation between the size of the stimulus set and the number of output neurons.

## 1.2   Improving Discrimination Performance with Feedback Inhibition

Consider a two layer network with an input and an output layer, and lateral inhibition between output neurons. What happens when the network is trained with a set of very similar stimuli? Typically the forward connections from the uninformative input neurons coding the overlap between stimuli will become much stronger compared to the connections coding features unique to certain stimuli (Fukushima, 1975; Földiák, 1990). Beyond a certain degree of stimulus similarity the output neurons only respond to the overlap, and thus fail to discriminate between the stimuli. Miyake and Fukushima (1984) proposed a mechanism to improve pattern selectivity fur such situations: they introduced a simple version of modifiable inhibitory feedback connections from the output units to the input units. These connections were paired with modifiable excitatory feedforward connections. When a feedforward connection was strengthened, the corresponding feedback connection was strengthened as well.

In this paper we show that this adaptive feedback inhibition can be generalized and adapted to a biologically more realistic network model with spiking neurons and *spike timing dependent plasticity (STDP)* based learning rule (Bi and Poo, 1998). We systematically varied the overlap between the patterns of the stimulus set and show how learning speed and selectivity increases after introducing modifiable inhibitory feedback connections.

Using spiking neural network models aims towards an understanding of how pattern recognition problems could be solved in the brain. If a mechanism can not be implemented with biologically realistic spiking neurons, then it is unlikely that this mechanism is used in the brain. Furthermore spiking neurons provide for high temporal precision, which is relevant for real-world applications. This is the case e.g. for spatio-temporal pattern recognition or for audio patterns.

## 2   Model

### 2.1   Network Architecture

The network is organized in two layers of spiking neurons: the *input layer* $U_0$ and the *representation layer* $U_1$ (Fig. 1). There are excitatory forward connections from $U_0$ to $U_1$ and lateral inhibitory connections between all $U_1$ neurons. These connections are adapted due to the correlation between presynaptic and postsynaptic spikes with a Hebbian and anti-Hebbian learning rule, respectively (Section 2.3). So far this is the standard architecture for competitive learning. Additionally, we introduce modifiable inhibitory feedback connections from $U_1$ to $U_0$. These inhibitory connections are also adapted using an anti-Hebbian learning rule.

### 2.2   Model Neurons

As a spiking model neuron we use the two dimensional system of differential equations proposed by Izhikevich (2003):

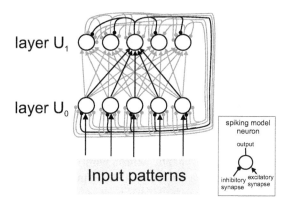

**Fig. 1.** Model architecture. The neurons of the input layer $U_0$ are activated when they are part of the current input pattern. $U_0$ neurons have modifiable excitatory connections to the representation layer $U_1$. $U_1$ neurons mutually inhibit each other. Additionally there are modifiable inhibitory feedback connections from $U_1$ to $U_0$. To better illustrate the network structure, connections from and to one of the neurons are plotted with black color while the other connections are plotted gray.

$$\frac{dV(t)}{dt} = 0.04V^2(t) + fV(t) + e - U(t) + I(t), \tag{1}$$

$$\frac{dU(t)}{dt} = a(bV(t) - U(t)) \tag{2}$$

with the auxiliary after-spike reseting:

$$\text{if } V(t) \geq 30mV, \text{ then } \begin{cases} V(t) \leftarrow c, \\ U(t) \leftarrow U(t) + d. \end{cases} \tag{3}$$

$V(t)$ and $U(t)$ are dimensionless variables. $V(t)$ represents the membrane potentials in $mV$. $I(t)$ is the synaptic input current. $a$, $b$, $c$, $d$, $e$ and $f$ are dimensionless parameters which determine the properties of the model neuron. In the simulations presented here we use a set of parameters which correspond to regular spiking cortical pyramidal neurons (example "L" in Izhikevich, 2004, a=0.02, b=-0.1, c=-55, d=6, e=108, f=4.1). The excitatory synaptic input $I_e$ is modelled as a current injection with additional noise $\sigma(t)$. The inhibitory input $I_i$ is modelled as a conductance based current. The excitatory synaptic input saturates at $I_{e,max}$. The inhibitory conductance saturates at $G_{i,max}$:

$$I = S_e(I_e) - S_i(G_i)(V - E_i), \tag{4}$$

$$S_e(I_e) = I_{e,max}\frac{I_e}{I_e + 1}, \tag{5}$$

$$S_i(G_i) = G_{i,max}\frac{G_i}{G_i + 1}, \tag{6}$$

$$\frac{d}{dt}I_e = -\frac{1}{\tau_e}I_e + \sum_{m=0}^{M-1} w_{e,m}\delta_m(t) + \sigma(t), \tag{7}$$

$$\frac{d}{dt}G_i = -\frac{1}{\tau_i}G_i + \sum_{m=0}^{M-1} w_{i,m}\delta_m(t). \tag{8}$$

The saturation constants were set to $I_{e,max} = 200$ and $G_{i,max} = 4.5$ to restrict excitatory and inhibitory input to a range where the numerical integration of the differential equations still works properly for $dt = 0.25ms$. The excitatory and inhibitory synaptic currents decrease exponentially with time constant $\tau_e$ and $\tau_i$ respectively, which were arbitrarily set to $5ms$. The biologically realistic range for the decay time constants of excitatory $AMPA$- and inhibitory $GABA_A$-currents is from 5 up to 50 ms. $w_{e,m}$ is the excitatory weight from the presynaptic neuron number $m$. $\delta_m(t)$ is 1 when a spike arrives at the presynaptic site, otherwise it is 0. $E_i$ is the reverse potential for the inhibitory current which was chosen to be 10 mV lower then the resting potential.

## 2.3   Learning Rules

The synaptic weight $w_{m,n}$ of the connection from presynaptic $U_0$ neuron $m$ to postsynaptic $U_1$ neuron $n$ is adapted according to a Hebbian learning rule:

$$\frac{d}{dt}w_{m,n} = \delta_n(t)RL_{pre,m}L_{post,n}, \tag{9}$$

$$L_{pre,m} = \sum_{t_{sm}} e^{-\frac{t-t_{sm}}{\tau_{pre}}}, \tag{10}$$

$$L_{post,n} = \sum_{t_{sn}} e^{-\frac{t-t_{sn}}{\tau_{post}}}. \tag{11}$$

$\delta_n(t)$ is 1 when a spike occurs in the postsynaptic neuron $n$. $t_{sm}$ and $t_{sn}$ denote the times of the past pre- and postsynaptic spikes. When a spike occurs, the pre- or postsynaptic *learning potentials* $L_{pre,m}$ or $L_{post,n}$ are increased by 1. They exponentially decrease with time constant $\tau_{pre} = 20ms$ and $\tau_{post} = 10ms$. $R$ is a constant corresponding to the learning rate and was tuned to allow for a weight change between 5 and 20 % after 10 stimulus presentations. For the excitatory connections from layer $U_0$ to $U_1$, we use a quadratic normalization rule:

$$w_{m,n}(t) = W\frac{w_{m,n}(t-dt)}{\sqrt{\sum_{m=0}^{M-1} w_{m,n}^2(t-dt)}}, \tag{12}$$

where $W$ is a constant value to adjust the quadratic weight sum. This prevents infinite growing of weights and introduces competition between the input synapses of a postsynaptic neuron. Physiological evidence for the existence of such heterosynaptic interactions were found, e.g., by Royer and Paré (2003). $W$ was set to a value which ensured a medium response activity at the beginning of the learning phase.

For the inhibitory connections we use the following anti-Hebbian learning rule:

$$\frac{d}{dt}w_{m,n} = R\left(\delta_n(t)L_{pre,m} - C\delta_m(t)w_{m,n}L_{post,n}\right), \tag{13}$$

$$L_{pre,m} = e^{-\frac{t-t_{sm}}{\tau_{pre}}}, \tag{14}$$

$$L_{post,n} = e^{-\frac{t-t_{sn}}{\tau_{post}}}. \tag{15}$$

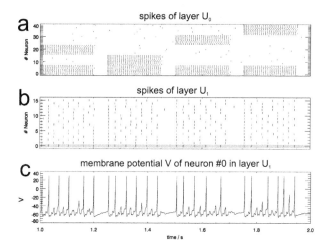

**Fig. 2.** Network without feedback inhibition, response before learning. a: Spikes of input layer $U_0$. b: Spikes of representation layer $U_1$. c: Membrane potential $V(t)$ of neuron #0 of $U_1$ (gray line in b).

The equations are very similar to the Hebbian learning rule (equation 9) but with an additional depression term. The decay time constants of the learning potentials were set to $\tau_{pre} = 30ms$ and $\tau_{post} = 100ms$. $C$ is a constant to adjust the ratio between potentiation and depression which determines the amount of inhibition. With lower $C$ the inhibitory connections will be stronger. $C$ was set to 0.005 for the feedback inhibition and 0.001 for the lateral inhibition. $t_{sm}$ and $t_{sn}$ denote the time of the last pre- and post- synaptic spike event respectively.

## 2.4   Stimuli

The input stimuli are binary spatial patterns that lead to additive modulation of excitatory synaptic current $I_e$ (equation 4) of layer $U_0$ neurons:

$$I_e(t) = \sum_{i \in N} p_n^{k_i} I_0 rect\left(\frac{t - i\tau_1}{\tau_2}\right),\tag{16}$$

$$rect(t) = \begin{cases} 1 : |t| < 0.5 \\ 0 : otherwise \,. \end{cases}\tag{17}$$

$p_{k_i}^n$ is 1 if the neuron $n$ is active for stimulus $k_i$, and 0 otherwise. $I_0$ is the input strength. $\tau_1$ is the time difference between stimulus onsets, $\tau_2$ is the duration of a single stimulus presentation (see Fig. 2 for an example). $k_1, k_2, ..., k_i$ is a random sequence of stimulus numbers.

For a systematic variation of the similarity between the input patterns, we constructed sets of stimuli as follows: each stimulus is a binary pattern $P_k$ of $N_{U_0}$ elements where $N_{U_0}$ is the number of neurons in the input layer.

$$P_k = (p_1^k, p_2^k, p_3^k, ..., p_{N_{U_0}}^k),\tag{18}$$

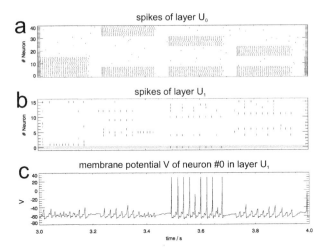

**Fig. 3.** Network without feedback inhibition, response after learning. a: Spikes of input layer $U_0$. b: Spikes of representation layer $U_1$. c: Membrane potential $V(t)$ of neuron #0 of $U_1$ (gray line in b).

$$p_m^k = \begin{cases} 1 \;, m \leq n_o \\ 1 \;, n_o + n_u(m-1) < m \leq n_o + n_u m \\ 0 \;, otherwise \;. \end{cases} \tag{19}$$

$n_a = f_a N_{U_0}$ is the number and $f_a$ the fraction of active neurons in each pattern. $n_o = f_o n_a$ is the number of neurons which are active in each pattern (overlap) and $n_u = n_a - n_o$ is the number of neurons which are unique for each pattern.

## 2.5  Performance Measure

In order to quantify the ability of the network to discriminate between the stimuli, we simulated a test phase after every learning phase. In the test phases the network was stimulated with the same input patterns as in the learning phases. We calculated the preferred stimulus $\kappa_n$ and a selectivity index $\eta_n$ for every $U_1$ neuron:

$$\kappa_n = \big\{ k : R_{n,k} = max(\{R_{n,1}, ..., R_{1,K}\}) \big\}, \tag{20}$$

$$\eta_n = \frac{R_{n,\kappa_n}}{\sum_{k=0}^{K} R_{n,k}} - \frac{1}{K} \;. \tag{21}$$

$K$ is the number of stimuli. $\kappa_n$ is the number of the stimulus which evokes the maximal response in $U_1$ neuron $n$. The selectivity index $\eta_n$ is 0 if all stimuli evoke the same response $R_{n,k}$, which means that this neuron bears no information about the identity of the stimulus. The maximum selectivity is $\frac{K-1}{K}$ when only one stimulus evokes a response but the others do not. From the following test phase we calculated how the activity of the $U_1$ neurons predict the identity of the input patterns: for each stimulus onset we derived the response $r_{n,i}$ for every $U_1$ neuron (number of spikes in a specified interval after stimulus onset), where $j$ is the number of the current stimulus. Combining

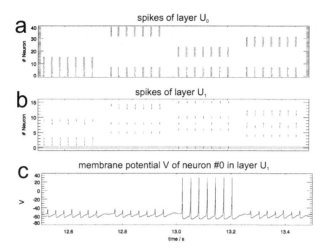

**Fig. 4.** Network with feedback inhibition, response after learning. a: Spikes of input layer $U_0$. b: Spikes of representation layer $U_1$. c: Membrane potential $V(t)$ of neuron #0 of $U_1$ (gray line in b). The feedback inhibition circuit causes rhythmic spike patterns in both layers.

these responses with the preference and the selectivity of the neurons, we calculated the stimulus $\nu_j$ predicted by this network activity:

$$\nu_j = \big\{ k : \xi_k = max(\{\xi_1, ..., \xi_K\}) \big\}, \tag{22}$$

$$\xi_k = \sum_{n \in \{i : \kappa_i = k\}} \eta_n r_{n,k} . \tag{23}$$

If $\nu_j = j$ then the prediction is correct, otherwise it is false. The performance $\rho$ is then $\rho = \frac{n_{hit}}{n_{hit} + n_{fail}}$ where $n_{hit}$ is the number of correct predictions and $n_{fail}$ the number of mistakes. The chance level is $\frac{1}{K}$.

## 3   Results

First we demonstrate the properties of the network without feedback inhibition for a stimulus set with little overlap (50%). The number of stimuli was $K = 4$. The numbers of neurons were: $N_{U_0} = 40$ and $N_{U_1} = 16$. Before learning, the network responds unselectively to the input stimuli (Fig. 2). The network quickly converges to a selective state: for each stimulus there is at least one $U_1$ neuron that selectively responds to it (Fig. 3).

When we systematically increased the overlap between the elements of the stimulus set the network needed longer to reach a selective state. When the overlap was very high it completely failed to discriminate between the stimuli (Fig. 5).

When we added the modifiable inhibitory feedback connections, the network took less time steps to reach a selective state. Even for high overlap, where it had failed without feedback inhibition, the network learned a selective representations (Fig. 6). Furthermore, the feedback inhibition causes rhythmic spike patterns in both layers and synchronizes the activated neurons (Fig. 4).

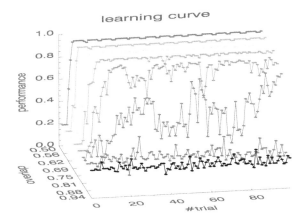

**Fig. 5.** Learning curves without feedback inhibition. A *trial* consisted of 40 stimulus presentations. For overlap up to 75% the network quickly learned a selective representation. For higher overlap it took longer training time to reach a selective state. For overlap higher than 88% the network stayed in an unselective state. Input strength: $I_0 = 0.008$.

Because the feedback inhibition reduces the spiking activity in $U_0$, we compensated this effect by increasing excitatory input strength $I_0$ (see equation 16) when turning on the feedback inhibition. To make sure that the differences in learning speed and learning performance were not caused by these parameter changes, we systematically tested the effect of different input strengths. We calculated a performance index for each $I_0$ value by averaging the performance values for the second half of learning trials over all overlap levels. Without feedback inhibition the maximum performance of the network (at $I_0 \approx 0.008$) was still lower than the maximum performance of the network with feedback inhibition (Fig. 7).

## 4   Discussion

Our simulations show that in a network of spiking neurons adaptive feedback inhibition can speed up learning of selective responses and enable discrimination of very similar input stimuli. The mechanism works as follows: While the network is in an unselective state, the correlation between the output units and these input units which code the overlap ($p_1^k...p_{n_o}^k$ in Eq. 18) is higher than the correlation between the output units and the input units which are unique for different patterns. Therefore, the inhibitory connections to the input neurons representing the overlap will grow stronger and the redundant activity will be reduced. In contrast, the input neurons coding the difference between the stimuli receive less inhibition. Thus, the network can use the discriminative information carried by these neurons to learn a selective representation.

The network parameters were chosen in a biologically realistic range. The input strength $I_0$ and the feed forward weight sum $W$ were set to obtain reasonable firing rates. The learning parameters that control the inhibitory connections ($C$, $\tau_{pre}$, $\tau_{post}$) must be guanrantee a substantial amount of inhibition. Overall the mechanism doesn't

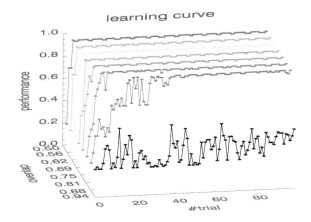

**Fig. 6.** Learning curves with feedback inhibition ; a *trial* consisted of 40 stimulus presentations. For the low overlap stimulus sets (50% - 81%) the network converged to a selective state faster than without feedback inhibition. Even for very high overlap (94%) the network still learned some selectivity. Input strength: $I_0 = 0.016$.

depend on the precise values of the parameters. Small or medium parameter changes do not qualitatively alter the properties of the network.

## 4.1 Comparison to Other Models

Miyake and Fukushima (1984) had already proposed a inhibitory feedback mechanism and showed how it could be included in their Cognitron model. They demonstrated the increased selectivity using stimulus pairs with up to 50% spatial overlap. As our simulations show, such an amount of overlap can still be separated using a network without feedback inhibition (Fig. 5).

Spratling (1999) had proposed a *pre-integration lateral inhibition* model. In this model for example an output neuron $O_i$ which has strong excitatory connection from input neuron $I_j$ will have strong inhibitory influence on the excitatory connections from $I_j$ to the other output neurons $O_{k \neq i}$. Spratling and Johnson (2002) showed that *pre-integration lateral inhibition* can enhance unsupervised learning. Spratling (1999) argues against the feedback inhibition model, that an output neuron cannot entirely inhibit the input to all other neurons without entirely inhibiting its own input. van Ooyen and Nienhuis (1993) point out a similar argument: With feedback inhibition the Cognitron model fails to elicit sustained responses for familiar patterns, because the corresponding input activity is deleted. But these drawbacks do not hold in our dynamic model: After strong activation of an output neuron $O_i$, the feedback inhibition will suppress the input and thus prevent all output neurons from firing including $O_i$. Inhibition is reduced, and excitatory input can grow again. Thus, for sustained input, the inhibitory feedback generates rhythmic chopping of both input and output layer neurons (Fig. 4). The strongest activated output neurons are able to fire output spikes before inhibition grows, while weakly activated output neurons are kept subthreshold. Furthermore, the

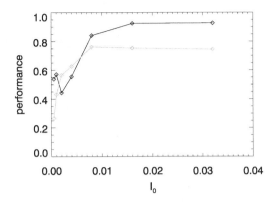

**Fig. 7.** Performance depends on input strength $I_0$. The data points show mean performance values, averaged over all overlap values and the second half of the learning trials. Black: Performance with feedback inhibition. Green (gray): Performance without feedback inhibition. Note that with feedback inhibition the network reaches higher performance values (90% compared to 75%).

common feedback inhibition tends to synchronize the activity of these input neurons which are part of the recognized pattern. Such a synchronization has been proposed to support object recognition through dynamic grouping of visual features (see e.g. Eckhorn, 1999; Eckhorn et al., 2004). In the model presented here, synchronization occurs as a consequence of successful pattern recognition.

The adaptive feedback inhibition model is in line with predictive coding models (Rao and Ballard, 1997). These models are based on the working principle of extended Kalman filters, where a prediction signal is subtracted from the input. Thus, in these models the predicted (expected) information is suppressed. This approach is the opposite to the *Adaptive-Resonance-Theorie (ART)*, which is based on enhancement of predicted information (Grossberg, 2001).

### 4.2   Physiological Equivalent

What could be a physiological basis for the proposed feedback inhibition mechanism? The main input to a cortical area arrives in layer 4 (Callaway, 1998). For example, layer 4 of the primary visual cortex receives input from the thalamic relay neurons of the lateral geniculate nucleus (LGN). Neurons in layer 2/3 have more complex receptive fields. They represent the main output of a cortical module to other cortical areas (Callaway, 1998). Thus, layer $U_0$ of our model corresponds to cortical layer 4 and layer $U_1$ to cortical layer 2/3.

Among direct input from thalamic relay neurons, layer 6 neurons receive feedback connections from layer 2/3. In visual area V1 they project back to the LGN but also have collaterals which project to layer 4, where they mainly target inhibitory interneurons (Beierlein et al., 2003). Thus, the anatomy of the neocortex provides the necessary connections for adaptive feedback inhibition: *layer 4 → layer 2/3 → layer 6 → inhibitory*

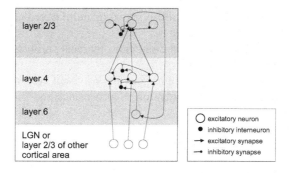

**Fig. 8.** Possible microcircuit underlying selective feedback inhibition: information enters the cortical module via layer 4, layer 2/3 learns selective representation of input patterns and projects back to layer 6, layer 6 neurons have projections to inhibitory interneurons in layer 4

*interneurons of layer 4.* This microcircuit could provide the basis for the suppression of uninformative input activity (Fig. 8).

We have shown, that adaptive feedback inhibition can increase learning speed and improve discrimination of highly similar patterns. For simplicity, we used a small set of simple stimulus patterns. The proposed mechanism can also be used for recognition of more complex patterns (e.g. 3d visual objects), if it is incorporated in a hierarchical multi-layer network architecture with feedback inhibition from higher to lower layers.

## Acknowledgements

This work was supported by DFG grant EC 53/11.

## References

**Beierlein, M., Gibson, J. R., Connors, B. W. (2003)**. Two dynamically distinct inhibitory networks in layer 4 of the neocortex. Journal of Neurophysiology 90, 2987–3000.

**Bi, G., Poo, M. (1998)**. Synaptic modifications in cultured hippocampal neurons: Dependence on spike timing, synaptic strength, and postsynaptic cell type. The Journal of Neuroscience 18 (24), 10464–10472.

**Callaway, E. M. (1998)**. Local circuits in primary visual cortex of the macaque monkey. Annual Review of Neuroscience 21, 47–74.

**Eckhorn, R. (1999)**. Neural mechanisms of scene segmentation: Recordins from the visual cortex suggest basic circuits for linking field models. IEEE Transactions on Neural Networks 10 (3), 464–479.

**Eckhorn, R., Bruns, A., Gabriel, A., Al-Shaikhli, B., Saam, M. (2004)**. Different types of signal coupling in the visual cortex related to neural mechanisms of associative processing and perception. IEEE Transactions on Neural Networks 15 (5), 1039–1052.

**Fukushima, K. (1975)**. Cognitron: A self-organizing multilayered neural network. Biological Cybernetics 20, 121–136.

**Földiák, P. (1990)**. Forming sparse representations by local anti-hebbian learning. Biological Cybernetics 64, 165–170.

**Grossberg, S. (2001)**. Linking the laminar circuits of visual cortex to visual perception: Development, grouping and attention. Neuroscience and Biobeavioral Revies 25, 513–526.

**Izhikevich, E. M. (2003)**. Simple model of spiking neurons. IEEE Transactions on Neural Networks 14 (6), 1569–1572.

**Izhikevich, E. M. (2004)**. Which model to use for cortical spiking neurons? IEEE Transactions on Neural Networks 15 (5), 1063–1070.

**Miyake, S., Fukushima, K. (1984)**. A neural network model for the mechanism of feature-extraction. A self-organizing network with feedback inhibition. Biological Cybernetics 50, 377–384.

**Rao, R. P. N., Ballard, D. H. (1997)**. Dynamic model of visual recognition predicts neural response properties in the visual cortex. Neural Computation 9, 721–763.

**Royer, S., Paré, D. (2003)**. Conservation of total synaptic weight through balanced synaptic depression and potentiation. Nature 422, 518–522.

**Spratling, M. W. (1999)**. Pre-synaptic lateral inhibition provides a better arcitecture for self-organizing neural networks. Network: Computation in Neural Systems 10, 285–301.

**Spratling, M. W., Johnson, M. H. (2002)**. Pre-integration lateral inhibition enhances unsupervised learning. Neural Computation 14 (9), 2157–2179.

**van Ooyen, A., Nienhuis, B. (1993)**. Pattern recognition in the neocognitron is improved by neuronal adaptation. Biological Cybernetics 70, 47–53.

# Supervised Batch Neural Gas

Barbara Hammer[1], Alexander Hasenfuss[1],
Frank-Michael Schleif[2], and Thomas Villmann[3]

[1] Clausthal University of Technology, Institute of Computer Science,
Clausthal-Zellerfeld, Germany
[2] University of Leipzig, Institute of Computer Science, Germany
[3] University of Leipzig, Clinic for Psychotherapy, Leipzig, Germany

**Abstract.** Recently, two extensions of neural gas have been proposed: a
fast batch version of neural gas for data given in advance, and extensions
of neural gas to learn a (possibly fuzzy) supervised classification. Here we
propose a batch version for supervised neural gas training which allows to
efficiently learn a prototype-based classification, provided training data
are given beforehand. The method relies on a simpler cost function than
online supervised neural gas and leads to simpler update formulas. We
prove convergence of the algorithm in a general framework, which also
incorporates supervised k-means and supervised batch-SOM, and which
opens the way towards metric adaptation as well as application to proximity data not embedded in a real-vector space.

## 1 Introduction

Prototype-based classification constitutes an intuitive machine learning technique which represents classes by typical prototype locations and assigns labels
to new data points by means of a winner-takes-all rule. Unlike feedforward networks or support vector machines (SVM), the method provides insight into the
classification behavior by an inspection of the prototypes. Interestingly, the generalization behavior of prototype-based techniques is quite robust, since generalization bounds which only depend on the hypothesis margin but not on the
number of parameters of the model (in particular the input dimensionality) can
be derived similar to SVMs [4].

One of the most popular learning techniques for prototype-based methods
is Kohonen's learning vector quantization (LVQ) and variants and extensions
thereof [7,10]. Thereby, LVQ is based on heuristics and applies Hebbian learning
to the respective winning prototype. Several extensions of the basic algorithm
substitute this heuristic by adaptation rules which are derived from a cost function [7]. However, these methods rely on local adaptations. Therefore they easily
get stuck in local optima if dealing with multimodal data. Modifications using
neighborhood cooperation avoid this problem, such as the proposal presented in
[6], which integrates the dynamics of unsupervised neural gas (NG) [12] into the
adaptation.

Another problem of LVQ type classifiers is given by the fact that class labels
are necessarily crisp in these learning algorithms. Fuzzy-labeled data cannot be

F. Schwenker and S. Marinai (Eds.): ANNPR 2006, LNAI 4087, pp. 33–45, 2006.

learned and it is not possible to indicate ambiguous regions of the data space by a fuzzy labeling of the prototypes. Recently, an extension of unsupervised neural gas clustering to a supervised fuzzy classifier, namely fuzzy labeled neural gas (FLNG), has been proposed [16]. Obviously, NG can trivially be expanded to a classifier by posterior labeling of the prototypes. However, in this case the prototype locations are not adapted according to the labels, but according to the data statistics only. The basic idea of FLNG consists in an extension of the NG cost function by a term measuring the deviation of the class labels from the data points and prototypes, whereby the latter are automatically adapted during training. Adaptation takes place by means of a stochastic gradient descent on the resulting cost function, whereas the class labels influence the prototype locations.

This general idea faces the problem that the extension of the NG cost function by the quantization error of the labels as proposed in [16] for discrete data is not differentiable at the borders of the receptive fields. Therefore, modifications are necessary. For continuous data the article [16] proposes approximations which are differentiable and which lead to quite complicated update terms for the prototypes and class labels. Here, we consider a different extension of the cost function and a different optimization scheme, batch learning, which allows a direct optimization of the quantization error and which yields very simple and intuitive update rules. In addition, it shares the fast convergence of (unsupervised) batch NG as introduced in [3]. We test the method on several data sets.

Similar to supervised batch NG, it is possible to extend other popular batch clustering algorithms such as k-means and the batch self-organizing map (SOM) [10] to supervised classification. We integrate these approaches into a common framework by means of the cost function, and we show convergence of general batch optimization. Thereby, the possibility to adapt metric parameters as has been used in recent LVQ versions [6] is also included. In addition, the application to general proximity data which is not embedded in a euclidian vector space becomes possible by median versions of the optimization scheme as introduced in [11]. We shortly discuss these possibilities covered by the general framework.

## 2  Unsupervised Clustering

Assume data vectors $\mathbf{v} \in \mathbb{R}^d$ are given as stimuli, distributed according to an underlying probability distribution $P(\mathbf{v})$. The aim of prototype-based unsupervised clustering is to find a number of prototypes or weight vectors $\mathbf{w}_i \in \mathbb{R}^d$, $i = 1, \ldots, n$ representing the data points faithfully, e.g. measured in terms of the average deviation of a data point from its respective closest prototype. There exist different possibilities to achieve this goal: The objective of neural gas [12] is a minimization of the cost function

$$E_{\mathrm{NG}}(W) = \frac{1}{2C(\lambda)} \sum_{i=1}^{n} \int h_\lambda(k_i(\mathbf{v}, W)) \cdot (\mathbf{v} - \mathbf{w}_i)^2 P(\mathbf{v}) d\mathbf{v}$$

where $k_i(\mathbf{v}, W) = |\{\mathbf{w}_j \,|\, (\mathbf{v} - \mathbf{w}_j)^2 < (\mathbf{v} - \mathbf{w}_i)^2\}|$ is the rank of prototype $i$, $h_\lambda(t)$ is a Gaussian shaped curve such as $h_\lambda(t) = \exp(-t/\lambda)$ with neighborhood range $\lambda > 0$, and $C(\lambda)$ is a normalization constant. Typically, online adaptation takes place by means of a stochastic gradient descent method. The resulting learning rule adapts all prototypes after the presentation of each stimulus by a small step, whereby the rank determines the adaptation strength. Recently, an alternative batch adaptation scheme for this cost function has been proposed which, for a given finite training set, in turn, determines the rank $k_i(\mathbf{v}, W)$ according to fixed prototype locations and the prototype locations as average of all training points weighted according to their rank, until convergence. Batch adaptation can be interpreted as Newton optimization of the cost function, and often a fast convergence can be observed compared to online adaptation.

K-means directly minimizes the quantization error

$$E_{\mathrm{k-means}}(W) = \frac{1}{2} \sum_{i=1}^{n} \int \chi_i(\mathbf{v}, W) \cdot (\mathbf{v} - \mathbf{w}_i)^2 P(\mathbf{v}) d\mathbf{v}$$

where $W$ denotes the set of prototypes and $\chi_i(\mathbf{v}, W)$ indicates the receptive field of prototype $\mathbf{w}_i$; i.e. it is one iff the data point $\mathbf{v}$ is closest to $\mathbf{w}_i$ and it is zero, otherwise. Typically, the function is optimized by a batch update scheme for a given finite set of training points $\mathbf{v}_1, \ldots, \mathbf{v}_p$ drawn according to $P(\mathbf{v})$. The algorithm iteratively assigns the given training points to their respective closest prototypes and sets the prototype locations $\mathbf{w}_i$ to the centers of gravity of the current receptive fields as indicated by the assignment, until convergence. This scheme can be interpreted as Newton optimization of $E_{\mathrm{k-means}}$ [1]. Unlike NG, k-means relies on the initialization of prototypes and typically fails to find a global or even good local optimum of $E_{\mathrm{k-means}}$ if the cost function is multimodal. Neural gas offers a very robust alternative that is insensitive to initialization due to neighborhood cooperation.

A third popular unsupervised learning scheme is given by the self-organizing map which includes neighborhood cooperation according to a priorly fixed lattice structure of the neurons. SOM is less flexible than NG, since the lattice topology need not fit the data topology. However, a fixed lattice offers the possibility of easy visualization e.g. using a two-dimensional regular lattice. The original SOM does not possess a cost function. A slight variation of SOM proposed by Heskes [8] has the cost function

$$E_{\mathrm{SOM}}(W) = \frac{1}{2C(\lambda)} \sum_{i=1}^{n} \int \chi_i^*(\mathbf{v}, W) \cdot \sum_{l=1}^{n} h_\lambda(\mathrm{nd}(i, l)) \cdot (\mathbf{v} - \mathbf{w}_l)^2 P(\mathbf{v}) d\mathbf{v}$$

where $C(\lambda)$ is again a constant, $\mathrm{nd}(i, j)$ denotes the neighborhood range of neuron $i$ and $j$ on the priorly fixed lattice, and $\chi_i^*(\mathbf{v}, W)$ is one for neuron $i$ iff the average $\sum_{l=1}^{n} h_\lambda(\mathrm{nd}(i, l)) \cdot (\mathbf{v} - \mathbf{w}_i)^2$ is minimum, otherwise it is zero. For SOM, batch as well as online adaptation schemes are used in practice. SOM constitutes a very popular method for data mining and data visualization [10].

For all formulations, batch adaptation schemes provide an interface towards clustering general proximity data for which only pairwise distances of the data points are given but in general no embedding within a real-vector space is available. The euclidian distance is substituted by the given proximities, and optimization of prototypes takes place within the discrete space given by the data points, as proposed in [3,11].

## 3   Supervised Batch NG

Often, additional information in the form of class labels is available. That means, additional class labels $y_i$ are given for every data point $\mathbf{v}_i$. We assume that $y_i \in \mathbb{R}^d$, $d$ being the number of classes. This notion subsumes crisp classification with unary encoded class information as well as fuzzy assignments to $d$ classes. The general aim of clustering provided additional label information can be twofold: either unsupervised clustering, mining, or visualization of the given data whereby the additional cluster information should be taken into account as much as possible to achieve a meaningful result; or direct supervised classification according to the given class labels. Both aims can be incorporated into prototype-based clustering by an extension of the overall cost function such that the information given by the class labels is taken into account. First promising steps into this direction can be found in the aproach [16] for online NG. Each prototype $\mathbf{w}_i$ is equipped with an additional vector $Y_i \in \mathbb{R}^d$ which should represent the class labels of data points in the receptive field as accurately as possible. The cost function of NG is extended to

$$\alpha \cdot E_{\mathrm{NG}}(W) + (1 - \alpha) \cdot E_{\mathrm{NG-Y}}(W, Y)$$

whereby $E_{\mathrm{NG}}(W)$, as beforehand, measures the quantization error of prototypes, $E_{\mathrm{NG-Y}}(W, Y)$ measures the error introduced by the difference of class labels of data points and prototypes, and $\alpha \in [0, 1]$ constitutes a weighting of the two objectives. A natural choice of the latter term is

$$E_{\mathrm{NG-Y}}(W, Y) = \frac{1}{2C(\lambda)} \sum_{i=1}^{n} \int h_\lambda(k_i(\mathbf{v}, W)) \cdot (y - Y_i)^2 P(\mathbf{v}) d\mathbf{v}$$

However, as pointed out in [16], this cost function is not differentiable at the borders of the receptive fields. The approach presented in [16] proposes to substitute the term $h_\lambda(k_i(\mathbf{v}, W))$ by an analytic approximation, which yields update rules for $W$ and $Y$.

Here, we consider a simpler solution. The cost function of supervised NG becomes

$$E_{\mathrm{BSNG}}(W, Y) = \alpha \cdot \frac{1}{2C(\lambda)} \sum_{i=1}^{n} \int h_\lambda(k_i(\mathbf{v}, y, W, Y)) \cdot (\mathbf{v} - \mathbf{w}_i)^2 P(\mathbf{v}) d\mathbf{v}$$

$$+ (1 - \alpha) \cdot \frac{1}{2C(\lambda)} \sum_{i=1}^{n} \int h_\lambda(k_i(\mathbf{v}, y, W, Y)) \cdot (y - Y_i)^2 P(\mathbf{v}) d\mathbf{v}$$

where $k_i(\mathbf{v}, y, W, Y) = |\{\mathbf{w}_j \mid \alpha(\mathbf{v} - \mathbf{w}_j)^2 + (1 - \alpha)(y - Y_j)^2 < \alpha(\mathbf{v} - \mathbf{w}_i)^2 + (1 - \alpha)(y - Y_i)^2\}|$ denotes the rank of prototype $i$ measured according to the closeness of the current data point and the prototype weight and labeling. Thus, it constitutes an average over the quantization error of the prototypes and labels, weighted according to the rank taken over both, prototype and label closeness. This cost function corresponds to original (unsupervised) NG applied to the embedded data points $(\sqrt{\alpha} \cdot \mathbf{v}, \sqrt{1 - \alpha} \cdot y)$, thus it is differentiable at borders of receptive fields.

Batch adaptation schemes suppose that a finite set of training data $(\mathbf{v}_1, y_1)$, $\ldots$, $(\mathbf{v}_p, y_p)$ is given in advance. The cost function becomes

$$\hat{E}_{\text{BSNG}}(W, Y) = \frac{1}{2C(\lambda)} \sum_{i=1}^{n} \sum_{j=1}^{p} h_\lambda(k_i(\mathbf{v}_j, y_j, W, Y))$$

$$\left(\alpha \cdot (\mathbf{v}_j - \mathbf{w}_i)^2 + (1 - \alpha) \cdot (y_j - Y_i)^2\right)$$

Batch optimization determines in turn the hidden variables $k_{ij} := k_i(\mathbf{v}_j, y_j, W, Y)$ and the weights and labels $W$ and $Y$ until convergence. This yields the following update rules of **supervised-batch-NG (BSNG)**:

**(1)** For given $W$, $Y$, set $k_{ij} = |\{\mathbf{w}_l \mid \alpha \cdot (\mathbf{v}_j - \mathbf{w}_l)^2 + (1 - \alpha) \cdot (y_j - Y_l)^2 \leq \alpha \cdot (\mathbf{v}_j - \mathbf{w}_i)^2 + (1 - \alpha) \cdot (y_j - Y_i)^2\}|$ as the rank of prototype $i$ given $\mathbf{v}_j$.
**(2)** For fixed $k_{ij}$, set $\mathbf{w}_i = \sum_j h_\lambda(k_{ij}) \cdot \mathbf{v}_j / \sum_j h_\lambda(k_{ij})$, and $Y_i = \sum_j h_\lambda(k_{ij}) \cdot y_j / \sum_j h_\lambda(k_{ij})$.

Note that the assignments of the receptive fields and the rank depend on the closeness of the prototype as well as the correctness of its class label. The new prototypes are determined as center of gravity of all data points weighted according to this rank, the same holds for the class labels.

One can consider this scheme as Newton optimization of the cost term $\hat{E}_{\text{BSNG}}(W, Y)$: the updates within a Newton scheme are $\Delta(W, Y) = -J \cdot H^{-1}$ where $J$ is the Jacobian of $\hat{E}$ and $H$ is the Hessian. Since $k_{ij}$ is locally constant, we get up to sets of measure zero $\partial \hat{E}_{\text{BSNG}}/\partial \mathbf{w}_i = (\alpha/C(\lambda)) \cdot \sum_j h_\lambda(k_{ij})(\mathbf{w}_i - \mathbf{v}_j)$ and $\partial \hat{E}_{\text{BSNG}}/\partial Y_i = (\alpha/C(\lambda)) \cdot \sum_j h_\lambda(k_{ij})(Y_i - y_j)$. The Hessian equals a diagonal matrix with entries $\partial^2 \hat{E}_{\text{BSNG}}/\partial \mathbf{w}_i^2 = (\alpha/C(\lambda)) \cdot \sum_j h_\lambda(k_{ij})$ and $\partial \hat{E}_{\text{BSNG}}/\partial Y_i^2 = (\alpha/C(\lambda)) \cdot \sum_j h_\lambda(k_{ij})$. Obviously, this corresponds to the batch updates of $W$ and $Y$.

Before proving convergence of supervised batch NG in a general framework, which also incorporates supervised batch SOM and supervised k-means, we test the algorithm on several datasets. So far, the experiments are preliminary, and further studies, in particular in combination with more powerful approaches as will be discussed in section 5, are the subject of future work.

## 3.1  Artificial Data

The main difference of NG with posterior labeling and BSNG consists in the fact that the rank assignments also take the fact into account whether the labels

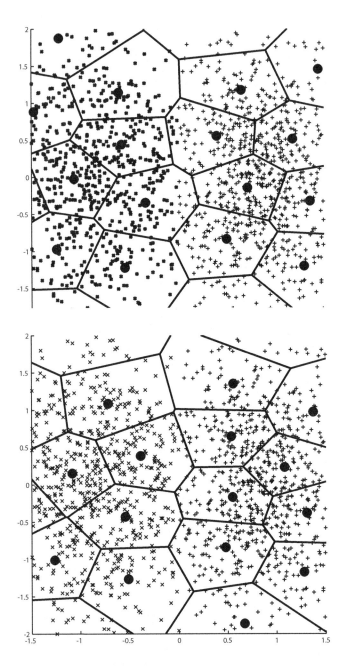

**Fig. 1.** Receptive fields obtained by batch NG (top) and BSNG (bottom) on an artificial two-dimensional data set. Obviously, the incorporation of the label information for BSNG yields a better separation of the two classes; the prototype locations follow the classification boundary

fit. This has the effect that the prototypes of BSNG better account for cluster borders of labeled data points, whereas NG only follows the overall statistics. The parameter $\alpha$ controls the strength of the label contribution, $\alpha = 1$ corresponds to standard NG. This effect can be clearly observed in the following example. We consider two Gaussian clusters labeled by 0 resp. 1, whereby points with x-component at least 0 are dropped for class 0, and points with x-component at most 0 are dropped for class 1. Hence, the classes are well separated, whereby a couple of data points lies close to the decision boundary. Fig. 1 shows a typical result of the receptive fields of the prototypes obtained by batch NG and BSNG with mixing parameter $\alpha = 0.1$, respectively. Thereby, prototypes of NG are labeled by a majority vote within the receptive field. Fuzzy labels for BSNG arise automatically during training, these are turned into crisp classes based on the largest component of the label vector. Obviously, BSNG well approximates the decision border, whereas NG yields a couple of errors at this region. This corresponds to the classification accuracy of 99.1% for BSNG and 97.8% for NG.

## 3.2   Iris Data

We train batch NG and BSNG using 9 prototypes on the well-known iris dataset [13], which consists in the task to classify 150 points characterized by 4 real-valued attributes into 3 classes of equal size. Class 1 is well separated from class 2 and 3, but classes 2 and 3 slightly overlap. For each run, the set is randomly divided into a training and test set of equal size, and averages over 50 runs are reported. The neighborhood range $\lambda$ is multiplicatively annealed starting from 4.5 over 100 training epochs. Different values of the mixing parameter $\alpha$ are

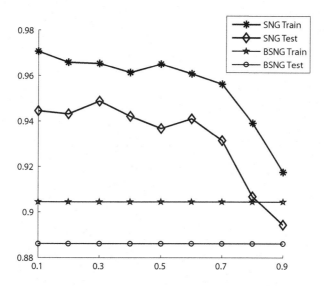

**Fig. 2.** Accuracy on the training and test set achieved by supervised batch NG (BSNG) and batch NG (BNG) on the iris dataset for different mixing parameters $\alpha$

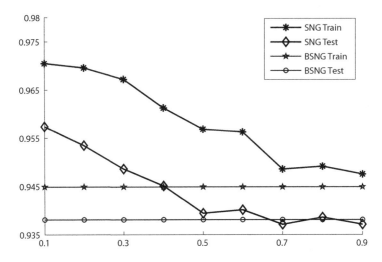

**Fig. 3.** Accuracy on the training and test set achieved by supervised batch NG (BSNG) and batch NG (BNG) on the Wisconsin breast cancer dataset for different mixing parameters $\alpha$

reported. The classification accuracy on the training and test set for BSNG and, in comparison, for NG with posterior labeling can be observed in Fig.2. Obviously, the classification accuracy becomes better for smaller $\alpha$, i.e. more emphasis of the given data labels. Thereby $\alpha$ must not become 0 which corresponds to a pure label adaptation without adaptation of the prototypes. $\alpha = 1$ corresponds to standard NG. Obviously, the classification accuracy of simple NG is inferior compared to the supervised version due to the overlap of classes 2 and 3 which is not accounted for by the overall statistics of the input vectors. The algorithm reported in [16] (Gaussian approximation) achieves (in a single run with parameter $\alpha = 0.5$) a training set accuracy of 0.85 and test set accuracy of 0.91 using 9 prototypes, thus it is better than post labeled NG, but worse compared to supervised batch NG for this parameter choice.

### 3.3   Wisconsin Breast Cancer

The Wisconsin breast cancer data consists of nearly 600 data points described by 30 real-valued input features which are to be separated into 2 classes. Training uses 20 prototypes and the same parameters as beforehand, starting with an initial neighborhood range 10. The results are presented in Fig.3. As before, a larger emphasis on the correctness of the labels yields a better classification accuracy which is superior to neural gas. Interestingly, the approach presented in [16] which relies on a different supervised extension of NG (Gaussian approximation of the rank) achieves an accuracy of 0.92 for the training set and 0.91 on the test set for a mixing parameter 0.5, which is in this case worse than the result obtained by NG with posterior labeling.

# 4   Perspectives – General Supervised Batch Clustering

Now, we introduce a general cost function and a batch adaptation scheme for supervised prototype-based clustering which extends SOM, NG, and k-means by two aspects: the integration and adaptation of a (possibly fuzzy) labeling and potential adaptation of metric parameters according to the overall objective. The proposal includes BSNG introduced above as a special case.

Note that, for a finite set of training data $\mathbf{v}_1, \ldots, \mathbf{v}_p$, the cost function of SOM, NG, and k-means can be written as

$$\hat{E}(W) = \sum_{i=1}^{n} \sum_{j=1}^{p} f_1(k_{ij}(W)) \cdot f_2^{ij}(W)$$

where (neglecting constants) $f_1(k_{ij}(W))$ is given by $\chi_i(\mathbf{v}_j, W)$, $h_\lambda(k_i(\mathbf{v}_j, W))$, or $\chi_i^*(\mathbf{v}_j, W)$, respectively, and $f_2^{ij}(W)$ constitutes the squared distance $(\mathbf{v}_j - \mathbf{w}_i)^2$ or the average $\sum_{l=1}^{n} h_\lambda(\mathrm{nd}(i, l)) \cdot (\mathbf{v}_j - \mathbf{w}_l)^2$, respectively. We extend this cost function in two respects: we assume that each training vector $\mathbf{v}_j$ is accompanied by a priorly given label $y_j$ and each prototype $\mathbf{w}_i$ is equipped by a label $Y_i$. The labels $Y$ are adapted according to the data labels $y$ during training such that $Y_i$ represents the class information of the data points in the receptive field of $\mathbf{w}_i$, as introduced for batch NG in the previous section. In addition, we extend the metric by possibly adaptive metric parameters $\Lambda$ which allow a better shaping of the classifier according to the given task. Adaptive metric parameters are quite common in supervised as well as unsupervised clustering [5,9,14,6,7], since the choice of the metric severely influences the final classification ability of the models. Therefore, this possibility should be included in a general framework.

The general cost function of supervised clustering becomes

$$\hat{E}(W, \Lambda, Y) = \sum_{i=1}^{n} \sum_{j=1}^{p} f_1(k_{ij}(W, \Lambda, Y)) \cdot \left( \alpha \cdot f_2^{ij}(W, \Lambda) + (1 - \alpha) \cdot d(Y_i, y_j) \right)$$

where $d$ measures the distance of the two labels (e.g. the squared euclidian distance) and $\alpha \in [0, 1]$ controls the weighting of the two parts of this cost function, unsupervised vector quantization and correct labeling of the prototypes. Thereby, the parameters might be subject to constraints, i.e. $\lambda \in X_\Lambda$, $W \in X_W$, and $Y \in X_Y$.

We introduce a general batch optimization scheme of $\hat{E}(W, \Lambda, Y)$ and we show its convergence. We assume that $k_{ij}(W, \Lambda, Y)$ constitutes a function which maps given parameter values to unique assignments (possibly after introducing some order) within a finite set $X_K$ such that it optimizes $\hat{E}$ for fixed parameters $W$, $\Lambda$, and $Y$. Thereby, constraints might apply: for SOM and k-means, the assignments $k_{ij}$ constitute unary vectors for fixed $j$; for NG, they constitute a permutation of $\{0, \ldots, n - 1\}$. This assumption allows us to optimize the cost function $\hat{E}$ consecutively for the parameters of $\hat{E}$ and hidden variables $k_{ij}$ connected to the function $k_{ij}(W, \Lambda, Y)$. General batch optimization of $\hat{E}$ proceeds in two steps;

after an initialization of the parameters, the following two optimization steps are performed until convergence

(1) for given $W$, $\Lambda$, $Y$, find $k_{ij}$ in $X_K$ (possibly subject to constraints) such that

$$\sum_{i=1}^{n}\sum_{j=1}^{p} f_1(k_{ij}) \cdot \left(\alpha \cdot f_2^{ij}(W, \Lambda) + (1-\alpha) \cdot d(Y_i, y_j)\right)$$

is minimum;

(2) for given $k_{ij}$, find $W \in X_W$, $\Lambda \in X_\Lambda$, and $Y \in X_Y$ such that

$$\sum_{i=1}^{n}\sum_{j=1}^{p} f_1(k_{ij}) \cdot \left(\alpha \cdot f_2^{ij}(W, \Lambda) + (1-\alpha) \cdot d(Y_i, y_j)\right)$$

is minimum.

To show convergence, consider the function

$$Q(W, \Lambda, Y, W', \Lambda', Y') :=$$
$$\sum_{i=1}^{n}\sum_{j=1}^{p} f_1(k_{ij}(W, \Lambda, Y)) \cdot \left(\alpha \cdot f_2^{ij}(W', \Lambda') + (1-\alpha) \cdot d(Y'_i, y_j)\right) .$$

Note that $\hat{E}(W, \Lambda, Y) = Q(W, \Lambda, Y, W, \Lambda, Y)$. Assume batch optimization starts with $W$, $\Lambda$, $Y$ and computes optimum $k_{ij}$ and $W'$, $Y'$, $\lambda'$ based thereon. We find

$$\hat{E}(W', \Lambda', Y') = Q(W', \Lambda', Y', W', \Lambda', Y') \leq Q(W, \Lambda, Y, W', \Lambda', Y')$$

because $k_{ij}(W', \Lambda', Y')$ are optimum assignments given $W'$, $Y'$, $\lambda'$. Further,

$$\hat{E}(W, \Lambda, Y) = Q(W, \Lambda, Y, W, \Lambda, Y) \geq Q(W, \Lambda, Y, W', \Lambda', Y')$$

since $W'$, $Y'$, $\lambda'$ are optimum assignments for given $k_{ij}$. Thus,

$$\hat{E}(W, \Lambda, Y) - \hat{E}(W', \Lambda', Y') =$$
$$Q(W, \Lambda, Y, W, \Lambda, Y) - Q(W, \Lambda, Y, W', \Lambda', Y')$$
$$+ Q(W, \Lambda, Y, W', \Lambda', Y') - Q(W', \Lambda', Y', W', \Lambda', Y') \geq 0,$$

i.e. the cost function does not increase in batch optimization. Since the assignments $k_{ij}$ are unique and they stem from a finite set, the algorithm must converge in a finite number of steps. This shows the convergence of the algorithm in a finite number of optimization steps for all optimization schemes of this form, in particular supervised batch NG.

Often, the values $W$ and $\Lambda$ stem from a real-vector space. In this case, it is possible to show that the algorithm, in general, converges to a local optimum of the cost function $\hat{E}$. For discrete $W$ and $\Lambda$, this is not possible since the term 'local optimum' is not defined without specifying an additional neighborhood relation in the discrete sets $X_W$ and $X_\Lambda$. Assume continuous $X_W$ and $X_\Lambda$ and assume, that for the final solution $W$, $\Lambda$, $Y$ of batch optimization an open neighborhood exists such that $k_{ij}(W, \Lambda, Y)$ is constant in this neighborhood (this is usually the case for any given finite data set). In this case $\hat{E}(\cdot)$ and $Q(W, \Lambda, Y, \cdot)$ coincide in a vicinity of the solution, i.e. a local optimum of the latter is also a local optimum of the first one. Thus, a local optimum of $\hat{E}$ has been found in this case.

## 5 Future Approaches

This general formulation opens the way towards a couple of concrete algorithms for different application areas. We shortly mention a few possibilities which seem particularly promising and which experimental investigation will be the subject of future research.

### 5.1 Supervised Batch SOM

As already mentioned, the general formulation of batch optimization includes the possibility to extend SOM by a supervised component. Since SOM is subject to a fixed lattice structure which need not fit the data topology, it can be expected that the classification accuracy is usually worse compared to supervised batch NG. However, supervised SOM offers the possibility of data visualization if a low dimensional regular lattice is used. In this case, supervised components can be naturally integrated into the visualization. This is beneficial in particular for high-dimensional data where accumulated noise might blur the information hidden in the data. Additional label information allows to focus on the relevant parts of the data and visualize these aspects. The principle of integration of additional information in unsupervised learning has been introduced in [9,14], for example. Unlike this proposal, supervised batch SOM offers a simple alternative for the special case of additional label information.

### 5.2 Relevance Learning

Clustering crucially depends on the choice of the underlying metrics which determines the winner for a given data point. If the chosen metric is not appropriate for the task at hand, the classification fails. This is particularly pronounced for high-dimensional data where noise can accumulate and disrupt the information available in the data. Because of this fact, the principle of relevance learning as introduced in [7] has proven beneficial for prototype based clustering. The basic idea is to substitute the standard euclidian metric by a weighted version

$$(\mathbf{v}_j - \mathbf{w}_i)^2_\Lambda = \sum_{l=1}^{k} \Lambda_l^2 ((v_j)_l - (w_i)_l)^2$$

where $\Lambda_l$ are relevance parameters with $\sum_l \Lambda_l = 1$ which scale the dimensions according to their significance for the given task. The general formulation of batch optimization as introduced above allows us to adapt the relevance parameters automatically during training such that they are optimum adapted according to the given cost function. For the diagonal metric, the optimization task in **(2)** can be solved analytically for $\Lambda$ and yields

$$\Lambda_l = \frac{\left( \sum_{ij} h_\lambda(k_{ij}) \cdot ((v_j)_l - (w_i)_l)^2 \right)^{-1}}{\sum_{l'} \left( \sum_{ij} h_\lambda(k_{ij}) \cdot ((v_j)_{l'} - (w_i)_{l'})^2 \right)^{-1}}$$

for NG, i.e. weight vectors similar to the diagonal Mahalanobis distance arise, whereby the rank of the prototypes weighted according to the appropriateness of the weight and label is taken into account.

### 5.3  Median Clustering

Often, data are not embedded in a euclidian vector space, rather, pairwise prox-imities $d_{ij}$ which describe the distance of $\mathbf{v}_i$ and $\mathbf{v}_j$ are available. A variety of clustering algorithms for proximity data has been proposed [3,11,15,17], however, only few possibilities to train prototype-based methods for supervised classifi-cation of proximity data are available. The general framework as introduced above opens the way towards a very simple and intuitive method: supervised median clustering. Thereby, optimization of $W$ is restricted to the discrete set $X_W = \{\mathbf{v}_1, \ldots, \mathbf{v}_p\}$ given by the training patterns. In the optimization step (2), the generalized median, i.e. the data point $\mathbf{v}_i$ which minimizes the considered sum is taken as $\mathbf{w}_j$. This principle has been introduced in [11] for SOM and, including a proof of convergence, in [3] for NG. The transfer to supervised NG or SOM is immediate, whereby optimization can take place either by extensive search, or incorporating (exact or approximate) acceleration as discussed in [2].

# References

1. L. Bottou and Y. Bengio (1995), Convergence properties of the k-means algorithm, in *NIPS 1994*, 585-592, G. Tesauro, D.S. Touretzky, and T.K. Leen (eds.), MIT.
2. B. Conan-Guez, F. Rossi, and A. El Golli (2005), A fast algorithm for the self-organizing map on dissimilarity data, in *Workshop on Self-Organizing Maps*, 561-568.
3. M. Cottrell, B. Hammer, A. Hasenfuss, and T. Villmann (2006), Batch and median neural gas, *Neural Networks*, to appear.
4. K. Crammer, R. Gilad-Bachrach, A. Navot, and N. Tishby (2002), Margin analysis of the LVQ algorithm, *NIPS'2002*.
5. I. Gath, and A.B. Geva (1989), Unsupervised optimal fuzzy clustering, *IEEE Transactions on Pattern Analysis and Machine Intelligence* **11**(7):773-781.
6. B. Hammer, M. Strickert, and T. Villmann (2005), Supervised neural gas with general similarity measure, *Neural Processing Letters* **21**(1), 21-44.
7. B. Hammer, and T. Villmann (2002), Generalized relevance learning vector quan-tization, *Neural Networks* **15**, 1059-1068.
8. T. Heskes (2001), Self-organizing maps, vector quantization, and mixture modeling, *IEEE Transactions on Neural Networks*, **12**:1299-1305.
9. S. Kaski and J. Sinkkonen (2004), Principle of learning metrics for data analysis, *Journal of VLSI Signal Processing*, special issue on Machine Learning for Signal Processing, **37**: 177-188.
10. T. Kohonen (1995), *Self-Organizing Maps*, Springer.
11. T. Kohonen and P. Somervuo (2002), How to make large self-organizing maps for nonvectorial data, *Neural Networks* **15**:945-952.
12. T. Martinetz, S.G. Berkovich, and K.J. Schulten (1993), 'Neural-gas' network for vector quantization and its application to time-series prediction, *IEEE Transac-tions on Neural Networks* **4**:558-569.

13. D.J. Newman, S. Hettich, C.L. Blake, and C.J. Merz (1998), UCI Repository of machine learning databases [http://www.ics.uci.edu/~mlearn/MLRepository.html]. Irvine, CA: University of California, Department of Information and Computer Science.
14. J. Peltonen, A. Klami, and S. Kaski (2004), Improved learning of Riemannian metrics for exploratory analysis, *Neural Networks*, **17**:1087-1100.
15. S. Seo and K. Obermayer (2004), Self-organizing maps and clustering methods for matrix data, *Neural Networks* **17**:1211-1230.
16. T. Villmann, B. Hammer, F. Schleif, T. Geweniger, and W. Herrmann (2006), Fuzzy classification by fuzzy labeled neural gas, *Neural Networks*, accepted.
17. S. Zhong and J. Ghosh (2003), A unified framework for model-based clustering, *Journal of Machine Learning Research* **4**:1001-1037.

# Fuzzy Labeled Self-Organizing Map with Label-Adjusted Prototypes

Thomas Villmann[1,*], Udo Seiffert[2], Frank-Michael Schleif[3,4], Cornelia Brüß[2], Tina Geweniger[4,5], and Barbara Hammer[6]

[1] University Leipzig, Medical Department
[2] IPK Gatersleben, Pattern Recognition Group
[3] BRUKER Daltonik Leipzig, Numerical Toolbox Group
[4] University Leipzig, Institute of Computer Science
[5] University of Applied Science Mittweida, Computer Science
[6] Clausthal University of Technology, Institute of Computer Science

**Abstract.** We extend the self-organizing map (SOM) in the form as proposed by Heskes to a supervised fuzzy classification method. On the one hand, this leads to a robust classifier where efficient learning with fuzzy labeled or partially contradictory data is possible. On the other hand, the integration of labeling into the location of prototypes in a SOM leads to a visualization of those parts of the data relevant for the classification.

## 1 Introduction

The self-organizing map (SOM) constitutes one of the most popular data mining and visualization methods, mapping a given possibly high-dimensional data set nonlinearly onto a low-dimensional regular lattice in a topology-preserving fashion [10]. It can be taken as an adaptive *unsupervised* learning scheme for prototype based vector quantization with the additional feature of topographic mapping. Several methods exist to extend the SOM model for supervised classification tasks. These approaches range from simple post-labeling to the well-known counterpropagation network [10],[7],[8]. However, all these methods have in common that the locations of the prototypes in the data space remain unchanged by the subsequent determination of the prototype labels.

In the following we will propose an extension of the SOM such that it can be used as a prototype based classification approach. Thereby, the position of the prototypes is explicitly influenced by the classification task. In this way a combination of statistical and class properties triggers the prototype and the related label learning. The learning rules for prototypes as well as prototype labels are obtained from a cost function which is a combination of a classification error and the energy function of the SOM according to the formulation introduced by HESKES [9]. Thereby, the class information of the data may be fuzzy. The resulting map allows a visualization of the classification process by

---

[*] Corresponding author.

F. Schwenker and S. Marinai (Eds.): ANNPR 2006, LNAI 4087, pp. 46–56, 2006.
© Springer-Verlag Berlin Heidelberg 2006

means of the properties of topology preserving mapping of SOMs, which leads to a better understanding of the classification scheme. Further, metric adaptation, as known from learning vector quantization [4],[3], can be easily incorporated into this approach to improve its flexibility.

## 2   The Self-Organizing Map

As mentioned above, SOMs can be taken as unsupervised learning of topographic vector quantization with a topological structure (grid) within the set of pro-totypes (codebook vectors). Thereby, roughly speaking, topology preservation means that similar data points are mapped onto identical or neighbored grid lo-cations (prototypes), see Fig 1. An exact mathematical definition is given in [12]. Successful tools for assessing this map property are the topographic function and the topographic product [12],[1].

There exists a wide range of applications in pattern recognition ranging from spectral image processing to bioinformatics. The mathematics behind the orig-inal model as proposed by KOHONEN is rather complicated, particularly due to the lack of an underlying cost function for continuous data distributions. How-ever, HESKES proposed a minor variant of the original algorithm which usually leads to the same results as the original SOM but for which a cost function can be established [9]. We will base our model on this formulation.

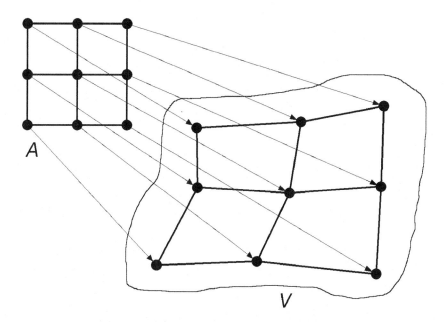

**Fig. 1.** Illustration of tropographic mapping by SOMs. A continuous change in the input space $\mathcal{V}$ leads to a representation by weight vectors, the neurons of which are neighbored in the grid space $A$.

Assume data $\mathbf{v} \in \mathcal{V}$ are given distributed according to an underlying distribution $P(\mathcal{V})$. A SOM is determined by a set $A$ of neurons/prototypes $\mathbf{r}$ equipped with weight vectors $\mathbf{w_r} \in \mathbb{R}^d$ and arranged on a lattice structure which determines the neighborhood relation $N(\mathbf{r}, \mathbf{r}')$ of neuron $\mathbf{r}$ and $\mathbf{r}'$. Denote the set of neurons by $\mathbf{W} = \{\mathbf{w_r}\}_{\mathbf{r} \in A}$. The mapping description of a trained SOM defines a function

$$\Psi_{\mathcal{V} \rightarrow A} : \mathbf{v} \mapsto s(\mathbf{v}) = \underset{\mathbf{r} \in A}{\operatorname{argmin}} \sum_{\mathbf{r}' \in A} h_\sigma(\mathbf{r}, \mathbf{r}') \xi(\mathbf{v}, \mathbf{w_{r'}}). \tag{1}$$

where

$$h_\sigma(\mathbf{r}, \mathbf{r}') = \exp\left(\frac{N(\mathbf{r}, \mathbf{r}')}{\sigma}\right) \tag{2}$$

determines the neighborhood cooperation with range $\sigma > 0$. $\xi(\mathbf{v}, \mathbf{w})$ is an appropriate distance measure, usually the standard Euclidean norm

$$\xi(\mathbf{v}, \mathbf{w_r}) = \|\mathbf{v} - \mathbf{w_r}\| = (\mathbf{v} - \mathbf{w_r})^2. \tag{3}$$

However, here we chose $\xi(\mathbf{v}, \mathbf{w})$ to be arbitrary supposing that it is a differentiable and symmetric function which measures some similarity. In this formulation, an input stimulus is mapped onto that position $\mathbf{r}$ of the SOM, where the distance $\xi(\mathbf{v}, \mathbf{w_r})$ is minimum, whereby the average over all neurons according to the neighborhood is taken. We refer to this neuron $s(\mathbf{v})$ as the winner.

During the adaptation process a sequence of data points $\mathbf{v} \in \mathcal{V}$ is presented to the map representative for the data distribution $P(\mathcal{V})$. Each time the currently most proximate neuron $s(\mathbf{v})$ according to (1) is determined. All weights within the neighborhood of this neuron are adapted by

$$\triangle \mathbf{w_r} = -\epsilon h_\sigma(\mathbf{r}, s(\mathbf{v})) \frac{\partial \xi(\mathbf{v}, \mathbf{w_r})}{\partial \mathbf{w_r}} \tag{4}$$

with learning rate $\epsilon > 0$. This adaptation follows a stochastic gradient descent of the cost function introduced by HESKES [9]:

$$E_{\text{SOM}} = \frac{1}{2C(\sigma)} \int P(\mathbf{v}) \sum_{\mathbf{r}} \delta_{\mathbf{r}}^{s(\mathbf{v})} \sum_{\mathbf{r}'} h_\sigma(\mathbf{r}, \mathbf{r}') \xi(\mathbf{v}, \mathbf{w_{r'}}) d\mathbf{v} \tag{5}$$

were $C(\sigma)$ is a constant which we will drop in the following, and $\delta_{\mathbf{r}}^{\mathbf{r}'}$ is the usual Kronecker symbol checking the identity of $\mathbf{r}$ and $\mathbf{r}'$.

One main aspect of SOMs is the visualization ability of the resulting map due to its topological structure. Under certain conditions the resulting non-linear projection $\Psi_{\mathcal{V} \rightarrow A}$ generates a continuous mapping from the data space $\mathcal{V}$ onto the grid structure $A$. This mapping can mathematically be interpreted as an approximation of the principal curve or its higher-dimensional equivalents [6]. Thus, as pointed out above, similar data points are projected on prototypes which are neighbored in the grid space $A$. Further, prototypes neighbored in the lattice space should code similar data properties, i.e. their weight vectors shoud be close together in the data space according to the metric $\xi$. This property of SOMs is called topology preserving (or topographic) mapping realizing the mathematical concept of continuity. For a detailed consideration of this topic we refer to [12].

## 3   Fuzzy Labeled SOM (FLSOM)

SOM is a well-established model for nonlinear data visualization which, due to its above mentioned topology preserving properties, can also serve as an adequate preprocessing step for data completion, classification or interpolation. For high-dimensional data sets, however, the result is often suboptimal if no further information about the data is present. In such cases, a default model and metric such as the Euclidean metric often accounts for the fact that only general properties, but not necessarily the parts relevant for the task at hand are represented. Often, auxiliary data in the form of (possibly partial or contradictory) labels are available. In this case, SOM can be used for a preprocessing step in classification by means of posterior labeling. Here, we seek for an integration of the label information such that the prototype locations are determined with respect to the auxiliary data. On the one hand, this improves the classification result if we are interested in supervised classification. On the other hand, information relevant for the classification can be visualized by means of the underlying SOM topology adapted towards the labeling.

Assume training point $\mathbf{v}$ is equipped with a label vector $\mathbf{x} \in [0, 1]^{N(c)}$ whereby the component $x_i$ of $\mathbf{x}$ determines the assignment of $\mathbf{v}$ to class $i$ for $i = 1, \ldots,$ $N(c)$. Hence, we can interpret the label vector as probabilistic or possibilistic fuzzy class memberships. Accordingly, we enlarge each prototype vector $\mathbf{w_r}$ of the map by a label vector $\mathbf{y_r} \in [0, 1]^{N(c)}$ which determines the portion of neuron $\mathbf{r}$ assigned to the respective classes. During training, prototype locations $\mathbf{w_r}$ and label vectors $\mathbf{x}_i$ are adapted according to the given labeled training data. For this purpose, we extend the cost function of the SOM as defined in (5) to a cost function for fuzzy-labeled SOM (FLSOM) by

$$E_{\text{FLSOM}} = (1 - \beta) E_{\text{SOM}} + \beta E_{\text{FL}} \tag{6}$$

where the factor $\beta \in [0, 1]$ is a balance factor to determine the influence of the goal of clustering the data set and the goal of achieving a correct labeling. One can simply choose $\beta = 0.5$, for example. As above, $E_{\text{SOM}}$ measures the quantization of the map taking topological constraints into account. $E_{\text{FL}}$ measures the error of the classification. We choose

$$E_{\text{FL}} = \frac{1}{2} \int P(\mathbf{v}) \sum_{\mathbf{r}} g_\gamma(\mathbf{v}, \mathbf{w_r}) (\mathbf{x} - \mathbf{y_r})^2 \, d\mathbf{v} \tag{7}$$

where $g_\gamma(\mathbf{v}, \mathbf{w_r})$ is a Gaussian kernel describing a neighborhood range in the data space:

$$g_\gamma(\mathbf{v}, \mathbf{w_r}) = \exp\left(-\frac{\xi(\mathbf{v}, \mathbf{w_r})}{2\gamma^2}\right). \tag{8}$$

This choice is based on the assumption that data points close to the prototype determine the corresponding label if the underlying classification is sufficiently smooth. Note that $g_\gamma(\mathbf{v}, \mathbf{w_r})$ depends on the prototype locations, such that $E_{\text{FL}}$ is influenced by both $\mathbf{w_r}$ and $\mathbf{y_r}$, and an adaptation yields to a different location of prototypes which is also influenced by the labels.

We obtain the update rules by taking the derivatives: Labels are only influenced by the second part $E_{FL}$, which yields

$$\frac{\partial E_{FL}}{\partial \mathbf{y_r}} = - \int P(\mathbf{v}) \, g_\gamma(\mathbf{v}, \mathbf{w_r}) (\mathbf{x} - \mathbf{y_r}) \, d\mathbf{v} \qquad (9)$$

and the corresponding learning rule

$$\triangle \mathbf{y_r} = \epsilon_l \beta \cdot g_\gamma(\mathbf{v}, \mathbf{w_r}) (\mathbf{x} - \mathbf{y_r}) \qquad (10)$$

with learning rate $\epsilon_l > 0$. This yields to a weighted average of the data fuzzy labels of those data close to the associated prototypes. However, in comparison to the usual SOM the receptive fields are different because the prototype update is determined by the gradient of (6) which yields $\frac{\partial E_{SOM}}{\partial \mathbf{w_r}} + \frac{\partial E_{FL}}{\partial \mathbf{w_r}}$ where

$$\frac{\partial E_{FL}}{\partial \mathbf{w_r}} = -\frac{1}{4\gamma^2} \int P(\mathbf{v}) \, g_\gamma(\mathbf{v}, \mathbf{w_r}) \frac{\partial \xi(\mathbf{v}, \mathbf{w_r})}{\partial \mathbf{w_r}} (\mathbf{x} - \mathbf{y_r})^2 \, d\mathbf{v} \qquad (11)$$

which takes the accuracy of fuzzy labeling into account for the weight update. The update rule for the weights thus becomes

$$\triangle \mathbf{w_r} = -\epsilon(1 - \beta) \cdot h_\sigma(\mathbf{r}, s(\mathbf{v})) \frac{\partial \xi(\mathbf{v}, \mathbf{w_r})}{\partial \mathbf{w_r}} \qquad (12)$$

$$+\epsilon \beta \frac{1}{4\gamma^2} \cdot g_\gamma(\mathbf{v}, \mathbf{w_r}) \frac{\partial \xi(\mathbf{v}, \mathbf{w_r})}{\partial \mathbf{w_r}} (\mathbf{x} - \mathbf{y_r})^2 \, .$$

As mentioned above, unsupervised SOMs generate a topographic mapping from the data space onto the prototype grid under specific conditions. If the classes are consistently determined with respect to the varying data, one can expect for supervised topographic FLSOMs that the labels become ordered within the grid structure of the prototype lattice. In this case the topological order of the prototypes should be transferred to the topological order of prototype labels such that we have a smooth change of the fuzzy probabilistic class labels between neighbored grid positions.

## 4    Relevance Learning

As mentioned above, $\xi(\mathbf{v}, \mathbf{w_r})$ is often chosen as squared Euclidean metric such that the term $\frac{\partial \xi(\mathbf{v}, \mathbf{w_r})}{\partial \mathbf{w_r}}$ becomes $-2(\mathbf{v} - \mathbf{w_r})$. However, the integration of adaptive relevance factors (metric parameters) seems particularly interesting because of an increased flexibility and interpretability of the model with almost the same cost as for the standard metric [5]. Generally, we consider a parametrized distance measure $\xi^\lambda(\mathbf{v}, \mathbf{w})$ with a parameter vector $\boldsymbol{\lambda} = (\lambda_1, \ldots, \lambda_M)$ with $\lambda_i \geq 0$ and normalization $\sum_i \lambda_i = 1$. The idea of relevance learning is to optimize the relevance factors $\boldsymbol{\lambda}$ of the distance measure with respect to the classification task [4],[3], i.e. we consider $\frac{\partial E_{FLSOM}}{\partial \lambda_l}$. Formal derivation yields

$$\frac{\partial E_{FLSOM}}{\partial \lambda_l} = (1 - \beta)\frac{\partial E_{SOM}}{\partial \lambda_l} + \beta \frac{\partial E_{FL}}{\partial \lambda_l} \qquad (13)$$

with

$$\frac{\partial E_{\text{SOM}}}{\partial \lambda_l} = \frac{1}{2} \int P(\mathbf{v}) \sum_{\mathbf{r}} \delta_{\mathbf{r}}^{s(\mathbf{v})} \sum_{\mathbf{r}'} h_{\sigma}(\mathbf{r}, \mathbf{r}') \cdot \frac{\partial \xi^{\lambda}(\mathbf{v}, \mathbf{w_r})}{\partial \lambda_l} d\mathbf{v} \qquad (14)$$

and

$$\frac{\partial E_{\text{FL}}}{\partial \lambda_l} = -\frac{1}{4\gamma^2} \int P(\mathbf{v}) \sum_{\mathbf{r}} g_{\gamma}(\mathbf{v}, \mathbf{w_r}) \frac{\partial \xi^{\lambda}(\mathbf{v}, \mathbf{w_r})}{\partial \lambda_l} (\mathbf{x} - \mathbf{y_r})^2 d\mathbf{v} \qquad (15)$$

for the respective parameter adaptation.

In case of $\xi^{\lambda}(\mathbf{v}, \mathbf{w})$ being the scaled Euclidean metric

$$\xi^{\lambda}(\mathbf{v}, \mathbf{w}) = \sum_i \lambda_i (v_i - w_i)^2 \qquad (16)$$

(with $\lambda_i \geq 0$ and $\sum_i \lambda_i = 1$), relevance learning ranks the input dimensions $i$ according to their relevance for the classification task at hand. Thus, $\frac{\partial \xi(\mathbf{v}, \mathbf{w}_i)}{\partial \mathbf{w}_i}$ becomes

$$\frac{\partial \xi(\mathbf{v}, \mathbf{w}_i)}{\partial \mathbf{w}_i} = -2 \cdot \Lambda \cdot (\mathbf{v} - \mathbf{w}_i) \qquad (17)$$

with diagonal matrix $\Lambda$ with $i$-th diagonal entry $\lambda_i$. The corresponding learning rule for the relevance parameters becomes

$$\triangle \lambda_l = -\epsilon_{\lambda} \frac{1 - \beta}{2} \sum_{\mathbf{r}} h_{\sigma}(s(\mathbf{v}), \mathbf{r}) \cdot (v_l - (w_{\mathbf{r}})_l)^2 \qquad (18)$$

$$+ \epsilon_{\lambda} \frac{\beta}{4\gamma^2} \sum_{\mathbf{r}} g_{\gamma}(\mathbf{v}, \mathbf{w_r})(v_l - (w_{\mathbf{r}})_l)^2 (\mathbf{x} - \mathbf{y_r})^2 \qquad (19)$$

(subscript $l$ denoting the component $l$ of a vector) with learning rate $\epsilon_{\lambda} > 0$. This update is followed by normalization to ensure $\lambda_i \geq 0$ and $\sum_i \lambda_i = 1$.

## 5    Experiments

### 5.1    Data Set

In order to demonstrate the practical properties of the proposed algorithm, a quite challenging application in the field of biological image segmentation has been chosen. Against the background of spatiotemporal 3-D modelling of cereal seeds based on up to 2.000 high-resolution images of histological cross-sections a processing transition from crisp to fuzzy segmentation is desirable.

For this purpose all image pixels are characterized by an extensive feature vector containing information on color, geometry and symmetry (such as Cartesian and polar coordinates, distance to centroid, absolute angle to symmetry axis) and particularly texture according to varying neighborhoods (such as Gaussian filters, histogram based features) and subsequently sorted into classes by a suitable classifier. A number of training pixels are used to set up a classification system. These training pixels commonly have a unique class label indicating that tissue which has previously been assigned by an expert. Since this assignment is often not univocal, due to slight transitions from one biological tissue to an adjacent one, some fuzzy image segmentation would retain much more biological knowledge. Further details about the biological background along with fuzzy segmentation using Fuzzy Labelled Neural Gas (FLNG) can be found in [2]. Tab. 1 summarizes those details of the data set relevant to this paper.

**Table 1.** Details of the utilized demonstration data set. The classes are non-uniformly distributed and usually multimodal.

| Number of inputs | Number of classes | SOM-grid size | Number of training examples | Number of test examples |
|---|---|---|---|---|
| 170 | 5 | $7 \times 7$ | ca. 10.000 | > 10.000.000 |

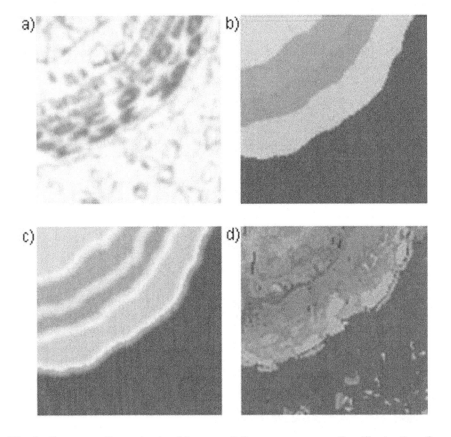

**Fig. 2.** Corresponding cutouts of images of the same cross-section illustrating the results of an automatic fuzzy classification: a) original colour image, b) manually crisply segmented image, c) manually fuzzily segmented image (see [2]), d) automatic classification using FLSOM.

## 5.2   Results

Since different areas of the images require more or less fuzzy segmentation, Fig. 2 shows a typical cutout from one complete microscope image containing several transitions of different tissues. In comparison to the crisp segmented image it can clearly be seen, that there are areas with predominantly crisp segmentation as well as areas with mainly fuzzy segmentation. Insofar, the classification system has to reach two partly contradictory goals, the mapping of structural image data onto the classes in a fuzzy manner and the observance of the statistical information about the data distribution. We used the scaled Euclidean distance (16) and a $7 \times 7$ SOM grid in the applications, which is chosen according to an optimal topology preserving mapping (the topographic product is approximately zero, indicating good topographic mapping [1]). The learning rate was $\epsilon = 0.01$, $\epsilon_\lambda = 0.1\epsilon$ and the balancing parameter $\beta = 0.6$ based on experimental experiences [2],[13]. Relevance learning was incorporated for optimal metric adaptation using the scaled Euclidean metric (16).

The resulted segmentation image based on FLSOM classification is depicted in Fig. 2d. The result shows that the obtained image mixes the original class information overlaid by the structural information (geometry, symmetries ...) contained in the original color image Fig. 2a. This impression is emphasized if the original color image is manually overlaid by the fuzzy classification target (fuzzy labeled) image Fig. 2c and after this compared to the FLSOM classification result. This comparison is shown in Fig. 3, which demonstrates a nice agreement. The segmentation result is comparable to a segmentation obtained by fuzzy labeled neural gas algoritm (FLNG), which also is a neural map based fuzzy classification scheme similar to FLSOM [2],[13]. Favored features of SOMs are the visualization abilities which are also available for FLSOM in advance compared to FLNG. Here, this property is used for investigation of the class structures. For

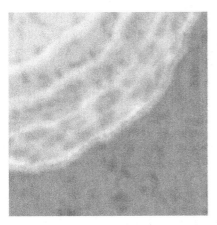

**Fig. 3.** Comparison of manually overlaid color image Fig. 2a and Fig. 2c (left) with FLSOM resulted classification Fig. 2d (right)

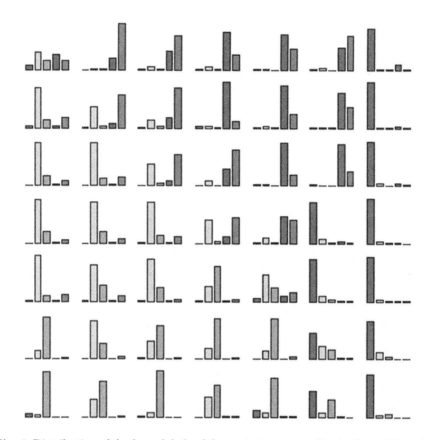

**Fig. 4.** Distribution of the fuzzy labels of the prototypes according to the grid locations. The topological order of labels performing label clusters can easily be detected.

this purpose, the fuzzy labels of prototypes are plotted according to the underlying topological structure of the $7 \times 7$-SOM-grid, Fig. 4. Obviously clear clusters of labels can be locally detected and separated with a smooth change between them. Because of the topology preservation of the SOM-mapping (proven by the topographic product) we can conclude here that a continuos change in the data space leads to a continuos change in the label space and hence classification decision.

Additionally, the adapted relevance profile of the scale parameters $\lambda_i$ of the scaled Euclidean metric (16) may offer new insights for further investigations, see Fig. 5. This particularly concerns the optimization of the feature vector currently used for the segmentation and the network training, respectively. From the relevance profile it can be concluded that a rather long feature vector is necessary to keep all the information required to distinguish between the different tissues (classes). Nevertheless, the used feature vector is subject to a further optimization based on the obtained relevance profiles at different runs. However, this is not trivial, since several runs at similar classification performance may yield

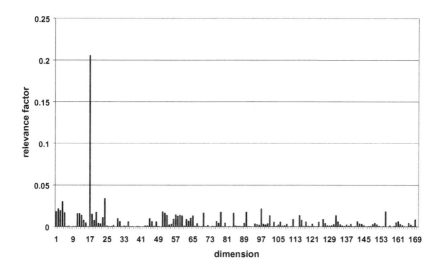

**Fig. 5.** Relevance profile of the values $\lambda_i$ for the scaled Euclidean metric used in the application

different relevance profiles. Generally though, this way FLSOM additionally offers a native and self-contained way to keep itself slim.

## 6    Conclusions

We presented an extension of the SOM for supervised classification tasks, which explicitly adapts the prototypes according to the classification task. It is derived as a gradient descent of a cost function obtained from the SOM formulation according to the HESKES-approach extended by an additional (balanced) term assessing the classification ability. In this way the statistical as well as label properties of the data influence prototype positions and fuzzy label learning. The visualization abilities of SOMs based on the topology preservation property of unsupervised SOMs then can be used for visual inspection of the class labels of the prototypes which may allow a better understanding of the underlying classification decision scheme.

In future work the connections to the unsupervised clustering in SOMs with auxiliary data information should be considered [11]. For this purpose one could interpret the fuzzy class labels as the auxiliary data space.

## Acknowledgements

The authors would like to thank Winfriede Weschke for providing expertise on the biological background of the demonstration application. This work was supported by a grant of the German Federal Ministry of Education and Research (No. 0312706A).

# References

1. H.-U. Bauer and K. R. Pawelzik. Quantifying the neighborhood preservation of Self-Organizing Feature Maps. *IEEE Trans. on Neural Networks*, 3(4):570–579, 1992.
2. C. Brüß, F. Bollenbeck, F.-M. Schleif, W. Weschke, T. Villmann, and U. Seiffert. Fuzzy image segmentation with fuzzy labeled neural gas. In M. Verleysen, editor, *Proc. Of European Symposium on Artificial Neural Networks (ESANN'2006)*, pages 563–568, Brussels, Belgium, 2006. d-side publications.
3. B. Hammer, M. Strickert, and T. Villmann. Supervised neural gas with general similarity measure. *Neural Processing Letters*, 21(1):21–44, 2005.
4. B. Hammer and T. Villmann. Generalized relevance learning vector quantization. *Neural Networks*, 15(8-9):1059–1068, 2002.
5. B. Hammer and T. Villmann. Classification using non-standard metrics. In M. Verleysen, editor, *Proc. Of European Symposium on Artificial Neural Networks (ESANN'2005)*, pages 303–316, Brussels, Belgium, 2005. d-side publications.
6. T. Hastie and W. Stuetzle. Principal curves. *J. Am. Stat. Assn.*, 84:502–516, 1989.
7. R. Hecht-Nielsen. Counterprogagation networks. *Appl. Opt.*, 26(23):4979–4984, December 1987.
8. R. Hecht-Nielsen. Applications of counterpropagation networks. *Neural Networks*, 1(2):131–139, 1988.
9. T. Heskes. Energy functions for self-organizing maps. In E. Oja and S. Kaski, editors, *Kohonen Maps*, pages 303–316. Elsevier, Amsterdam, 1999.
10. T. Kohonen. *Self-Organizing Maps*, volume 30 of *Springer Series in Information Sciences*. Springer, Berlin, Heidelberg, 1995. (Second Extended Edition 1997).
11. J. Sinkkonen and S. Kaski. Clustering based on conditional distributions in an auxiliary space. *Neural Computation*, 14:217–239, 2002.
12. T. Villmann, R. Der, M. Herrmann, and T. Martinetz. Topology Preservation in Self–Organizing Feature Maps: Exact Definition and Measurement. *IEEE Transactions on Neural Networks*, 8(2):256–266, 1997.
13. T. Villmann, B. Hammer, F.-M. Schleif, and T. Geweniger. Fuzzy classification by fuzzy labeled neural gas. *Neural Networks*, page in press, 2006.

# On the Effects of Constraints in Semi-supervised Hierarchical Clustering

Hans A. Kestler[1,2], Johann M. Kraus[1,2],
Günther Palm[1], and Friedhelm Schwenker[1]

[1] Department of Neural Information Processing, University of Ulm,
89069 Ulm, Germany
hans.kestler@uni-ulm.de, friedhelm.schwenker@uni-ulm.de
[2] Department of Internal Medicine I, University Hospital Ulm, Robert-Koch-Str. 8,
89081 Ulm, Germany

**Abstract.** We explore the use of constraints with divisive hierarchical clustering. We mention some considerations on the effects of the inclusion of constraints into the hierarchical clustering process. Furthermore, we introduce an implementation of a semi-supervised divisive hierarchical clustering algorithm and show the influence of including constraints into the divisive hierarchical clustering process. In this task our main interest lies in building stable dendrograms when clustering with different subsets of data.

## 1 Background

The aim of cluster analysis is to explore a collection of data items and to group *similar* objects together. Similarity can be measured in many different ways, for example by the Euclidean distance. Every information used in an unsupervised learning technique comes from the data themselve, which means no external teaching signal guides the algorithm. During the past years several modifications were proposed to incorporate additional background knowledge into clustering algorithms [1–9]. The main idea is that in some tasks prior information about a small amount of data is known and should support the clustering process. This background information is usually provided as a set of constraints between pairs of data items [2]. Real class labels seem not feasible in clustering because of the inherent discrepancy between labels and clusters. Pairwise constraints are typically encoded as *must-links* and *cannot-links* [2] either indicating two points belong to the same cluster or to different clusters.

Up to now different clustering algorithms were adapted to make use of semi-supervised clustering. Constraint-based approaches modify the cluster search, either by including constraints into the objective function [1] or by initalizing and constraining during the clustering process [10, 3, 9]. Metric-based approaches first train the cluster metric to satisfy the constraints using shortest-path algorithm [4], expectation maximization [5], gradient descent [6], convex optimization [7, 8] or combinations of constraint-based and metric-based methods [11].

F. Schwenker and S. Marinai (Eds.): ANNPR 2006, LNAI 4087, pp. 57–66, 2006.

Many real-world unsupervised learning tasks may profit from an inclusion of background knowledge, e.g. image processing, text mining or even lane finding using GPS data. Another important field for data mining using semi-supervised clustering is the functional grouping of genes. For this problem we are not only interested in one particular clustering as built by partitioning clustering algorithms, such as K-means or SOM, but in getting a hierarchy of partitions (dendrogram).

Our main emphasis lies on building robust hierarchical clusterings for DNA microarray data. Here we are interested in the resulting dendrogram and focus on the question of creating stable dendrograms. In this setting one of the problems that frequently arise is the change of the branching structure when computing several runs with different data subsets. Since the inclusion of background knowledge seems to enhance the accuracy of clustering algorithms, we studied its effect on the dendrogram stability. In Section 2 we explain some basic annotations on the effects of constraints in semi-supervised hierarchical clustering. In Section 3 we introduce our new algorithm for divisive hierarchical clustering with a-priori information and section 4 shows our results from semi-supervised clustering in hierarchical algorithms.

## 2    Background Knowledge in Hierarchical Clustering

### 2.1    Constraints

Background knowledge may be available in different forms, e.g. as labels or constraints. Following Wagstaff & Cardie [2] we use *cannot-link* and *must-link* constraints to insert a-priori information into our clustering algorithm. We don't use labels, because they indicate class memberships and a class can consist of different and distant clusters. As mentioned above, *must-links* indicate two data items being arranged in one cluster and *cannot-links* allude not to assign two data items to the same group.

### 2.2    Effects from Constraints in Hierarchical Clustering

Constraints indicate a relationship between two data items. When a partition of a data set into $k$ cluster is computed, we may profit from including this form of background knowledge, because constraints seem to support the clustering algorithm to define the clusters of this partition more accurate. Computing a hierarchy of partitions is a different task. Here we are confronted with a sequence of refinements of clusters. A hierarchy of partitions is either computed by a subsequent assembly of two clusters or by a subsequent division of one cluster. Whereas each partition is formed by a different number of clusters there is a different set of relations between the data items in these clusters, i.e. every partition provides its own set of constraints, see Figure 1. In the following we present two scenarios which should point up the effects of constraints in hierarchical clustering.

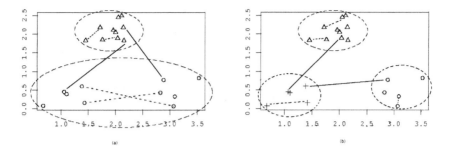

**Fig. 1.** Basic example for a data set with two clusters (Subfigure a, clusters △, o) and its refinement into three clusters (Subfigure b, clusters △, + , o). Additionally each partitioning provides its own set of constraints (lines = *cannot-links*, dashed lines = *must-links*).

**Effects from *Cannot-Links*:** In our first scenario we want to show the effects of *cannot-links* in hierarchical clustering. Imagine we want to compute a dendrogram for a data set using a divisive hierarchical clustering algorithm. To simplify matters we only look on the first two levels of the computed dendrogram. These two levels propose two partitions of the data set. On the first level we see a partition into two clusters and on the second level one of these clusters is split again. Additionally we can provide two different sets of *cannot-link* constraints.

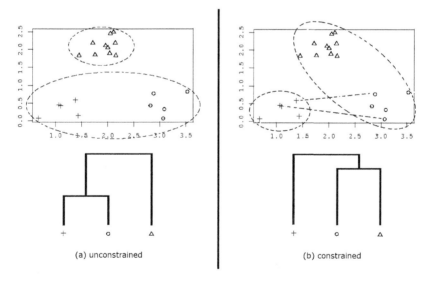

**Fig. 2.** Different branching structures when providing a few *cannot-links* between clusters on a lower level. Subfigure (a) shows a clustering into two (dashed circles) and three clusters (△, + , o) and the corresponding dendrogram. Adding *cannot-links* (dashed lines) between some elements from cluster + and cluster o results in a different clustering on the second level, see Subfigure (b).

The first set indicates relationships between data items from the partitioning into two clusters and the second set contains *cannot-links* from the partitioning into three clusters.

When incorporating the first set of constraints we may get a more accurate clustering into two clusters, because *cannot-links* for data items on the boundaries of the clusters could guide the algorithm to improve the shape of the clusters. Since all of these *cannot-links* could be resolved in the first clustering step, we don't use them in the further steps any more.

On the other hand we probably want to make use of the second set of constraints. The possible effect of the inclusion of this set of constraints could be seen in Figure 2. In this example we see two initial clusters, one of them builds a supercluster that could be refined again. After providing some *cannot-links* indicating this refinement in the first step of the clustering procedure the algorithm tries to resolve even these *cannot-links*. As a result either the constrained items could not be assigned to the correct supercluster or actually a complete different supercluster is built.

**Effects from *Must-Links*:** In this scenario we want to describe the effect of adding *must-links*. Again we only look at the first two levels of the dendrogram, but this time we only have one set of constraints containing *must-links* deduced from the first level. Similar to the inclusion of *cannot-links* we can distinguish between two effects. When we use *must-links* from clusters on the second level, the dendrogram on the first level may profit from a finer definition of the shapes of these two clusters.

Contrary to the above, in the next refinement steps these constraints hinder the clustering algorithm. Figure 3 shows the results from adding *must-links* to the divisive clustering algorithm. In this example two *must-links* could not be correctly split.

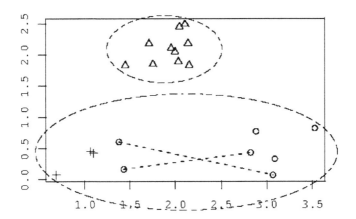

**Fig. 3.** Partitioning into three clusters ($\triangle$, $+$, $o$) after including *must-links* (dashed lines) between elements from a partitioning into two clusters (dashed circles). When splitting the lower cluster the two *must-links* hinder a correct refinement.

## 3  Semi-supervised Divisive Hierarchical Clustering

In microarray data mining studies we are usually confronted with low-cardinality data. Computing dendrograms after removing or adding some samples could easily contradict a previous constructed hierarchy.

Figure 4 shows a simple two-dimensional example for this behaviour. Three clusters were formed using Gaussian distribution. Randomly removing three items results in different subsets of the data. Subfigures (a) and (b) show two possible subsets. A hierarchical clustering of these two subsets results in two contradictory dendrograms, where either cluster **a** and cluster **b** or cluster **a** and cluster **c** are proposed to be similar. Applied to the task of gene functional grouping, no unique branching structure can be predicted when working on incomplete data sets, even though a correct clustering is found. In this section we introduce our attempts to enhance the dendrogram stability by including background knowledge into the clustering process.

### 3.1  Constraints

According to the considerations described in Section 2 we decided to restrict the use of constraints. To avoid mixing constraints from different levels of the

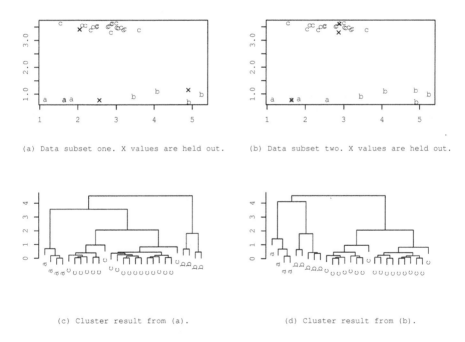

(a) Data subset one. X values are held out.    (b) Data subset two. X values are held out.

(c) Cluster result from (a).    (d) Cluster result from (b).

**Fig. 4.** Subfigures (a) and (b) show two different subsets of a simple two-dimensional data set containing clusters **a**, **b** and **c**. The subsets are built by holding out three items, for clarity marked by X. Clustering both subsets results in two different dendrograms. In Subfigure (c) cluster **a** and **c**, in Subfigure (d) cluster **a** and **b** are deduced from one combined cluster.

dendrogram we only add constraints for one particular partition of the data set. Furthermore, we use our set of constraints only for the clustering on this predefined level. This means for example providing a set of constraints that include *cannot-links* for a partition of three clusters, we only use these constraints on the second level of the dendrogram. In the task of building more stable dendrograms, we are mainly interested in the dendrogram stability on the first level. Therefore, we additionally decided to use only constraints from the first level. Nevertheless, our algorithm could easily be expanded to make use of constraints from different levels of the dendrogram. Furthermore, we build the combined transitive closure [10] over all constraints to get the most from our background knowledge and to avoid presenting contradictory constraints.

## 3.2 Algorithm: Constrained-Divisive

Divisive hierarchical clustering starts the clustering procedure with the complete data set in one cluster. The largest available cluster is then at each subsequent step divided into two clusters until finally all clusters contain only one single data item. To identify the largest available cluster, usually the diameters of all clusters are compared. To find out where to split the chosen cluster, its element with the largest average distance to all other elements can be used as the initial item of the new cluster. According to a user-defined distance measure all remaining points are assigned to their most similar cluster.

Our implementation of CONSTRAINED-DIVISIVE modifies this basic divisive algorithm. Only on the first partitioning, i.e. the clustering into two clusters, we have to include the constraints, on all other steps the constraints are not used

---

**Algorithm 1.** Constrained-Divisive

---

CONSTRAINED-DIVISIVE(data set $D = \{d_1, \ldots, d_n\}$, *must-links* $Con_= \subseteq D \times D$, *cannot-links* $Con_{\neq} \subseteq D \times D$)

1. Let $C$ be the initial cluster group: $C = \{D\}$.
2. Select the cluster $C_m \in C$ with the largest dissimilarity between any two of its objects. Divide $C_m$ following (3) to (7).
3. Select the element $s_z$ with the highest average dissimilarity to all other elements and, if clustering the first level, with an unresolved *cannot-link*. $s_z$ initiates the splinter group $S$. If clustering the first level:
   $\forall d \in C_m, s \in S :$ If $(d_i, s_j) \in Con_=$, move $d_i$ to $S$.
4. $\forall d$ still $\in C_m, s \in S :$ Compute the difference of distances:
   $Diff(i) = [averagedistance(d_i, d_j)] - [averagedistance(d_i, s_j)]$.
   Select the element $d_h$ with the greatest difference $Diff(h)$.
   If clustering the first level: If $\exists s_j \in S : (d_h, s_j) \in Con_{\neq}$, set $Diff(h) = 0$.
   If $Diff(h) > 0$, move $d_h$ to the splinter group $S$.
5. Repeat (4) and (5) until all differences $Diff(h)$ are negative.
6. Now the original cluster ist split into two clusters. One is the splinter group $S$, the other is formed by the remaining elements in $C_m$.
7. Iterate between (2) and (7) until all clusters $\{C_1 \ldots C_k\}$ contain only a single element.

---

any more and we compute the dendrogram according to the basic algorithm. In the following we comment the clustering process from the first step more precisely. We include *cannot-links* into two decisions. When looking for the first element to split we could use an element with a *cannot-link* and a large average distance to all other elements. Secondly we avoid violating *cannot-links* when assigning elements to a chosen cluster. In addition we use *must-links* when assigning elements to a new cluster by moving all linked elements at once. This proceeding guaranties not not violate any constraints during the clustering into two clusters.

Our clustering algorithm could easily be expanded to make use of constraints from different levels. Therefore, one set of constraints for each level and an indicator for the context (the level) of this set must be included. Every set of constraints then should only be used in its context.

## 4    Experiments and Results

### 4.1    Data Sets

The first data set we analyzed is an artificial example of a two-dimensional problem containing three different clusters. We built each cluster by the use of a Gaussian distribution as seen in Figure 4. A partition into three clusters is easy to compute, because the clusters are obviously separable. Nevertheless, when removing some data items the partition into two clusters is not stable.

Our second data set comes from gene expression profiles from the pancreas (see Buchholz et al. [12]). This data set provides two classes (pancreas cancer vs. pancreatitis/normal) for 62 samples. Each sample is characterized by 169 gene expression values.

### 4.2    Evaluation Method

There is no gold standard for evaluating clustering results and therefore it is necessary to define the basic problem. In our study we want to compare the results from different clusterings. Jain & Dubes [13] suggest to use a relative criterion to measure the agreement between two clusterings. We do not measure the totally agreement of two dendrograms, but the agreement on a selected partition. As we have the a-priori information about the cluster membership of all samples on the first levels, we can measure the stability of the clustering algorithm by comparing the cluster results with this *external* clustering. On the other hand we can measure the stability on the lower levels by comparing all clusterings from the different subsets with each other.

We make use of the Rand Index [14]. Given a set of $n$ items and two partitions $P$ and $Q$ there are four ways to compare clusters in these different partitions. Let $a$ be the number of all pairs of items in the same cluster in $P$ and in the same cluster in $Q$, $b$ be the number of all pairs of items in the same cluster in $P$ but not in the same cluster in $Q$, $c$ be the number of all pairs of items not in the same cluster in $P$ but in the same cluster in $Q$ and $d$ the number of all pairs of items in different clusters in both partitions. The scores $a$ and $d$ therefore represent agreements, the scores $b$ and $c$ disagreements in the partitions. The Rand Index is the sum of the correct decisions compared to all decisions:

$$\frac{a+d}{a+b+c+d} \qquad (1)$$

The value for perfect agreement of two partitions is 1. One advantage of computing the Rand Index is the possibility to include the constraints into the evaluation result. As we count pairwise clustering decisions, we omit the constrained pairs from the computation of the Rand Index. This Corrected Rand Index is a better indicator for the improvement of the clustering algorithm, because it only counts *real* decisions.

### 4.3   Results

For our artificial data set we only measure the stability on the first level. Here we want to get a more stable partition into two clusters. We compare all results from CONSTRAINED-DIVISIVE to the external label. Table 1 shows the results for this test. After removing randomly 10% of the data items ten times and adding 3% and 5% random constraints we computed the Corrected Rand Index for each run. By adding constraints we could improve the stability of the dendrogram on the first level.

Table 2 shows the results for the microarray data set. Here we not only measured the stability on the first level of the dendrograms but also analyzed the effect from the constraints on the stability on the lower levels of the dendrograms. We computed the Rand Index for the results on each level over all runs.

**Table 1.** Stability results for CONSTRAINED-DIVISIVE on the first data set. After removing 10% of the data items and adding 3% and 5% randomly constrained pairs from partitioning into two clusters the stability on the first level increases. The value of the Corrected Rand Index is the median from 50 runs. The second value counts the number of correct partitionings into two clusters according to the external label.

| Constraints | Corrected Rand Index | Correct decisions |
|-------------|----------------------|-------------------|
| without     | 0.89                 | 23                |
| 3%          | 1                    | 28                |
| 5%          | 1                    | 33                |

**Table 2.** Stability results for CONSTRAINED-DIVISIVE on the pankreas data set. After removing 10% of the data items and adding 5% and 10% constrained pairs from partitioning into two clusters the stability on the first level increases. The value of the Rand Index is the median from 50 runs. The further rows show the median for the Rand Index from comparing the different partitionings on the lower levels.

| Constraints | Rand Index | Level 5 | Level 10 |
|-------------|------------|---------|----------|
| without     | 0.96       | 0.96    | 0.94     |
| 5%          | 1          | 0.98    | 0.93     |
| 10%         | 1          | 0.98    | 0.94     |

The median from these values indicates that the constraints improve the stability even for some lower levels.

## 5    Discussion and Conclusion

Clustering of gene expression profiles is an important task in DNA microarray analysis. As hierarchical clustering algorithms can predict a basic branching structure they are often used in this context [15]. Nevertheless, clustering different subsets of DNA data or adding some new samples to the data set may result in getting contradictory dendrograms. Since we are interested in getting stable dendrograms to provide a prediction of the branching structure, we tried to improve the dendrogram stability by including background knowledge.

Davidson & Ravi [9] presented an agglomerative hierarchical clustering algorithm using constraints and demonstrated the enhancement in the cluster accuracy. Their algorithm stops if no more agglomerations according to the *cannot-links* can be performed. This results in root-less dendrograms. Additionally they provided constraints from one particular partitioning and then used these constraints during the complete clustering process. In Section 2 we pointed out that this kind of constraining holds the risk of inducting wrong constraints. As a result their approach is not able to provide a rough estimation of the branching stucture on the top levels in the dendrogram and may lead to variable dendrograms.

In microarray data analysis a rough estimation of the subgrouping is best seen at the top of the dendrogram, whereas the detailed hierarchy in the lower levels is often not as important. We implemented a divisive hierarchical clustering algorithm and included background knowledge in the form of constraints. On the basis of our considerations about the effects of constraints in the hierarchical clustering process we decided to restrict the use of constraints on the first level of the dendrogram and did not to use constraints from the lower levels. By comparing the results from unconstrained and constrained divisive hierarchical clusterings we could show that this inclusion of constraints in the divisive hierarchical clustering algorithm results in more stable dendrograms. Furthermore, the positive effect of the constraints from the first level of the dendrogram even seem to improve the stability of the lower levels.

## Acknowledgments

This work is supported by the Stifterverband für die Deutsche Wissenschaft (HAK) and the German Science Foundation, SFB 518, Project C5 (HAK and GP).

## References

1. Demiriz, A., Bennett, K., Embrechts, M.: Semi-supervised clustering using genetic algorithms. In: Artificial Neural Networks in Engineering, New York, Troy (1999) 809–814

2. Wagstaff, K., Cardie, C.: Clustering with instance-level constraints. In: Proceedings of the 17th International Conference on Machine Learning, San Francisco, CA, USA, Morgan Kaufmann Publishers Inc. (2000) 1103–1110
3. Basu, S., Banerjee, A., Mooney, R.: Semi-supervised clustering by seeding. In: Proceedings of 19th International Conference on Machine Learning. (2002) 19–26
4. Klein, D., Kamvar, S., C.Manning: From instance-level constraints to space-level constraints: Making the most of prior knowledge in data clustering. In: Proceedings of 19th International Conference on Machine Learning. (2002) 307–314
5. Bilenko, M., Mooney, R.: Adaptive duplicate detection using learnable string similarity measures. In: Proceedings of the Ninth ACM SIGKDD International Conference on Knowledge Discovery and Data Mining. (2003) 39–48
6. Cohn, D., Caruana, R., McCallum, A.: Semi-supervised clustering with user feedback. Technical report, Cornell University (2003)
7. Xing, E., Ng, A., Jordan, M., S.Russell: Distance metric learning, with application to clustering with side-information. In: Advances in Neural Information Processing Systems 15. (2003) 505–512
8. Bar-Hillel, A., Hertz, T., Shental, N., Weinshall, D.: Learning distance functions using equivalence relations. In: Proceedings of 20th International Conference on Machine Learning. (2003) 11–18
9. Davidson, I., Ravi, S.: Agglomerative hierarchical clustering with constraints: Theoretical and empirical results. In: Knowledge Discovery in Databases: 9th European Conference on Principles and Practice of Knowledge Discovery in Databases. Volume 3721 of Lecture Notes in Computer Science., Springer (2005) 59–70
10. Wagstaff, K., Cardie, C., Rogers, S., Schroedl, S.: Constrained k-means clustering with background knowledge. In: Proceedings of 18th International Conference on Machine Learning. (2001) 577–584
11. Bilenko, M., S.Basu, Mooney, R.: Integrating constraints and metric learning in semi-supervised clustering. In: Proceedings of the 21st International Conference on Machine Learning. (2004)
12. Buchholz, M., Kestler, H., Bauer, A., Böck, W., Rau, B., Leder, G., Kratzer, W., Bommer, M., Scarpa, A., Schilling, M., Adler, G., Hoheisel, J., Gress, T.: Specialized dna arrays for the differentiation of pancreatic tumors: A solution for a common diagnostic dilemma. Clin Cancer Res **11** (2005) 8048–8054
13. A.K.Jain, Dubes, R.: Algorithms for Clustering Data. Prentice Hall, New Jersey (1988)
14. Rand, W.: Objective criteria for the evaluation of clustering methods. Journal of the American Statistical Association **66** (1971) 846–850
15. Eisen, M., Spellman, P., Brown, P., Botstein, D.: Cluster analysis and display of genome-wide expression patterns genetics cluster analysis and display of genome-wide expression patterns. PNAS **95** (1998) 14863–14868

# A Study of the Robustness of KNN Classifiers Trained Using Soft Labels

Neamat El Gayar[1], Friedhelm Schwenker[2], and Günther Palm[2]

[1] Cairo University
Faculty of Computers and Information
12613 Giza, Egypt
`n.elgayar@fci-cu.edu.eg`
[2] University of Ulm
Department of Neural Information Processing
D-89069 Ulm, Germany
{`friedhelm.schwenker, guenther.palm`}`@uni-ulm.de`

**Abstract.** Supervised learning models most commonly use crisp labels for classifier training. Crisp labels fail to capture the data characteristics when overlapping classes exist. In this work we attempt to compare between learning using soft and hard labels to train K-nearest neighbor classifiers. We propose a new technique to generate soft labels based on fuzzy-clustering of the data and fuzzy relabelling of cluster prototypes. Experiments were conducted on five data sets to compare between classifiers that learn using different types of soft labels and classifiers that learn with crisp labels. Results reveal that learning with soft labels is more robust against label errors opposed to learning with crisp labels. The proposed technique to find soft labels from the data, was also found to lead to a more robust training in most data sets investigated.

## 1   Introduction

Dealing with vagueness is a common problem in many pattern recognition problems. This vagueness is sometimes due to the existence of overlapping classes. In supervised learning models (classifier design) crisp labels are mainly used for training. Crisp labels indicate the membership of a training pattern to a single class. Such labels can be hard to obtain in real applications and fail to reflect the natural grouping or uncertainty that is available among classes.

Few attempts have been made in the machine learning community to discuss the necessities, approaches and virtues of using soft labels for classifier training [1,2]. Soft labels allow a pattern to belong to multiple classes with different degrees. A soft label can be considered fuzzy, probabilistic or possibilistic according to what its entries indicate. A review of hard, fuzzy and probabilistic and possibilistic labels can be found in [3].

Using soft labels can be very useful in cases where the feature space has overlapping or ill-defined classes, to accommodate the uncertainty of an external teacher about certain patterns, to model the opinions of several experts, and to

F. Schwenker and S. Marinai (Eds.): ANNPR 2006, LNAI 4087, pp. 67–80, 2006.

deal with linguistic features [1]. In some real world applications like in medicine, a clear (crisp) classification of training data may be difficult or impossible: Assignments of a patient to a certain disorder frequently can be done only in a probabilistic (fuzzy) manner [4].

In most cases however, data sets are most commonly labeled with crisp labels. Nevertheless, soft labels can be generated to provide more realistic memberships of the training patterns to ensure robust training [5]. In [2] Kuncheva reviews various schemes for generating soft labels and discusses whether using soft labels for learning can improve the classifier performance. Results of a detailed experimental investigation for the *K-nearest neighbor classifier* (KNN) indicates that although there is no clear winner amongst the *K*-nearest neighbor classifier and the *Fuzzy-K-nearest neighbor classifier* (FKNN) using fuzzy labels; the FKNN can be a useful choice for some applications because it provides additional information about the certainty of the classification decision. Keller et al [6] claim that the improvement on the error rate might not be the main benefit from using the FKNN model. More importantly, the model offers a degree of certainty which can be used with a "refuse-to-decide" option. Thus objects with overlapping classes can be detected and processed separately.

Few work has been devoted to study learning under noisy test instances [7,8,9] and was mainly restricted to studying noise imposed on hard labels. In this study we attempt to compare between the robustness of classifiers trained using soft labels opposed to classifiers trained with hard labels against errors in the labels. In our problem we mainly are interested to study cases where the classes are not mutually exclusive and therefore each training sample is allowed several class labels. This is different for the multiple-label problem; where multiple candidate class labels are associated with each training instance and it is assumed that only one of the candidates is the correct label [10]. Our work also introduces a new labeling technique based on the *Generalized Nearest prototype Classifier* (GNPC) proposed in [11]. The GNPC has be shown to unify disparate classification techniques like clustering and relabeling, *Parzen's classifier*, *radial basis function networks* (RBF), *Learning vector quantization* (LVQ) type classifiers; and nearest neighbor rules. In this study we focus on one family of the GNPC to use it for generating soft labels which is based on clustering and relabeling. In particular our approach uses fuzzy clustering of data points and fuzzy relabeling of prototypes to assign soft labels to data vectors.

Experiments were conducted on five data sets to compare the classifier performances that learn using crisp labels and different types of soft labels. Experiments were conducted at different noise levels imposed on the data labels. The classifiers used in this study to learn using crisp/soft labels are KNNs. KNN models are simple, wide applicable models and are usually recognized as good competitors to many neural network models and other classification paradigms [11]. The KNN variations that learn using soft labels (i.e FKNN) have been investigated in detail [2] while, most neural model and other known classification techniques were mainly devised to work with crisp labels. Our study will be extended in future work to other classification paradigms working with soft labels including MLP and RBF learning with fuzzy labels [5,1] and recently the work of LVQ models learning with soft labels [12].

The paper is organized as follows; Section 2 reviews two methods to generate soft labels based on a KNN classification. Section 3 proposes a new technique based on GNPC using fuzzy clustering and fuzzy relabelling. Section 4, describes the used data sets, and outlines details of the experiments conducted. In Section 5, results are illustrated, summarized and discussed. Finally, the paper is concluded in Section 6.

## 2    Soft Labels

A crisp label $y(x)$ of a pattern vector $x \in \mathbb{R}^d$ denotes the class to which this pattern belongs. On the other hand, if $l(x)$ is a soft label of $x$, then $l(x)$ is a $M$-dimensional vector with entries in $[0,1] \subset \mathbb{R}$ indicating the degree with which pattern $x$ is a member of each class. Here $M$ is the number of classes in the application at hand. The problem of determining a soft label can hence be stated as follows: Given a labeled data set $Z$ of $N$ samples $Z = \{x_1, \ldots, x_i, \ldots, x_N\} \subset \mathbb{R}^d$, where each $x_i$ is associated with a crisp label $y(x_i) \in \{C_1, C_2, \ldots, C_M\}$, where $C_i$, $i = 1, \ldots, M$ are the available class labels. Calculate for each $x_i$ a soft label, $l(x_i) \in (l_{i1}, l_{i2}, \ldots, l_{iM}) \in [0,1]^M$ representing the degrees of class memberships to the classes $\{C_1, C_2, \ldots, C_M\}$ respectively, i.e. $l_{ij} = l(x_i)_j$ denotes the degree with which pattern $x_i$ belongs to class $C_j$. As follows, two schemes to assign soft labels using a KNN classifier are briefly described. In the next section we introduce a soft labeling technique based on Generalized nearest prototype classifier (GNPC).

### 2.1    K-Nearest Neighbor Soft Labels

The KNN soft labels for any $x_i \in Z$ are calculated as follows: First the $k$ points in $Z$ closest to $x_i$ are determined, and then the membership of pattern $x_i$ to class $C_j$ is calculated through the relative frequencies:

$$l(x_i)_j = \frac{k_j}{k} \tag{1}$$

Here $k_j$ is the number of elements $x \in Z$ amongst the $k$ closest neighbors to $x_i$ which are labeled with classes $y(x) = C_j$.

### 2.2    Keller Soft Labels

The Keller et al. soft labeling scheme [6] is similar to the KNN labeling scheme but guarantees that all objects retain their true class labels if the soft labels are "hardened" by the maximum membership rule. This scheme will affect only those objects which are close to classification boundaries by diminishing the "certainty" for their own class at the expense of increasing the certainty for the bordering class (or classes). The soft labels are computed as follows:

$$l(x_i)_j = \begin{cases} 0.51 + 0.49\frac{k_j}{k} & : \text{ if } C_j \text{ is the crisp class label of } x_i \\ 0.49\frac{k_j}{k} & : \text{ otherwise} \end{cases} \qquad (2)$$

Again, $k_j$ is the number of elements amongst the $k$ closest neighbors $x \in Z$ to $x_i$ which are labeled with class $C_j$.

## 3   Generating Soft Labels by GNPC

Prototype based classification is perhaps the simplest and most intuitively motivated pattern recognition paradigm. There are many classification techniques
that are based implicitly or explicitly on similarity to point prototypes, for example RBF networks, LVQ and some recent extensions of the LVQ with soft
assignments to data vectors to prototypes [12,13,14,15]. Like the K-nearest neighbor method Nearest Prototype Classifier (NPC) is a local classification method
in the sense that classification boundaries are approximated locally. Instead of
making use of all the data points of a training set, however, NPC relies on a
set of appropriately chosen prototype vectors. This makes the method computationally more efficient, because the number of items which must be stored and
to which a new data point must be compared for classification is considerably
less. In [10] an integrated framework for a generalized nearest prototype classifier
(GNPC) is proposed. Five large families of classifiers are shown to fit within the
GNPC framework. The five families differ most importantly in the way prototypes are obtained and not in their formal GNPC representation. The definition
of a GNPC is listed below.

**Definition 1 [10]:** The generalized Nearest Prototype Classifier (GNPC) is the
5-tuple $(V, L_V, s, T, S)$ where:

a) $V = \{v_1, \ldots, v_p\}$, $v_i \in \mathbb{R}^d$ is the set of $p$ prototypes;
b) $L_V$ is the $M \times p$ label matrix of the $p$ prototypes for $M$ classes ;
c) $s(\cdot, \cdot)$ is a similarity measure defined on $\mathbb{R}^d$ that calculates the similarity
    between data point $x$ and prototypes $v_k$.
d) $T$ is any $t$-norm defined over fuzzy sets, and $S$ is an aggregation operator.

Given an unlabeled vector $x \in \mathbb{R}^d$, the similarity of $x$ to all $p$ prototypes is calculated to produce the similarity vector $s = (s(x, v_1), \ldots, s(x, v_p)) = (s_1, \ldots, s_p)$
The label of a vector $x$ to class $C_j$ is assigned as follows

$$l(x)_j = S_{k=1}^p L_V(j, k) T s_k$$

According to the GNPC, $x$ is then assigned to the class which corresponds to the
maximum entry in the label vector. The GNPC framework can be categorized
into 5 families of different classifiers according to the determination $V, L_V, s(x, v)$
and the operators $T$ and $S$ in the Definition above. It is shown that for the five
families of the classifiers studied in [10] the type of operations used for $T$ is the
*product*; while the $S$ is either defined as the *maximum* or the *average* operation.

As follows we introduce an approach to generate soft labels based on Generalized nearest prototype classifier (GNPC). In particular our proposed method is
linked to the first family of classifiers which is based on clustering and re-labeling.

## 3.1 Soft Labels with GNPC Using Fuzzy Clustering and Fuzzy Re-labeling

Our proposed method to assign soft labels to a previously labeled data set is summarized in Table 1.

**Table 1.** The GNPC Algorithm

**Input**
- $Z$ a set of $N$ crisp labeled training examples $x$
- $M$ classes $C_1, C_2, \ldots, C_M$.
- Each $x$ is associated with a crisp label $y(x_i) \in \{C_1, C_2, \ldots, C_M\}$

**1. Fuzzy Clustering FCM step**
  1. Initialize $p$, the number of clusters of $Z$
  2. Cluster analysis of $Z$ using the FCM algorithm
  3. For each $x_i \in Z$, obtain its cluster membership $\mu(x_i)$

**2. Calculating soft labels for the $p$ clusters**
  1. Initialize the $M \times p$ matrix $L = 0$
  2. For each point $x_i \in Z$ and it's label $y(x_i) = C_q$: $L_q = L_q + \mu(x_i)$
    here $L_q$ is the $q$-th row of $L$.
  3. Normalize the columns of $L$ to sum to 1
  4. Normalize the rows of $L$ to sum to 1

**3. Infer a soft label of a pattern from the soft labels of the clusters**
For data point $x_i$, calculate its fuzzy label as follows:
  1. Find $\mu(x_i)$ from FCM in previous step
  2. Calculate soft label using fuzzy composition: $l(x_i) = L \circ \mu(x_i)$.

As follows we describe the algorithm in details linking it to the GNPC described above. In Step 1 of the algorithm, the prototypes are defined in the data using clustering. Each cluster is represented by a single prototype. Data vectors in the same cluster are supposed to possess much more similarity to each other than to the patterns in other groups. Data vectors are clustered disregarding their labels. Here we choose to employs fuzzy C-means clustering (FCM) [16] which is probably the most popular fuzzy clustering method that attempts to cluster feature vectors by iteratively minimizing an objective function. The fuzzy *c-means* generates for each element $x_i$ in the data a membership vector

$$\mu(x_i) = (\mu_{i1}, \ldots, \mu_{ip})$$

that describes how strong it belongs to each cluster. Here $\mu_{ik}$ denotes the similarity of pattern $x_i$ to the cluster prototype $v_k$ and is calculated using the FCM as follows:

$$\mu_{ik} = \frac{1}{\sum_{q=1}^{p} \left(\frac{d_{ik}}{d_{iq}}\right)^{\frac{1}{\beta-1}}}$$

$\beta > 1$ is the fuzzifier, $d_{iq}$ can be calculated by any distance measure; here we use the Euclidean distance.

The membership values of the patterns generated using the FCM method are distributed over the clusters in a normalized fashion The number of clusters for a given dataset is computed using cluster validity measures [17]; where different numbers of clusters are experimented with and the clustering with the maximum cluster validity is selected [18].

Step 2, of the algorithm corresponds to finding soft labels for cluster proto-types denoted by the $M \times p$ prototype label matrix $L_V$. This is often referred to in the literature as relabelling. Crisp relabelling schemes minimizes overall number of resubstituition misclassifications to label each cluster prototype with the class held by the majority of the vectors within that cluster [10]. An advantage can be gained making soft relabeling [10,19]; thereby providing soft connections between prototypes and classes; value $L_V(j, k)$ can hence be regarded as the strength of the association of $v_k$ with class $C_j$.

In step 2.2 of Table1 the fuzzy labeling procedure for the prototypes is described which uses the membership functions of the patterns generated from the FCM step and the crisp labels information to derive soft labels for the cluster prototypes. Here restrict the sum of label vector for the prototypes $v_k$ to one and therefore we add the normalization step in 2.3-4. The resulting label matrix $L_V$ can be regarded as a "fuzzy relation" on $C \times V$ [20] expressing the association between the classes and the prototypes.

Finally, in step 3 for a given data point its soft label can be inferred from the prototype label matrix $L_V$ and the similarity of $x$ to the given prototypes denoted by the FCM membership function vector $\mu(x)$ using a "composition" operation $\circ$ used for fuzzy-logic inference mechanism [20] The soft label of the vector $x$ is hence calculated as follows: $l(x) = L \circ \mu(x)$ or $l(x)_j = S_{k=1}^{p} L_V(j, k) T \mu_k$. Typically $T$ is an intersection operation (a $t$-norm) and $S$ is either a union or a mean $n$-place operation. In our implementation we use $T$ as product and the $S$ as maximum operation.

## 4   Data and Experiments

Experiments were performed on five different data sets. All data sets share the characteristics that there exist some classes overlapping to some extent. The first data set is the Iris data set containing 4 features and 3 classes. We also used two benchmark synthetic data sets [2] which are two dimensional. The first syntactic data set, the Normal-mixtures data, consists of two classes and is generated from a mixture of two normal distributions with the same covariance matrices. The class distribution has been chosen to allow a best possible error rate of 8%. The second syntactic data set, the Cone-torus data set consist of 3 classes and is generated from three differently shaped distributions; where patterns from each class is not equal but are rather distributed with a frequency of 0.25, 0.25 and 0.5. We also use a set of object images, COIL data, obtained from Columbia Object Image Library [21]. The dataset contains 8 features of the images of 20 different objects, for each object 72 training samples are available.

Table 2 summarizes the characteristics of the data sets used. In addition, we use the Satimage data from the ELENA database [22]; which represents Landsat Multi-Spectral Scanner image data, consisting 6435 patterns each of 36 attributes representing 6 different classes (red soil, cotton crop, grey soil , damp grey soil, soil with vegetation stubble and very damp grey soil). Table 2 summarizes some of the characteristics of the data sets used.

**Table 2.** Summary of data sets used in the numerical experiments

| Data set | No of features | No of classes | No of data points | pattern/class |
|---|---|---|---|---|
| Iris | 4 | 3 | 150 | equal |
| Normal-mixtures | 2 | 2 | 1000 | equal |
| Cone-torus | 2 | 3 | 400 | different |
| COIL | 8 | 20 | 1440 | equal |
| Satimage | 36 | 6 | 1000 | different |

We mainly use the K-nearest neighbor classifier (KNN) in the numerical experiments. The KNN classifier is popular for its simplicity to use and implementation, robustness to noisy data and its wide applicability in a lot of appealing applications [23]. We used a simple version of the FKNN [2] that is trained using soft labels. The KNN trained with crisp labels was compared to the FKNN trained with the different soft labels described in Section 2. Experiments were repeated for the five data sets described above. To evaluate the robustness of the different labels we forced errors on the training sets with different percentages and examined the performance of the classifiers trained with crisp labels and the three variations of the soft labels. The errors were introduced to the crisp training data set and then mapped by the corresponding labeling scheme into soft labels. The accuracy of the compared techniques was calculated using a 10-fold cross validation [24]. Note the K-nearest neighbor value, $k$ used in equations 1 and 2 to generate the KNN soft labels and the Keller soft labels, respectively are not necessary the same as the K-nearest neighbor value, used for the KNN and the FKNN classifiers used for the final classification; we will therefore refer to the latter value as $K$ to avoid confusion. We investigated the affect of the choice of $k$ (for soft label generation) and $K$ (for final classifiers) in our experimentation. In particular we generate the soft labels using KNN soft labels and the Keller soft labels for $k = 3, 5, 7, 9, 11, 13, 15$. For the KNN and FKNN classifiers we repeat the experiments for $K = 3, 5, 7, 9$ for all data sets. In the following section experimental results are presented and discussed.

## 5   Results and Discussion

Figures 1, 2, 3, 4 and 5 illustrate the results on the Isis data set, the Normal mixtures data set, the Cone Torus data set, the Coil data set and the Satimage data set, respectively. The figures compare the accuracy of the KNN classifier trained with crisp labels and the accuracy of the FKNN classifier trained with the

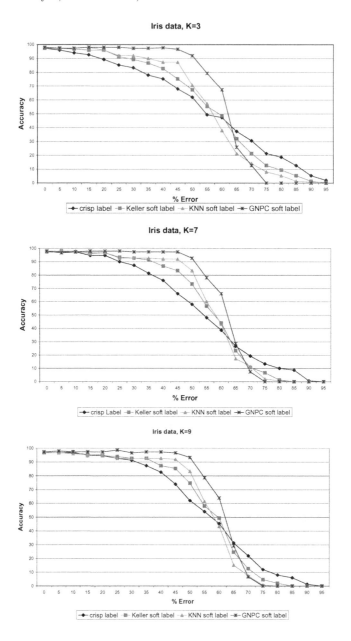

**Fig. 1.** Results of the IRIS data

KNN soft labels, Keller et al. soft labels and the proposed GNPC soft labels. The accuracies for the different techniques are calculated when noise was introduced to the class labels. In the experiments, from 5-95% of the class labels have been flipped at random using the uniform distribution. Results for KNN and FKNN classifier at $K = 3$ are presented for all data sets as the results on other values

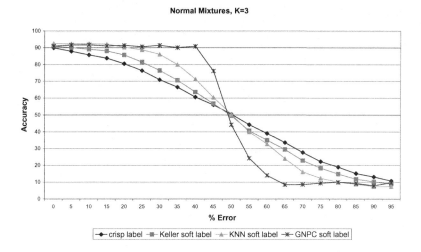

**Fig. 2.** Results of the Mixtures data set

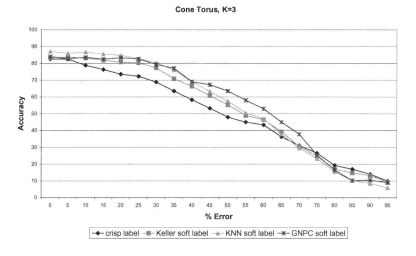

**Fig. 3.** Results of the Cone-torus data set

of K resulted in a more or less similar relative behavior for all techniques when different labeling techniques are compared. Figure 1 outlines the results for the Iris data set for $K = 3, 7, 9$. The performance of the classifiers trained with Keller soft labels and KNN soft labels showed sensitivity for the choice of k ; where the results of the classifiers trained with KNN soft labels were generally more sensitive to the choice of $k$. Different data sets behaved differently under the choice of $k$ (and the choice of the $K$ for the classifiers) but generally experiments have shown that a reasonable choice of $k$ would be 7 or 9 for all data and classifier models under investigation. In figures 1-5 we fix k to 7. Figures 6 and 7

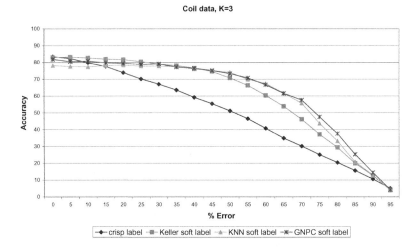

**Fig. 4.** Results of the COIL data set

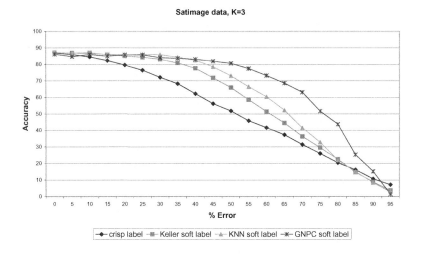

**Fig. 5.** Results of the Satimage data set

investigate the performance of the classifiers trained with Keller soft labels and KNN soft labels with $k = 3, 5, 7, 9, 11, 13, 15$ for the Iris and the Satimage data sets, respectively. For the GNPC soft labels we used an adaptive technique to find the optimal number of clusters "p" for each data set as mentioned before. For the Iris data set we used 10 clusters, the Normal Mixtures data with 20 clusters, the Cone torus data with 45 clusters, the Coil data with 300 clusters and the Satimage data with 120 clusters.

The performance the classifiers trained with the FCM soft labels were affected by the number of clusters "p" chosen and there is a relation between the number

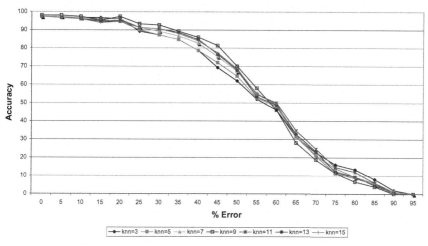

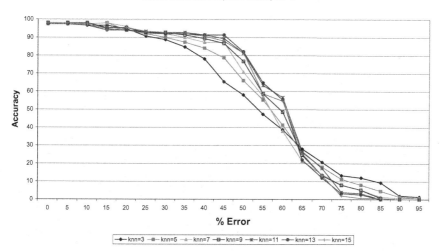

**Fig. 6.** Effect of the parameter $k$ for the Iris data when using Keller soft labels and KNN soft labels

of classes available in the data and the number of adequate clusters. We recommend starting with number of clusters that are a multiple of 10 of the number of classes. For the GNPC soft labels we also used for the FCM algorithm a fuzzification constant of 2, except for the Coil and the Satimage data sets where we reduced the fuzzification constant to 1.1 to prevent soft labels produced by the FCM clustering to be to diffuse among multiple classes. To infer the soft labels of a given data point we used a max-product [20] composition operator.

Examining the results illustrated in figures 1 through 5, it is obvious that the accuracy of the KNN classifier trained with crisp labels is generally less

**Keller soft labels, Satimage, K=3**

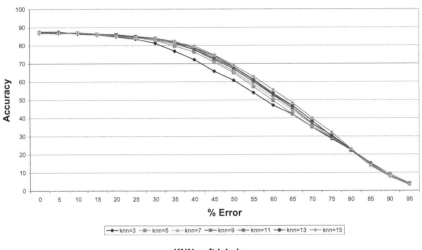

**KNN soft labels**

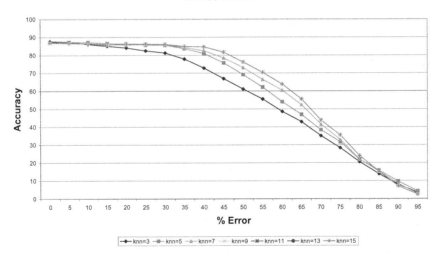

**Fig. 7.** Effect of the parameter $k$ for the Satimage data when using Keller soft labels and KNN soft labels

robust to errors on the labels compared to the FKNN classifier trained with different soft labels. The FKNN trained with soft labels seems to be able to sustain a robust performance up to 65% error rate for the Iris data, 45 % error rate for the Normal Mixtures data, 75% error for the Cone torus data and finally until 95% for both the Coil data and the Satimage data; compared to the KNN trained with crisp labels. In the same time, the FKNN classifier trained with the GNPC soft label is able in most cases to maintain a more stable accuracy compared to the other KNN and the Keller soft label for most data sets under investigation.

# 6   Conclusion and Future Work

In this work we propose a new technique to obtain soft labels from available crisp labels that is based on fuzzy clustering of the data and fuzzy relabeling of the cluster prototypes. Fuzzy labels are obtained through fuzzy logic based inference. The proposed method is extended from a GNPC family which unifies many disparate classification techniques.

The robustness of the classifiers trained with crisp and soft labels is tested. Experiments were conducted on five data sets to compare the behavior of the classifiers when errors are available in the data labels. Results reveal the robustness of the KNN classifier trained with soft labels opposed to classifiers trained with crisp labels. The proposed soft labeling scheme based of fuzzy clustering and fuzzy relabelling was found in general be most robust to error on labels and less sensitive to the choice of parameters (like the k parameter in the KNN and Keller soft labeling techniques) and the KNN classifier model. In our future work we intend to examine more alternatives to generate soft labels by exploring and extending other families of the GNPC framework and to study the effectiveness of other classifier models (MLP, RBF, LVQ and SVM) that learn with soft labels.

We particularly also intend to investigate other alternatives for soft labels in cases where the data set is incompletely labeled or is labeled using different sources of information. We also aim towards using soft labels in the framework of multiple classifier systems and similarly test their usefulness in the context of accuracy and robustness.

## Acknowledgement

This research has been partially supported by the DFG (German Research Society) grant SCHW 623/3-2 and SCHW 623/4-2.

## References

1. El Gayar, N.F.: Fuzzy Neural Network Models for Unsupervised and Confidence-Based Learning. PhD thesis, University of Alexandria, Dept. of Comp. Sc. (1999)
2. Kuncheva, L.: Fuzzy classifier design. Physica-Verlag (2000)
3. Bezdek, J., Pal, N.: Two soft relatives of learning vector quantization. Neural Networks 8(5) (1995) 729–743
4. Villmann, T., Hammer, B., Schleif, F.M., Geweniger, T.: Fuzzy labeled neural gas for fuzzy classification. In: Proceedings of WSOM 2005. (2005) 283–290
5. Pal, S., Mitra, S.: Multilayer perceptron, fuzzy sets and classification. IEEE Transactions on Neural Networks 3 (1992) 683–697
6. Keller, J., Gray, M., Givens, J.: A fuzzy k-nearest algorithm. IEEE Transactions on Pattern Analysis and Machine Intelligence 7 (1985) 693–699
7. Angluin, D., Laird, D.: Learning from noisy examples. Machine Learning 2(4) (1987) 343–370
8. Lam, P., Stork, D.: Evaluating classifiers by means of test data with noisy labels. In: Proceedings of the International Joint Conference on Artificial Intelligence. (2003) 513–518

9. Bernadt, J., Soh, L.: Authoritative citation knn learning with noisy training datasets. In: Proceedings of the International Conference on Artificial Intelligence. (2004) 916–931
10. Jin, R., Ghahramani, Z.: Learning with multiple labels. In: Advances in Neural Information Processing Systems. Volume 15. (2003)
11. Kuncheva, L., Bezdek, J.: An integrated frame work for generalized nearest prototype classifier design. International Journal of Uncertainty, Fuzziness and Knowledge-based System 6(5) (1998) 437–457
12. Villmann, T., Schleif, F.M., Hammer, B.: Fuzzy labeled soft nearest neighbor classification with relevance learning. In: Proceedings of ICMLA 2005, IEEE Press (2005) 11–15
13. Karayiannis, N.: Repairs to GLVQ: A new family of competitive learning schemes. IEEE Transaction on Neural Networks 7 (1996) 1062–1071
14. Seo, S., Bode, M. Obermayer, K.: Soft nearest prototype classification. IEEE Transaction on Neural Networks 14 (2003) 390398
15. Seo, S., Obermayer, K.: Soft learning vector quantization. 15 (2003) 15891604
16. Melin, P., Castillo, O.: Hybrid Intelligent Systems for Pattern Recognition Using Soft Computing. Springer-Verlag (2005)
17. Xie, X., Beni, G.: A validity measure for fuzzy clustering. IEEE Trans. on Pattern Analysis and Machine Intelligence 13(8) (1991) 841–847
18. Czogala, E., Leski, J.: Fuzzy And Neuro-Fuzzy Intelligent Systems. Physica-Verlag (2000)
19. Van de Wouwer, P., Scheunders, P., van Dyck, M., De Bodt, M., Wuyts, F., Van de Heyning, P.: Wavelet-filvq classifier for speech analysis. In: Proc. of the Int. Conf. Pattern Recognition, IEEE Press (1996) 214218
20. Klir, G., Yuan, B.: Fuzzy Sets and Fuzzy Logic, Theory and Applications. Prentice-Hall of India (2002)
21. Nene, S.A., Nayar, S.K., Murase, H.: Columbia object image library (coil-20). Technical report, Technical Report CUCS-005-96 (1996)
22. ELENA: (ftp.dice.ucl.ac.be, directory: pub/neural-nets/elena/databases)
23. Duda, R., Hart, P., Stork, D.: Pattern Classification. John Wiley and Sons (2004)
24. Kuncheva, L.: Combining pattern classifiers. John Wiley and Sons (2004)

# An Experimental Study on Training Radial Basis Functions by Gradient Descent

Joaquín Torres-Sospedra, Carlos Hernández-Espinosa,
and Mercedes Fernández-Redondo

Departamento de Ingenieria y Ciencia de los Computadores, Universitat Jaume I,
Avda. Sos Baynat s/n, C.P. 12071, Castellon, Spain
{jtorres, espinosa, redondo}@icc.uji.es

**Abstract.** In this paper, we present experiments comparing different training
algorithms for Radial Basis Functions (RBF) neural networks. In particular we
compare the classical training which consist of an unsupervised training of centers followed by a supervised training of the weights at the output, with the full
supervised training by gradient descent proposed recently in same papers. We
conclude that a fully supervised training performs generally better. We also compare *Batch training* with *Online training* and we conclude that *Online training*
suppose a reduction in the number of iterations.

## 1 Introduction

A RBF has two layer of neurons. The first one, in its usual form, is composed of neurons
with Gaussian transfer functions (GF) and the second has neurons with linear transfer
functions.

The output of a RBF can be calculated with equations (1) and (2).

$$\hat{y}_{i,k} = \mathbf{w}_i^T \cdot \mathbf{h}_k = \sum_{j=1}^{c} w_{ij} \cdot h_{j,k} \tag{1}$$

$$h_{j,k} = \exp\left(-\frac{\|\mathbf{x}_k - \mathbf{v}_j\|^2}{\sigma^2}\right) \tag{2}$$

Where $\mathbf{v}_j$ are the center of the Gaussian transfer functions, $\sigma$ control the width of the
Gaussian transfer functions and $\mathbf{w}_i$ are the weights among the Gaussian units (GU) and
the output units.

As (1) and (2) show, there are three elements to design in the neural network: the
centers and the widths of the Gaussian units and the linear weights among the Gaussian
units and output units.

There are two procedures to design the network. One is to train the networks in two
steps. First we find the centers and widths by using some unsupervised clustering algorithm and after that we train the weights among hidden and output units by a supervised
algorithm. This process is usually fast [1-4].

The second procedure is to train the centers and weights in a full supervised fashion, similar to the algorithm Backpropagation (BP) for Multilayer Feedforward. This

F. Schwenker and S. Marinai (Eds.): ANNPR 2006, LNAI 4087, pp. 81–92, 2006.

procedure has the same drawbacks of Backpropagation, long training time and high computational cost. However, it has received quite attention recently [5-6].

In [5-6] it is used a sensitivity analysis to show that the traditional Gaussian unit (called "*exponential generator function*") of the RBF network has low sensitivity for gradient descent training for a wide range of values of the widths. As an alternative two different transfer functions are proposed. They are called in the papers "*lineal generator function*" and "*cosine generator function*". Unfortunately, the experiments shown in the papers are performed with only two databases and the RBF networks are compared with equal number of Gaussian unit.

In contrast, in this paper we present more complete experiments with nine databases from the *UCI Repository*, and include in the experiments four traditional unsupervised training algorithms and a fully gradient descent training with the three transfer functions analysed in papers [5-6].

Furthermore, we also presents experiments with *Batch* and *Online learning*, in the original references the training was performed in *Batch* mode and we show that Online Traning is the best alternative under the point of view of training speed.

## 2  Theory

### 2.1  Training by Gradient Descent

**"Exponential (EXP) Generator" Function.** This RBF has the usual Gaussian transfer function described in (1) and (2). The equation for adapting the weights by gradient descent is in (3).

$$\Delta \mathbf{w}_p = \eta \cdot \sum_{k=1}^{M} \varepsilon_{p,k}^0 \cdot \mathbf{h}_k \tag{3}$$

Where $\eta$ is the learning rate, $M$ the number of training patterns and $\varepsilon_{p,k}^0$ is the output error, the difference between target and output as in equation (4).

$$\epsilon_{p,k}^o = t_{p,k} - o_{p,k} \tag{4}$$

The equation for adapting the centers by gradient descent is the following:

$$\Delta v_q = \eta \cdot \sum_{k=1}^{M} \varepsilon_{p,k}^h \cdot (\mathbf{x}_k - \mathbf{v}_q) \tag{5}$$

Where $\eta$ is the learning rate and $\varepsilon_{p,k}^h$ is the hidden error given by equation (6) and (7).

$$\varepsilon_{p,k}^h = \alpha_{q,k} \cdot \sum_{i=1}^{n_o} \varepsilon_{i,k}^0 \cdot w_{iq} \tag{6}$$

$$\alpha_{q,k} = \frac{2}{\sigma^2} \cdot \exp\left(-\frac{\|\mathbf{x}_k - \mathbf{v}_q\|^2}{\sigma^2}\right) \tag{7}$$

In the above equations $n_o$ is the number of outputs and these equation are for *Batch training*, i.e., we adapt the variables of the network after the presentation of all the patterns of the training set.

The equations for *Online training* are basically the same, we only have to omit the sum for k=1, to M in the expressions.

For example, equation (5) in the *Online training* would be the following:

$$\Delta v_q = \eta \cdot \varepsilon_{p,k}^h \cdot (\mathbf{x}_k - \mathbf{v}_q) \tag{8}$$

And we would have to adapt $v_q$ after each presentation of a training pattern to the network.

**"Linear (LIN) Generator" Function.** In this case the transfer function of the hidden units is the following:

$$h_{j,k} = \left( \frac{1}{\|\mathbf{x}_k - \mathbf{v}_j\|^2 + \gamma^2} \right)^{\frac{1}{m-1}} \tag{9}$$

Where we have used $m = 3$ in our experiments and $\gamma$ is a parameter that should be determined by trial and error and cross-validation.

The above equations (3), (4), (5) and (6) are the same, but in this case $\alpha_{q,k}$ is different and is given in (10).

$$\alpha_{q,k} = \frac{2}{m-1} \cdot \left( \|\mathbf{x}_k - \mathbf{v}_q\|^2 + \gamma^2 \right)^{\frac{m}{1-m}} \tag{10}$$

**"Cosine (COS) Generator" Function.** In this case the transfer function is the following:

$$h_{j,k} = \frac{a_j}{\left( \|\mathbf{x}_k - \mathbf{v}_j\|^2 + a_j^2 \right)^{1/2}} \tag{11}$$

Equations (3), (4) and (5) are the same, but in this case the hidden error is different as in equation (12).

$$\varepsilon_{p,k}^h = \left( \frac{h_{j,k}^3}{a_j^2} \right) \cdot \sum_{i=1}^{no} \varepsilon_{i,k}^0 \cdot w_{iq} \tag{12}$$

The parameter $a_j$ is also adapted during training, the equation is (13).

$$\Delta a_j = \left( \frac{\eta}{a_j} \right) \cdot \sum_{i=1}^{no} h_{j,k} \cdot (1 - h_{j,k}^2) \cdot \varepsilon_{p,k}^h \tag{13}$$

## 2.2   Training by Unsupervised Clustering

**Algorithm 1.** This training algorithm is the simplest one. It was proposed in [1]. It uses adaptive k-means clustering to find the centers of the gaussian units. The process is iterative, we successively present an input pattern and after each presentation we find the closest center and adapt this center toward the input pattern, according to equation (14).

$$c(n+1) = c(n) + \eta \cdot (x - c(n)) \tag{14}$$

Where $x$ is the input pattern, $c$ is the closest center and $\eta$ the adaptation step.

After finding the centers, we should calculate the widths of the Gaussian units. For that, it is used a simple heuristic; we calculate the mean distance between one center and one of the closest neighbors, $P$, for example, the first closest neighbor ($P = 1$), the second ($P = 2$), the third ($P = 3$) or the fourth ($P = 4$).

We need a quite important trial and error procedure to design the network because the number of centers of k-means clustering should be fixed a priori and also the value $P$ for the heuristic of the widths. In our experiments we have tried all the combinations of the followings number of centers and widths. For the centers the values 10, 20, 30, 40, 50, 60, 70, 80, 90, 100 and 110 and for the widths we have used $P = 1, 2, 3, 4$.

**Algorithm 2.** This algorithm is proposed in reference [2]. However, we have slightly modified the algorithm. In the original reference it is used a truncation for the Gaussian functions and non-RBF functions in the hidden layer. We have applied the algorithm without truncation in the Gaussian functions and with only RBF units in the hidden layer.

Basically the algorithm is the following. The Gaussian units are generated incrementally, in stages $k$, by random clustering. Let $k = 1, 2, 3, \cdots$ denote a stage of this process. A stage is characterized by a parameter $\delta_k$ that specifies the maximum radius for the hypersphere that includes the random cluster of points that is to define the Gaussian unit; this parameter is successively reduced in every stage $k$ ( $\delta_k = \alpha \cdot \delta_{k-1}$, with $\alpha$ in the range 0.5-0.8). The Gaussian units at any stage $k$ are randomly selected in the following way. Randomly select an input vector $x_i$ from the training set I and search for all other training vectors within the $\delta_k$ neighborhood of $x_i$. The training vector are used to define the Gaussian unit $Q$ (the mean $C_Q$ is the center, and the standard deviation $w_Q$ the width) and then removed from the training set, forming what is called the remaining training set $R$. To define the next Gaussian unit $Q + 1$ another input vector $x_i$ is randomly selected from $R$ and the process repeated. This process of randomly picking an input vector $x_i$ is repeated until the remaining training set $R$ is empty. Furthermore, when the number of points in the cluster $N_j$ is less than a certain parameter $\beta$ no Gaussian unit is created. The stages are repeated until the cross-validation error increases.

The algorithm is described in procedure 1. Where, $\rho$ is the standard deviation of the distances of the training points from their centroid, $\gamma$ is a lower limit for the length of the neighborhood $\delta_k$ (a parameter), $TRE_k$ is the training set error at stage $k$ and $TSE_k$ is the cross-validation set error.

**Algorithm 3.** It is proposed in reference [3]. They use a one pass algorithm called *APC-III*, clustering the patterns class by class instead of the entire patterns at the same time. The *APC-III* algorithms uses a constant radius to create the clusters. In the reference this radius is calculated as the mean minimum distance between training patterns multiplied by a constant $\alpha$ , see equation (15).

$$R_0 = \alpha \cdot \frac{1}{P} \cdot \sum_{i=1}^{P} \min_{i \neq j}(\|x_i - x_j\|) \tag{15}$$

**Procedure 1.** Algorithm 2

1. Initialize counters and constants: $k = 0, Q = 0, \delta_1 = \rho, \alpha$ = some fraction between 0.5 and 0.8.
2. Increment stage counter $k = k + 1$. Reduce neighborhood radius: if $k > 1, delta_k = \alpha \cdot delta_{k-1}$. If $k < \gamma$ stop.
3. Select Gaussian units for the $k$-th stage: $j = 0, R = I$.
    (a) Set $j = j + 1$.
    (b) Select an input vector $x_i$ at random from $R$, the remaining training set.
    (c) Search for all vectors in $R$ within the $\delta_k$ neighborhood of $x_i$. Let this set of vectors be $V_j$.
    (d) Remove the set $V_j$ from $R : R = R - V_j$. If $N_j < \beta$, go to (f).
    (e) Increment Gaussian counter: $Q = Q + 1$. Compute the center $C_Q$ and width $w_Q$ of the $Q$-th Gaussian unit: $C_Q$ = centroid of the set $V_j$, and $w_Q$ = standard deviation of the points in the random cluster $V_j$.
    (f) If R is not empty, go to (a), else go to (4).
4. Calculate the RBF neural network output weights with $Q$ number of Gaussian units.
5. Compute $TSE_k$ and $TRE_k$.
    (a) If $TSE_k < TSE_{k-1}$, go to 2).
    (b) If $TSE_k > TSE_{k-1}$ and $TRE_k > TRE_{k-1}$, go to 2).
    (c) Otherwise, stop. Overfitting has occurred. Use the net generated in the previous stage.

The algorithm is described in procedure 2. The widths are calculated with the following heuristic: find the distance to the center of the nearest cluster which belongs to a different class and assign this value multiplied by $\beta$ to the width.

**Procedure 2.** Algortihm 3

1. Select one input pattern and construct the first cluster with center equal to this pattern.
2. Repeat steps 3 to 5 for each pattern.
3. Repeat step 4 for each cluster.
4. If the distance between the pattern and the clusters is less than $R_0$ include the pattern in the cluster and recalculate the new center of the cluster. Exit the loop.
5. If the pattern is not included in any cluster then create a new cluster with center in this pattern.

**Algorithm 4.** This algorithm is proposed in reference [4]. However, we have slightly modified the algorithm, in the original reference it is used a truncation for the Gaussian units and a hard limiting function for the output layer. We have applied the algorithm without these modifications of the normal RBF network.

The description of the algorithm is as follows. The Gaussian units are generated class by class $k$, so the process is repeated for each class. In a similar way to algorithm 2 the Gaussian units are generated in stages $h$. A stage is characterized by its majority criterion $\rho_h$, a majority criterion of 60% implies that the cluster of the Gaussian unit must have at least 60% of the patterns belonging to its class, this percentage of patterns is called $PC_j^r(k)$. The method will have a maximum of six stages; we begin with a majority criterion $h$ of 50% and end with 100%, by increasing 10% in each stage $\Delta \rho$. The

---

**Procedure 3.** Algorithm 4

---

0. Initialize constants:
   (a) $delta_{max} = 10\rho$,
   (b) $\Delta\theta =$ some constant (10% in the reference)
   (c) $\delta_0 =$ some constant (0 or $0.1 \cdot \rho$),
   (d) $\Delta\delta = (\delta_{max} - \delta_0)/s$, ($s = 25$ in the reference).

1. Initialize class counter: $k = 0$.
2. Increment class counter: $k = k + 1$. If $k > K$, stop. Else, initialize cumulative Gaussian counters: $S_k = 0$ (empty set), $q = 0$.
3. Initialize stage counter: $h = 0$.
4. Increment stage counter: $h = h+1$. Increase majority criterion: If $h > 1$, $\phi_h = \phi_{h-1} + \Delta\phi$, otherwise $\phi_h = 50\%$. If $\phi_h > 100\%$, go to (2) to mask the next class.
5. Select Gaussian units for the $h$th stage: $j = 0$, $R = I$.
   (a) Set $j = j + 1, r = 1, r = 0$.
   (b) Select an input pattern vector $x_i$ of class $k$ at random from $R$, the remaining training set.
   (c) Search for all pattern vectors in $R$ within a $\delta_r$ radius of $x_i$. Let this set of vectors be $V_j^r$.
       i. If $PC_j^r(k) < \phi_h$ and $r > 1$, set $r = r - 1$, go to (e).
       ii. If $PC_j^r(k) > \phi_h$ and $r > 1$, go to (d) to expand the neighborhood.
       iii. If $PC_j^r(k) < \phi_h$ and $r = 1$, go to (h).
       iv. If $PC_j^r(k) > \phi_h$ and $r = 1$, go to (d) to expand the neighborhood.
   (d) Set $r = r + 1, \delta_r = \delta_{r-1} + \Delta\delta$. If $\delta_r > \delta_{max}$, set $r = r - 1$, go to (e). Else, go to (c).
   (e) Remove class $k$ patterns of $V_j^r$ from $R$. If $N_j^r < \beta$, go to (g).
   (f) Set $q = q + 1$. Compute the center $C_q^k$ and width $w_q^k$ of the $q$-th Gaussian for class $k$. Add $q$th Gaussian to the set $S_k$. $C_q^k =$ centroid of class $k$ patterns in the set $V_j^r$ $w_q^k =$ standard deviation of the distances from the centroid $C_q^k$ of the class $k$ patterns in $V_j^r$.
   (g) If $R$ is not empty of class $k$ patterns, go to (a), else go to (6).
   (h) Remove class $k$ patterns of the $V_j^r$ from $R$. If $R$ is not empty of class $k$ patterns, go to (a), else go to (6).
6. From the set $S_k$, eliminate similar Gaussian units (those with very close centers and widths). Let $Q_k$ be the number of Gaussian units after this elimination.
7. Calculate the output weights of the net for class $k$.
8. Compute $TSE_h$ and $TRE_h$ for class $k$. If $h = 1$, go to (4). Else:
   (a) If $TSE_h < TSE_{h-1}$, go to (4).
   (b) If $TSE_h > TSE_{h-1}$ and $TRE_h > TRE_{h-1}$, go to (4).
   (c) Otherwise, overfitting has occurred. Use the mask generated in the previous stage as class $k$ mask. Go to (2) to mask next class.

---

Gaussian units for a given class $k$ at any stage $h$ are randomly selected in the following way. Randomly pick a pattern vector $x_i$ of class $k$ from the training set $I$ and expand the radius of the cluster $\delta_r$ until the percentage of patterns belonging to the class $k$, $PC_j^r(k)$, falls below the majority criterion, then the patterns of class $k$ are used to define the Gaussian unit (the mean $C_q^k$ is the center and the standard deviation $w_q^k$ is the width) and are removed from the training set, forming what it is called the remaining training set $R$. When the number of patterns in the cluster $N_j^r$ is below than a parameter,

$\beta$, no Gaussian unit is created. To define the next gaussian another pattern $x_i$ of class $k$ is randomly picked from the remaining training set $R$ and the process repeated. The successive stage process is repeated until the cross-validation error increases.

The algorithm can be summarized in the steps described in procedure 3. Where, $\phi$ is the maximum of the class standard deviations that are the standard deviations of the distances from the centroid of the patterns of each class, $K$ is the number of classes, $TRE_h$ is the training set error at stage $h$ and $TSE_h$ is the cross-validation set error.

## 3   Experimental Results

We have applied the training algorithms to nine different classification problems from the UCI repository of machine learning databases.

They are Balance Scale, Cylinders Bands, Liver Disorders, Credit Approval, Glass Identification, Heart Disease, The Monk's Problems and Voting Congresional Records. The complete data and a full description can be found in the repository http://www.ics. uci.edu/~ mlearn/MLRepository.html) [7].

### 3.1   Results

The first step was to determine the appropriate parameters of the algorithms by trial and error and cross-validation. We have used an extensive trial procedure and the final value of the parameters we have used in the experiments is in Table 1.

After that, with the final parameters we trained ten networks with different partition of data in training, cross-validation and test set, also with different random initialization of parameters. With this procedure we can obtain a mean performance in the database (the mean of the ten networks) and an error by standard error theory.

These results are in Table 2, 3, 4, 5 and 6. We have included for each database and training algorithm the mean percentage of correct classification with its error (column Perc.) and the number of gaussian transfer units under the column $Nunit$. In the case of unsupervised training algorithms number 2, 3 and 4 (Tables 5 and 6) the number in the column $Nunit$ is a value and an error. The reason is that the final number of Gaussian transfer units changes from one trial to another and we have included the mean value of the number of Gaussian units and the standard desviation as the error.

### 3.2   Interpretation of Results

Comparing the results of the same algorithm trained by gradient descent in the case of *Batch training* and *Online training*, we can see that the differences in performance are not significant. The fundamental difference between both training procedures is in the number of iterations and the value of the learning step. For example, 8000 iterations, $\eta$=0.001 in *EXP Batch* for Bala and 6000 iterations, $\eta$=0.005 in *EXP Online*. The final conclusion is that *online training* is more appropriate that *Batch training* for gradient descent of RBF.

Comparing *EXP*, *LIN* and *COS* generator functions, we can see that the general performance is quite similar except in the case mok1 where the performance of *EXP* is

**Table 1.** Optimal parameters of the different algorithms determined by trial and error

| Method | Params. | Database | | | | |
|---|---|---|---|---|---|---|
| | | bala | band | bupa | cred | glas |
| EXP Batch | Clusters | 45 | 110 | 35 | 40 | 125 |
| | $\sigma$ | 0.6 | 1.2 | 0.6 | 1.8 | 0.4 |
| EXP Online | Clusters | 60 | 40 | 40 | 30 | 110 |
| | $\sigma$ | 0.6 | 1 | 0.4 | 2 | 0.4 |
| LIN Batch | Clusters | 45 | 30 | 10 | 10 | 35 |
| | $\gamma$ | 0.4 | 0.1 | 0.4 | 0.9 | 0.1 |
| LIN Online | Clusters | 50 | 35 | 15 | 10 | 30 |
| | $\gamma$ | 0.6 | 0.3 | 0.8 | 0.1 | 0.2 |
| COS Batch | Clusters | 25 | 120 | 15 | 10 | 105 |
| | $a_j\_ini$ | 0.5 | 1.1 | 0.5 | 0.2 | 0.8 |
| COS Online | Clusters | 40 | 125 | 40 | 25 | 15 |
| | $a_j\_ini$ | 0.5 | 0.5 | 1.1 | 1.1 | 0.8 |
| UC Alg.1 | Clusters | 30 | 60 | 10 | 20 | 100 |
| | $P$ | 4 | 2 | 3 | 2 | 1 |
| UC Alg.2 | $\beta$ | 5 | 3 | 5 | 3 | 5 |
| | $\alpha$ | 0.8 | 0.65 | 0.8 | 0.8 | 0.8 |
| UC Alg.3 | $\beta$ | 5 | 7 | 5 | 6 | 5 |
| | $\alpha$ | 1.7 | 1.3 | 1.3 | 1.7 | 1.2 |
| UC Alg.4 | $\beta$ | 5 | 3 | 3 | 3 | 3 |

| Method | Params. | Database | | | |
|---|---|---|---|---|---|
| | | hear | mok1 | mok2 | vote |
| EXP Batch | Clusters | 155 | 60 | 80 | 35 |
| | $\sigma$ | 1.8 | 0.8 | 0.6 | 2 |
| EXP Online | Clusters | 20 | 30 | 45 | 5 |
| | $\sigma$ | 2 | 0.8 | 0.6 | 1.8 |
| LIN Batch | Clusters | 15 | 15 | 25 | 25 |
| | $\gamma$ | 0.3 | 0.2 | 0.5 | 0.1 |
| LIN Online | Clusters | 10 | 15 | 50 | 10 |
| | $\gamma$ | 0.1 | 0.1 | 0.2 | 0.3 |
| COS Batch | Clusters | 25 | 100 | 125 | 20 |
| | $a_j\_ini$ | 0.2 | 0.2 | 0.2 | 0.5 |
| COS Online | Clusters | 15 | 145 | 45 | 10 |
| | $a_j\_ini$ | 0.5 | 1.1 | 0.2 | 0.2 |
| UC Alg.1 | Clusters | 100 | 90 | 90 | 40 |
| | $P$ | 1 | 2 | 2 | 4 |
| UC Alg.2 | $\beta$ | 3 | 3 | 8 | 3 |
| | $\alpha$ | 0.8 | 0.8 | 0.8 | 0.65 |
| UC Alg.3 | $\beta$ | 5 | 5 | 5 | 5 |
| | $\alpha$ | 1.7 | 1.7 | 1.4 | 1.7 |
| UC Alg.4 | $\beta$ | 3 | 3 | 3 | 5 |

clearly better. In other aspect, *EXP* and *LIN* functions need a higher number of trials for the process of trial and error to design the network, because cosine generator functions adapt all parameters. But in contrast, the number of iterations needed to converge

**Table 2.** Performance of Gradient Descent with Exponential Generator Functions

| | Training Algorithm | | | |
|---|---|---|---|---|
| | **Exp Batch** | | **Exp Online** | |
| **Database** | **Percentage** | $Nunit$ | **Percentage** | $Nunit$ |
| **bala** | 90.2±0.5 | 45 | 90.2±0.5 | 60 |
| **band** | 74.1±1.1 | 110 | 74.0±1.1 | 40 |
| **bupa** | 69.8±1.1 | 35 | 70.1±1.1 | 40 |
| **cred** | 86.1±0.7 | 40 | 86.0±0.8 | 30 |
| **glas** | 92.9±0.7 | 125 | 93.0±0.6 | 110 |
| **hear** | 82.0±1.0 | 155 | 82.0±1.0 | 20 |
| **mok1** | 94.7±1.0 | 60 | 98.5±0.5 | 30 |
| **mok2** | 92.1±0.7 | 80 | 91.3±0.7 | 45 |
| **vote** | 95.6±0.4 | 35 | 95.4±0.5 | 5 |

**Table 3.** Performance of Gradient Descent with Linear Generator Functions

| | Training Algorithm | | | |
|---|---|---|---|---|
| | **Lineal Batch** | | **Lineal Online** | |
| **Database** | **Percentage** | $Nunit$ | **Percentage** | $Nunit$ |
| **bala** | 90.1±0.5 | 45 | 90.6±0.5 | 50 |
| **band** | 74.5±1.1 | 30 | 73.4±1.0 | 35 |
| **bupa** | 71.2±0.9 | 10 | 69.7±1.3 | 15 |
| **cred** | 86.2±0.7 | 10 | 85.8±0.8 | 10 |
| **glas** | 91.4±0.8 | 35 | 92.4±0.7 | 30 |
| **hear** | 82.1±1.1 | 15 | 81.8±1.1 | 10 |
| **mok1** | 93.2±0.7 | 15 | 94.5±0.7 | 15 |
| **mok2** | 82.8±1.2 | 25 | 89.6±1.2 | 50 |
| **vote** | 95.6±0.4 | 25 | 95.6±0.4 | 10 |

**Table 4.** Performance of Gradient Descent with Cosine Generator Functions

| | Training Algorithm | | | |
|---|---|---|---|---|
| | **Cosine Batch** | | **Cosine Online** | |
| **Database** | **Percentage** | $Nunit$ | **Percentage** | $Nunit$ |
| **bala** | 89.9±0.5 | 25 | 90.0±0.7 | 40 |
| **band** | 75.0±1.1 | 120 | 74.9±1.1 | 125 |
| **bupa** | 69.9±1.1 | 15 | 70.2±1.1 | 40 |
| **cred** | 86.1±0.8 | 10 | 86.1±0.8 | 25 |
| **glas** | 93.5±0.8 | 105 | 92.6±0.9 | 15 |
| **hear** | 82.1±1.0 | 25 | 81.9±1.1 | 15 |
| **mok1** | 89.8±0.8 | 100 | 90.2±1.0 | 145 |
| **mok2** | 87.9±0.8 | 125 | 86.6±1.1 | 45 |
| **vote** | 95.6±0.4 | 20 | 95.4±0.4 | 10 |

by *COS* functions is usually larger (for example: *EXP*, band= 10000 iterations; *LIN*, band= 15000; *COS*, band= 75000), so globally speaking the computational cost can be considered similar.

**Table 5.** Performance of Unsupervised Algorithms 1 and 2

| | Training Algorithm | | | |
|---|---|---|---|---|
| | UC Alg. 1 | | UC Alg. 2 | |
| Database | Percentage | $Nunit$ | Percentage | $Nunit$ |
| bala | 88.5±0.8 | 30 | 87.6±0.9 | 88.5±1.6 |
| band | 74.0±1.5 | 60 | 67±2 | 18.7±1.0 |
| bupa | 59.1±1.7 | 10 | 57.6±1.9 | 10.3±1.5 |
| cred | 87.3±0.7 | 20 | 87.5±0.6 | 95±14 |
| glas | 89.6±1.9 | 100 | 79±2 | 30±2 |
| hear | 80.8±1.5 | 100 | 80.2±1.5 | 26±4 |
| mok1 | 76.9±1.3 | 90 | 72±2 | 93±8 |
| mok2 | 71.0±1.5 | 90 | 66.4±1.7 | 26±4 |
| vote | 95.1±0.6 | 40 | 93.6±0.9 | 53±5 |

**Table 6.** Performance of Unsupervised Algorithms 3 and 4

| | Training Algorithm | | | |
|---|---|---|---|---|
| | UC Alg. 3 | | UC Alg. 4 | |
| Database | Percentage | $Nunit$ | Percentage | $Nunit$ |
| bala | 88.0±0.9 | 94.7±0.5 | 87.4±0.9 | 45±7 |
| band | 67±4 | 97.2±0.3 | 65.8±1.4 | 4.5±1.3 |
| bupa | 60±4 | 106.2±0.3 | 47±3 | 11±5 |
| cred | 87.9±0.6 | 161.10±0.17 | 86.4±0.9 | 32±4 |
| glas | 82.8±1.5 | 59.9±0.7 | 81.2±1.8 | 22±2 |
| hear | 72±4 | 71.8±0.6 | 78±3 | 10±2 |
| mok1 | 68±3 | 97.4±0.6 | 64±2 | 23±6 |
| mok2 | 66.5±0.8 | 143±0 | 71.6±1.5 | 20±2 |
| vote | 94.1±0.8 | 120.30±0.15 | 76±5 | 5.0±1.1 |

**Table 7.** Performance of Multilayer Feedforward with Backpropagation

| Database | N. Hidden | Percentage |
|---|---|---|
| bala | 20 | 87.6±0.6 |
| Bands | 23 | 72.4±1.0 |
| bupa | 11 | 58.3±0.6 |
| cred | 15 | 85.6±0.5 |
| glas | 3 | 78.5±0.9 |
| hear | 2 | 82.0±0.9 |
| mok1 | 6 | 74.3±1.1 |
| mok2 | 20 | 65.9±0.5 |
| vote | 1 | 95.0±0.4 |

In the original reference *LIN* and *COS* transfer functions were proposed as an improvement to the traditional *EXP* transfer function. We have not observed any improvement in our results.

Comparing unsupervised training algorithms among them, it seems clear that the classical algorithm 1, $k$-means clustering shows the better performance.

Finally, comparing unsupervised training with gradient descent we can see that the best alternative (under the performance point of view) is supervised training by gradient descent, it achieves a better performance in 6 of 9 databases.

In order to perform a further comparison, we have included the results of Multilayer Feedforward with Backpropagaion in Table 7. We can see that the results of RBF are better. This is the case in all databases except cred, hear and vote where the performance of both networks is similar.

## 4   Conclusions

In this paper we have presented a comparison of unsupervised and fully supervised training algorithms for RBF networks. The algorithms are compared using nine databases. Our results show that the fully supervised training by gradient descent may be the best alternative under the point of view of performance. The results of RBF are also compared with Multilayer Feedforward with Backpropagation.

In the case of fully supervised training algorithms we have performed experiments with three different transfer functions in the hidden units and the performance is similar. We have not observed an improvement in performance with *LIN* and *COS* functions as pointed out in the bibliography.

Furthermore under the point of view of training speed the alternative of *Online Training* is better than *Batch Training*.

Finally, we have included the performance on the same datasets of the network Multilayer Feedforward with Backpropagation and it seems that the performance of RBF trained by Gradient Descent is in general better.

## Acknowledgments

This research was supported by project *P1 ·1B2004-03* of Universitat Jaume I - Bancaja in Castellón de la Plana, Spain.

## References

1. J. Moody, and C.J. Darken, "Fast Learning in Networks of Locally-Tuned Procesing Units." *Neural Computation*, vol.1, pp 281-294, 1989.
2. A. Roy, S. Govil et alt, "A Neural-Network Learning Theory and Polynomial Time RBF Algorithm." *IEEE Trans. on Neural Networks*, vol.8, no. 6, pp.1301-1313, 1997.
3. Y. Hwang and S. Bang, "An Efficient Method to Construct a Radial Basis Function Neural Network Classifier." *Neural Network*, Vol.10 no. 8, pp.1495-1503, 1997
4. A. Roy, S. Govil et alt, "An Algorithm to Generate Radial Basis Function (RBF)-Like Nets for Classification Problems.", *Neural Networks*, vol.8, no. 2, pp.179-201, 1995.
5. N. Krayiannis, "Reformulated Radial Basis Neural Networks Trained by Gradient Descent." *IEEE Trans. on Neural Networks*. vol.10, no. 3, pp.657-671, 1999.

6. N. Krayiannis and M. Randolph-Gips, "On the Construction and Training of Reformulated Radial Basis Functions." *IEEE Trans. Neural Networks*. vol.14, no. 4, pp.835-846, 2003.
7. D.J. Newman, S. Hettich, C.L. Blake and C.J. Merz, "UCI Repository of machine learning databases.", http://www.ics.uci.edu/~mlearn/MLRepository.html, University of California, Irvine, Dept. of Information and Computer Sciences, 1998.

# A Local Tangent Space Alignment Based Transductive Classification Algorithm

Jianwei Yin[1], Xiaoming Liu[1], Zhilin Feng[1, 2], and Jinxiang Dong[1]

[1] Department of Computer Science and Technology, Zhejiang University, China
[2] Zhijiang College, Zhejiang University of Technology, Hangzhou 310024, China
zjuyjw@zju.edu.cn, liuxiaoming@cs.zju.edu.cn, djx@cs.zju.edu.cn

**Abstract.** LTSA (local tangent space alignment) is a recently proposed method for manifold learning, which can efficiently learn nonlinear embedding low-dimensional coordinates of high-dimensional data, and can also reconstruct high dimensional coordinates from embedding coordinates. But it ignores the label information conveyed by data samples, and can not be used for classification directly. In this paper, a transductive manifold classification method, called QLAT (LDA/QR and **LTSA** based **T**ransductive classifier) is presented, which is based on LTSA and TCM-KNN (transduction confidence machine-k nearest neighbor). In the algorithm, local low-dimensional coordinates is constructed using 2-stage LDA/QR method, which not only utilize the label information of sample data, but also conquer the singularity problem of traditional LDA, then the global low-dimensional embedding manifold is obtained by local affine transforms, finally TCM-KNN method is used for classification on the low-dimensional manifold. Experiments on labeled and unlabeled mixed data set illustrate the effectiveness of the method.

**Keywords:** manifold learning; local tangent space alignment; transductive inference; LDA/QR.

## 1 Introduction

Dimension reduction has long been an important problem in the fields of pattern classification, data mining and machine learning. With the development of information technology, especially the development of internet, more and more high-dimensional data, such as gene data, images and video emerges, the requirement of dimension reduction becomes more urgent.

Many high-dimensional data in real-world applications can be modeled as sets of points or vectors lying close to a low-dimensional nonlinear manifold. Discovering the structure of the manifold from such a sample of data points is a very challenging problem. Many dimension reduction algorithms have been proposed, and can be classified to two classes roughly: linear methods and nonlinear methods. PCA (principal component analysis) and LDA (linear discriminant analysis) are the most popular linear dimension reduction methods. While they have the advantages of easy understandable, simple to implement and can catch the linear structure of data, they can

F. Schwenker and S. Marinai (Eds.): ANNPR 2006, LNAI 4087, pp. 93–106, 2006.
© Springer-Verlag Berlin Heidelberg 2006

not discover the nonlinear structure of data. In reality, many higher dimension data is embedded in a low nonlinear manifold, and there have some cues to show the low-dimensional embedding is consistent with human perception[1]. To address the shortcomings of the linear methods, kernel PCA method and kernel LDA method have been proposed by many researchers. Recently, there has been considerable interest in developing efficient algorithms, the so called manifold learning methods, to construct nonlinear low-dimensional manifolds from sample data points in high-dimensional spaces, and these methods have been regarded as effective approaches for nonlinear dimension reduction. In Isomap algorithm [2], pairwise *geodesic* distances of the data points instead of the Euclid distance are used with MDS (multidimensional scaling). The LLE (locally linear embedding) method [3] constructs a local geometric structure that is invariant to translations and orthogonal transformations in a neighborhood of each data point, and seeks to project the data points into a low-dimensional space that best preserves those local geometries. (A related method using Hessian matrices is presented in [4]). LTSA (local tangent space alignment) [5] methods constructs a local tangent space for each data point, and obtains the global low-dimensional embedding through affine transformation of the local tangent spaces.

While the LTSA algorithm can learn the low-dimensional nonlinear embedding coordinates of the higher-dimensional data, and can reconstruct the higher-dimensional coordinates from the low-dimensional coordinates. But as pointed out in [6], the best representative features are not always the best discriminant features for general classification task. In LTSA, class label information of data is ignored and so it can not be applied for classification directly. In the paper, we try to use the class label information and extend the LTSA algorithm from dimension reduction to classification problem. Traditional classification algorithms try to make the trained classifier optimal for all possible future data samples, but in practical, it is not needed and the classifier is usually only required to be optimal for specific unseen data sets. Transductive inference[7,8] learns the classification for unseen data directly from known data, and is more economic than traditional algorithms. Integrating LTSA and the idea of transductive inference, we proposed a TCM-KNN (transduction confidence machine-k nearest neighbor) [7,8 ] based manifold classification algorithm, called QLAT (LDA/**QR** and **LTSA** based **T**ransductive classifier). The algorithm uses improved 2-stage LDA/QR algorithm [9] to construct local low-dimensional coordinate, then use LTSA method to retrieve the global embedding map for dimension reduction, finally, uses TCM-KNN on the low-dimensional embedding space for classification.

The rest of the paper is organized as follows: in Section 2, preliminary backgrounds are introduced, including LDA/QR, LTSA and TCM-KNN. In section 3, we describe in detail our proposed QLAT algorithm. Experiments result on synthetic and real data sets are presented in section 4. In section 5, we conclude and predict future work.

## 2  Preliminaries

QLAT algorithm is based on LTSA and TCM-KNN, which use the idea of LTSA to construct global embedding coordinates through affine transformation of the local space. TCM-KNN is the transductive version of KNN algorithm, LTSA and TCM-KNN are introduced in 2.2 and 2.3 sections respectively. In the first stage of the original LTSA, PCA is used to construct the local coordinate, LDA is required to utilize the class label information. An intrinsic limitation of classical LDA is the so-called singularity problem, to deal with the singularity problem and improve the performance of the algorithm, we use 2-stage LDA/QR algorithm instead of classical LDA to construct the local embedding space. In section 2.1, LDA/QR algorithm is introduced briefly.

## 2.1 LDA/QR Algorithm

LDA/QR is a 2-stage dimension reduction algorithm proposed by Ye etc [9]. In the first stage of the algorithm, the separation of different classes is maximized via QR decomposition on the small matrix composed of class centers. This stage can be used independently as a dimension reduction, and the distinct property of this stage is the low time/space complexity. The second stage of LDA/QR refines the first stage by addressing the issue of within-class distance, and can be solved using the similar method for classical LDA, that is, by applying eigen-decomposition method.

## 2.2 LTSA Algorithm

LTSA is a nonlinear dimension reduction algorithm operated on tangent space. Data are assumed to lie on noised nonlinear low-dimensional manifold in the algorithm. Local tangent spaces are constructed for every data point with their k nearest neighborhoods. The final global coordinates are obtained through transfer, scaling, rotation and alignment of the local tangent spaces. During the alignment process, the local coordinates of a data point in the neighborhood with respect to the tangent space are to be preserved by all means. Min etc in [10] have proved that the local tangent space can be constructed with the eigen-vectors of the local covariance matrix, so the local tangent space projection problem can be converted into local PCA problem. Finally, the problem of obtaining global embedding coordinates can be converted into eigen-value problem of matrix.

## 2.3 TCM-KNN

TCM-KNN is a transductive algorithm. Transductive inference is a type of local inference that moves from particular to particular. In contrast to inductive inference where one uses given empirical data to find the approximation of a functional dependency and then uses the obtained approximation to evaluate the values of a function at the points of interest, one estimates the values of a function only at the points of interest in one step. The transductive inference approach uses the whole training set to infer a rule for each new exemplar. Transductive inference has a strong connection with Kolmogorov complexity, and is related with the notion of randomness deficiency, which is a measure of randomness. TCM-KNN is a transductive version of KNN method.

## 3  LDA/QR and LTSA Based Transductive Classifier (QLAT)

QLAT is based on LTSA and TCM-KNN. Firstly, local tangent space is constructed for each sample data using its nearest neighborhoods, discriminant analysis is performed on local tangent space, and low-dimensional local coordinates are obtained for nearest neighborhoods. Then, global low-dimensional coordinates are achieved through affine transforming of local spaces. Finally, TCM-KNN algorithm is performed on the low-dimensional manifold space. The procedure of construct low-dimensional manifold is similar with the LTSA, but the mathematic induce process have some differences for class label information is ignored in LTSA. In the following, we give the detail induce process.

**Notation.** We use I to denote the identity matrix, e to denote the column vector with all the element 1, $\|*\|_2$ denotes the 2-norm of a vector or matrix, $\|*\|_F$ denotes the Frobenius norm, $A^T$ denotes the transpose of A, and $A^+$ denotes the Moore-Penrose generalized inversion.

Sample data set X, containing L labeled data and U unlabeled data, are assumed to evenly sampled from a noised low-dimensional manifold. That is, $X = X_L \cup X_U$, where $X_L = \{(x_1, y_1), ..., (x_L, y_L)\}$, $X_U = \{x_{L+1}, ..., x_{L+U}\}$, $y_i \in C = \{c_1, ..., c_{|C|}\}$, C is the class label set, let N=L+U, then $x_i = f(\tau_i) + \varepsilon_i$, $\tau_i \in R^d$, $x_i \in R^D$, i=1,...,N, and $D \geq d$. The classification problem is : given the labeled data set $X_L$ and unlabeled data set $X_U$, label the sample data $x_j$ in $X_U$ with $y_j$, $y_j \in C$, $j = L+1, ..., N$.

To obtain the local coordinate of a data point p, LTSA uses the k nearest neighborhoods of p, and the local coordinates can be obtained with local PCA. As mentioned above, this local coordinate is not optimal for the problem of classification. Discriminant analysis is needed to utilize the class label information of data points, furthermore, data samples of each class are required to perform discriminant analysis on the local tangent space. However, in practice, labeled data is usually small and most data are unlabeled, so the direct applying of LDA is not appropriate. So, we use the method of PCA+LDA to obtain the local coordinates using nearest neighborhoods, and obtain the global embedding coordinate through affine transformations of the local coordinates. For a data point p, k nearest neighborhoods are used in LTSA, but the k nearest neighborhood can not guarantee the needed sample number of each class, that is, LDA may not be applicable, CK-NN construction method is proposed in paper [11] to deal this problem for Isomap algorithm, and we apply a simple extension of KNN local space construction here. For each point p, find $k_1$ the nearest neighborhoods $p_j^i$ for each class $C_i$, i=1,...,|C|, j=1,...,$k_1$, and $p_j^i \in X_L$, then, LDA is performed with these data points, while PCA is performed with the $k'_1$ unlabeled nearest neighborhoods $p_j$ (j=1,...,$k'_1$) of p, $p_j \in X_U$, usually $k'_1=k_1$. The calculation of optimal d dimensional approximation of data point p in the affine space is equal to the optimizing problem:

$$\min_{x,\theta,Q} \sum_{j=1}^{k_1'} \| p_j - (x+Q\theta_j) \|_2^2 + \lambda \frac{|Q^T S_W^p Q|}{|Q^T S_B^p Q|} = \min_{x,\Theta,Q} \| X^{p'} - (xe^T + Q\Theta) \|_F^2 + \lambda \frac{|Q^T S_W^p Q|}{|Q^T S_B^p Q|} \qquad (1)$$

where Q is a D×d dimensional orthogonal matrix, $\Theta = [\theta_1,...,\theta_{k'}]$, $X^{p'}$ is the $k'_1$ unlabeled nearest neighborhoods of p, $S_W^p$ is the within-class scatter matrix of p and $S_B^p$ is the between-class scatter matrix. The definitions of $S_W^p$ and $S_B^p$ are:

$$S_W^p = \frac{1}{N^p} \sum_{i=1}^{|C|} \sum_{x \in X_i^p} (x - m_i^p)(x - m_i^p)^T \ , \quad S_B^p = \frac{1}{N^p} \sum_{i=1}^{|C|} N_i^p (m_i^p - m^p)(m_i^p - m^p)^T \ , \text{ where}$$

$N^p$ is the labeled data number near to p, $N^p=|C| \times k_1$, $N_i^p$ is the sample number near to p and belonging to class $C_i$, $m_i^p$ is the mean of $X_i^p$, $m^p$ is the overall mean of labeled data near to p.

The direct solving of above optimizing problem is difficult, and the problem can not be solved when $S_B$ is singular, so we change the target function. There are many improvement of classical LDA, for example Pseudoinverse LDA, PCA+LDA, LDA/GSVD, LDA/QR. Among them, LDA/QR is a recently proposed 2-stage LDA algorithm by Ye etc, between-class distance is maximized during the first stage, and the optimization problem is $G = \arg\max_{G^T G = I_d} trace(G^T S_B G)$, which can be solved using QR decomposition. Within-class distance is minimized during the second stage, and the target optimization problem is $W = \underset{W}{\arg\min} \, trace((W^T \widehat{S}_B W)^{-1}(W^T \widehat{S}_W W))$, where $\widehat{S}_B$ and $\widehat{S}_W$ are the reduced between-class and within-class scatter matrices respectively, and can be solved using eigen-decomposition of $\widehat{S_b^{-1} S_w}$ . During the first stage of the original LDA/QR algorithm, only information of labeled data is utilized, that is, $S_B$ is only related with labeled samples and information of large unlabeled sample is not utilized. We utilize the information of unlabeled data with LDA/QR algorithm, that is, change the optimization problem into

$$G = \underset{G^T G = I_d}{\arg \max} trace(G^T S_B G + \lambda G^T S_T G) \tag{2}$$

Where $S_T$ is the total scatter matrix of unlabeled data set near to p, $S_T = \sum_{x_j^p \in X^{p'}} (x_j^p - m^p)(x_j^p - m^p)^T$ , $\lambda$ is a parameter used to adjust the weight of labeled samples and unlabeled samples in the construction of local coordinates, which in fact, is also the adjust of weight between LDA and PCA. The second stage of LDA/QR is the same. When the LDA/QR finished, the low-dimensional representation of $x_i$ is

$z_i = G^T x_i = G^T(x_i - \bar{x} + \bar{x}) = G^T \bar{x} + G^T(x_i - \bar{x})$, where G is a D×d matrix. Comparing it with LTSA, the local coordinates in the low-dimensional space of $x_j^i$ near to $x_i$ is

$\theta_j^{(i)} = G^T(x_j^i - \bar{x^i})$ , so $x_j^i = \bar{x}_i + G\theta_j^i + \zeta_j^i$ , where $\zeta_j^i = (I - GG^T)(x_j^i - \bar{x^i})$ is the reconstruction error, and $\theta_j^{(i)}$ is the local coordinates of $x_j^i$ in the low-dimensional space near $x_i$.

Now consider constructing the global coordinates $\tau_i$ , i=1,...,N, in the low-dimensional embedding space based on the local coordinates $\theta_j^{(i)}$ which represents the local geometry. Assuming the global coordinates can be obtained with affine transform of the local coordinates. Let $\tau_{ij}$ is the global embedding coordinate of $x_{ij}$, then $\tau_{ij} = \bar{\tau}_i + L_i \theta_j^{(i)} + \varepsilon_j^{(i)}$ , j=1,...,N$_i$, i=1,...,N, N$_i$ is the number of nearest neighborhoods used during constructing the local coordinates of $x_i$, $N_i$ is not related with data point $x_i$, and $N_i=|C|*k_1+k'_1=(|C|+1)*k_1$ if $k'_1=k_1$, denote $M=N_i$, $\overline{\tau}_i$ is the mean of $\tau_{ij}$, $j=1,...,M$, $L_i \in R^{d \times d}$ is a local affine transformation matrix that needs to be determined, $\varepsilon_j^{(i)} \in R^d$ is the local reconstruction error. Denoting $T_i = [\tau_{i1},...,\tau_{iM}] \in R^{d \times M}$, $E_i = [\varepsilon_1^{(i)},...,\varepsilon_M^{(i)}] \in R^{d \times M}$ and $\Theta_i = [\theta_1^{(i)},...,\theta_M^{(i)}] \in R^{d \times M}$, we have $T_i = \frac{1}{M} T_i ee^T + L_i \Theta_i + E_i$, and the local reconstruction error matrix $E_i$ has the form:

$$E_i = T_i(I_M - \frac{1}{M}ee^T) - L_i\Theta_i \in R^{d \times M} \tag{3}$$

To preserve as much as possible the local geometry in the global low-dimensional space, we seek to find $\tau_{ij}$ and $L_i$ to minimize the reconstruction errors $\varepsilon_j^{(i)}$, i.e.,

$$\sum_i \|E_i\|_2^2 \triangleq \sum_i \left\| T_i(I - \frac{1}{M}ee^T) - L_i\Theta_i \right\|_2^2 = \min \tag{4}$$

Obviously, the optimal alignment matrix $L_i$ that minimizes the local reconstruction error $\| E_i \|_F$ for a fixed $T_i$, is given by $L_i = T_i(I - \frac{1}{M}ee^T)\Theta_i^+$, and therefore,

$$E_i = T_i(I - \frac{1}{M}ee^T)(I - \Theta_i^+\Theta_i).$$

Let $T=[\tau_1,...,\tau_N] \in R^{d \times N}$ and $S_i \in R^{N \times N}$ be the 0-1 selection matrix such that $TS_i=T_i$, where $\tau_i$ is the global low-dimensional embedding coordinates of $x_i$, $i=1,...,N$. We then need to find T to minimize the overall reconstruction error $\sum_{i=1}^{N} \|E_i\|_F^2 = \|TSW\|_F^2$, where $S = [S_1,\cdots,S_N] \in R^{N \times N^2}$, and $W=diag(W_1,\cdots;W_N) \in R^{N^2 \times N^2}$ with

$$W_i = (I_N - \frac{1}{N}ee^T)(I_N - \Theta_i^+\Theta_i) \in R^{N \times N} \tag{5}$$

To uniquely determine T, we will impose the constraints $TT^T=I_d$. It turns out that the vector e of all ones is an eigen-vector of

$$B \triangleq SWW^T S^T \tag{6}$$

corresponding to the zero eigen-value. Therefore the optimal T is given by the d eigenvectors of B corresponding to the $2^{nd}$ to $d+1^{st}$ smallest eigen-values, i.e., $T = [\tau_1,...,\tau_N] = [u_2^T,...,u_{d+1}^T]^T$, where $\tau_i$ is a d-dimensional column vector and $u_j$ is the corresponding eigenvector of the jth smallest eigen-value of matrix B. There, the low-dimensional embedding coordinate of $x_i$ is $\tau_i$, i=1,...,N.

After obtaining the global embedding coordinates, classification can be applied on the low-dimensional manifold space. We adopt the TCM-KNN[7,8] for the classification task. As mentioned before, TCM-KNN is a transductive inference method, and it seeks to find, from all possible labelings L(W) on the working set W, the one that yields the largest randomness deficiency, i.e., the most probable labeling. Randomness deficiency is, however, not computable. One has to approximate it instead, using a slightly modified Martin-Lof test for randomness and the values taken by such randomness tests are called p-values. Given a sequence of distances from exemplar i to other exemplars, the strangeness of i with putative label y is defined as:

$$\alpha_y(i) = (\sum_{j=1}^{k} d_{ij}^y)(\sum_{j=1}^{k} d_{ij}^{-y})^{-1} \tag{7}$$

The strangeness measure $\alpha_y(i)$ is the ratio of the sum of the k nearest distance d from the same class (y) divided by the sum of the k nearest distances from all the other classes (-y). The strangeness of an exemplar increases when the distance from the exemplars of the same class becomes larger and when the distance from the other classes becomes smaller. The smaller the strangeness, the larger its randomness deficiency is. The p-value for a working exemplar j (with putative label y) can be computed as:

$$p_y(j) = \frac{f(\alpha_1)+\cdots+f(\alpha_l)+f(\alpha_{new}^y)}{(l+1)f(\alpha_{new}^y)} \tag{8}$$

where l is the cardinality of the training set T, $\alpha_{new}^y$ is the strangeness measure of classifying a new sample into putative class y, f is monotonic nondecreasing function with f(0)=0, which can be defined as f($\alpha$)=$\alpha$. TCM-KNN classify a sample j into class y, if

$$p_y(j) = \arg\max_y(p_y(j)) \tag{9}$$

With the above explanation, the procedure of QLAT can be presented as follows:

**Table 1.** QLAT Algorithm

| |
|---|
| Input: Data set X (including labeled data set $X_L$ and unlabeled data set $X_U$), target embedding low-dimension d, number of nearest neighborhoods $k_l$ and $k'_l$ (usually equals to $k_l$) of LDA/QR, weight parameter $\lambda$, and k in TCM-KNN. Output: class label $y'_i$ of data in $X_U$, low embedding coordinates T of samples in X. |
| 1. dimension reduction with QR decomposition for each data point i in high-dimensional data space, maximizing the local between-class distances; 2. processing with the second stage of LDA/QR for each data point, minimizing the within-class distance; 3. affine transforming the local coordinates, the global embedding coordinate $\tau_i$ of data point i is given by the eigenvectors corresponding to 2~d+1 minimal eigenvalues of matrix B; 4. with the global low embedding coordinates, calculating the $p_y(x_i)$ of samples in $X_U$ with TCM-KNN algorithm, and classifying it with the class label $y_i = \arg\max_y p_y(x_i)$. |

During the first stage of LDA/QR, QLAT utilize the information of labeled data set and unlabeled data set simultaneously, not only maximizing the betweem-class distances, but also utilizing the geometry information of data distribution. Compared with original LDA/QR algorithm, it utilizes the geometry information of sample data more effectively, and compared with original LTSA algorithm, it utilizes the class label information of sample data more effectively.

## 4   Experimental Setup and Results

In order to evaluate QLAT method, we have conducted several experiments on synthetic data sets and real datasets. Experiment results on Swiss-roll 3D data set, 2D synthetic data set, MNIST data set, ORL data set and Yale B data set are presented in this section.

### 4.1   Synthetic Data

Swiss-roll data set [3] was sampled evenly from noiseless 3D Swiss-roll surface, the data set does not have class label information, we use the data set to test the low-dimensional embedding capability of QLAT. The generating function is as follows:

$t = (3 * pi / 2) * (1 + 2 * rand(1, N))$ ;
$s = 21 * rand(1, N)$ ;
$X = [t.*\cos(t); s; t.*\sin(t)]$ ;

LDA/QR+LTSA is used, TCM-KNN is not used, and only the first stage of LDA/QR is used, i.e., LDA is not used. Experiment results with different $k_l$ values are shown in Fig.1, N=4000, d=2 in the experiments. Similar results of LTSA with N=2000, d=2 and different k values are presented in paper [5]. From the result, it can be seen that QLAT algorithm can effectively discover the low-dimensional embedding structure of high-dimensional data.

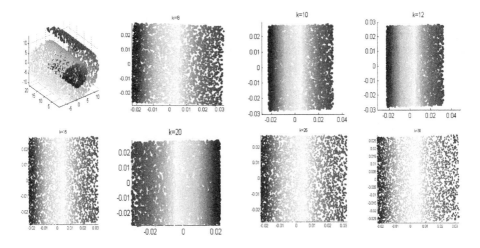

**Fig. 1.** 3D swiss roll data. Generating coordinates and computed coordinates by QLAT with different $k_l$ values, $k_l$=8,10,12,15,20,25,30 respectively.

The 2D synthetic data set [9] contains 200 data points from two classes (each has 100 points) in the 2D space. Data in the first class is generated from a Gaussian whose mean is [0,0], and data in the second class is generated from a mixture of two Gaussians: The first one has 30 points with the mean $[2,2] - [\frac{\sqrt{2}}{2}, -\frac{\sqrt{2}}{2}]\mu$, and the second one has 70 points with the mean $[2,2] + [\frac{\sqrt{2}}{2}, -\frac{\sqrt{2}}{2}]\mu$ (for some $\mu$). All these Gaussians have covariance $0.5I_2$. The low-dimensional embedding results with different $\mu$ are presented in Fig.2, TCM-KNN is not used, and $k_l = k'_l = 5$. It can be seen that QLAT can reduce the dimension of the data, meanwhile, keeping the separability of data of different classes.

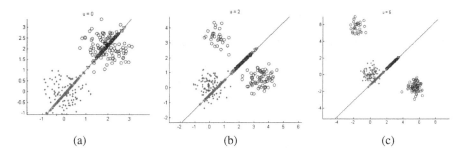

**Fig. 2.** Visualization of 2D synthetic data with different μ and their projections via QLAT, μ=0, 2, 5 corresponding to (a),(b) and (c)

### 4.2   MNIST Data Set, ORL Data Set and Yale B Data Set

The MNIST database of handwritten digits has a training set of 60,00 examples, and a test set of 10,000 examples. The sample numbers of each class in training set varies from 5842 to 6742, and the sample number of each class in test set is 1,000. It is a subset of a large set available from NIST. The digits have been size-normalized and centered in a fixed-size image. The ORL face data set contains 400 face images of 40 individuals. The image size is 92×112. The face images are perfectly centralized. The major challenge on this data set is the variation of the face post. There is no lighting variation with minimal facial expression variations and no occlusion. We use the whole image as an instance, that is, the dimension of an instance is 92×112=10,304. The Yale B data set contains 5760 single light source images of 10 subjects each seen under 576 viewing conditions (9 poses × 64 illumination conditions). The difference of viewing conditions dramatically increases the within-class variations of the data set. In this study, we use a subset of Yale B data set, which contains 1,280 face images, that is, each person with 4 poses and 32 illumination conditions. Its image size is 640 × 480. We crop the image from the row 80 to 480 and the column 150 to 450, and then subsample the cropped images with sample step 4×4. The dimension of each instance is 101×76=7,676.

In these experiments, we explore the performance of QLAT and compare it with other methods, including PCA-KNN, PCA+LDA-KNN, TCM-KNN, LDA/QR-TCM. Some parameters in the experiments are set as follows: the component number in PCA and the PCA stage in PCA+LDA are set as p=100, the output dimension for LDA is k-1, where k is the number of class labels here. Furthermore, in QLAT method, the $k_l$ and λ need to be decided, the performance of QLAT with different $k_l$ and λ on MNIST are presented in Tab.2, k is set to be 1 during the TCM-KNN step. To explore the utilizing of unlabeled samples in QLAT, label information of half labeled training samples are discarded, i.e., half of the training samples have class labels and the other half do not have. It can be seen that the classification performance is best when $k_l$ is between 8 and 12, and λ is about 1.0. If the $k_l$ is too small, the estimation error of between-class scatter matrix will become large when analyzing the local structure. While if the $k_l$ is too big, the influence of remote data points is improperly enlarged, which can not represent the locality of the analysis, besides, which increases the amount of computation. As to $\lambda$, which balance PCA and LDA during the local analysis. If $\lambda$ is taken too small, QLAT is similar to LDA/QR and can not utilize the information of unlabeled samples. While if $\lambda$ is taken too large, which can not take advantage of labeled samples. Of course, the most optimal values of $k_l$ and $\lambda$ are related with the specific data set to be classified. In the next experiment, we take $k_l=10$ and $\lambda=1.0$.

**Table 2.** Classification error of QLAT on MNIST with different $k_l$ and $\lambda$ (K=1)

| k \ λ | 0 | 0.2 | 0.6 | 1.0 | 3.0 | 5.0 | 10.0 |
|---|---|---|---|---|---|---|---|
| 5 | 3.28 | 3.24 | 2.89 | 2.74 | 3.15 | 3.84 | 4.78 |
| 8 | 3.18 | 3.41 | 2.38 | 2.24 | 2.93 | 4.12 | 4.32 |
| 10 | 3.82 | 3.17 | 2.53 | 2.32 | 3.18 | 5.02 | 4.22 |
| 12 | 3.46 | 3.25 | 3.51 | 2.23 | 2.84 | 5.41 | 6.74 |
| 20 | 9.25 | 7.54 | 4.83 | 2.34 | 3.52 | 8.64 | 10.32 |
| 30 | 10.36 | 8.44 | 5.81 | 4.32 | 6.23 | 10.21 | 12.4 |

Figure 3 shows the classification error results of different methods on MNIST, ORL and Yale B data sets. For the MNIST and Yale B data sets, class label information of 1/3 training sample is discarded, while for the ORL data set, all the class label information of training data set is used. The most interesting result lies in the classification accuracy results on Yale B data set. We observe that PCA+LDA-KNN, PCA+LDA-TCM, LDA/QR-TCM and QLAT distinctly outperform the PCA-KNN method. Recall that the images in the Yale B data set contains large variations of poses and illumination conditions, whose direct consequence is the large within-class variation of each individual. The effort of minimizing the within-class variation achieves distinct success in this situation. While PCA does not have the effort in minimizing the within-class variation, which predicts its poor performance in this situation.

Besides the major observation mentioned above, it can also be seen that TCM-KNN outperforms traditional KNN. In all the methods above, QLAT can achieve the best

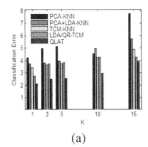    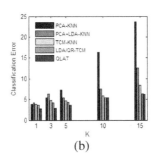    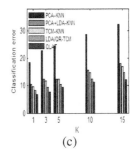

(a)                          (b)                          (c)

**Fig. 3.** Performance comparison of different methods on 3 data sets, (a) for MNIST, (b) for ORL and (c) for Yale B

performances on all the three data sets, especially on the Yale B data set. As to the ORL data set, the performance improvement of QLAT compared to LDA/QR-TCM is not significant. On ORL data set, the performances of most methods can achieve above 90%. This is mainly due to the relatively small within-class variations in these data. Recall that ORL face images contains small pose variations and have no obstruction. Finally, it can be seen that KNN with k=1 usually performs the best by all algorithms on all three image data sets.

## 5 Conclusions and Future Work

We have described QLAT, a classification algorithm based on LTSA and TCM-KNN, which extends the usage field of LTSA algorithm from dimension reduction to classification problem. Compared with LTSA, it not only utilize the geometry information of unlabeled data set, also utilize the class label information of labeled data, and utilizes 2-stage LDA/QR instead of traditional LDA during constructing the local embedding coordinates. Compared with traditional KNN, QLAT uses TCM-KNN algorithm for classification on low-dimensional manifold and can effectively utilize the distribution information of testing samples. Experiment results show that QLAT is an effective manifold classification method.

In future, we plan to investigate improvement in QLAT algorithm. Such as the parameter values of $k_l$ and $\lambda$ during constructing local embedding coordinates need to be decided in QLAT, how to obtain the optimal values for a specific data set need further investigation. Furthermore, the integration of LTSA and other transductive inference algorithms also needs investigation.

## Acknowledgement

The work has been supported by the National High-Tech. R&D Program for CIMS, China (No.2003AA411021) and the highlight R&D Program of Zhejiang Province (No.2004C11053, No. 2005C21078).

## References

1. Seung, S., Daniel, D.L., The manifold ways of perception. Science, 2000, 290(5500): 2268-2269.
2. Tenenbaum, J.B., de Silva, V., and Langford, J.C.,, A Global Geometric Framework for Nonlinear Dimensionality Reduction. Science, 2000, 290(5500): 2319-2323.
3. Roweis, S.T. and Saul, L.K., Nonlinear dimensionality reduction by locally linear embedding. Science, 2000, 290(5500): 2323-2326.
4. David, L.D., Caroe, G., Hessian eigenmaps Locally linear embedding techniques for high-dimensional data. Proceedings of the National Academy of Sciences of the United States of America, 2003. 100(10): 5591-5596.
5. Zhang, Z.Y., Zha, H.Y., Principal manifolds and nonlinear dimensionality reduction via tangent space alignment. SIAM Journal of Scientific Computing, 2004. 26(1): 313-338.

6.  Yan, S.C., Zhang, H.J., Hu, Y.X., etc, Discriminant Analysis on Embedded Manifold. Proceeding of the 8$^{th}$ Europe Conference on Computer Vision-ECCV 2004, LNCS, 3021:121-132.
7.  Proedrou, K., Nouretdinov, I., Vovk, V,, etc, Transductive Confidence Machines for Pattern Recognition. Proceedings of the 13th European Conference on Machine Learning, 2002, LNAI, 2430:381-390
8.  Li, F.Y., Wechsler, H., Open Set Face Recognition Using Transduction. IEEE Transactions on Pattern Analysis and Machine Intelligence, 2005. 27(11): 1686-1697.
9.  Ye, J.P., Li, Q., A two-stage linear discriminant analysis via QR-decomposition. IEEE Transactions on Pattern Analysis and Machine Intelligence, 2005, 27(6): 929-941.
10. Min, W.L., Lu K., HE X.F., Locality pursuit embedding, Pattern Recognition, 2004. 37(4): 781-788.
11. Wu, Y.M., Chan, K.L., Wang, L., Face recognition based on discriminative manifold learning. in Proceedings of the 17th International Conference on Pattern Recognition. 2004, 4:171-174.

# Incremental Manifold Learning Via Tangent Space Alignment

Xiaoming Liu[1], Jianwei Yin[1], Zhilin Feng[1,2], and Jinxiang Dong[1]

[1] Department of Computer Science and Technology, Zhejiang University, China
[2] Zhijiang College, Zhejiang University of Technology, Hangzhou 310024, China
liuxiaoming@zju.edu.cn, zjuyjw@zju.edu.cn

**Abstract.** Several algorithms have been proposed to analysis the structure of high-dimensional data based on the notion of manifold learning. They have been used to extract the intrinsic characteristic of different type of high-dimensional data by performing nonlinear dimensionality reduction. Most of them operate in a "batch" mode and cannot be efficiently applied when data are collected sequentially. In this paper, we proposed an incremental version (ILTSA) of LTSA (Local Tangent Space Alignment), which is one of the key manifold learning algorithms. Besides, a landmark version of LTSA (LLTSA) is proposed, where landmarks are selected based on LASSO regression, which is well known to favor sparse approximations because it uses regularization with $l_1$ norm. Furthermore, an incremental version (ILLTSA) of LLTSA is also proposed. Experimental results on synthetic data and real word data sets demonstrate the effectivity of our algorithms.

**Keywords:** manifold learning, LTSA, incremental learning, LASSO.

## 1 Introduction

The purpose of dimensionality reduction is to transform a high-dimensional data set into a low-dimensional space, while retaining most of the underlying structure in the data. Dimensionality reduction has long been an important problem in the field of pattern classification, data mining and machine learning. It is important for several reasons, with the most important being to circumvent the curse of dimensionality: many classifiers perform poorly in a high-dimensional space given a small number of training samples. Dimensionality reduction can also be used to visualize the data by transforming the data into two or three dimensions.

Many dimension reduction algorithms have been proposed, and can be classified into two classes roughly: linear methods and nonlinear methods. PCA (Principal Component Analysis) and LDA (Linear Discriminant Analysis) are the most popular linear dimensionality reduction methods. While they are easy understandable, simple to implemented and can catch the linear structures of data, they can not discover the nonlinear structures of the data. In reality, many high dimension data is embedded in a

F. Schwenker and S. Marinai (Eds.): ANNPR 2006, LNAI 4087, pp. 107–121, 2006.

low nonlinear manifold, and there are some cues that the low-dimensional embedding is consistent with human perception [1]. To address the shortcomings of the linear methods, kernel PCA method and kernel LDA method have been proposed by many researchers. Recently, there has been considerable interest in developing efficient algorithms, the so called manifold learning methods, to construct nonlinear low-dimensional manifolds from sample data points in high-dimensional spaces, and these methods have been regarded as effective approaches for nonlinear dimension reduction. In ISOMAP algorithm [2], pairwise geodesic distances of the data points instead of the Euclid distance are used with MDS (multidimensional scaling). The LLE (locally linear embedding) method [3] constructs a local geometric structure that is invariant to translations and orthogonal transformations in a neighborhood of each data point, and seeks to project the data points into a low-dimensional space that best preserves those local geometries. (A related method using Hessian matrices is presented in [4]). LTSA (local tangent space alignment) [5] methods constructs a local tangent space for each data point, and obtains the global low-dimensional embedding through affine transformation of the local tangent spaces.

Most of above nonlinear algorithms operate in a batch mode, meaning that all the data points need to be available during training. In applications like surveillance, where image data are collected sequentially, batch methods is computationally demanding: Repeating running the "batch" version whenever new data points become available is time consuming. Data accumulation is particularly beneficial to manifold learning algorithms due to their nonparametric nature. Another benefit for developing incremental methods is that the gradual changes in the data manifold can be detected. An incremental algorithm can be easily modified to be adaptive by incorporating "forgetting" effect. Another situation where incremental learning is useful is when there is an unbounded stream of possible data to learn from.

There have been some tries to create incremental manifold algorithms from their batch mode. In [6] Martin and Anil proposed two incremental algorithms considering the original ISOMAP and landmarked ISOMAP. An incremental LLE algorithm is proposed by Olga etc in [7]. In this paper, we have modified the LTSA algorithm so that it can update the low-dimensional representation of data points. Inspired by the landmarks using with the ISOMAP, we proposed an landmarked LTSA algorithm to reduce time complexity and memory requirement. Two incremental algorithms are proposed corresponding to the algorithms.

The main contribution of this study includes:

1. An landmark version of LTSA algorithm, where the landmark selection is based on LASSO [9]. This contrasts with previous work like [11], where random points are selected as landmark points.
2. Two incremental LTSA algorithms corresponding to original LTSA and landmark LTSA.
3. An incremental eigen-decomposition problem with increasing matrix size is solved by subspace iteration with Ritz acceleration. This is much efficient than solving a SVD problem from scratch.

## 2  LTSA

Given a set of data points $x_1,\ldots,x_N$ in a m-dimensional space $R^m$, LTSA assumes that the data lie on a (Reimannian) manifold and maps $x_i$ to its d-dimensional representation $\tau_i$ in such a way that the local geometry information of $x_i$ is reserved as much as possible. The local geometry information of $x_i$ is defined as the local coordinates of the data points $x_j$s in the neighborhood with respect to the tangent space of $x_i$. The power of LTSA can be demonstrated by the three-dimensional "Swiss-roll" data set in Fig.1, where points are colored according to their location on the manifold. When PCA is used to reduce the dimension to two (Figure 1b), points with different colors are mixed together, so disconnected regions on the manifold are mapped to similar locations. In LTSA (Figure 1c), the color of the points change gradually, indicating that the representation discover by LTSA faithfully corresponds to the structure of the curved manifold.

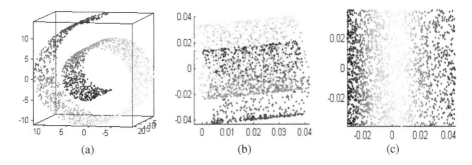

**Fig. 1.** LTSA on "Swiss roll" with 2,000 points, using knn neighborhood with k=8. (a) Points are colored according to their positions on the manifold. (b) Points with different colors are mixed together when they are plotted by the two PCA coordinates. (c) LTSA coordinates, a clear trend of the color is observed, indicating the structure of the manifold is recovered.

The LTSA algorithm has three stages. First, local information are extracted. LTSA requires the user to specify a parameter k, which is the number of neighborhoods used to construct local tangent spaces. For each $x_i$, let $X_i=[x_{i1},\ldots,x_{ik}]$ be a matrix consists of its k-nearest neighbors including $x_i$, say in terms of the Euclidean distance and $\overline{x_i}$ be the mean of $X_i$. LTSA determines $X_i$ for each $x_i$ firstly, then extracts local geometry information around $x_i$. Let $F = f(\Omega)$ is a parameterized manifold with $f : \Omega \subset R^d \to R^m$, while the Jacobi matrix of $f$ at $\tau$ cannot be explicitly computed without knowing the function $f$, the local tangent space $T_\tau$ at a fixed $\tau$ can be approximated using points in a neighbor set in the high-dimensional input space. Let $Q_t$ be an orthonomal basis matrix of $T_\tau$ and $\theta_t^*(\overline{\tau})$ the local coordinate of $\overline{\tau}$ corresponding to $T_\tau$. Then, $Q_t$ and $\theta_t^*(\overline{\tau})$ can be calculated with SVD, so the local reconstruction error $E_i$ can also be estimated.

LTSA proceeds to construct the alignment matrix. At the end of the first stage, a data point $x_{ij}$ near $x_i$ can be represented as $x_{ij} = \overline{x}_i + Q_i\theta_j^{(i)} + \varepsilon_j^{(i)}$ , where $\varepsilon_j^{(i)} = (I - Q_iQ_i^T)(x_{ij} - \overline{x}_i)$ denotes the reconstruction error. The global coordinates $\tau_i$, $i=1,...,N$ in the low-dimensional space are constructed based on the local coordinates $\theta_j^{(i)}$ which represents the local geometry. The local geometry information embedding by the $\theta_j^{(i)}$ are preserved as much as possible in the global coordinates.

The final step of LTSA recovers embedding coordinates $\tau_i$. To uniquely determine T, the constraint $TT^T = I_d$ is imposed. The optimal T is given by the d eigenvectors of alignment matrix corresponding to the 2nd to d+1st small eigenvalues.

## 3 Incremental Version of LTSA (ILTSA)

The major computation cost of LTSA involves the computation of the smallest eigenvectors of the symmetric positive semidefined alignment matrix B. As new data arrive, these quantities usually do not change much: a new data point often changes the neighbors among only a subset of vertices, and the simple eigenvectors and eigenvalues of a slightly perturbed real symmetric matrix stay close to their original values. This justifies the reuse of the current transform matrix and coordinates for update. Compared to the incremental version of ISOMAP [6], the incremental LTSA is more suitable since it does not need the time consuming graph reconstruction problem, which is needed to calculate the geodesic distance between data points. More specificly, the structure of alignment matrix B in LTSA is highly local, and the influence of a new data is more local, which makes the updating of matrix very simple.

The problem of incremental LTSA can be described as follows. Assume that the low-dimensional coordinates $t_i$ of $x_i$ for the first n points are given. As a new sample $x_{n+1}$ is observed, how should we update the existing set of $t_i$ and find $t_{n+1}$? Our solution consists of three stages. The local geometry information are first updated in view of the new coming data $x_{n+1}$. The local coordinates of $x_{n+1}$ with respect to subset of the existing points are then used to estimate $t_{n+1}$. Finally, all $t_i$ are updated in view of the coming data $x_{n+1}$.

The modification of the original LTSA for incremental updates will be described in section 3.1. In section 3.2, we proposed a new variant of LTSA (LLTSA) that utilizes the LASSO and LARS algorithms to select landmark points, because of LTSA is nonparametric, the data points themselves need to be stored, which limit the LTSA usage in huge data set. Compared to [6], where an incremental version of ISOMAP is proposed, the big difference is the landmarks are selected somewhat randomly, while in our method, the landmarks are selected following a more principal approach, as in [12]. An incremental version of LLTSA is also proposed in section 3.2.

## 3.1 Incremental LTSA (ILTSA)

When the new data $x_{n+1}$ is observed, it only affects directly the coordinates of points which includes $x_{n+1}$ in their k nearest neighborhoods, using $X_A$ denotes this set of points. However, as the local tangent space of a point $x_i \in X_A$ is modified by the new point $x_{n+1}$, all the local coordinates of its neighbors need update. For each $x_i \in X_A$, let $X_i=[x_{i1},...,x_{ik}]$ be a neighborhood matrix consisting of its k-nearest neighbors including $x_i$. The d-dimensional affine subspace approximation for data point in $X_i$ is computed as

$$\min_{x,\theta,Q} \sum_{j=1}^{k} \left\| x_{ij} - (x + Q\theta_j) \right\|_2^2 = \min_{x,\theta,Q} \left\| X_i - (xe^T + Q\Theta) \right\|_2^2 \qquad (1)$$

where Q is of d columns and is orthonormal and $\Theta = [\theta_1,...,\theta_k]$. Similar to PCA analysis, the optimal x is given by $\overline{x}_i$, the mean of all the $x_{ij}$'s and the optimal Q is given by $Q_i$, the matrix of d left singular vectors of $X_i(I - ee^T/k)$ corresponding to its d largest singular values, and $\Theta$ is given by $\Theta_i$ defined as

$$\Theta_i = Q_i^T X_i (I - ee^T/k) = [\theta_1^{(i)},...,\theta_k^{(i)}], \ \theta_j^{(i)} = Q_i^T (x_{ij} - \overline{x}_i), \qquad (2)$$

and $\theta_j^{(i)}$ incorporates local geometry information near $x_i$.

What we need is to construct the global coordinate $\tau_{n+1}$ in the low-dimensional space based on the given global coordinates $\tau_i$, i=1,...,n, and the local coordinates $\theta_j^{(i)}$. In the same spirit of original LTSA, the principal of locating $\tau_{n+1}$ is to minimize the reconstruction errors $\varepsilon_j^{(i)}$, which is defined as

$$\varepsilon_j^{(i)} = \tau_{ij} - [\overline{\tau}_i + L_i \theta_j^{(i)}] \text{ ,j=1,...,k, } x_i \in X_A \qquad (3)$$

where $\overline{\tau_i}$ is the mean of $\tau_{ij}$'s, $L_i$ is a local affine transformation matrix that need to be determined and $\varepsilon_j^{(i)}$ the local reconstruction error. Denoting $T_i = [\tau_{i1}, ..., \tau_{ik}]$ and $E_i = [\varepsilon_1^{(i)}, ..., \varepsilon_k^{(i)}]$, then we have $T_i = \frac{1}{k} T_i e e^T + L_i \Theta_i + E_i$, and the local reconstruction error matrix $E_i$ then has the form

$$E_i = T_i(I - ee^T/k) - L_i \Theta_i. \tag{4}$$

To best preserve the local geometry information in the low-dimensional space, $\tau_i$ and $L_i$ are sought to minimize the reconstruction errors $\varepsilon_{n+1}^{(i)}$, i.e.,

$$\sum_{x_i \in X_A} \left\| \varepsilon_{n+1}^{(i)} \right\|_2^2 = \sum_{x_i \in X_A} \left\| \tau_{n+1}(I - ee^T/k) - L_i \theta_{n+1}^{(i)} \right\|_2^2 = \min \tag{5}$$

The optimal alignment matrix $L_i$ that minimize the local reconstruction error $\| E_i \|_F$ for a fixed $\tau_i$ is given by $L_i = T_i(I - ee^T/k)\Theta_i^+$, and there for

$$E_i = T_i(I - \frac{1}{k}ee^T)(I - \Theta_i^+ \Theta_i).$$

To get the coordinates of $\tau_{n+1}$ given n known coordinates of $x_i$, i=1,...,n. We seek to minimize the local reconstruction error of $x_{n+1}$ for each point $x_i \in X_A$, which is written as

$$\| \varepsilon_{n+1}^{(i)} \|_2^2 = \| \tau_{n+1}^{(i)} - [\overline{\tau_i} + L_i \theta_{n+1}^{(i)}] \|_2^2 = \| \tau_{n+1}^{(i)} - [\overline{\tau_i} + T_i \Theta_i^+ \theta_{n+1}^{(i)}] \|_2^2. \tag{6}$$

As in LTSA, in the global low-dimensional coordinates, we want to minimize the reconstruction error:

$$\min_{\tau_{n+1}} \| \varepsilon_{n+1}^{(i)} \|_2^2 = \min_{\tau_{n+1}} \| \tau_{n+1} - [\overline{\tau_i} + T_i \Theta_i^+ \theta_{n+1}^{(i)}] \|_2^2, for\ x_i \in X_A, \tag{7}$$

$\tau_{n+1}$ is obtained by solving the above equations in the least square sense.

A related procedure is applied in [7] for LLE to calculate the coordinates of new data point. The eigenvalues of new data distance matrix are assumed the same as old data set. However, the assumption does not always hold in practice. In reality, if $x_{n+1}$ is very near to a point $x_i$, the local geometry information of $x_i$ will change enormously and so the eigenvalues. Our method does not assume the assumption, so it can overcome this situation.

After get the low-dimensional coordinates of new data point $x_{n+1}$, we need update the coordinates $\tau_i$ in view of the modified alignment matrix. This can be viewed as an incremental eigenvalue problem, since $\tau_i$ is obtained by eigen-decomposition. However, since the size of alignment matrix is increasing, traditional updating methods with same matrix size cannot be applied directly. An iterative scheme is used to update T by finding the eigenvales and eigenvectors of alignment matrix $B_{new}$. A good initial guess for the subspace of dominant eigenvectors of $B_{new}$ is the column space of $T^T$. A better eigen-space is found by subspace iteration together with Rayleigh-Ritz acceleration [13]:

1. Compute $Z=B_{new}T^T$ and perform QR decomposition on Z, i.e., $Z=QR$ and let $V=Q$.
2. Form $Z^*=V^TB_{new}V$ and perform eigen-decomposition of the d by d matrix $Z^*$, let $\lambda_i$ and $u_i$ be the ith eigenvalue and the corresponding eigenvector.
3. $V_{new}=V[u_2...u_{d+1}]$ is the improved set of eigenvectors of $B_{new}$.

## 3.2  LTSA with Landmark Points

One drawback of the original LTSA is the quadratic memory requirement: the distance matrix is of size $O(n^2)$, making LTSA infeasible for large data sets. The same problem occurs in ISOMAP algorithm. In [11] landmark ISOMAP was proposed to reduce the memory requirement while lowering the computation cost and an incremental version of L-ISOMAP was proposed in [6]. In landmark ISOMAP, instead of finds all the pairwise geodesic distances, the methods finds a mapping that preserves the geodesic distances originating from a small set of landmark points. In the original L-ISOMAP, random points are used as landmark points. In the [6], the vectors corresponding to the largest d singular value of centered geodesic distance matrix are used as landmark points. Least Absolute value Subset Selection Operator(LASSO) [9] is a shrinkage and selection method for linear regression. It minimizes the usual sum of squared errors with a bound on the sum of the absolute values of the coefficients. Finding the LASSO solutions used to require solving a quadratic programming problem, until the development of the Least Angle Regression(LARS) procedure [10], which is much faster and not only gives the LASSO solutions but also provides an estimator of the risk as a function of the regularization tuning parameter. LASSO with the LARS are used in [12] to select landmarks for ISOMAP algorithm. We follows the similar procedures to select landmarks for LTSA algorithm.

### 3.2.1 Landmark Selection Based on LASSO and LARS

Let X be the n data points set in $R^m$, i.e., $X = [x_1...x_n]$, and T be the corresponding n d-dimensional point set in low-dimensional space. The sacristy of LTSA in achieved by finding an estimate $\hat{\beta}$ that minimizes the function

$$E = \| \theta - K\hat{\beta} \|^2 + \gamma \| \hat{\beta} \|_q^q \tag{8}$$

where $K = \{k_{ij}\}, k_{ij} = \exp(-\dfrac{\| x_i - x_j \|}{2\sigma_k^2})^2$ is a Gaussian kernel, $\theta \in R^n$ and $\hat{\beta} \in R^n$, $\gamma$ is

a tunning parameter that controls the amount of regularization. $\hat{\beta}$ is the parameter

column vector, and $\| \hat{\beta} \|_q$ denotes the $l_q$ norm of $\hat{\beta}$, i.e., $\sqrt{\sum_{i=1}^{n} | \hat{\beta}_i |^q}$. For the most

sparseness, the ideal value of q would be zero. However, minimizing E with the $l_0$ norm is prohibitive in computational terms. A sub-optimal strategy is to use q=1 instead. This is the usual formulation of a LASSO regressive problems, which is traditionally solved using quadratic programming. The recent development of the LARS method has made this unnecessary.

An important factor of the method is the choose of $\theta$, which influences the process

of landmark points selecting. In [12], the $\theta$ is chosen as $\theta = [\theta_1...\theta_n]^T$, where $\theta_j$

equals to the maximum principal angle between $T_{x_u}(M)$ and $T_{x_j}(M)$, $x_j$ is the jth

column of X and $x_u$ is the mean of X, $T_{x_u}(M)$ and $T_{x_j}(M)$ are the tangent subspace at

$x_u$ and $x_j$ respectively. The principal angles and efficient algorithms to compute them can be found in [14]. The local tangent subspace can be found by local SVD, which is calculated during the original LTSA, so there would be litter extra computational burden. A big difference between our method compared with the method in [12], is that

the $\theta_j$ in our method is more local, here $\theta_j$ is defined as the maximum principal angle

between $T_{\bar{x}_{ju}}$ and $T_{x_j}$, where $\bar{x}_{ju}$ is the mean of $X_j$, which is the neighbor set of $x_j$. The

choice is in the same spirit as LTSA, which in principal is more local compared with

ISOMAP, and also note the geometry information near a point $x_i$ embedding in LTSA is determined by its near neighbors.

Briefly, LARS starts with $\hat{\beta} = 0$ and adds covariates (the column of K) to the model according to their correlation with the prediction error vector, $\theta - K\hat{\beta}$, setting the corresponding $\hat{\beta}_j$ to a value such that another covariate becomes equally correlated with the error and is, itself, add to the model. LARS then proceeds in a direction equiangular to all the active $\hat{\beta}_j$ and the process is repeated until all covariates have been added. There are a total of m steps, each of which adds a new $\hat{\beta}_j$, making it non-zero. With slight modification, these steps correspond to a sampling of the tuning parameter $\gamma$ in (8) under LASSO. Furthermore, the risk is shown can be estimated as

$R(\hat{\beta}_p) = \| \theta - K\hat{\beta}_p \|^2 / \bar{\sigma}^2 - m + 2p$, where p is the number of non-zero of $\hat{\beta}_j$, and $\bar{\sigma}^2$

can be found from the unconstrained least square solution.

The landmarks are the columns $x_j$ of X with the same index j as non-zero element of $\hat{\beta}_j$, where $p = \arg\min_p R(\hat{\beta}_p)$. There are $n' = p$ landmarks, as there are p non-zero elements in $\hat{\beta}_p$.

### 3.2.2  Incremental Landmark LTSA (ILLTSA)

Without the generality, let the first u points, i.e., $x_1,\ldots,x_u$ be the landmark points, denote the point set with $X_L$. For a data point $x_i$, instead of finding the k minimal distance among all the data point X, the landmark LTSA(LLTSA) finds the k minimal distance neighbors among the small set landmark points $X_L$, and use this information to construct local tangent space. In the LLTSA, the size of distance matrix D ={$d_{ij}$} is u*n, where $d_{ij}$ is the distance between $x_i$(a landmark point) and $x_j$. The local tangent space of $x_{n+1}$ is constructed with the local geometry information with $X_L$. The coordinate of the new point $x_{n+1}$ is determined by solving a Least-Square problem similar to that in section 3.1. The difference is that the columns among $X_L$ instead of X, are used. Finally, subspace iteration together with Ritz acceleration is used to improve singular vector estimates. The steps are the following:

1. Perform SVD on the matrix BT, $U_1 S_1 V_1^T = BX$ .

2. Perform SVD on the matrix $B^T U_1$, $U_2 S_2 V_2^T = B^T U_1$ .

3. Set $T_{new} = U_2 (S_2)^{1/2}$ and $Q_{new} = U_1 (S_2)^{1/2}$ .

Similarly, the updated coordinates are the eigenvectors corresponding to 2~d+1 smallest eigenvalues.

# 4  Experiments

In order to evaluate the methods proposed, we have conducted several experiments on synthetic data sets and real datasets. The main algorithm is implemented in Matlab. The running time is measured on a 2.1 GHz PC with 1G memory running Windows XP.

## 4.1  Incremental LTSA(ILTSA)

The accuracy and the efficiency of the basic incremental algorithm is evaluated by comparing it with the batch version on several data sets. The first experiment is on the 3 dimensional Swiss roll data set, the data set is also used in the original LTSA. Initialization is done by finding the coordinate estimate $x_i$ for 100 randomly selected points using the original "batch" LTSA, with the neighborhood size k=8. Random points from the S-curve data set are then added one by one, until 2,000 points are accumulated. The incremental algorithm described in Section 3.1 is used to update the coordinates. Figure 2 shows several snapshots of the algorithm. In the first column, the circles and cross in the figures represent the coordinates estimated by the batch and the incremental version ILTSA respectively. The second column contains scatter plots, where the color of the points correspond to the coordinates of the first column. The third column illustrates the neighborhood structure graphs. Snapshots with 100, 500, 1,000 points are shown. The cross and the circles match very well, indicating that the coordinates updates by the incremental LTSA follow closely with the coordinates estimated by the batch version for different number of points.

To quantify the accuracy of the coordinate update of the incremental algorithm ILTSA, we adopt an error measure[6] defined as the square root of the mean square

error between $\hat{\tau}_i^{(n)}$ and $\tau_i^{(n)}$ , normalized by the total sample variance:

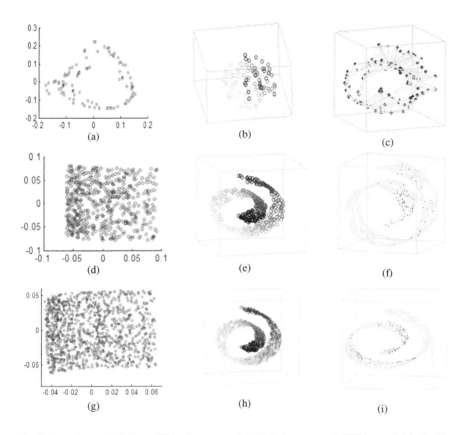

**Fig. 2.** Snapshots of "Swiss roll" for incremental LTSA. Incremental LTSA was initialized by running the "batch" LTSA with 100 points((a) to (c)). Snapshots with 500 and 1,000 are shown in (d) to (f) and (g) to (i) respectively.

$$\varepsilon_n = \sqrt{\frac{1}{n}\sum_{i=1}^{n} \| \tau_i^{(n)} - \hat{\tau}_i^{(n)} \|^2 / \sum_{i=1}^{n} \| \tau_i^{(n)} \|^2}$$ . $\varepsilon_n$ against the number of data point n for

Swiss roll data set is presented in Figure 3a. From the figure, we can see that the proposed updating method is fairly accurate with an average error of 0.08 percent. The computation time is show in Table 1. Our incremental approach has significant saving in main aspects of LTSA: the global coordinates update. Note that both the batch and incremental versions need the same number of distance computations.

Similar experimental procedure is applied to other data sets. The "S-curve" data set contains points in a 3D space with an effective dimensionality of two, which is a standard benchmark for manifold learning. The "rendered face" data set contains 698 face images with size 64*64 rendered at different illumination and pose conditions.

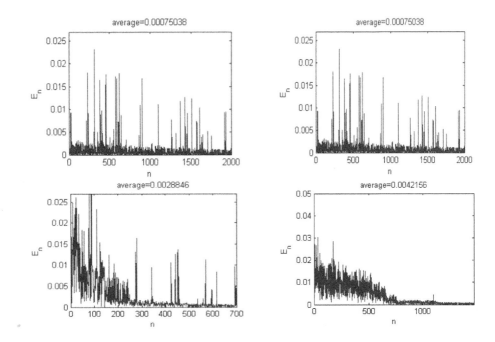

**Fig. 3.** Approximation error ($\varepsilon_n$) between the coordinates estimated by the basic incremental LTSA and the basic batch LTSA for different numbers of data points (n). (a) Swiss roll, (b) S-curve, (c) Rendered Faces. (d) MNIST digit 2.

**Table 1.** Runtime (Seconds) for Batch and incremental LTSA

|  | Swiss roll | | S-curve | | Rendered face | | MNIST 2 | |
|---|---|---|---|---|---|---|---|---|
|  | Batch | Incr. | Batch | Incr. | Batch | Incr. | Batch | Incr. |
| Computing $t_{n+1}$ | 31.76 | 0.43 | 28.96 | 0.56 | 3.47 | 0.07 | 32.85 | 0.52 |
| Updating $t_i$ | | 5.12 | | 5.53 | | 0.86 | | 4.38 |

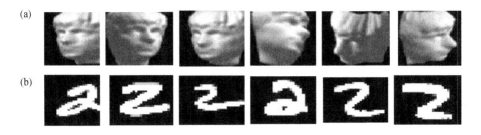

**Fig. 4.** Example images of data sets. (a) rendered face. (b) MNIST digit 2.

"MNIST digit 2" is a 576-dimensional data set derived from the digit images "2" from MNIST and contains 28 by 28 digit images. Some examples for "rendered face" and "MNIST digit 2" are shown in Figure 4. All the above data set are also used in [6]. The neighborhood size for MNIST digit 2 and "rendered face" is set to 10 to demonstrate that the proposed approach is efficient and accurate irrespective of the neighborhood used. The approximation error and the computation time for these data set are shown in Figure 3 and Table 1. We can see that the incremental LTSA is accurate and efficient for updating the coordinates in all these data sets.

## 4.2  Experiments on Landmark LTSA

A similar experimental procedure is applied to the incremental landmark LTSA described in Section 3.2 for Swiss roll, S-curve, rendered face, MNIST digit2 data sets. 300 randomly points from the data set are selected at start, points are then added one by one randomly until 5,000 points are accumulated. For the data set less than 5000, the procedure stops when all the data point are used. 100 points from the initial 300 points are selected to be the landmark points following the LASSO procedure in section 3.2.1. The snapshots for incremental LLTSA are fairly similar to those for incremental LTSA in Fig.2 and are omitted here. The approximation error and the computation time for the batch and incremental version of landmark LTSA are shown in Fig. 5 and Table 2 respectively. Once again, the coordinates estimated by the incremental version are accurate with respect to the batch version, and the computation time is much less.

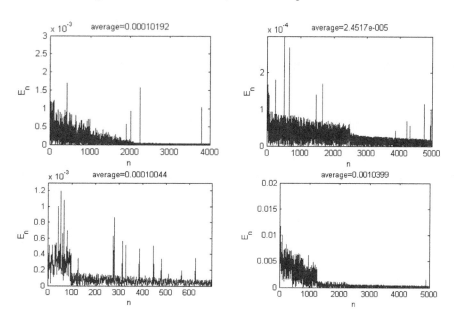

**Fig. 5.** Approximation error ($\varepsilon_n$) between the coordinates estimated by the incremental landmark LTSA and the batch landmark LTSA for different numbers of data points (n). (a) Swiss roll. (b) S-curve. (c) Rendered Faces. (d) MNIST digit 2.

**Table 2.** Runtime (Seconds) for Batch and incremental Landmark LTSA

|  | Swiss roll | | S-curve | | Rendered face | | MNIST 2 | |
|---|---|---|---|---|---|---|---|---|
|  | Batch | Incr. | Batch | Incr. | Batch | Incr. | Batch | Incr. |
| Computing $t_{n+1}$ | 11.72 | 0.35 | 12.06 | 0.72 | 2.13 | 0.09 | 10.58 | 0.42 |
| Updating $t_i$ |  | 3.21 |  | 3.54 |  | 0.87 |  | 2.76 |

## 5   Conclusion

Nonlinear dimensionality reduction is an important problem with applications in pattern recognition, computer vision and data mining. We have proposed an algorithm (ILTSA) for incremental nonlinear mapping problem by modifying the LTSA algorithm. The core idea is to efficiently reestimate the eigenvectors using the previous computation results. A landmark version of LTSA (LLTSA) is also proposed, where the landmark points are selected based on LASSO and LARS regression. The proposed algorithm finds geometrically meaningful landmarks and avoids expensive quadratic programming computations. Furthermore, an incremental LLTSA (ILLTSA) algorithm is also proposed for the landmark version of LTSA. The proposed methods have been validated on synthetic and real datasets.

## Acknowledgement

The work has been supported by the National High-Tech. R&D Program for CIMS, China (No.2003AA411021) and the highlight R&D Program of Zhejiang Province (No.2004C11053, No. 2005C21078).

## References

1. Seung, S., Daniel, D.L., The manifold ways of perception. Science, 2000, 290(5500): 2268-2269.
2. Tenenbaum, J.B., de Silva, V., and Langford, J.C.,, A Global Geometric Framework for Nonlinear Dimensionality Reduction. Science, 2000, 290(5500): 2319-2323.
3. Roweis, S.T. and Saul, L.K., Nonlinear dimensionality reduction by locally linear embedding. Science, 2000, 290(5500): 2323-2326.
4. David, L.D., Caroe, G., Hessian eigenmaps Locally linear embedding techniques for high-dimensional data. Proceedings of the National Academy of Sciences of the United States of America, 2003. 100(10): 5591-5596.
5. Zhang, Z.Y., Zha, H.Y., Principal manifolds and nonlinear dimensionality reduction via tangent space alignment. SIAM Journal of Scientific Computing, 2004. 26(1): 313-338.
6. Martin H.C. Law, A.K.J., Incremental Nonlinear Dimensionality Reduction by Manifold Learning. IEEE Transactions on Pattern Analysis and Machine Intelligence, 2006. 28(3): p. 377-391.

7. Olga Kouropteva, O.O., Matti Pietikainen, Incremental locally linear embedding. Pattern Recognition, 2005. 38: p. 1764-1767.
8. ZhenYue Zhang, H.Z. A Domain Decomposition Method for Fast Manifold Learning. in Advances in Neural Information Processing Systems. 2006: MIT Press.
9. T. Hastie, R. Tibshirani, and J. H. Friedman. The Elements of Statistical Learning. Springer, 2001.
10. B. Efron, T. Hastie, I. Johnstone, and R. Tibshirani. Least angle regression. Annals of Statistics, 2003.
11. V. de Silva, J.B.T. Global versus Local Approaches to Nonlinear Dimensionality Reduction. in Advances in Neural Information Processing Systems 15. 2003.
12. Jorge Gomes da Silva, J.S.M., Jo?o Manuel Lage de Miranda Lemos. Selecting Landmark Points for Sparse Manifold Learning. in Advances in Neural Information Processing Systems. 2006. Vancouver, Canada: MIT Press.
13. G.H. Golub, C.F.V.L., Matrix Computations. 1996: Johns Hopkins University Press.
14. A. Bjorck, G.H.G., Numerical methods for computing angles between linear subspaces. Mathematics of Computation, 1973. 27(123): p. 579-594.

# A Convolutional Neural Network Tolerant of Synaptic Faults for Low-Power Analog Hardware

Johannes Fieres, Karlheinz Meier, and Johannes Schemmel

Ruprecht-Karls University, Heidelberg, Germany
fieres@kip.uni-heidelberg.de
http://kip.uni-heidelberg.de/vision

**Abstract.** Recently, the authors described a training method for a convolutional neural network of threshold neurons. Hidden layers are trained by by clustering, in a feed-forward manner, while the output layer is trained using the supervised Perceptron rule. The system is designed for implementation on an existing low-power analog hardware architecture, exhibiting inherent error sources affecting the computation accuracy in unspecified ways. One key technique is to train the network on-chip, taking possible errors into account without any need to quantify them. For the hidden layers, an on-chip approach has been applied previously. In the present work, a chip-in-the-loop version of the iterative Perceptron rule is introduced for training the output layer. Influences of various types of errors are thoroughly investigated (noisy, deleted, and clamped weights) for all network layers, using the MNIST database of hand-written digits as a benchmark.

## 1 Introduction

Many models of the human visual system assume a hierarchical set of feature detectors to play a fundamental role in invariant object recognition [13,17,12,18]. The idea is that a visual representation of a natural object is composed of a number of smaller shapes which, each taken by themselves, appear more invariant under transformations than the entire object as a whole. Using a hierarchical system, where complex features are inferred from the presence or absence of many simpler features, recognition can be performed more robustly and with less computational effort compared to learning each single visual representation of the whole object.

Inspired by biology, convolutional neural networks apply this idea in the engineering field: The first layer usually detects simple features, e.g., oriented line segments. By successive feature extraction through the layer hierarchy, more and more complex shapes, and finally entire objects can be recognized in higher layers. Such networks have been shown to be robust image classifiers, provided the details of the network topology are correctly chosen and an appropriate training strategy is applied [3,8,16,6,11].

While convolutional neural networks usually possess a huge absolute number of computable connections, they make heavy use of a concept called *weight*

F. Schwenker and S. Marinai (Eds.): ANNPR 2006, LNAI 4087, pp. 122–132, 2006.

*sharing*, reducing the actual amount of adjustable parameters: Large groups of neurons have identical weights. Thus, the same operation ("compute the dot-product with a given weight vector") must be applied over and over again to different data. Moreover, the tree-like connection topology (see Fig. 1) makes parallel evaluation straight-forward. These facts lead naturally to the idea to employ a dedicated, possibly parallely working, hardware device optimized for this simple type of operation. A custom hardware solution was applied success-fully for speeding up a convolutionary network several years ago [7]. Nowadays, where almost arbitrary amounts of computing speed can be bought off-the-shelf, e.g., in form of Linux clusters, the development of non-standard computing de-vices is motivated more by the desire for small, low-power solutions, as needed for example in mobile applications, or when economic mass production justifies the development effort (e.g., in automotive industry). In the long run, custom analog solutions could be an alternative to standard processors in terms of production yield, especially in the field of "soft" computing techniques: While inevitable de-fects occurring on microchips constitute a serious issue in large digital designs, one can envisage trainable systems working as well on imperfect, or even partly damaged, substrates.

A mixed-signal analog/digital Very-Large-Scale Integration neural network architecture has been developed by some of the authors [15]. A prototype chip is available and has been applied successfully to real-world tasks [4]. Connecting multiple chips by digital links allows smooth scalability[1]. The authors proposed a convolutional network implementation for this hardware architecture [2]. The threshold neurons provided by the hardware render gradient based methods inap-plicable. Instead, a mixture of self-organized clustering and Perceptron learning is employed. The present paper focuses on techniques for assuring robustness of the algorithm against variations of the hardware substrate.

## 2  General Setup and Training

*Input Layer.* In order to be processed by the hard-threshold network, the grey-level input images are transformed into a binary representation by applying a threshold at half the maximum pixel value.

*Hidden Layers.* Network layers consist of a stack of *feature planes*, each of which is a rectangular grid of neurons (see Fig. 1). A group of neurons from adjacent planes within the same layer, located at the same grid position, will be referred to as a *hyper column*. The neurons in a given hyper column receive input con-nections from the same local neighborhood of neurons in the preceding layer (which will be called their *input region*), but are each tuned to detect a different feature. All hyper-columns within a given layer are identical with respect to their neurons' synaptic weights (*weight sharing*), while receiving inputs from shifted input regions, depending on their own grid position.

Four layers of this kind are present, where—alternatingly—the odd-numbered are S-type (or *recognition*) layers, and the even-numbered are C-type (or

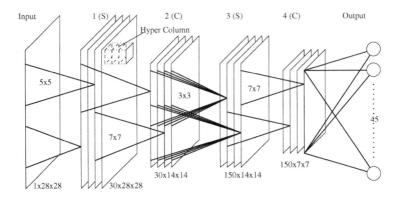

**Fig. 1. Network topology** Layers are organized in feature planes, which are regular grids of neurons. Neurons receive input connections from a local neighborhood in the previous layer.

*blurring*) layers. The S/C notation is adopted from [3].[1] The S-layer weights are adjusted during training, whereas the C-layer neurons have all their weights fixed to 1. Another particularity of C-layers is that neurons receive input only from the corresponding plane in the preceding S-layer. This way, a C-layer spatially blurs the S-layer's activation pattern. The blurring operation results in local shift invariance [3] and thus in higher-order invariances in higher network layers. In the C-layers, layer dimensions are sub-sampled by a factor of 2. Together with the connection topology, this leads to growing *receptive fields* in higher-layer neurons. The receptive field of a neuron denotes the area in the input layer from which this neuron eventually receives input. For computing border cells, the previous layer is padded with the background value (-1).

All neurons compute their output according to

$$O = \beta \left( \mathbf{w} \cdot \mathbf{I} - t \right), \tag{1}$$

where $\mathbf{w} = [w_1, \ldots, w_N]$ and $t$ are the neuron's weights resp. threshold, $\mathbf{I} = [I_1, \ldots, I_N]$ are the current input values $I_i \in \{-1, 1\}$, and $\beta(x)$ is the bipolar step function (1 for $x > 0$, $-1$ otherwise).[2] The threshold $t$ is not incorporated in the training process (see below), but is set explicitly afterwards. For the S-layers, $t$ is set to a fraction of the respective neuron's maximally achievable activation $t = T_S \sum_i |w_i|$. For C-layers, $t = T_C$. The constants $T_S$ and $T_C$ are optimized for each layer.

Training of the S-layers proceeds bottom-up. Assume that layer $n$, consisting of $K$ feature planes, is to be trained. Only the weights of one prototype hyper column are identified, which is then duplicated to the full layer dimensions

---

[1] Fukushima named the layer types after the Simple and Complex cells found in the mammalian visual cortex by Hubel and Wiesel (1968).

[2] The hardware [15] uses 0/1 neurons. Before transferring the weights to the hardware, they are converted accordingly which is possible by a simple transformation.

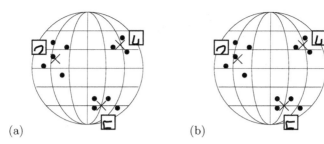

**Fig. 2.** Schematic visualization of the clustering process. Dots represent the input vectors $\mathcal{I}$, located on a hyper sphere, crosses represent the weight vectors $w_k$. Input vectors are clustered around typical shape features. **(a)** Before training, $w_k$ are initialized with random members from $\mathcal{I}$. **(b)** After training, $w_k$ have settled in cluster centers.

(weight sharing). For each training image (index $j$) and for each grid position in layer $n$ (indices $x, y$), there is one input vector $\mathbf{I}^j_{xy}$ to the hyper column at that position. Let $\mathcal{I} := \{\mathbf{I}^j_{xy}/||\mathbf{I}^j_{xy}||\}$ be the set of all those (normalized) input vectors. These vectors lie on a unit hyper-sphere in the input space, and, since the training images contain the objects to be recognized, the vectors are likely to be clustered around shape features which are typical for the objects in question and which can be recognized in layer $n$. Consequently, $K$ clusters in $\mathcal{I}$ are identified and the cluster centers are set as the weight vectors of the $K$ neurons in the prototype hyper column (see Figure 2 for an illustration). This consideration does not depend on certain shape features to appear always at the same positions on the input layer, since $\mathcal{I}$ includes data from all grid positions.

For clustering, the K-Means algorithm is used (see e.g. [5]), where the angle between two vectors is taken as the distance measure. This training scheme is equivalent to competitive Hebbian learning [14]. The algorithm stops if either only a small fraction (0.5%) of patterns switched their cluster assignments in the previous epoch or a maximum of 100 epochs has elapsed. The exact definition of the termination criterion does not seem critical. Only a subset of the training images (200 per class) is considered for clustering. Taking 400 per class instead does not improve results.

*Output Layer.* The output layer is a pairwise linear classifier, fully connected to the last intermediate layer. Each output cell is trained to discriminate only two classes. For 10 pattern classes, and considering every possible combination of two classes, there are 45 output units. When evaluating an unseen pattern, each unit votes for one of the two classes it was trained with. The class receiving the most overall votes wins. Training is done using standard Perceptron learning, where after each pattern presentation, a neuron's weights and threshold $\mathbf{v} = [w_1, \ldots, w_N, t]$ are updated according to:

$$\mathbf{v} \leftarrow \begin{cases} \mathbf{v} - O\mathbf{J}, \text{ if } O \text{ is incorrect} \\ \mathbf{v}, \text{ if } O \text{ is correct} \end{cases}, \tag{2}$$

where $\mathbf{J} = [I_1, \ldots, I_N, -1]$ is the current input vector plus an additional constant component to account for the bias $t$ in $\mathbf{v}$, and $O$ is the neuron's current output. Patterns are presented in random order and the training is terminated if the output is correct for a pre-defined number of consecutive pattern presentations, The required number of consecutive correct patterns is 10,000 in all of the experiments, resulting almost always in termination after about 1-2 million pattern presentations.

*Meta-Parameters.* For a concrete network implementation, various details regarding the network topology, as well as the threshold constants $T_S$ and $T_C$, must be fixed. The meta-parameters needed for one adjacent S/C layer pair are defined now: $K$ denotes the number of feature planes per layer. For the S-layers, the input region is a square of hyper-columns of size $D_S \times D_S$. C-neurons have a circular input region with diameter $D_C$ with all their weights fixed to 1. The threshold parameters $T_S$ and $T_C$ have already been discussed above.

## 3   On-Chip Training

Before operating the hardware, the neural weight values are loaded onto the network chip. Due to substrate imperfections and inherent device variations of the analog computing units, network results generally differ from the ones expected from exact computation. Here, it is assumed that variations in the weight values constitute the dominating effect in the considered hardware architecture. More specifically, we assume that the actual *effective weights* on the chip differ from the explicitly *programmed weights*, according to some distortion model. In order to account for these weight perturbations, on-chip training techniques are employed. On-chip training approaches are able to compensate only for fixed-pattern errors (i.e., perturbations which do not vary over time), which however, according to experiences with the prototype chip, seem to play the major role.

*Hidden Layers.* As detailed in section 2, network layers are trained sequentially, bottom-up. Weight training (clustering) happens in software, based on the output of the previous layer. If, after training a given layer, the trained weights are loaded onto the chip, the chip's result can be used as training input for consecutive layers. Since this way succeeding layers "learn" to live with the imperfections of the previous one, more robust behavior is expected compared to loading a completely software-trained network onto the chip.

*Output Layer.* The straight-forward method just described does not work for the output layer because no further layer exists which could compensate for possible errors. Thus, the output layer must be configured such that the effective weights on the hardware (in contrast to the programmed weights) are optimal. For this aim, the Perceptron learning algorithm is applied in a "chip-in-the-loop" fashion: Let $\hat{\mathbf{v}}$ be the effective weight vector after the hardware has been configured with the programmed weights $\mathbf{v}$. Then, the update rule (2) is applied, with the difference that the actual output $O$ is now computed on the hardware:

$$O = O(\hat{\mathbf{v}}(\mathbf{v})). \tag{3}$$

If the algorithm converges, $\hat{\mathbf{v}}$ will be optimal. Note that no explicit knowledge about $\hat{\mathbf{v}}$ is necessary, i.e., there is no need for quantitative error analysis.

Certainly, the crucial part is "if the algorithm converges", which is not guaranteed any more even if the data are linearly separable. For example, a malfunctioning synapse could cause the corresponding weight to grow infinitely if one or more patterns keep being classified incorrectly due to this synapse failure. However, heuristically, no ill behavior is observed in the presented experiments.

Although all 32,000 synapses of the network chip can be reconfigured in about a tenth of a millisecond, updating the weights after each single pattern is not very effective, due to the necessary data transfer to and from the hardware, and other overhead associated with one network run. Minimal training speed can be achieved by evaluating a few thousand patterns at once and then updating the weights with the accumulated modification. Nevertheless, in the experiments presented here, the cingle-pattern update rule is used.

## 4   Results

*Performance with Ideal Synapses.* The MNIST data set [9] is used as a benchmark recognition problem. It consists of 28x28 pixel grey-value images of the hand-written digits "0" through "9". Samples are shown in Fig. 3. 60,000 images are provided for training, 10,000 for testing. For finding the optimal metaparameters, the training images are split further into a training set (50,000) and a validation set (10,000), each with equal distribution of digit classes. With the parameters found to perform best on the validation set (Table 1), 100 networks are trained with the patterns of the training and validation set combined, and tested on the test set. The average error rate obtained on the test set is 1.74%±0.10% (best network: 1.49%, worst network: 1.97%). Here, the error is given as the standard deviation within the ensemble of the 100 networks.

*Performance with Faulty Synapses.* The network's robustness is tested by artificially applying three different kinds of synaptic errors to the programmed weights.
**"Noise":** All effective synaptic weights are subject to perturbations by adding random normally distributed offsets to the programmed weights.

**Table 1.** Topology and training meta-parameters

|          | $K$  | $D_S$ | $T_S$ | $D_C$ | $T_C$ |
|----------|------|-------|-------|-------|-------|
| Layers 1-2 | 30 | 5 | 0.5 | 7 | 1 |
| Layers 3-4 | 150 | 3 | 0.4 | 7 | 0 |

**Fig. 3.** Sample digits from the MNIST data base (binarized version)

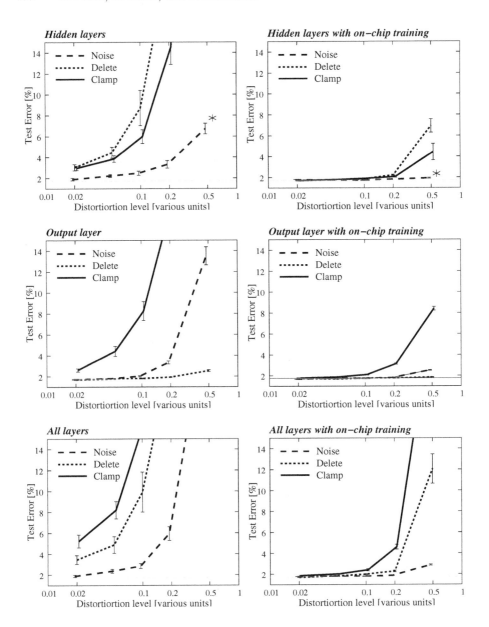

**Fig. 4.** Different types of synaptic errors in the hidden layers (top), the output layer (middle), and all layers (bottom). Left: Errors are applied to completely trained network. Right: Errors are incorporated in the training (on-chip approach). The x-axis denotes the width of weight perturbation for the "noise" error type, resp. the fraction of affected synapses for the "delete" and "clamp" error types. Logarithmic scale for convenience. The shaded line corresponds to network performance with ideal synapses $(1.74\% \pm 0.01\%)$. Here, errors are given as errors of the average value of an ensemble $(\text{stdev}/\sqrt{\#\text{trials}})$. * Marked curves appear also in [2].

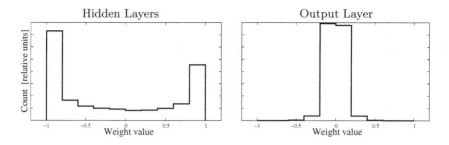

**Fig. 5.** Distribution of synaptic weights typically observed in the hidden layers and the output layer. Weights are forced to the interval [-1,1] by scaling each neuron's weight vector to unit maximum norm after training. Histrograms are over all weights in one trained network.

**"Delete":** A given fraction of all weights is set to 0, corresponding to disabled synapses.
**"Clamp":** A given fraction of all weights is set to the extreme positive or negative value (-1,1, each 50% chance), corresponding to clamped synapses, e.g., as caused by electric shortcuts.

All presented results are obtained using a software implementation of the described network model. This is mostly due to the fact that the parallelly ongoing development of the hardware system has not quite kept pace with the requirements of the presented application. In particular, the prototype chip is too small for large networks as used here (see also section 5). Looking at it positively, this way the properties of the network model and training method are evaluated isolated from the particularities of a concrete hardware substrate, and reproducibility is ensured.

All three error types are applied separately to the hidden layers and the output layer, and, in a third setting, to the entire network. All settings are first evaluated when applying the synapse errors to a fully trained network (Fig. 4, left diagrams), and then with employing the on-chip training (Fig. 4, right diagrams). Each data point represents the average test error rate from a series of 10 independently trained and distorted networks. Clearly, the on-chip training approach is to a large extent able to compensate for the tested synaptic errors.

It is interesting to observe that the hidden layers show relatively high sensitivity to the deletion of synapses, but can cope quite well with large amounts of noise, while the output layer behaves the opposite way. This fact can be understood from the different training strategies applied: The hidden layers are trained by correlation-based learning, which is known to tend to produce extreme synaptic weights, c.f., [10]. Fig. 5, left hand side, shows a typical weight distribution in the hidden layers. In such a bi-modal weight distribution, adding noise will not easily destroy the overall behavior of a neuron, but setting synapses to zero (i.e., deleting), is very likely to strongly affect a neuron's behavior. On the other hand, a typical weight distribution in the output layer is depicted in Fig. 5, right side. Here, most weights are close to zero, so deleting synapses will with a high probability do not much harm to a neuron, while adding noise with an absolute width will likely alter a synapse's stength by a large relative factor.

It should be noted that the low sensitivity of the output layer to synapse deletion might also be promoted by the large number of synapses present per neuron: Each output neuron receives more than 7,000 inputs which are highly inter-correlated, because of the blurring C-layers, neighboring pixels on a feature plane tend to be in an equal state. When working with pruned networks in the future (see Outlook), this effect can be better quantified.

## 5    Conclusion and Outlook

A neural network consisting of binary threshold neurons, trained using a combination of self-organization and supervised learning, is applied to hand-written digits classification. With regard to the envisaged analog hardware implementation, robustness to computation errors is required. Therefore, the influences of various modes of synaptic malfunction are thoroughly evaluated. Two on-chip approaches are described for coping with fixed-pattern errors. Although initially not obvious, a simple chip-in-the-loop version of the Perceptron learning rule produces satisfying results. With the on-chip learning, the network shows to be remarkably resistant to unknown, but temporally invariable, synaptic errors. However, it should be noted that even with spontaneous synaptic errors which were not seen during training, the performance degrades gracefully (Fig. 4, plots to the left). For example, even with 10% randomly deleted synapses in all layers, still over 90% of all digits are correctly classified.

The error rates achieved on the MNIST data set do not quite reach the best rates reported for convolutional networks trained by back-propagation, see [9] for a "high score". But taking into account the simplicity of the training methods, the low complexity of evaluating the network (threshold neurons), and the focus on robustness, the presented method can certainly be said to be competitive. Moreover, it has been shown previously that by adding a preprocessing stage (expanding the training data set by elastic distortions), the test error can be further decreased [2].

The final aim is to implement the system on a mixed-signal hardware architecture. Setups for recognizing simple geometric shapes have been already run successfully on the prototype chip. This chip however features a maximum number of 128 inputs per neuron, which limits the number of feature planes in the first convolutional layer to 14 (corresponding to 3 x 3 x 14 = 125 inputs to the 3rd layer), and restricts also the number of possible inputs to the output layer. The evaluation of a network as shown in this paper has to be postponed for a larger implementation of the hardware architecture. However, in order to allow the most realistic evaluation of the hardware system using the prototype chip, methods are being developed for pruning the network size with comparably little drawback in performance.

# Acknowledgments

This work was funded in part by the European Union, contracts nos. IST-2001-34712 (SenseMaker) and IST-2004-2.3.4.2 (FACETS). The first author was supported by a scholarship of the Landesgraduiertenförderung, Baden-Württemberg. We thank all persons who contributed to this work with useful comments.

# References

1. J. Fieres, A. Grubl, S. Philipp, K. Meier, J. Schemmel, F. Schürmann: A platform for parallel operation of VLSI neural networks. Conference on Brain Inspired Cognitive Systems (BICS 2004), Stirling, Scotland (2004)
2. J. Fieres, J. Schemmel, K. Meier: Training convolutional neural networks of threshold neurons suited for low-power hardware implementation. Int. Joint Conference on Neural Networks (IJCNN 2006), Vancouver, CA, (accepted) (2006)
3. K. Fukushima: Neocognitron: A hierarchical neural network capable of visual pattern recognition. Neural Networks 1, 119-130 (1988)
4. S. G. Hohmann, J. Fieres, K. Meier, J. Schemmel, T. Schmitz, F. Schürmann: Training Fast Mixed-Signal Neural Networks for Data Classification. Proceedings of the 2004 International Joint Conference on Neural Networks (IJCNN'04), 2647-2652, IEEE Press (2004)
5. J.-S. R. Jang, C.T. Sun, E. Mizutani: Neuro-Fuzzy and Soft Computing, Prentice-Hall (1997)
6. S. Lawrence, C.L. Giles, A.C. Tsoi, A.D. Back: Face recognition: a convolutional neural network approach. Transactions on Neural Networks 8(1) 98-113 (1997)
7. Y. LeCun, L. D. Jackel, B. Boser, J.S. Denker, H. P. Graf, I. Guyon, D. Henderson, R.E. Howard, W. Hubbard: Handwritten digit recognition: Applications of neural net chips and automatic learning. IEEE Communications Magazine, November 1989, 41-46 (1989)
8. Y. LeCun, L. Bottou, Y. Bengio, P. Haffner: Gradient-Based Learning Applied to Document Recognition. Proceedings of the IEEE, 86(11), 2278-2324 (1998)
9. Y. LeCun: The MNIST database of handwritten digits. http://yann.lecun.com/exdb/mnist
10. R. Linsker: From basic network principles to neural architecture. (Series of 3 papers) Proc. Natl. Sci. USA 83, 7508-7512 (1983)
11. C. Neubauer: Evaluation of convolutional neural networks for visual recognition. Transactions on Neural Networks 9(4), 685-696 (1998)
12. M.W. Oram, D.I. Perret: Modeling visual recognition from neurobiological constraints. Neural Networks (7) 945-972 (1994)
13. M. Riesenhuber, T. Poggio: Hierarchical Models of Object Recognition in Cortex. Nature Neuroscience 2 , 1019-1025 (1999)
14. D. E. Rumelhart, D. Zipser: Feature discovery by competitive learning. Cognitive Science, 9, 75-112 (1985)
15. J. Schemmel, S. Hohmann, K. Meier, F. Schurmann: A mixed-mode analog neural network using current-steering synapses. Analog Integrated Circuits and Signal Processing 38, 233-244 (2004)

16. P.Y. Simard, D. Steinkraus, J.C. Platt: Best Practices for Convolutional Neural Networks Applied to Visual Document Analysis. Intl. Conf. Document Analysis and Recognition, 958-962 (2003)
17. K. Tanaka: Inferotemporal cortex and object vision. Ann. Rev. Neuroscience 19, 109-139 (1996)
18. S. Ullmann, S. Soloviev: Computation of pattern invariance in brain-like structures. Neural Networks 12, 1021-1036, (1999)

# Ammonium Estimation in a Biological Wastewater Plant Using Feedforward Neural Networks

Hilario López García and Iván Machón González

Universidad de Oviedo. Escuela Politécnica Superior de Ingeniería. Departamento de Ingeniería Eléctrica, Electrónica de Computadores y Sistemas. Edificio Departamental 2. Zona Oeste. Campus de Viesques s/n. 33204 Gijón (Asturias). Spain

**Abstract.** Mathematical models are normally used to calculate the component concentrations in biological wastewater treatment. However, this work deals with the wastewater from a coke plant and it implies inhibition effects between components which do not permit the use of said mathematical models. Due to this, feed-forward neural networks were used to estimate the ammonium concentration in the effluent stream of the biological plant. The architecture of the neural network is based on previous works in this topic. The methodology consists in performing a group of different sizes of the hidden layer and different subsets of input variables.

## 1 Introduction

The main objective of this paper is the application of a feed-forward neural network to estimate the effluent ammonium concentration in a biological wastewater treatment plant which is composed of two serial reactors. There is a sedimentator or clarifier after each reactor. In the first reactor, there is a removal of COD, thiocyanate and phenol. On the other hand, there is an elimination of COD, ammonium and thiocyanate in the second reactor.

Although mathematical models are usually used to estimate the substrate concentrations in this type of treatment, inhibition effects between substrates can appear in certain types of wastewater. In this case, the wastewater from a coke plant of the steel industry must be treated biologically and the associated inhibition effects do not permit the use of classical mathematical models. For this reason, universal approximators such as feed-forward neural networks were used to model the biological treatment.

This work is part of the KNOWATER II project "Implementation of a Knowledge Based System for Control of Steelworks Waste Water Treatment Plant", which is sponsored by ECSC and their agreement number is 7210-PR-234. The contractors are Centro Sviluppo Materiali S.p.A., Corus RT&D, Betrieb Forschung Institut (BFI) and Universidad de Oviedo. The main objective of the KNOWATER II project is the development of plant supervision techniques for implementation in wastewater treatment plants.

F. Schwenker and S. Marinai (Eds.): ANNPR 2006, LNAI 4087, pp. 133–143, 2006.

## 2    Work Undertaken

### 2.1    Process Understanding and Comprehension of the Data

The first step is the acquisition of all the process knowledge. Technical reports, scientific articles related to the topic and expert advice must be taken into account.

The final objective is the development of an estimation of the ammonia concentration in the effluent stream of a wastewater biological treatment plant which is composed of two serial biological reactors. Taking this objective into account a feed-forward neural network was considered to estimate this concentration.

Fig. 1 to 5 represent the values of the available process variables. The measurement units are not relevant provided that the measurement has always been taken using the same unit since the data will be normalized later.

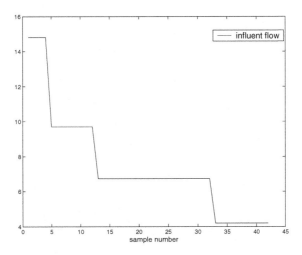

**Fig. 1.** Influent flow

### 2.2    Selection of Variables

One of the key tasks is the selection of the process variables to model the system. Applying the knowledge acquired during the first task mentioned above is necessary in order to obtain this selection. The physical process has to be carefully studied and the most significant process variables must be chosen. Moreover, the analysis of several combinations of process variables, which are suspected to form the training data set, will be necessary. Feeding the neural network with the significant process variables is very important.

Beforehand, the influent flow is a key variable. The higher the influent flow the lower the hydraulic residence time in a continuous reactor. Therefore the organisms might not have had enough time to reduce the concentrations of the toxic

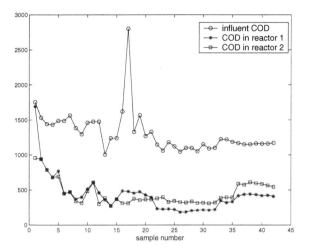

**Fig. 2.** Chemical oxygen demand (COD)

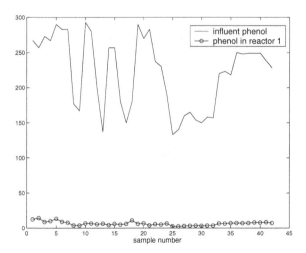

**Fig. 3.** Phenol concentration

substances. Thus, the influent flow and the hydraulic residence time are completely correlated and related to the reactor volume. Only one of these variables is chosen as training variable. The other would not contribute any additional information.

Fig. 1 to 5 show the available data: influent flow, organic material expressed as COD, ammonium, thiocyanate and phenol. All these variables might influence the ammonium removal.

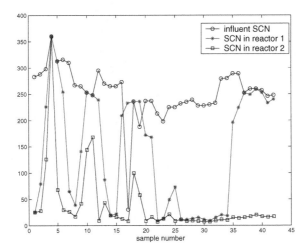

**Fig. 4.** Thiocyanate concentration

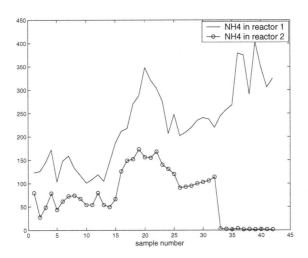

**Fig. 5.** Ammonium concentration

The organic material expressed as COD may influence since an increase of its concentration would demand a biological activity increment to eliminate the same rate of ammonium. For that reason, at first, this variable will be considered in two data sets.

Phenol may have the same importance given to the COD and, moreover, due to its factor of toxicity that would contribute to the treatment. However, it seems to be deduced in Fig. 3 that its influence on ammonium is minimum due to its complete removal in the first reactor whereas the ammonium is transformed into nitrate in the second reactor. For that reason the phenol concentration has not been considered to be integrated into the data set for training.

**Table 1.** Training variables

| Set number | Process variables |
|---|---|
| Variable set No 1 | Influent flow, influent ammonium concentration, influent thiocyanate concentration and influent COD |
| Variable set No 2 | Influent flow, influent ammonium concentration and influent COD |
| Variable set No 3 | Influent flow and influent ammonium concentration |
| Variable set No 4 | Influent flow, influent ammonium concentration and influent thiocyanate concentration |

The same mentioned above is valid for the thiocyanate but its elimination happens in both reactors and is not complete. Thus, it is considered to form part of the training data set.

Finally, the influent ammonium concentration must be considered since it obviously influences the effluent ammonium concentration.

Taking the above mentioned into account, four variable sets will be analyzed as input variables which are described in table 1. Several models of neural networks will be trained using these four variable sets to select the best model that minimizes the estimation error.

## 2.3 Data Preprocessing and Training

The data are normalized to a zero mean and a unitary variance. This allows all the features to move in the same ranges and, hence, be treated by the neural network in the same way.

The next step consists in establishing the architecture of the neural network which is composed of a single hidden layer with hyperbolic tangent as activation function and a single neuron with linear activation function as output layer, see Fig. 6.

The activation function of the neurons of the hidden layer is a hyperbolic tangent. In this way, this type of function allows the network to learn non linear

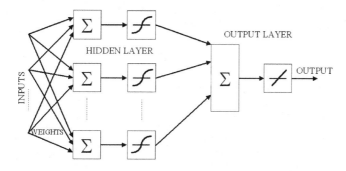

**Fig. 6.** Architecture of the neural network

relationships. The activation function of the output layer is linear enabling the network to take any value.

This network topology can be used as a general approximator for any function that has a finite number of discontinuities whenever the hidden layer has a sufficient number of neurons and non linear activation function, see [1], [2],[3] and [4].

The training of the neural network was carried out using the Levenberg-Marquardt algorithm [5], [6] and [7].

After training, the network is pruned removing the weights that have the lowest saliences [8]. At this stage a data set different from that used for training is employed. This utilized data set is the testing data set.

## 3   Methodolgy of Model Validation

The prediction of the model must be as accurate as possible for all the process working zones. The model validation to achieve this requirement attempts to select the best model according to the mean square error (mse). The mse for different assays (both training and pruning) were carried out. In this work, 60 assays were done for each variable data set and different number of hidden neurons. The minimum value, the mean value and the standard deviation of the mse of these 60 assays are registered. The mean square error is calculated as (1)

$$e_t = \frac{1}{N} \sum_{i=1}^{N} (\hat{y}_i - y_i)^2 \tag{1}$$

where $y$ is the real value, $\hat{y}$ is the estimated value, $e$ is the estimation error. These three values are calculated for each sample $i$. $N$ is the total number of samples. The autocorrelation of the prediction error is useful as well [9].

The objectives of this validation process are:

1. Discover the minimum number of input variables that yield the best estimation of the objective variable (effluent ammonium concentration).
2. The architecture of the neural network: Number of layers, number of neurons in each layer and activation functions.

Discovering the input variables that optimize the approximation to the objective function is the first task based on the topology described above. The mean square error and the autocorrelation between the output variable and the error are useful to carry out this task. Once the best combination of input variables has been selected, the number of hidden neurons must be determined. A low number of neurons does not provide enough parameters to train the neuronal network correctly. On the other hand, an excessive number of neurons leads to overtraining problems and its computational cost is higher.

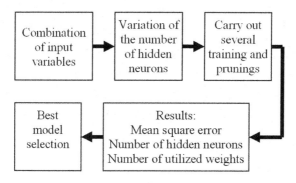

**Fig. 7.** Methodology for training and validation

The training and pruning of the neuronal network has been carried out using the toolbox named "Neural Based Network Identification System" developed by the Technical University Helsinki [10] and [11].

Fig. 7 represents the methodology. The number of neurons in the hidden layer is increased gradually for each combination of input variables, making several tests with each of them (60 assays were carried out in this work). After pruning, the results are registered as the number of neurons in the hidden layer, the testing and training errors, the average and variance of these errors and the final number of utilized weights.

## 4   Results

Fig. 8 shows the minimum value, mean value and standard deviation of the mean square error in function of the number of utilized weights calculated for each combination of variables of table 1.

It can be seen that the higher the number of weights the lower the training error whereas at the beginning the testing error decreases, although it rises later. Therefore an optimum number of weights must be found.

Variable set No 4 or the influent flow, the influent ammonium concentration and the influent thiocyanate concentration have been chosen as input variables based on the minimum value, the mean value and the standard deviation of the testing mean square error. The best results take place in a number of utilized weights equal to 18 which correspond to an original model of 8 hidden neurons. Problems of local minima have been detected in some models.

An iterative loop is established to search for the best model that minimizes the testing mean square error after pruning and considering the selected input variables and a number of hidden neurons equal to 8. Fig. 9 represents the best model after pruning. Four of the eight neurons are not used as can be observed.

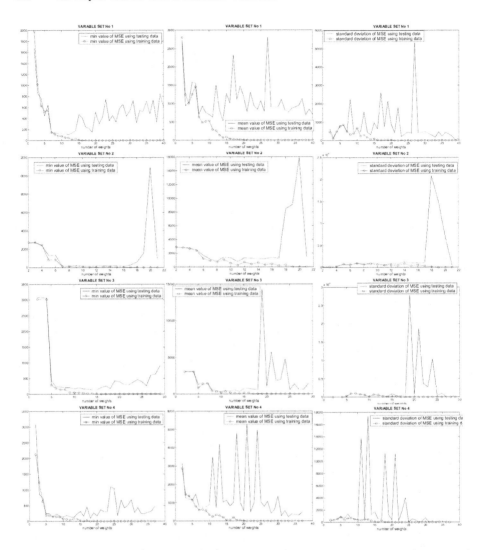

**Fig. 8.** Minimum value, mean value and standard deviation of the mse in function of the number of utilized weights for each variable set

However, it is necessary to start training with a high enough number of neurons and then stop the procedure and remove the pruned weights.

Fig. 10 shows the real data, both training and testing data, corresponding to effluent ammonium concentration and the values estimated by the neural network. The autocorrelation of the estimation error is good tending quickly to zero and the distribution is also good with most of the samples centered in the origin according to Fig. 11.

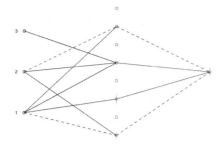

**Fig. 9.** Best of model of the neural network

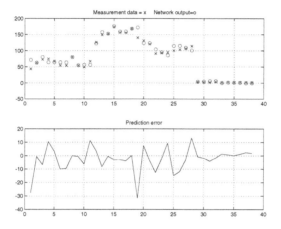

**Fig. 10.** Estimated and real effluent ammonium concentration

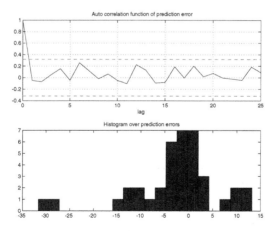

**Fig. 11.** Autocorrelation of the estimated error

# 5   Conclusions

A neural network model has been developed to estimate the ammonium concentration in the effluent stream of a wastewater plant whose treatment is biological. There are mathematical models well known for biological treatment such as the Activated Sludge Model (ASM). These can be formulated using kinetic dynamics (Haldane, Monod) and material balances to configure the particular structure of the plant. However, in this case these models are not very useful because of the existence of inhibition between substances. In this sense, the use of ANNs has been recommended. Neural networks are widely used to estimate key parameters of physical processes.

In this paper, a feed-forward neural network is outlined to obtain a satisfactory approach to estimate the effluent ammonium concentration of the treatment plant. The methodology consists in performing a group of different sizes of the hidden layer and different subsets of input variables.

The developed model is useful to obtain simulations under varying conditions of the influent stream. In this way, the effluent ammonium concentration can be estimated. This neural network achieves better results than the classical mathematical models for biological wastewater treatment due to the problematic composition of the coke wastewater.

## Acknowledgments

Our warmest thanks are expressed to the following for their financial support: The Commission of the European Communities, European Coal and Steel (ECSC), supporting KNOWATER II project "Implementation of a Knowledge Based System for Control of Steelworks Waste Water Treatment Plant" with 7210-PR-234 as agreement number.

## References

1. Hornik, K., Stinchcombe, M., White, H.: Multilayer feedforward networks are universal approximators. Neural Networks. **2** (1989) 359–366
2. Funahashi, K.: On the approximate realization of continuous mappings by neural networks. Neural Networks. **2** (1989) 192–193
3. Cybenko, G.: Approximation by superpositions of a sigmoidal function. Mathematics of Control, Signals, and Systems. **2** (1989) 303–314
4. Hartman, E., Keeler, J., Kowalski, J.: Layered neural networks with gaussian hidden units as universal approximations. Neural Computation **2** (1990) 210–215
5. Levenberg, K.: A method for the solution of certain problems in least squares. Quart. Appl. Math. (1944) 164–168
6. Marquardt, D.: An algorithm for least-squares estimation of nonlinear parameters. SIAM J. Appl. Math. **11** (1963) 431–441
7. Moré, J.: The levenberg-marquardt algorithm: Implementation and theory. Numerical Analysis. **630** (1977) 105–116

8. LeCun, Y., Denker, J., Solla, S. Optimal brain damage. Advances in Neural Information Processing Systems. **2** (1990) 598–605

9. López, H., González, R., Machón, I., Ojea, G., Peregrina, S., González, J., de Abajo, N.: Identification of melting and brightening section of a tinplate facility by means of neural networks. Proc. European Control Conference. Porto, (2001)

10. Norgaard, M., Ravn, O., Poulsen, N., Hansen, L.: Neural Networks for Modelling and Control of Dynamic Systems. London: Springer-Verlag (2000)

11. Norgaard, M., Ravn, O., Poulsen, N.: Nnsysid-toolbox for system identification with neural networks. Mathematical and Computer Modelling of Dynamical Systems. **8** (2002) 1–20

# Support Vector Regression
# Using Mahalanobis Kernels

Yuya Kamada and Shigeo Abe

Graduate School of Science and Technology
Kobe University
Rokkodai, Nada, Kobe, Japan
abe@eedept.kobe-u.ac.jp
http://www2.eedept.kobe-u.ac.jp/~abe

**Abstract.** In our previous work we have shown that Mahalanobis kernels are useful for support vector classifiers both from generalization ability and model selection speed. In this paper we propose using Mahalanobis kernels for function approximation. We determine the covariance matrix for the Mahalanobis kernel using all the training data. Model selection is done by line search. Namely, first the margin parameter and the error threshold are optimized and then the kernel parameter is optimized. According to the computer experiments for four benchmark problems, estimation performance of a Mahalanobis kernel with a diagonal covariance matrix optimized by line search is comparable to or better than that of an RBF kernel optimized by grid search.

## 1   Introduction

Support vector regressors (SVRs) have been used for various applications as a powerful function approximation tool. One of the problems of SVRs is that model selection, in which the values of the margin parameter, the error threshold, and the kernel parameter are optimized, is time consuming. There are several approaches to ease model selection but the most reliable method is cross-validation [1].

In most cases radial basis function network (RBF) kernels are used for SVRs. But Mahalanobis kernels [2,3], which are an extension of RBF kernels, and which exploit the data distribution information more than RBF kernels do, are used to ease model selection for pattern classification problems [4].

In this paper, based on [4] we propose model selection of SVRs using Mahalanobis kernels. Namely, using all the training data, we calculate the covariance matrix for the Mahalanobis kernel. We then optimize the margin parameter, the error threshold, and the kernel parameter that scales the Mahalanobis distance by line search: after optimizing the margin parameter and the error threshold by cross-validation, we optimize the kernel parameter by cross-validation. We show the usefulness of Mahalanobis kernels over RBF kernels using benchmark data sets.

F. Schwenker and S. Marinai (Eds.): ANNPR 2006, LNAI 4087, pp. 144–152, 2006.

In Section 2, we summarizes the SVRs, and in Section 3, we discuss Mahalanobis kernels. Then, in Section 4 we discuss model selection using Mahalanobis kernels. Finally in Section 5, we compare performance of Mahalanobis kernels with RBF kernels using some benchmark data sets.

## 2    Support Vector Regressors

In this section we briefly summarize the architecture of support vector regressors.

Let the $M$ input-output pairs be $(\mathbf{x}_i, y_i)$ $(i = 1, \ldots, M)$ and the mapping function be $\mathbf{g}(\mathbf{x})$, in which the input vector $\mathbf{x}$ is mapped into the $l$-dimensional feature space. Then the approximation function $f(\mathbf{x})$ is given by

$$f(\mathbf{x}) = \mathbf{w}^T \mathbf{g}(\mathbf{x}) + b, \tag{1}$$

where $\mathbf{w}$ is the $l$-dimensional vector and $b$ is the bias term.

For the loss function:

$$E(y, f(\mathbf{x})) = \begin{cases} 0 & \text{for } |y - f(\mathbf{x})| \leq \varepsilon, \\ |y - f(\mathbf{x})| - \varepsilon & \text{otherwise,} \end{cases} \tag{2}$$

where $\varepsilon$ is a user-defined error threshold, the dual problem of the SVR is given by

$$\text{maximize} \quad -\frac{1}{2} \sum_{i,j=1}^{M} (\alpha_i - \alpha_i^*)(\alpha_j - \alpha_j^*) H(\mathbf{x}_i, \mathbf{x}_j)$$

$$-\varepsilon \sum_{i=1}^{M} (\alpha_i + \alpha_i^*) + \sum_{i=1}^{M} y_i(\alpha_i - \alpha_i^*) \tag{3}$$

$$\text{subject to} \quad \sum_{i=1}^{M} (\alpha_i - \alpha_i^*) = 0, \tag{4}$$

$$0 \leq \alpha_i, \ \alpha_i^* \leq C, \tag{5}$$

where $H(\mathbf{x}_i, \mathbf{x}_j) = \mathbf{g}^T(\mathbf{x}) \mathbf{g}(\mathbf{x})$ is a kernel, and $\alpha_i$ and $\alpha_i^*$ are Lagrange multipliers associated with $\mathbf{x}_i$.

The obtained approximation function is given by

$$f(\mathbf{x}) = \sum_{i=1}^{M} (\alpha_i - \alpha_i^*) H(\mathbf{x}_i, \mathbf{x}) + b. \tag{6}$$

## 3    Mahalanobis Kernels

In function approximation we consider that all the training data belong to one cluster. For the cluster we define the Mahalanobis distance between a datum $\mathbf{x}$ and the center vector of the cluster:

$$d(\mathbf{x}) = \sqrt{(\mathbf{x} - \mathbf{c})^T Q^{-1} (\mathbf{x} - \mathbf{c})}, \tag{7}$$

where the center vector and the covariance matrix of the data are given, respectively, by

$$\mathbf{c} = \frac{1}{M} \sum_{i=1}^{M} \mathbf{x}_i, \tag{8}$$

$$Q = \frac{1}{M} \sum_{i=1}^{M} (\mathbf{x}_i - \mathbf{c}) (\mathbf{x}_i - \mathbf{c})^T. \tag{9}$$

The Mahalanobis distance is linear translation invariant [5]. Thus we need not worry about the scales of input variables.

Another interesting characteristic is that the average of the square of Mahalanobis distances is $m$ [5]:

$$\frac{1}{M} \sum_{i=1}^{M} (\mathbf{x}_i - \mathbf{c})^T Q^{-1} (\mathbf{x}_i - \mathbf{c}) = m. \tag{10}$$

Then, we define the Mahalanobis kernel by

$$H(\mathbf{x}, \mathbf{x}') = \exp\left(-\frac{\delta}{m} (\mathbf{x} - \mathbf{x}')^T Q^{-1} (\mathbf{x} - \mathbf{x}')\right), \tag{11}$$

where $\delta (> 0)$ is the scaling factor to control the Mahalanobis distance. Here, the Mahalanobis distance is calculated between $\mathbf{x}$ and $\mathbf{x}'$, not between $\mathbf{x}$ and $\mathbf{c}$. The Mahalanobis kernel is an extension of the RBF kernel. Namely, by replacing $\delta Q^{-1}/m$ by $\gamma I$, where $\gamma(> 0)$ is a parameter for slope control and $I$ is the $m \times m$ unit matrix, we obtain the RBF kernel:

$$\exp(-\gamma \|\mathbf{x} - \mathbf{x}'\|^2). \tag{12}$$

From (10), by dividing the square of the Mahalanobis distance by $m$, it is normalized to 1 irrespective of the number of input variables. Although (11) is an approximation of the Mahalanobis kernel, this may enable to limit the search of the optimal $\delta$ value in a small range.

If we use the full covariance matrix, it will be time-consuming for a large number of input variables. Thus we consider two cases: Mahalanobis kernels with diagonal covariance matrices and Mahalanobis kernels with full covariance matrices. Hereafter we call the former diagonal Mahalanobis kernels and the latter non-diagonal Mahalanobis kernels.

## 4   Model Selection

Model selection is to optimize kernels and parameters to obtain the high generalization ability of SVRs. In this section, we discuss model selection for RBF kernels and Mahalanobis kernels by cross-validation.

### 4.1   RBF Kernels

For RBF kernels, we need to determine the values of $\varepsilon$, $\gamma$, and $C$ by grid search. To set the proper search range of $\gamma$, it is better to normalize the input ranges into $[0, 1]$. Thus, because the maximum value of $\|\mathbf{x} - \mathbf{x}'\|^2$ is $m$, we use the following RBF kernels instead of (12) [6]:

$$\exp\left(-\frac{\gamma}{m}\|\mathbf{x} - \mathbf{x}'\|^2\right). \tag{13}$$

Because RBF kernels are not scale invariant, rescaling of the range into $[0, 1]$ is not always optimal.

### 4.2   Mahalanobis Kernels

For Mahalanobis kernels, we need to determine the values of $\varepsilon$, $\delta$, and $C$. But because Mahalanobis kernels given by (11) are determined according to the data distribution and normalized by $m$, the initial value of $\delta = 1$ is a good selection. Thus, we can carry out model selection by line search not by grid search. Namely, the model selection is done as follows:

1. Set $\delta = 1$ and determine the values of $C$ and $\varepsilon$ by cross-validation for the values of $C$ and $\varepsilon$ on grid points. We call this the first stage.
2. Setting the values of $C$ and $\varepsilon$ as those determined by the first stage, determine the value of $\delta$ by cross-validation. We call this the second stage.

Because $\delta = 1$ is a good initial value, we may search the optimal value around 1. In addition, because Mahalanobis kernels are normalized by the co-variance matrix, it is scale invariant. Therefore, unlike RBF kernels, the scale transformation of input variables does not affect the approximation error of SVRs.

## 5   Performance Evaluation

In this section, we evaluate the proposed model selection method. For this purpose, we performed model selection using Mahalanobis kernels and RBF kernels by grid search and line search and investigated whether the Mahalanobis kernel by line search performs well both from the approximation ability and model selection speed.

### 5.1   Evaluation Conditions

We used the benchmark data sets listed in Table 1. The water purification data set [7,8] is to estimate coagulant to be added to purify water. The Mackey-Glass data set [8,9] is a time series data set with chaotic behaviors. The Boston 5 and 14 data sets are from the Boston data set [10,11]. The Boston 5 data set predicts the nitrous oxide level, which is the 5th variable in the Boston data and Boston

**Table 1.** Parameter setting

| Data | Inputs | Train. | Test |
|---|---|---|---|
| Water Purification | 10 | 241 | 237 |
| Mackey-Glass | 4 | 500 | 500 |
| Boston 5 | 13 | 506 | — |
| Boston 14 | 13 | 506 | — |

14 data set predicts the median value of a home price, which is the 14th variable in the Boston data set. Since the Boston data set is not divided into training and test data sets, we randomly divided the set into two with almost equal sizes.

We ran c programs on a Xeon 2.8G personal computer with Linux operating systems. We trained the SVRs using the primal-dual interior-point method without using the decomposition technique. We used 5-fold cross-validation both for grid search and line search in determining the kernel parameter $\gamma$ or $\delta$, $\varepsilon$, and $C$.

## 5.2  Water Purification Data

We performed 5-fold cross-validation changing $C = \{1, 5, 10, 50, 100, 500, 1000, 3000, 5000, 10000, 50000, 100000\}$ and $\varepsilon = \{0.001, 0.005, 0.01, 0.05, 0.1\}$ for both kernels, $\gamma = \{0.1, 0.5, 1.0, 5.0, 10, 15\}$ for RBF kernels, and $\delta = \{0.1, 0.2, \ldots, 1.0, \ldots, 1.9, 2.0\}$ for Mahalanobis kernels.

Table 2 shows the results. "G" and "L" denote that the grid search and line search are performed for model selection and "Diag" and "Non-Diag" denote that the diagonal and non-diagonal covariance matrices are used for Mahalanobis kernels, respectively. The "Optimal" columns list the parameter values selected by model selection. The "Time" column lists the time for model selection by cross-validation. Approximation errors were evaluated by the average error and the maximum approximation error.

From the table, by grid search, the model selection time using Mahalanobis kernels is about three times longer than that using RBF kernels. But by line search they are almost comparable. The average estimation errors for the test data using a kernel by line search are worse than those using the same kernel by grid search but the maximum errors are smaller. Although the results are different for different kernels and different model selection methods, the difference is small.

## 5.3  Mackey-Glass Data

We performed 5-fold cross-validation changing $C=\{1, 10, 100, 500, 1000, 3000, 5000, 8000, 10000, 50000, 100000\}$ and $\varepsilon = \{10^{-7}, 10^{-6}, 10^{-5}, 10^{-4}, 0.001, 0.01\}$ for both kernels, $\gamma = \{0.1, 0.5, 1.0, 5.0, 10, 15\}$ for RBF kernels, and $\delta = \{0.1, 0.2, \ldots, 1.0, \ldots, 1.9, 2.0\}$ for Mahalanobis kernels.

**Table 2.** Performance comparison for water purification data

| Kernel | Optimal | | | Time | Train. Error | | Test Error | |
|---|---|---|---|---|---|---|---|---|
| | $C$ | $\varepsilon$ | $\gamma/\delta$ | [s] | Ave | Max | Ave | Max |
| RBF (G) | 5 | 0.05 | 10. | 4384 | 0.779 | 16.1 | 0.892 | 6.22 |
| RBF (L) | 100 | 0.001 | 1.0 | 827 | 0.852 | 17.9 | 0.954 | 6.04 |
| Diag (G) | 5 | 0.05 | 0.4 | 13050 | 0.806 | 16.4 | 0.919 | 6.27 |
| Diag (L) | 1 | 0.05 | 1.1 | 808 | 0.844 | 15.4 | 0.936 | 5.88 |
| Non-Diag (G) | 5 | 0.1 | 0.4 | 12611 | 0.706 | 14.6 | 0.942 | 5.57 |
| Non-Diag (L) | 1 | 0.001 | 0.8 | 770 | 0.817 | 15.1 | 0.965 | 4.40 |

**Table 3.** Performance comparison for Mackey-Glass data

| Kernel | Optimal | | | Time | NRMSE | |
|---|---|---|---|---|---|---|
| | $C$ | $\varepsilon$ | $\gamma/\delta$ | [s] | Train. | Test |
| RBF (G) | $10^5$ | $10^{-5}$ | 15.0 | 105173 | 0.00172 | 0.00215 |
| RBF (L) | $10^5$ | $10^{-4}$ | 15.0 | 14796 | 0.00191 | 0.00213 |
| Diag (G) | $10^5$ | $10^{-7}$ | 2.0 | 176293 | 0.00027 | 0.00272 |
| Diag (L) | $10^5$ | $10^{-5}$ | 2.0 | 13166 | 0.00025 | 0.00280 |
| Non-Diag (G) | 500 | $10^{-4}$ | 1.2 | 169645 | 0.00284 | 0.00231 |
| Non-Diag (L) | 500 | $10^{-7}$ | 0.9 | 11367 | 0.00390 | 0.00313 |

We evaluated the estimation performance of the Mackey-Glass data set by the Normalized Root Mean Square Error (NRMSE), i.e. the root-mean-square error divided by the standard deviation of the time series data.

Table 3 shows the results for the Mackey-Glass data set. The optimal values of $\varepsilon$ are very small because the data set does not include noise. Both for RBF and diagonal Mahalanobis kernels, grid search and line search do not give much difference in estimation error but the estimation errors for the diagonal Mahalanobis kernels are a little worse. Non-diagonal Mahalanobis kernels by line search show worst estimation error.

Model selection by grid search for Mahalanobis kernels is slower than that for RBF kernels, but model selection time by line search is comparable for three kernels.

### 5.4 Boston Data

Since the Boston data set is not divided into training and test data sets, we randomly divided the set into 20 training and test data sets with almost equal sizes. And we determined the optimal parameter values by 5-fold cross-validation using training data sets and evaluated the average errors and their standard deviation for the training and test data sets. In cross-validation we changed $C$ = {1, 10, 100, 1000, 5000, 10000, 50000, 100000} and $\varepsilon$ = {0.001, 0.01, 0.1} for both kernels, and $\gamma$ = {0.1, 0.5, 1.0, 5.0, 10, 15} for RBF kernels, and $\delta$ = {0.1, 0.2,..., 1.0,..., 1.9, 2.0} for Mahalanobis kernels.

Table 4 lists the results for the Boston 5 data set. The optimal values of the parameters show the most frequently selected values among 20 trials. "Time" column lists the average time for model selection for 20 trials. We evaluated the estimation performance by average errors and their standard deviations. The boldface numbers show the best performance group, in which there are no statistical difference in both averages and variances among the members of the group. And the italic numerals show the second performance group, in which the averages are statistically different from the best group although there is no statistical difference in the variances. This means that estimation performance of RBF kernels by line search is inferior to that of RBF kernels by grid search. But estimation performance of Mahalanobis kernels shows the best irrespective of a diagonal or non-diagonal covariance matrix or line search or grid search. In addition since model selection is speeded up by line search, the line search strategy is suitable for Mahalanobis kernels for this data set.

**Table 4.** Performance comparison for Boston 5 data

| Kernel | Optimal $C$ | $\varepsilon$ | $\gamma/\delta$ | Time [s] | Error & Stand. Dev. Train. | Test |
|---|---|---|---|---|---|---|
| RBF (G) | $10^5$ | 0.001 | 5.0 | 3473 | 0.0273 ± 0.0060 | *0.0371 ± 0.0024* |
| RBF (L) | $10^5$ | 0.001 | 1.0 | 609 | 0.0369 ± 0.0229 | 0.0469 ± 0.0219 |
| Diag (G) | 1 | 0.001 | 0.9 | 6330 | 0.0154 ± 0.0052 | **0.0287 ± 0.0022** |
| Diag (L) | 1 | 0.001 | 0.8 | 504 | 0.0130 ± 0.0036 | **0.0280 ± 0.0021** |
| Non-Diag (G) | 1 | 0.001 | 0.4 | 7035 | 0.0123 ± 0.0037 | **0.0287 ± 0.0021** |
| Non-Diag (L) | 1 | 0.001 | 0.5 | 586 | 0.0119 ± 0.0034 | **0.0286 ± 0.0020** |

Table 5 shows the results for the Boston 14 data set. Since the optimal values show the most frequently selected values, although they are the same for the RBF kernels with grid search and line search, the average errors and the standard deviations are different. The boldface numerals show the best estimation performance group and the italic numerals show the second best group. Therefore, for this data set, estimation performance of Mahalanobis kernels is statistically better than that of RBF kernels. And the diagonal Mahalanobis kernel by line search is a good choice from the standpoint of estimation performance and model selection speed.

**Table 5.** Performance comparison for Boston 14 data

| Kernel | Optimal | | | Time | Error & Stand. Dev. | |
|---|---|---|---|---|---|---|
| | $C$ | $\varepsilon$ | $\gamma/\delta$ | [s] | Train. | Test |
| RBF (G) | $10^5$ | 0.1 | 15. | 2870 | $2.20 \pm 0.173$ | $2.84 \pm 0.206$ |
| RBF (L) | $10^5$ | 0.1 | 15. | 639 | $2.19 \pm 0.151$ | $2.83 \pm 0.196$ |
| Diag (G) | 100 | 0.1 | 0.3 | 7020 | $1.46 \pm 0.295$ | $\mathbf{2.40 \pm 0.153}$ |
| Diag (L) | 10 | 0.1 | 0.7 | 639 | $1.57 \pm 0.362$ | $\mathbf{2.48 \pm 0.187}$ |
| Non-Diag (G) | 100 | 0.1 | 0.2 | 8061 | $1.20 \pm 0.250$ | $\mathbf{2.50 \pm 0.151}$ |
| Non-Diag (L) | 10 | 0.1 | 0.6 | 842 | $1.48 \pm 0.326$ | *2.63 ± 0.187* |

### 5.5 Discussions

In cross-validation, we used 6 parameter values for RBF kernels and 20 for Mahalanobis kernels, which is more than three times larger. But according to the experiments, for the Mahalanobis kernels model selection by line search was 10 to 16 times faster. In addition, model selection for Mahalanobis kernels by line search was three to five times faster than that for RBF kernels by grid search, although model selection for Mahalanobis kernels by grid search was slower than that for RBF kernels by grid search.

For the 4 benchmark data sets, diagonal Mahalanobis kernels by line search showed stable estimation performance and especially for Boston data sets Mahalanobis kernels by line search belonged to the best estimation group in a statistical sense. But RBF kernels and non-diagonal Mahalanobis kernels by line search showed inferior estimation performance in some cases.

Therefore, from estimation performance and model selection speed, the Mahalanobis kernels by line search can be alternative kernels for RBF kernels. In addition, the diagonal Mahalanobis kernels are enough for this purpose.

## 6   Conclusions

We discussed model selection using the Mahalanobis kernels for function approximation. We calculate the covariance matrix using the training data and determine the optimum values of the margin parameter, the error threshold, and the kernel parameter by line search. Namely, first we determine the margin parameter and the error threshold by grid search fixing the value of the kernel parameter, and then we determine the value of the kernel parameter. The computer experiments showed that the performance of the Mahalanobis kernels by line search was comparable to, or better than that of RBF kernels by grid search.

# References

1. K. Duan, S. S. Keerthi, and A. N. Poo. An Empirical Evaluation of Simple Performance Measures for Tuning SVM Hyperparameters. *Proc. ICONIP-2001*, Paper ID# 159, 2001.
2. R. Herbrich. *Learning Kernel Classifiers: Theory and Algorithms*. MIT Press, Cambridge, MA, 2002.
3. F. Friedrichs and C. Igel. Evolutionary Tuning of Multiple SVM Parameters. *Proc. ESANN 2004*, pp. 519–524, 2004.
4. S. Abe. Training of Support Vector Machines with Mahalanobis Kernels. *Proc. ICANN 2005*, pp. 571-576, 2005.
5. S. Abe. *Pattern Classification: Neuro-Fuzzy Methods and Their Comparison*. Springer-Verlag, London, 2001.
6. S. Abe. *Support Vector Machines for Pattern Classification*. Springer-Verlag, London, 2005.
7. K. Baba, I. Enbutu, and M. Yoda. Explicit Representation of Knowledge Acquired from Plant Historical Data Using Neural Network. *Proc. IJCNN 1990*, Vol. 3, pp. 155–160, 1990.
8. S. Abe. *Neural Networks and Fuzzy Systems: Theory and Applications*. Kluwer, Boston, MA, 1997.
9. R. S. Crowder. Predicting the Mackey-Glass Time Series with Cascade-Correlation Learning. *Proc. 1990 Connectionist Models Summer School*, pp. 117–123, Carnegie Mellon University, 1990.
10. D. Harrison and D. L. Rubinfeld. Hedonic Prices and the Demand for Clean Air. *Journal of Environmental Economics and Management*, Vol. 5, pp. 81-102, 1978.
11. http://www.cs.toronto.edu/~delve/data/datasets.html

# Incremental Training of Support Vector Machines Using Truncated Hypercones

Shinya Katagiri and Shigeo Abe

Graduate School of Science and Technology
Kobe University
Rokkodai, Nada, Kobe, Japan
abe@eedept.kobe-u.ac.jp
http://www2.eedept.kobe-u.ac.jp/~abe

**Abstract.** We discuss incremental training of support vector machines in which we approximate the regions, where support vector candidates exist, by truncated hypercones. We generate the truncated surface with the center being the center of unbounded support vectors and with the radius being the maximum distance from the center to support vectors. We determine the hypercone surface so that it includes a datum, which is far away from the separating hyperplane. Then to cope with non-separable cases, we shift the truncated hypercone along the rotating axis in parallel in the opposite direction of the separating hyperplane. We delete the data that are in the truncated hypercone and keep the remaining data as support vector candidates. In computer experiments, we show that we can delete many data without deteriorating the generalization ability.

## 1 Introduction

The high generalization ability of support vector machines (SVMs) [1,2] lies in mapping of the input space to a high dimensional feature space, maximizing margins of separating hyperplanes in the feature space, and use of proper kernels to specific applications. Training by solving a quadratic programming problem leads to the global optimum solution. But since we need to solve a problem with the variables equal to the number of training data, training becomes slow for a large sized problem. In addition, in an incremental training environment, where training data are incrementally obtained, efficient incremental training methods are required. In SVMs, only support vectors, which are near class boundaries and which determine the decision functions, are required for training. Thus, if we can detect support vectors or support vector candidates in future incremental training, we can alleviate slow training by deleting unnecessary data before training.

In [3,4], training data other than support vectors are deleted at the incremental training step. However, this method may delete support vector candidates and thus may lead to degradation of generalization ability. Therefore, to maintain the generalization ability comparable to that of batch training, we need

F. Schwenker and S. Marinai (Eds.): ANNPR 2006, LNAI 4087, pp. 153–164, 2006.
© Springer-Verlag Berlin Heidelberg 2006

to retain support vector candidates. Under the assumption that the separating hyperplane after incremental training does not change much, in [5] support vector candidates are selected from the data that are near the separating hyperplane. But if the separating hyperplane rotates after retraining, this method may fail in keeping support vector candidates. To cope with the rotation of separating hyperplanes, in [6,7] class regions are approximated by hyperspheres using one-class SVMs [8] and data near hyperspheres are kept as support vector candidates.

In this paper, we propose an incremental training method that is robust for rotation of separating hyperplanes, approximating the regions for support vector candidates by truncated hypercones. Since support vectors are at the vertexes of convex hulls, we can keep support vector candidates if we retain the vertexes of the convex hulls for the classes. But since it is difficult to generate a convex hull in the feature space, and the vertexes that are far away from the convex hull are unlikely to be support vectors in the future, we approximate the region of data that are near the separating hyperplane by truncated hypercones.

For each class, we generate a truncated surface with the center at the center of unbounded support vectors and with the radius being the maximum distance from the center to support vectors. The rotating axis goes through the center and is perpendicular to the truncated surface. We generate the surface of a hypercone so that it includes the datum that is far away from the separating hyperplane and the distance from the rotating axis is maximum. The data that are inside of the truncated hypercone are deleted and the remaining data are kept as support vector candidates.

In Section 2, we summarize SVMs and in Section 3, we explain two conventional methods. Then in Section 4, we propose an incremental training method using truncated hypercones and in Section 5 we compare our proposed method and the conventional methods from the standpoint of generalization ability and the deletion ratio of training data.

## 2   Support Vector Machines

In SVMs, the input $\mathbf{x}$ is mapped into the high dimensional feature space using the mapping function $\phi(\mathbf{x})$. For $M$ input-output pairs $(\mathbf{x}_i, y(\mathbf{x}_i))$, $i = 1, ..., M$, let $y(\mathbf{x}_i) = 1$ if $\mathbf{x}_i$ belongs to class 1, and $y(\mathbf{x}_i) = -1$ if $\mathbf{x}_i$ belongs to class 2. We consider the following decision function in the feature space:

$$f(\phi(\mathbf{x})) = \mathbf{w}^T \phi(\mathbf{x}) + b, \tag{1}$$

where $\mathbf{w}$ is a coefficient vector, $b$ is a bias term, and if $\mathbf{x}$ is correctly classified, $y(\mathbf{x}_i)f(\phi(\mathbf{x}_i)) > 0$. If all the training data are correctly classified, $f(\phi(\mathbf{x})) = \mathbf{0}$ is called *separating hyperplane* and the minimum distance between the separating hyperplane and the training data is called *margin*.

In SVMs, the separating hyperplane is determined so that the margin is maximized while minimizing the classification error of the training data:

Minimize

$$Q(\mathbf{w}, \boldsymbol{\xi}) = \frac{1}{2}||\mathbf{w}||^2 + C\sum_{i=1}^{M}\xi_i \tag{2}$$

subject to

$$y(\mathbf{x}_i)(\mathbf{w}^T\phi(\mathbf{x}_i) + b) \geq 1 - \xi_i \quad \text{for} \quad i = 1, ..., M, \tag{3}$$

where $C$ is a margin parameter to control the tradeoff between maximization of margins and minimization of classification errors and $\xi_i$ are slack variables associated with $\mathbf{x}_i$.

Introducing the Lagrange multipliers, the following dual problem is obtained:

Maximize

$$Q(\boldsymbol{\alpha}) = \sum_{i=1}^{M}\alpha_i - \frac{1}{2}\sum_{i,j=1}^{M} y(\mathbf{x}_i)y(\mathbf{x}_j)\alpha_i\alpha_j K(\mathbf{x}_i, \mathbf{x}_j) \tag{4}$$

subject to

$$\sum_{i=1}^{M} y(\mathbf{x}_i)\alpha_i = 0, \quad 0 \leq \alpha_i \leq C. \tag{5}$$

Here $K(\mathbf{x}, \mathbf{x}')$ is called *kernel function*:

$$K(\mathbf{x}, \mathbf{x}') = \phi(\mathbf{x})^T\phi(\mathbf{x}'). \tag{6}$$

In our study we use polynomial kernels with degree $d$:

$$K(\mathbf{x}, \mathbf{x}') = (\mathbf{x}^T\mathbf{x}' + 1)^d, \tag{7}$$

and RBF (Radial Basis Function) kernels:

$$K(\mathbf{x}, \mathbf{x}') = \exp(-\gamma||\mathbf{x} - \mathbf{x}'||^2), \tag{8}$$

where $\gamma > 0$.

For the solution of (4) and (5), if $\alpha_i > 0$, $\mathbf{x}_i$ are called *support vectors*. Especially if $\alpha_i = C$, *bounded support vectors* and if $0 < \alpha_i < C$, *unbounded support vectors*. The most important characteristic is that we can obtain the same solution using only support vectors.

Using support vectors, the decision function is expressed by

$$f(\phi(\mathbf{x})) = \sum_{i \in S} y(\mathbf{x}_i)\alpha_i K(\mathbf{x}_i, \mathbf{x}) + b, \tag{9}$$

where $S$ is the support vector indices and $\mathbf{w}$ is given by

$$\mathbf{w} = \sum_{j \in S} y(\mathbf{x}_j)\alpha_j\phi(\mathbf{x}_j). \tag{10}$$

Margin $\delta$ is given by

$$\delta = \frac{1}{||\mathbf{w}||} = \frac{1}{\sqrt{\displaystyle\sum_{j,k \in S} y(\mathbf{x}_j)y(\mathbf{x}_k)\alpha_j\alpha_k K(\mathbf{x}_j, \mathbf{x}_k)}}. \tag{11}$$

# 3   Conventional Incremental Training Methods

In [5], support vector candidates are selected if

$$y(\mathbf{x})f(\phi(\mathbf{x})) \leq \beta + 1 \tag{12}$$

is satisfied, where $\beta (> 0)$ is a user defined parameter. If the separating hyperplane does not change much after retraining, future support vectors are kept by (12). But if the separating hyperplane rotates after retraining, support vector candidates tend to be deleted if the value of $\beta$ is not properly selected.

In [6,7], concentric hyperspheres are used to approximate the regions for support vector candidates.

For class $j$ $(j = 1, 2)$, we generate the minimum-volume hypersphere with radius $R_j$ that includes all the training data in that class. Then we generate a concentric hypersphere with radius $\rho R_j$, where $\rho (0 < \rho < 1)$ is a user defined parameter. Then we generate a hypercone with the vertex at the center of the hypersphere, which opens on the opposite side of the separating hyperplane. The openness of the hypercone is controlled by the angle, $\theta (-90 < \theta < 90)$, between the surface of the hypercone and the hyperplane that goes thorough the vertex of the hypercone and that is parallel to the separating hyperplane. We delete data that are inside of the hypersphere with radius $\rho R_j$ or in the hypercone unless they are not support vectors.

# 4   Proposed Method

## 4.1   Relations Between Support Vector Candidates and Vertexes of Convex Hulls

We consider what data should we keep to cope with the rotation of the separating hyperplane when data are added. To make matters simple we consider the separable case shown in Fig. 1. In the figure, the regions of the two classes are shown as convex hulls. The optimal separating hyperplane for this problem is shown in the figure. Now suppose that data are added but that these data are not in the regions of different classes. Then the separating hyperplane after incremental training will exist in the shaded region. Thus the data, which are the vertexes of the convex hulls and which are in the shaded region, are support vector candidates. Therefore, if we keep all the data that are vertexes, we can hold all the support vector candidates.

However, since usually we map the input space into the feature space and we do not explicitly treat variables in the feature space, generation of convex hulls is very difficult. In addition, by this method, redundant data on the vertexes that are far away from the separating hyperplane will be retained, which is inefficient. Thus, to solve this problem, we use truncated hypercones, which include the vertexes of the convex hulls but delete data that are far away from the separating hyperplane.

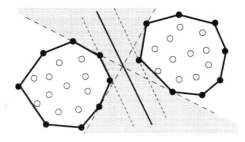

**Fig. 1.** Possible locations of separating hyperplanes and vertexes of convex hulls

## 4.2   Data Deletion Using Truncated Hypercones

Consider the case where a classification problem is linearly separable in the feature space as shown in Fig. 2. To keep the data whose images are near the separating hyperplane, we generate the truncated hypercones as shown in the figure and delete the data whose images are inside of the truncated hypercones. Data in black disks are retained and data in white disks are deleted.

Now we explain how to generate truncated hypercones. First, we generate truncated surface, whose center is the mean vector of mapped support vectors and the radius $r_i$ $(j = 1, 2)$ is the maximum distance among the distances from the center to mapped support vectors. The rotating axis is the line that goes through the center and that is perpendicular to the separating hyperplane. If there is only one support vector like the right class in Fig. 2, a truncated hypercone shrinks to a hypercone with the mapped support vector being the center and with radius $r_2 = 0$.

For each class, among the mapped data whose distances from the separating hyperplane are longer than that of the class center of mapped training data, calculate the maximum distance from the rotating axis, $R_i$ $(i = 1, 2)$. Use this as the radius that determine the slope of the truncated hypercone and generate the truncated hypercone. The reason why we exclude the mapped data that are nearer to the separating hyperplane than the class center of mapped training data is that these data are consider to be the candidate of support vectors.

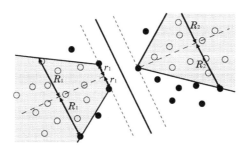

**Fig. 2.** Deletion of data using truncated hypercones

Generation of hypercones discussed so far is for separable problems such as shown in Fig. 2. For non-separable problems, mapped data inside of the convex hulls could be support vector candidates. To cope with this, we move the truncated hypercone in parallel along the rotating axis as shown in Fig. 3.

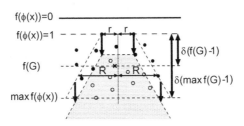

**Fig. 3.** Parallel movement of a truncated hypercone

To control parallel shifts we introduce three parameters: $f(\mathbf{G}_{fs})$, max $f(\phi(\mathbf{x}))$, and $f(\phi(\mathbf{G}_{is}))$, where $f(\mathbf{G}_{fs})$ is the output of the decision function for the center vector of the mapped training data that are kept at an incremental training step, max $f(\phi(\mathbf{x}))$ is the output of the decision function for $\mathbf{x}$, whose associated distance from $\phi(\mathbf{x})$ to the separating hyperplane is the maximum among the data that are kept at an incremental training step, and $f(\phi(\mathbf{G}_{is}))$ is the output of the decision function for the center vector of the training data added so far. If we calculate $f(\mathbf{G}_{fs})$ using the data that are added so far we need to keep all the data. Thus, $f(\phi(\mathbf{G}_{is}))$ is to approximate $f(\mathbf{G}_{fs})$ calculated using all the data added so far.

Using these parameters we shift hyperplane by $m_1\,\delta\,(f(\mathbf{G}_{fs}) - 1)$, $m_2\,\delta\,(\text{max } f(\phi(\mathbf{x})) - 1)$, or $m_3\,\delta\,(f(\phi(\mathbf{G}_{is})) - 1)$, where $m_1, m_2(0 \leq m_2 \leq 1)$, and $m_3$ are user defined parameters.

The flow of incremental training using truncated hypercones is as follows:

1. Train an SVM using the initial training set $X_a$.
2. Add incremental data set $X_b$ to $X_a$: $X_a = X_a \cup X_b$.
3. Using the data in $X_a$ that satisfy $y(\mathbf{x})f(\phi(\mathbf{x})) \geq 1$, generate the truncated hypercones and shift them in parallel along rotating axes. If $\mathbf{x}$ does not satisfy $y(\mathbf{x})f(\phi(\mathbf{x})) \leq 1$ and $\phi(\mathbf{x})$ is included in the shifted truncated hypercone, delete $\mathbf{x}$: $X_a = X_a - \{\mathbf{x}\}$.
4. If there is $\mathbf{x}$ in $X_a$ that satisfies $y(\mathbf{x})f(\phi(\mathbf{x})) \leq 1$, retrain the SVM.
5. Iterate Steps 2, 3, and 4 during incremental training.

In Step 3, we keep the data that satisfy $y(\mathbf{x})f(\phi(\mathbf{x})) \leq 1$ because they are bounded support vectors and are support vector candidates after training. In Step 4, if there are no data that satisfy $y(\mathbf{x})f(\phi(\mathbf{x})) \leq 1$, the separating hyperplane after retraining is the same. Thus, we do not retrain the SVM.

### 4.3    Determination of Inside of Truncated Hypercones

We judge whether a mapped datum is inside or outside of a truncated hypercone using $r_i$ and $R_i$.

The center of the truncated surface, $\mathbf{a}_i$, for class $i$ is given by

$$\mathbf{a}_i = \frac{1}{|S_i'|} \sum_{j \in S_i'} \phi(\mathbf{x}_j), \tag{13}$$

where $S_i'$ is the index set of unbounded support vectors for class $i$ and $|S_i'|$ is the number of unbounded support vectors for class $i$. Using (13), $r_i$ is given by

$$r_i = \max_{j \in S_i'} \|\phi(\mathbf{x}_j) - \mathbf{a}_i\|$$

$$= \max_{j \in S_i'} \sqrt{K(\mathbf{x}_j, \mathbf{x}_j) - \frac{2}{|S_i'|} \sum_{k \in S_i'} K(\mathbf{x}_j, \mathbf{x}_k) + \frac{1}{|S'_i|^2} \sum_{k' \in S_i'} \sum_{k \in S_i'} K(\mathbf{x}_{k'}, \mathbf{x}_k)}. \tag{14}$$

We use the following two center vectors to check if the distance from the separating hyperplane to a mapped datum $\phi(\mathbf{x})$ is longer than that to the center vector:

1. The use of $f(\mathbf{G}_{\text{fs}})$ and max $f(\phi(\mathbf{x}))$ for the truncated hypercone shift
   The center vector in the feature space at an incremental training step is calculated using a set of class $i$ data, $X_i$:

$$\mathbf{G}_{\text{fs}} = \frac{1}{|X_i|} \sum_{j \in X_i} \phi(\mathbf{x}_j). \tag{15}$$

And the decision function $f(\mathbf{G}_{\text{fs}})$ is given by

$$f(\mathbf{G}_{\text{fs}}) = \mathbf{w}^T \mathbf{G}_{\text{fs}} + b = \frac{1}{|X_i|} \sum_{j \in X_i} \sum_{k \in S} y(\mathbf{x}_k) \alpha_k K(\mathbf{x}_j, \mathbf{x}_k) + b. \tag{16}$$

For $\mathbf{x}$ that satisfies $y(\mathbf{x})f(\phi(\mathbf{x})) \geq 1$ and $f(\phi(\mathbf{x})) > f(\mathbf{G}_{\text{fs}})$, we calculate the distance from the rotating axis to $\phi(\mathbf{x})$ for the possible candidate of the radius of the truncated hypercone.

2. The use of $f(\phi(\mathbf{G}_{\text{is}}))$ for the parallel shift
   For the set of data, $X_{\text{old}}$, that includes the deleted data for class $i$, let the center vector be $\mathbf{G}_{\text{old}}$. Assume that a set of data, $X_{\text{add}}$, is added. Then the center vector, $\mathbf{G}_{\text{is}}$, after addition is given by

$$\mathbf{G}_{\text{is}} = \frac{1}{|X_{\text{old}}| + |X_{\text{add}}|} (|X_{\text{old}}| \mathbf{G}_{\text{old}} + \sum_{k \in X_{\text{add}}} \mathbf{x}_k). \tag{17}$$

In this way, we can update the center vector in the input space without storing deletable data. Although mapping of the center vector into the feature space does not coincide with the center vector in the feature space, it could be an approximation. The decision function for $\mathbf{G}_{\mathrm{is}}$ is given by

$$f(\phi(\mathbf{G}_{\mathrm{is}})) = \mathbf{w}^T \phi(\mathbf{G}_{\mathrm{is}}) + b = \frac{1}{|S|} \sum_{k \in S} y(\mathbf{x}_k) \alpha_k K(\mathbf{G}_{\mathrm{is}}, \mathbf{x}_k) + b. \qquad (18)$$

For $\mathbf{x}$ that satisfies $y(\mathbf{x})f(\phi(\mathbf{x})) \geq 1$ and $f(\phi(\mathbf{x})) > f(\phi(\mathbf{G}_{\mathrm{is}}))$, we calculate the distance between the rotating axis and $\phi(\mathbf{x})$ for the possible candidate of the radius of the truncated hypercone.

Among $\mathbf{x}$ that satisfies $f(\phi(\mathbf{x})) > f(\mathbf{G}_{\mathrm{fs}})$ or $f(\phi(\mathbf{x})) > f(\phi(\mathbf{G}_{\mathrm{is}}))$, the maximum distance among the distances between the rotating axis and $\phi(\mathbf{x})$ is selected as the radius of the truncated hypercone. From Fig. 4, $R_i$ is given by

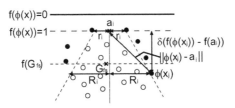

**Fig. 4.** Calculation of radius $R_i$

$$R_i = \max_{j \in X_i} \sqrt{||\phi(\mathbf{x}_j) - \mathbf{a}_i||^2 - \{\delta(f(\phi(\mathbf{x}_j)) - f(\mathbf{a}_i))\}^2}, \qquad (19)$$

where

$$||\phi(\mathbf{x}_j) - \mathbf{a}_i|| = K(\mathbf{x}_j, \mathbf{x}_j) - \frac{2}{|S'_i|} \sum_{k \in S'_i} K(\mathbf{x}_j, \mathbf{x}_k)$$

$$+ \frac{1}{|S'_i|^2} \sum_{k \in S'_i} \sum_{k \in S'_i} K(\mathbf{x}_k, \mathbf{x}_k), \qquad (20)$$

$$f(\mathbf{a}_i) = \mathbf{w}^T \mathbf{a}_i + b = \frac{1}{|S'_i|} \sum_{j \in S'_i} \sum_{k \in S} y(\mathbf{x}_k) \alpha_k K(\mathbf{x}_j, \mathbf{x}_k) + b. \qquad (21)$$

Similar to the calculation of $R_i$, for $\mathbf{x}$ the distance, $d(\mathbf{x})$, between the rotating axis and $\phi(\mathbf{x})$ is given by

$$d(\mathbf{x}) = \sqrt{||\phi(\mathbf{x}) - \mathbf{a}_i||^2 - \{\delta(f(\phi(\mathbf{x})) - f(\mathbf{a}_i))\}^2}. \qquad (22)$$

The radius $L_i$ of the truncated hypercone, at which points the output of the decision function is the same with $f(\phi(\mathbf{x}))$ is given as follows.

1. The use of $f(\mathbf{G}_{fs})$ for the truncated hypercone shift
   For $\mathbf{x}$ that satisfies $f(\phi(\mathbf{x})) > 1 + m_1(f(\mathbf{G}_{fs}) - f(\mathbf{a}_i))$, we calculate $L_i$ by

$$L_i = r_i + (R_i - r_i) \times \frac{\left( f(\phi(\mathbf{x})) - m_1\{f(\mathbf{G}_{fs}) - f(\mathbf{a}_i)\} \right) - f(\mathbf{a}_i)}{f(R_i) - f(\mathbf{a}_i)}. \quad (23)$$

2. The use of max $f(\phi(\mathbf{x}))$ for the truncated hypercone shift
   For $\mathbf{x}_j (j \in X_i)$ belonging to class $i$, we calculate $\max_{j \in X_i} f(\phi(\mathbf{x}_j))$. Then for $\mathbf{x}$ that satisfies $f(\phi(\mathbf{x})) > 1 + m_2(\max_{j \in X_i} f(\phi(\mathbf{x}_j)) - f(\mathbf{a}_i))$, we calculate $L_i$ by

$$L_i = r_i + (R_i - r_i) \times \frac{\left( f(\phi(\mathbf{x})) - m_2\{\max_{j \in X_i} f(\phi(\mathbf{x}_j)) - f(\mathbf{a}_i)\} \right) - f(\mathbf{a}_i)}{f(R_i) - f(\mathbf{a}_i)}. \quad (24)$$

3. The use of $f(\phi(\mathbf{G}_{is}))$ in the truncated hypercone shift
   For $\mathbf{x}$ that satisfies $f(\phi(\mathbf{x})) > 1 + m_3(f(\phi(\mathbf{G}_{is})) - f(\mathbf{a}_i))$, we calculate the following $L_i$:

$$L_i = r_i + (R_i - r_i) \times \frac{\left( f(\phi(\mathbf{x})) - m_3\{f(\phi(\mathbf{G}_{is})) - f(\mathbf{a}_i)\} \right) - f(\mathbf{a}_i)}{f(R_i) - f(\mathbf{a}_i)}. \quad (25)$$

If we set $m_1, m_2, m_3$ to 0, we delete data without shifting truncated hypercones. If $d(\mathbf{x}) < L_i$
is satisfied we delete $\mathbf{x}$.

## 5   Performance Evaluation

We evaluated the effectiveness of the proposed method using the two-class benchmark problems listed in Table 1.[1] Each problem consists of 100 or 20 training and test data sets. Except for banana, ringnorm, and thyroid data sets, we normalized the input range into $[0, 1]$.

For each of 100 or 20 training data sets in a two-class problem, we generated the incremental training data sets, dividing each training data set into subsets with 5% of the training data. In each incremental training step, we added a subset to the classifier.

Training of SVMs was done by the primal-dual interior-point method combined with the decomposition techniques.

We compared the proposed and conventional methods for the optimal kernel and margin parameter $C$. We determined the optimal kernel by 5-fold cross-validation using the first five training data sets for the polynomial kernels with $d = [2, 3, 4]$ and RBF kernels with $\gamma = [0.1, 1, 10]$, and the margin parameter $C =$

---

[1] http://ida.first.fraunhofer.de/projects/bench/benchmarks.htm

**Table 1.** Specifications of two-class data sets

|          | Trn  | Test | Inputs | Classes | Sets |
|----------|------|------|--------|---------|------|
| Banana   | 400  | 4900 | 2      | 2       | 100  |
| B. cancer| 200  | 77   | 9      | 2       | 100  |
| Diabetes | 468  | 300  | 8      | 2       | 100  |
| German   | 700  | 300  | 20     | 2       | 100  |
| Heart    | 170  | 100  | 13     | 2       | 100  |
| Image    | 1300 | 1010 | 18     | 2       | 20   |
| Ringnorm | 400  | 7000 | 20     | 2       | 100  |
| F. solar | 666  | 400  | 9      | 2       | 100  |
| Splice   | 1000 | 2175 | 60     | 2       | 20   |
| Thyroid  | 140  | 75   | 5      | 2       | 100  |
| Twonorm  | 400  | 7000 | 20     | 2       | 100  |
| Waveform | 400  | 4600 | 21     | 2       | 100  |

**Table 2.** Parameter setting

| Data     | Kernel | Batch | Hplane | Sphere | | Tcone-1 | Tcone-2 | Tcone-3 |
|----------|--------|-------|--------|--------|---|---------|---------|---------|
|          |        | $C$   | $\beta$| $\rho$ | $\theta$ | $m_1$ | $m_2$ | $m_3$ |
| Banana   | $\gamma 1$   | 10   | 2    | 0.5 | 0 | 0.5 | 0.08 | 0.5 |
| B. cancer| $\gamma 1$   | 1    | 0.01 | 0.5 | 0 | 0.5 | 0.08 | 0.5 |
| Diabetes | $d2$         | 50   | 0.5  | 0.5 | 0 | 0.5 | 0.08 | 0.5 |
| German   | $\gamma 1$   | 10   | 0.1  | 0.5 | 0 | 0.5 | 0.08 | 0.5 |
| Heart    | $\gamma 1$   | 50   | 0.5  | 0.5 | 0 | 0.5 | 0.08 | 0.5 |
| Image    | $\gamma 1$   | 1000 | 2    | 0.5 | 0 | 0.5 | 0.08 | 0.5 |
| Ringnorm | $\gamma 0.1$ | 1    | 0.1  | 0.5 | 0 | 0.5 | 0.08 | 0.5 |
| F. solar | $d2$         | 10   | 0.5  | 0.5 | 0 | 0.5 | 0.08 | 0.5 |
| Splice   | $\gamma 10$  | 1    | 0.1  | 0.5 | 0 | 0.5 | 0.08 | 0.5 |
| Thyroid  | $d2$         | 1    | 1    | 0.5 | 0 | 0.5 | 0.08 | 0.5 |
| Twonorm  | $d4$         | 50   | 2    | 0.5 | 0 | 0.5 | 0.08 | 0.5 |
| Waveform | $\gamma 1$   | 1    | 0.1  | 0.5 | 0 | 0.5 | 0.08 | 0.5 |

$[1, 10, 50, 100, 500, 1000, 2000, 3000, 5000, 8000, 10000, 50000, 100000]$. (Please refer to [7] for the detailed selection procedure.)

For the conventional method that uses the hyperplane (Hplane), we set $\beta$ so that the generalization ability is comparable with that of batch training. This parameter setting is to compare the numbers of deletable data and is not realizable. For the conventional method that uses hyperspheres (Sphere) we set $\rho = 0.5$ and $\theta = 0$ [7].

For the proposed method, since $m_1$ and $m_3$ are not upper bounded, we set $m_1$ and $m_3 = [0.1, 0.2, 0.3, 0.4, 0.5, 0.6, 0.7, 0.8, 0.9, 1, 3, 5, 8, 10]$. Since $m_2$ satisfies $0 \leq m_2 \leq 1$, we set $m_2 = [0.01, 0.03, 0.05, 0.08, 0.1, 0.2, 0.3, 0.4, 0.5, 0.6, 0.7, 0.8, 0.9, 1]$. As an initial test, using the diabetes data set, which has the medium number of training data and the medium number of the input variables (8 variables), the twonorm data set with 20 input variables, and waveform with

**Table 3.** Performance comparison (%)

| Data | Term | Batch | Hplane | Sphere | Tcone-1 | Tcone-2 | Tcone-3 |
|---|---|---|---|---|---|---|---|
| Banana | Test | 89.31±0.53 | 89.31±0.53 | 89.31±0.53 | *88.40±1.92* | *88.20±1.83* | 89.31± 0.53 |
| | Trn | 91.95±1.30 | 91.93±1.30 | 91.93±1.30 | 91.14±2.45 | 91.03±2.24 | 91.94±1.30 |
| | Del | 73.6±2.3 | 64.3±3.7 | **69.8±2.7** | 70.5±4.1 | 71.5±3.2 | 54.2±5.4 |
| B. cancer | Test | 73.25±4.53 | 73.25±4.53 | 73.25±4.53 | 73.25±4.53 | 73.25±4.53 | 73.25±4.53 |
| | Trn | 82.80±1.72 | 82.80±1.72 | 82.80±1.72 | 82.80±1.71 | 82.80±1.72 | 82.80±1.72 |
| | Del | 34.6±2.7 | 0.1±0.3 | 0.1±0.2 | 0.0±0.1 | 0.0±0.2 | 0.0±0.0 |
| Diabetes | Test | 76.46±1.85 | 76.46±1.85 | 76.46±1.85 | 76.44±1.88 | 76.44±1.88 | 76.39±1.90 |
| | Trn | 78.48±1.22 | 78.48±1.22 | 78.48±1.22 | 78.52±1.18 | 78.48±1.23 | 78.43±1.27 |
| | Del | 45.5±1.7 | 15.7±8.3 | **27.8±13.4** | **31.4±16.1** | 26.9±16.6 | **31.6±16.2** |
| German | Test | 76.63±2.14 | 76.70±2.26 | 76.63±2.14 | 76.63±2.14 | 76.65±2.17 | 76.63±2.12 |
| | Trn | 81.14±1.27 | 80.94±1.41 | 81.14±1.27 | 81.14±1.27 | 81.14±1.29 | 81.14±1.30 |
| | Del | 43.8±1.5 | 33.8±5.7 | **35.5±3.7** | 30.8±6.8 | 33.4±4.7 | 21.4±6.7 |
| Heart | Test | 83.68±3.39 | 83.68±3.39 | 83.68±3.39 | 82.84±4.58 | 82.83±5.57 | 83.34±3.43 |
| | Trn | 85.95±1.92 | 85.95±1.92 | 85.95±1.92 | 85.29±3.90 | 85.32±4.00 | 85.74±2.18 |
| | Del | 56.3±3.4 | 24.9±21.9 | **32.4±27.6** | **35.4±25.8** | **32.3±23.2** | **36.0±26.1** |
| Image | Test | 97.14±0.48 | 97.12±0.47 | 97.13±0.48 | *96.30±0.71* | *96.48±0.50* | *96.03±1.11* |
| | Trn | 98.60±0.18 | 98.60±0.17 | 98.60±0.18 | 97.82±0.44 | 98.08±0.31 | 97.41±0.80 |
| | Del | 88.3±0.7 | **60.2±3.8** | **61.7±4.7** | 80.6±4.7 | 83.4±1.9 | 83.1±5.4 |
| Ringnorm | Test | 98.41±0.10 | 98.41±0.10 | 98.41±0.10 | 98.41±0.10 | 98.41±0.10 | 98.41±0.10 |
| | Trn | 99.91±0.15 | 99.91±0.15 | 99.91±0.15 | 99.91±0.15 | 99.91±0.15 | 99.91±0.15 |
| | Del | 61.5±2.3 | **45.6±16.3** | 31.0±11.1 | 31.5±11.7 | 35.9±13.0 | 24.2±9.6 |
| F. solar | Test | 68.29±1.85 | 68.29±1.85 | 68.29±1.85 | *67.44±2.34* | 68.30±1.85 | *67.47±2.56* |
| | Trn | 68.19±1.26 | 68.19±1.26 | 68.19±1.26 | 67.82±1.84 | 68.19±1.26 | 67.81±1.85 |
| | Del | 18.9±1.9 | 4.5±3.5 | **11.5±8.6** | 12.8±10.5 | **11.4±9.7** | 11.5±10.5 |
| Splice | Test | 88.66±0.71 | 88.66±0.72 | 88.66±0.71 | 88.66±0.71 | 88.66±0.71 | 88.66±0.71 |
| | Trn | 99.09±0.24 | 99.09±0.24 | 99.09±0.24 | 99.09±0.24 | 99.10±0.24 | 99.09±0.24 |
| | Del | 26.5±1.3 | **11.9±10.7** | **13.2±12.0** | **13.5±12.2** | **13.6±12.3** | 8.4±7.7 |
| Thyroid | Test | 96.31±1.90 | 96.31±1.90 | 96.31±1.90 | 96.31±1.90 | 95.84±2.29 | 95.33±4.34 |
| | Trn | 99.34±0.49 | 99.34±0.49 | 99.34±0.49 | 98.50±2.03 | 98.82±1.02 | 97.84±4.70 |
| | Del | 88.9±1.3 | 66.5±11.3 | 60.9±6.7 | **83.0±3.6** | **82.0±7.4** | 78.1±17.3 |
| Twonorm | Test | 97.57±0.12 | 97.57±0.12 | 97.57±0.12 | 97.56±0.13 | 97.57±0.12 | 97.57±0.12 |
| | Trn | 98.24±0.55 | 98.24±0.55 | 98.24±0.55 | 98.23±0.56 | 98.24±0.55 | 98.24±0.55 |
| | Del | 79.1±1.6 | 57.5±6.4 | 51.2±6.8 | 47.6±5.8 | **71.3±7.5** | 47.4±5.6 |
| Waveform | Test | 90.00±0.45 | 90.00±0.45 | 90.00±0.45 | 90.00±0.43 | 90.00±0.44 | 90.00±0.44 |
| | Trn | 93.51±1.37 | 93.51±1.37 | 93.51±1.37 | 93.52±1.38 | 93.51±1.38 | 93.51±1.39 |
| | Del | 61.6±2.2 | **36.8±28.0** | **38.2±25.7** | **37.3±25.2** | **39.8±26.8** | **34.1±23.0** |

21 input variables, we incrementally trained the SVM with the optimal kernel and the optimal value of $C$ for the above parameter setting of $m_1$, $m_2$, and $m_3$ and selected $m_1 = 0.5$, $m_2 = 0.08$, and $m_3 = 0.5$, by which setting sufficient data deletion was done with the generalization performance comparable to that of batch training.

Table 2 lists the parameter values used in the experiments. In the table, "Kernel" denotes the kernel and the parameter value determined by cross-validation. For instance, $\gamma1$ means RBF kernels with $\gamma = 1$ and $d2$ means polynomial kernels with degree $d = 2$. The results are shown in "Batch," "Hplane," "Sphere," and "Tcone" columns. For the proposed method, "Tcone-$i$" ($i = 1, 2, 3$) denotes that the parameter $m_i$ is used. From the table, the optimal value of $\beta$ changes as the classification problem changes.

Table 3 lists the results. "Test" and "Trn" rows show the average recognition rates and their standard deviations of the test and training data when incremental training is finished. The "Del" row shows the number of deleted training data divided by the number of training data. For batch training, the number of deleted training data is calculated by the number of training data minus the number of support vectors. Thus, the "Del" value for batch training is the upper bound of that of incremental training if all the support vectors are kept by incremental training.

The recognition rates of the test data shown in italic are statistically different from those of batch training with the significance level of 0.05. The deletion ratios in boldface are the group that realizes the best deletion of data, in which the deletion ratio of any member of the group is statistically the same.

From Table 3, Sphere and Tcone-2 show the best performance and Tcone-1, Tcone-3, and Hplane show the second best. Although the recognition rates of the test data for Sphere are comparable with those of batch training, those for Tcone are in some cases lower. Thus, the parameter selection of Sphere is more robust than that of Tcone.

## 6  Conclusions

In this paper, to reduce memory cost by deleting unnecessary data, we proposed an incremental training method for SVMs, which is robust for rotation of separating hyperplanes after incremental training.

Based on the fact that support vectors form vertexes of convex hulls for classes, we use truncated hypercones to keep the data that are near the separating hyperplanes. We generate the truncated surface with the center being the center of unbounded support vectors and the radius being the maximum distance between the center and unbounded support vectors. The rotating axis goes through the center and is perpendicular to the truncated surface. The rotating surface includes the datum, which is far away from the separating hyperplane and which is farthest from the rotating axis. We delete data that are inside of the truncated hypercone and keep the remaining data.

For two-class problems, we showed that, in most cases, we could delete many training data while keeping the generalization ability comparable to that of batch training.

## References

1. V. Vapnik, *Statistical Learning Theory*, John Wiley & Sons, 1998.
2. V. Vapnik, *The Nature of Statistical Learning Theory*, Springer-Verlag, 1995.
3. P. Mitra, C. A. Murthy, S. K. Pal, "Data Condensation in Large Databases by Incremental Learning with Support Vector Machines," *Proc. ICPR 2000*, pp. 2708–2711, 2000.
4. C. Domeniconi and D. Gunopulos, "Incremental Support Vector Machine Construction," *Proc. ICDM 2001*, pp. 589–592, 2001.
5. G. Cauwenberghs and T. Poggio, "Incremental and Decremental Support Vector Machine Learning," In T. K. Leen, T. G. Dietterich, and V. Tresp, Eds., *Advances in Neural Information Processing Systems 13*, pp. 409–415, MIT Press, 2000.
6. S. Katagiri and S. Abe, "Selecting Support Vector Candidates for Incremental Training," *Proc. SMC 2005*, pp. 1258–1263, 2005.
7. S. Katagiri and S. Abe, "Incremental Training of Support Vector Machines Using Hyperspheres," *Pattern Recognition Letters* (accepted).
8. D. M. J. Tax and R. P. W. Duin, "Outliers and Data Descriptions," *Proc. Seventh Annual Conference of the Advanced School for Computing and Imaging*, pp. 234–241, 2001.

# Fast Training of Linear Programming Support Vector Machines Using Decomposition Techniques

Yusuke Torii[1] and Shigeo Abe[2]

[1] Kobe University, Rokkodai, Nada, Kobe, Japan
057t238n@stu.kobe-u.ac.jp
[2] Kobe University, Rokkodai, Nada, Kobe, Japan
abe@kobe-u.ac.jp

**Abstract.** Decomposition techniques are used to speed up training support vector machines but for linear programming support vector machines (LP-SVMs) direct implementation of decomposition techniques leads to infinite loops. To solve this problem and to further speed up training, in this paper, we propose an improved decomposition techniques for training LP-SVMs. If an infinite loop is detected, we include in the next working set all the data in the working sets that form the infinite loop. To further accelerate training, we improve a working set selection strategy: at each iteration step, we check the number of violations of complementarity conditions and constraints. If the number of violations increases, we conclude that the important data are removed from the working set and restore the data into the working set. The computer experiments demonstrate that training by the proposed decomposition technique with improved working set selection is drastically faster than that without using the decomposition technique. Furthermore, it is always faster than that without improving the working set selection for all the cases tested.

## 1 Introduction

Decomposition techniques [1] are widely used to speed up training of support vector machines (SVMs) [2,3] for large size problems. Stable convergence to solutions by decomposition techniques is verified both by computer experiments and theoretical analysis [4,5]. In [5], the sequential minimum optimization technique, which uses a decomposition technique with a working set size of two, is shown to converge asymptotically if the most violating variables are selected.

But for a linear programming support vector machine (LP-SVM), in which the quadratic objective function in an SVM is replaced with a linear function [6], direct implementation of decomposition techniques sometimes leads to infinite loops. But this phenomenon has not been discussed so far.

In this paper, we propose decomposition techniques for training an LP-SVM that resolve infinite loops and speed up training by improved working set selection. In training an LP-SVM by decomposition techniques, first, we select the

F. Schwenker and S. Marinai (Eds.): ANNPR 2006, LNAI 4087, pp. 165–176, 2006.
© Springer-Verlag Berlin Heidelberg 2006

initial working set randomly, and optimize the subproblem. Using the primal and dual solutions, we check if each of the training data satisfies the complementarity conditions and the constraints. And if all the training data satisfy the complementarity conditions and the constraints, we finish training.

But if there exist training data that do not satisfy the complementarity conditions or the constraints, we select the working set again. In selecting the working set, we detect the variables, in the fixed set, that do not satisfy complementarity conditions, and move them to the working set. And we detect the data, in the working set, that is not support vectors of the subproblem, and move them to the fixed set. Then, we optimize the new subproblem and iterate the algorithm until all the training data satisfy the complementarity conditions and the constraints.

The above training method sometimes leads to infinite loops, in which the same sequence of working sets repeatedly appears. To resolve infinite loops, if an infinite loop is detected, we include in the new working set all the data that are in the working sets that form the infinite loop. This working set strategy works to resolve infinite loops but according to our experiments, many iteration steps are spent before the solution goes into an infinite loop. Thus, to further speed up training, we propose an improved working set selection strategy. Namely, at each iteration step, we check the number of violations of the complementarity conditions and constraints. If the number of violations increases at some step, we conclude that important data were removed at the previous step of working set selection and add those data to the next working set.

The structure of this paper is as follows. In Section 2, we summarize the architecture of LP-SVMs, and in Section 3, we discuss the proposed method. In Section 4, we show the simulation results using benchmark data sets and in Section 5, we describe the conclusions.

## 2   Linear Programming Support Vector Machines

Let $m$-dimensional training inputs $\mathbf{x}_i$ $(i = 1, ..., M)$ belong to Class 1 or 2 and the associated labels be $y_i = 1$ for Class 1 and $-1$ for Class 2, where $M$ is the number of training inputs. In the normal SVMs [7], we determine the decision function by

$$D(\mathbf{x}) = \mathbf{w}^T \mathbf{g}(\mathbf{x}) + b, \tag{1}$$

where $\mathbf{w}$ is an $l$-dimensional vector, $b$ is a scalar, and $\mathbf{g}(\mathbf{x})$ is the mapping function that maps $m$-dimensional vector $\mathbf{x}$ into the $l$-dimensional feature space. The optimal separating hyperplane can be obtained by solving the following quadratic programming problem:

$$\text{Minimize} \quad Q(\mathbf{w}, \boldsymbol{\xi}) = \frac{1}{2}\|\mathbf{w}\|^2 + C \sum_{i=1}^{M} \xi_i \tag{2}$$

$$\text{subject to} \quad y_i(\mathbf{w}^t \mathbf{g}(\mathbf{x}_i) + b) \geq 1 - \xi_i \quad \text{for} \ \ i = 1, ..., M, \tag{3}$$

where $C$ is the margin parameter that determines the tradeoff between the maximization of the margin and minimization of the classification error, and $\xi_i$ is the nonnegative slack variable for $\mathbf{x}_i$.

By replacing the L2-norm $\|\mathbf{w}\|_2^2 = w_1^2 + w_2^2 + \cdots + w_l^2$ in the objective function (2) with an L1-norm $\|\mathbf{w}\|_1 = |w_1| + |w_2| + \cdots + |w_l|$, the SVM becomes as follows:

$$\text{Minimize} \quad Q(\mathbf{w}, \boldsymbol{\xi}) = \sum_{i=1}^{l} |w_i| + C \sum_{i=1}^{M} \xi_i \tag{4}$$

$$\text{subject to} \quad y_i(\mathbf{w}^t \mathbf{g}(\mathbf{x}_i) + b) \geq 1 - \xi_i \quad \text{for } i = 1, ..., M. \tag{5}$$

By this formulation, for the linear kernel, i.e., $\mathbf{g}(\mathbf{x}) = \mathbf{x}$, we can solve the problem by linear programming. However, for the kernels other than linear kernels, we need to treat the feature space explicitly.

To apply linear programming to the feature space, we define the decision function in the dual form as follows [8]:

$$D(\mathbf{x}) = \sum_{i=1}^{M} \alpha_i H(\mathbf{x}, \mathbf{x}_i) + b, \tag{6}$$

where $\alpha_i$ and $b$ take on real values. Thus, we need not use label numbers. And $H(\mathbf{x}, \mathbf{x}')$ is a kernel function that is given by

$$H(\mathbf{x}, \mathbf{x}') = \mathbf{g}(\mathbf{x})^T \mathbf{g}(\mathbf{x}'). \tag{7}$$

The kernels that are used in our study are as follows:

- polynomial kernels: $H(\mathbf{x}, \mathbf{x}') = (\mathbf{x}^T \mathbf{x}' + 1)^d$, where $d$ is a positive integer,
- RBF kernels: $H(\mathbf{x}, \mathbf{x}') = \exp(-\gamma \|\mathbf{x} - \mathbf{x}'\|^2)$, where $\gamma$ is a positive parameter.

Then we consider solving the following linear programming problem:

$$\text{Minimize} \quad Q(\boldsymbol{\alpha}, \boldsymbol{\xi}) = \sum_{i=1}^{M} (|\alpha_i| + C\xi_i) \tag{8}$$

$$\text{subject to} \quad y_j \left( \sum_{i=1}^{M} \alpha_i H(\mathbf{x}_j, \mathbf{x}_i) + b \right) \geq 1 - \xi_j \quad \text{for } j = 1, \ldots, M, \tag{9}$$

where $\boldsymbol{\alpha} = (\alpha_1, \ldots, \alpha_M)^T$ and $\boldsymbol{\xi} = (\xi_1, \ldots, \xi_M)^T$. Letting $\alpha_i = \alpha_i^+ - \alpha_i^-$ and $b = b^+ - b^-$, where $\alpha_i^+ \geq 0$, $\alpha_i^- \geq 0$, $b^+ \geq 0$, $b^- \geq 0$, we can solve (8) and (9) for $\boldsymbol{\alpha}$, $b$, and $\boldsymbol{\xi}$ by linear programming. Furthermore, we introduce the slack variables $u_i$ ($i = 1, \ldots, M$) into (9). Then (8) and (9) become as follows:

$$\text{Minimize} \quad Q(\boldsymbol{\alpha}^+, \boldsymbol{\alpha}^-, \boldsymbol{\xi}) = \sum_{i=1}^{M} (\alpha_i^+ + \alpha_i^- + C\xi_i) \tag{10}$$

subject to

$$y_j \left( \sum_{i=1}^{M} (\alpha_i^+ - \alpha_i^-) H(\mathbf{x}_j, \mathbf{x}_i) + b^+ - b^- \right) + \xi_j = 1 + u_j \quad \text{for } j = 1, \ldots, M. \tag{11}$$

And the decision function (6) becomes

$$D(\mathbf{x}) = \sum_{i=1}^{M}(\alpha_i^+ - \alpha_i^-)H(\mathbf{x}, \mathbf{x}_i) + b^+ - b^-. \tag{12}$$

But we must notice that since $\mathbf{w} = \sum_{i=1}^{M} \alpha_i \, \mathbf{g}(\mathbf{x}_i)$, minimization of the sum of $|\alpha_i|$ does not lead to maximization of the margin measured in the L1 norm.

Let (10) and (11) be a primal problem. Then the dual problem is given as follows:

$$\text{Maximize} \quad \sum_{i=1}^{M} z_i, \tag{13}$$

$$\text{subject to} \quad \sum_{i=1}^{M} y_i H(\mathbf{x}_i, \mathbf{x}_j) z_i + v_j^+ = 1 \quad \text{for } j = 1, \ldots, M, \tag{14}$$

$$\sum_{i=1}^{M} y_i H(\mathbf{x}_i, \mathbf{x}_j) z_i = v_j^- - 1 \quad \text{for } j = 1, \ldots, M, \tag{15}$$

$$\sum_{i=1}^{M} y_i z_i = 0, \tag{16}$$

$$z_j + w_j = C \quad \text{for } j = 1, \ldots, M, \tag{17}$$

where $z_i \geq 0$ ($i = 1, \ldots, M$) are dual variables, and $v_i^+ \geq 0$, $v_i^- \geq 0$, $w_i \geq 0$ ($i = 1, \ldots, M$) are slack variables.

By this formulation, in the primal problem, the number of variables is $4M+2$ and the number of equality constrains is $M$. In the dual problem, the number of variables is $4M$ and the number of equality constrains is $3M+1$. Thus for a large number of training data, training becomes slow even by linear programming. Therefore, we need to use decomposition techniques.

We can solve above primal problem (10) and (11) or dual problem (13)–(17) by linear programming. If we optimize a linear programming problem by the simplex method, we need only to solve the primal or dual problem. If we solve one, the other is also solved [10,11]. Therefore, in this paper, we solve only the primal problem.

By solving (10) and (11), we obtain the primal and dual solutions. If these solutions are optimal, they satisfy the following complementarity conditions:

$$\alpha_i^+ v_i^+ = 0 \quad \text{for } i = 1, \ldots, M, \tag{18}$$
$$\alpha_i^- v_i^- = 0 \quad \text{for } i = 1, \ldots, M, \tag{19}$$
$$\xi_i w_i = 0 \quad \text{for } i = 1, \ldots, M, \tag{20}$$
$$u_i z_i = 0 \quad \text{for } i = 1, \ldots, M. \tag{21}$$

The training data $\mathbf{x}_i$ that satisfy

$$\alpha_i = \alpha_i^+ - \alpha_i^- = 0, \tag{22}$$

$$\xi_i = 0, \tag{23}$$
$$z_i = 0, \tag{24}$$

do not affect the solution even if they are removed. Namely, the training data $\mathbf{x}_i$ that do not satisfy (22)–(24) are support vectors.

## 3   Proposed Method

In this section, we discuss the decomposition technique for the LP-SVM. If we directly implement the strategy for working set selection developed for normal SVMs [1], the solution often goes into an infinite loop. Even if it does not, the convergence is usually slow. To overcome these, in Subsection 3.1, we discuss a strategy for working set selection to avoid infinite loops, and in Subsection 3.2, we further refine the working set selection to speed up training.

### 3.1   Decomposition Techniques for LP-SVMs

In decomposition techniques for an LP-SVM, we iterate optimizing subproblems that are smaller than the original optimization problem (10) and (11). Namely, we decompose the index set $T = \{1, \ldots, M\}$ into two sets $W$ and $F$, where $W$ is a working set and $F$ is a fixed set. Here, $W \cup F = \{1, \ldots, M\}$ and $W \cap F = \phi$. Then we decompose $\boldsymbol{\alpha}^+ = \{\alpha_i^+ | i = 1, \ldots, M\}$ into $\boldsymbol{\alpha}_W^+ = \{\alpha_i^+ | i \in W\}$ and $\boldsymbol{\alpha}_F^+ = \{\alpha_i^+ | i \in F\}$. Likewise, we decompose the remaining variables, i.e., decompose $\boldsymbol{\alpha}^-$ into $\boldsymbol{\alpha}_W^-$ and $\boldsymbol{\alpha}_F^-$, $\boldsymbol{\xi}$ into $\boldsymbol{\xi}_W$ and $\boldsymbol{\xi}_F$, $\mathbf{u}$ into $\mathbf{u}_W$ and $\mathbf{u}_F$, $\mathbf{v}^+$ into $\mathbf{v}_W^+$ and $\mathbf{v}_F^+$, $\mathbf{v}^-$ into $\mathbf{v}_W^-$ and $\mathbf{v}_F^-$, $\mathbf{w}$ into $\mathbf{w}_W$ and $\mathbf{w}_F$, and $\mathbf{z}$ into $\mathbf{z}_W$ and $\mathbf{z}_F$.

And we define the following subproblem. Fixing $\boldsymbol{\alpha}_F^+$ and $\boldsymbol{\alpha}_F^-$,

$$\text{minimize} \quad Q(\boldsymbol{\alpha}_W^+, \boldsymbol{\alpha}_W^-, \boldsymbol{\xi}_W) = \sum_{i \in W} (\alpha_i^+ + \alpha_i^- + C\xi_i) \tag{25}$$

subject to

$$y_j \left( \sum_{i \in W} (\alpha_i^+ - \alpha_i^-) H(\mathbf{x}_i, \mathbf{x}_j) + b^+ - b^- + \sum_{i \in F} (\alpha_i^+ - \alpha_i^-) H(\mathbf{x}_i, \mathbf{x}_j) \right) + \xi_j$$
$$= 1 + u_j \quad \text{for} \quad j \in W. \tag{26}$$

Solving (25) and (26), we obtain $\boldsymbol{\alpha}_W^+$, $\boldsymbol{\alpha}_W^-$, $\boldsymbol{\xi}_W$, $\mathbf{u}_W$, $\mathbf{v}_W^+$, $\mathbf{v}_W^-$, $\mathbf{w}_W$, and $\mathbf{z}_W$. These vectors constitute the optimal solution for the subproblem associated with the working set $W$. But the optimal solution for the subproblem may not be optimal for the entire problem (10) and (11). To check if the obtained solution is optimal for the entire problem, we need to determine the values for the variables in the fixed set.

First, we obtain primal variables $\boldsymbol{\alpha}_F^+$, $\boldsymbol{\alpha}_F^-$, $\boldsymbol{\xi}_F$, and $\mathbf{u}_F$. Fixing $\boldsymbol{\alpha}_F^+ = \mathbf{0}$ and $\boldsymbol{\alpha}_F^- = \mathbf{0}$, we obtain $\boldsymbol{\xi}_F$ and $\mathbf{u}_F$ by the following constraints

$$y_j \left( \sum_{i \in W, F} (\alpha_i^+ - \alpha_i^-) H(\mathbf{x}_i, \mathbf{x}_j) + b^+ - b^- \right) + \xi_j = 1 + u_j \quad \text{for} \quad j \in F. \tag{27}$$

Here, (27) is a subset of (11). Using the decision function (12), the constraints (27) become

$$y_j D(\mathbf{x}_j) + \xi_j = 1 + u_j \quad \text{for} \quad j \in F. \tag{28}$$

Then we obtain $\boldsymbol{\xi}_F$ and $\mathbf{u}_F$ as follows:

1. If $y_j D(\mathbf{x}_j) > 1$, $\xi_j = 0$. Therefore, from (28), $u_j = y_j D(\mathbf{x}_j) - 1$.
2. If $y_j D(\mathbf{x}_j) \leq 1$, $\xi_j = 1 - y_j D(\mathbf{x}_j)$. Therefore from (28), $u_j = 0$

Secondly, we obtain the dual variables $\mathbf{v}_F^+$, $\mathbf{v}_F^-$, $\mathbf{w}_F$, and $\mathbf{z}_F$. Fixing $\mathbf{z}_F = \mathbf{0}$, we obtain $\mathbf{v}_F^+$, $\mathbf{v}_F^-$, and $\mathbf{w}_F$ by the following constraints:

$$v_j^+ = 1 - \sum_{i=1}^{M} y_i H(\mathbf{x}_i, \mathbf{x}_j) z_i \quad \text{for} \quad j \in F, \tag{29}$$

$$v_j^- = 1 + \sum_{i=1}^{M} y_i H(\mathbf{x}_i, \mathbf{x}_j) z_i \quad \text{for} \quad j \in F, \tag{30}$$

$$w_j = C \quad \text{for} \quad j \in F. \tag{31}$$

Here, (29)–(31) are obtained from (14), (15), and (17). We must notice that when we obtain $v_j^+$, $v_j^-$ ($j \in F$) from (29) and (30), they may take negative values.

In this way, we obtain $\boldsymbol{\alpha}_F^+$, $\boldsymbol{\alpha}_F^-$, $\boldsymbol{\xi}_F$, $\mathbf{u}_F$, $\mathbf{v}_F^+$, $\mathbf{v}_F^-$, $\mathbf{w}_F$, and $\mathbf{z}_F$. Next, we check if each of the variables satisfies the complementarity conditions (18)–(21) and the constraints. But after solving the subproblem whose variables constitute the working set, the variables satisfy both the complementarity conditions and the constraints because they are the optimal solution of the subproblem. Thus we need to check only the variables in the fixed set. As is apparent from the foregoing discussions, the variables in the fixed set satisfy the constraints (27), (29)–(31), but $v_j^+$, $v_j^-$ ($j \in F$) may take negative values. This is the violation of the constraints $v_j^+ \geq 0$ and $v_j^- \geq 0$. Furthermore, variables in the fixed set may violate the complementarity conditions (18)–(21). Therefore, we detect the variables that do not satisfy the complementarity conditions or the constraints in the fixed set. If they exist, we add them to the working set. Meanwhile, in the working set, we detect the data that are not support vectors of the subproblem, i.e., the data that satisfy (22)–(24). And we move the data that are not support vectors of the subproblem from the working set to the fixed set. And we iterate training until all the training data satisfy the complementarity conditions and the constraints.

We also finish training in the case where the value of the objective function changes little from the previous iteration, i.e., $|Q_k - Q_{k-1}| < \epsilon$, where $Q_k$ is the value of the objective function at the $k$th iteration and $\epsilon$ is a small positive parameter.

The above mentioned working set selection strategy, however, often leads to an infinite loop. In the infinite loop, the same working set is selected repeatedly.

The detail of the infinite loop is as follows. Let the working set sequence be

$$\cdots, \; W_k, \; W_{k+1}, \cdots, \; W_{k+t}, \; W_{k+t+1}, \; W_{k+t+2}, \cdots, W_{k+2t+1}, \cdots,$$

where $W_k$ is the working set at the $k$th iteration. If

$$W_k = W_{k+t+1}, \quad W_{k+1} = W_{k+t+2}, \quad \cdots \quad , W_{k+t} = W_{k+2t+1},$$

the same sequence of working sets is repeated infinitely. Namely, an infinite loop occurs. Infinite loops occur because some data that are removed at some iteration step violate the complementarity conditions or constraints in the subsequent step and move back to the working set. Thus the simplest way to avoid an infinite loop is as follows. If we find an infinite loop at the $(k + 2t + 1)$th iteration, we set $W_{k+2t+2} = W_k \cup W_{k+1} \cup \cdots \cup W_{k+t}$.

According to the above discussion, a procedure for training an LP-SVM using the decomposition techniques that avoids infinite loops is as follows.

**Step 1**

We initialize $\boldsymbol{\alpha}^+ = \mathbf{0}$, $\boldsymbol{\alpha}^- = \mathbf{0}$, $\mathbf{z} = \mathbf{0}$, and $k = 1$, where $k$ is the iteration number.

**Step 2**

We set $q$ points from the training data set to $W_1$, where $q$ is a positive integer and $W_1$ is an initial working set.

**Step 3**

We optimize the subproblem for the working set $W_k$.

**Step 4**

We obtain variables in the fixed set by (28)–(31).

**Step 5**

We check if each of the training data in the fixed set satisfies the complementarity conditions (18)–(21) and the constraints $v_i^+ \geq 0$, $v_i^- \geq 0$ ($i = 1, \ldots, M$). If there exist training data that violate the complementarity conditions or the constraints, we go to Step 6. If all the training data satisfy the complementarity conditions and the constraints or $|Q_k - Q_{k-1}| < \epsilon$, we finish training.

**Step 6**

We check if the infinite loop exists. If it exists, we add all the data in the working sets that form the infinite loop to the next working set $W_{k+1}$. And we add 1 to $k$ and go to Step 3. Otherwise we go to Step 7.

**Step 7**

In the fixed set, we detect the variables that violate the complementarity conditions or the constraints, and move at most $q$ points to the working set $W_{k+1}$. In the working set, we detect the data that are not support vectors of the subproblem, and move them to the fixed set. And we add 1 to $k$ and go to Step 3.

## 3.2   Improving Working Set Selection

The decomposition technique for an LP-SVM discussed in Subsection 3.1 can resolve infinite loops. But according to our experiments, usually an infinite loop appears after long iteration steps. Therefore, if an infinite loop appears, training is usually very slow. In this subsection, we discuss how to accelerate training by improving the working set selection strategy.

The data that are support vectors of the entire problem are very important because if all of these data are in the working set, the optimal solution for the subproblem is the optimal solution for all the training data. In selecting a working set, it often occurs that these important data, i.e., support vectors of the entire problem, go out of the working set. But in many cases, these important data return back to the working set in the subsequent iteration step. In particular, when an infinite loop occurs, these important data repeatedly go out of and return back to the working set.

Let $V_k$ be the number of data that violate the complementarity conditions or the constraints at the $k$th iteration. In general, $V_k$ is large in early stage of training. And as training proceeds while selecting the working set, $V_k$ gets smaller and smaller until it reaches 0, at which step we finish training. But if we observe the value of $V_k$ during training, it sometimes increases. This is attributed to the fact that important data for training go out of the working set.

Therefore, when $V_k$ increases, i.e., $V_k \geq V_{k-1}$, we can conclude that the data that were in $W_{k-1}$ went out of $W_{k-1}$ at the $(k-1)$th iteration and violate the complementarity conditions or the constraints after training using $W_k$. That is, these data try to go back to the working set soon after they go away since these data are important for training. Therefore, our new strategy is to return back these data to the working set $W_{k+1}$. Here, we must notice that for $V_k \geq V_{k-1}$ we do not remove any data from $W_k$. We only return back data into the working set. This is because if we remove the data from $W_k$, important data may be removed.

By implementing this process, we can stop important data from going in and out of the working set. Thus, it leads to accelerating training. A procedure for training an LP-SVM using the improved decomposition technique is as follows.

**Step 1**
   We initialize $\boldsymbol{\alpha}^+ = \mathbf{0}$, $\boldsymbol{\alpha}^- = \mathbf{0}$, $\mathbf{z} = \mathbf{0}$, and $k = 1$, where $k$ is the iteration number.
**Step 2**
   We set $q$ points from the training data set to $W_1$, where $q$ is a positive integer and $W_1$ is an initial working set.
**Step 3**
   We optimize the subproblem for the working set $W_k$.
**Step 4**
   We obtain variables in the fixed set by (28)–(31).
**Step 5**
   We check if each of the training data in the fixed set satisfies the complementarity conditions (18)–(21) and the constraints $v_i^+ \geq 0$, $v_i^- \geq 0$ ($i =$

$1, \ldots, M$). If there exist training data that violate the complementarity conditions or the constraints, we go to Step 6. If all the training data satisfy the complementarity conditions and the constraints or $|Q_k - Q_{k-1}| < \epsilon$, we finish training.

**Step 6**

We check if we are in the infinite loop. If so, we add all the data in the working sets that form the infinite loop to the next working set $W_{k+1}$. And we add 1 to $k$ and go to Step 3. Otherwise we go to Step 7.

**Step 7**

If $V_k < V_{k-1}$, we go to Step 8. Otherwise, we detect the data that were in $W_{k-1}$ but went out of $W_{k-1}$ at the $(k-1)$th iteration and violate the complementarity conditions or the constraints at the $k$th iteration. If there exist such data, we add these data to the working set $W_{k+1}$. And we add 1 to $k$ and go to Step 3. But if no such data exist, we go to Step 8.

**Step 8**

In the fixed set, we detect the variables that violate the complementarity conditions or the constraints, and move at most $q$ points to the working set $W_{k+1}$. From the working set, we detect the data that are not support vectors of the subproblem and move them to the fixed set. And we add 1 to $k$ and go to Step 3.

## 4  Simulation Experiments

In this section, we show two experimental results. In the first experiment, we show the effectiveness of the improved decomposition techniques discussed in Subsection 3.2 over training without decomposition. In the second experiment, we compare the improved decomposition technique with the original decomposition technique discussed in Subsection 3.1.

Linear programming can be solved either by the simplex method or the primal-dual interior-point method. But in our experiments, we use the "lp.c" [9], which is a program for the simplex method.

The data sets used to evaluate the performance are multiclass data sets: the numeral data for license plate recognition [12], the blood cell data [13], the thyroid data [14], and hiragana data [15,16]. Table 1 shows the numbers of inputs, classes, training data, and test data of the benchmark data sets. We use one-against-all support vector machines [7]. Therefore, all the training data are used for training.

**Table 1.** Benchmark data specification

| Data | Inputs | Classes | Trn. | Test |
|---|---|---|---|---|
| Numeral | 12 | 10 | 810 | 820 |
| Blood cell | 13 | 12 | 3097 | 3100 |
| Thyroid | 21 | 3 | 3772 | 3428 |
| Hiragana-50 | 50 | 39 | 4610 | 4610 |
| Hiragana-13 | 13 | 38 | 8375 | 8356 |

### 4.1  Effect of the Decomposition Techniques

We evaluate the speedup by using the improved decomposition technique.

Figure 1 shows the training time for the change of $q$, namely the number of data added to the working set, using the blood cell data. We use polynomial kernels with $d = 3$ and fix the margin parameter $C = 1000$. From the figure, it is seen that training is accelerated most when $q$ is around 100.

Table 2 shows the optimum value of $q$ and the speedup by the improved decomposition techniques. "Dec.," "No-Dec.," and "Speedup" denote that the decomposition technique is used, not used, and the speedup obtained by the improved decomposition technique. From the table, it is seen that we can speed up training drastically by the improved decomposition technique for all the data sets.

**Table 2.** Optimum value of $q$ and the speedup by the improved decomposition techniques

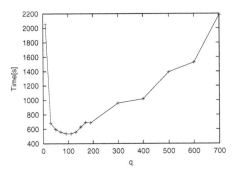

**Fig. 1.** Training time for the change of $q$

| Data | Term | Dec. | No-Dec. |
|------|------|------|---------|
| Numeral | Optimum $q$ | 30 | – |
| | Rate[%] | 99.51 | 99.51 |
| | Time[s] | 1.2 | 361 |
| | Speedup | 301 | 1 |
| Blood cell | Optimum $q$ | 110 | – |
| | Rate[%] | 92.58 | 92.58 |
| | Time[s] | 536 | 45840 |
| | Speedup | 86 | 1 |
| Thyroid | Optimum $q$ | 90 | – |
| | Rate[%] | 97.17 | 97.17 |
| | Time[s] | 840 | 58887 |
| | Speedup | 70 | 1 |

### 4.2  Comparison Between Original and Improved Decomposition Techniques

In Table 3, we list performance comparison of the original and improved decomposition techniques. We use polynomial kernels with $d = 3$ and RBF kernels with $\gamma = 1$. The value of $C$ is 10 and 10000. We set $q$ as 80 for all the cases. From the table, it is seen that the improved decomposition techniques is faster than the original decomposition techniques for all the cases.

Figures 2 and 3 show the numbers of violations of complementarity conditions and constraints for the original and improved methods, respectively. The results are obtained for Class 1 against others using the numeral data with polynomial kernels with $d = 3$ and $C = 1000$. In Fig. 2, the numbers of violations fluctuate very much and the convergence is very slow. As explained previously, this is because the important data are removed from the working set. But in Fig. 3, the fluctuation is quickly subdued because important data are restored when the number of violations increases.

**Table 3.** Comparison between original and improved decomposition techniques

| Data | Parameter | Original Rate[%] | Time[s] | Improved Rate[%] | Time[s] | Speedup |
|------|-----------|------------------|---------|------------------|---------|---------|
| Numeral | $d3, C10$ | 89.39(92.47) | 15.5 | 99.51(100) | 1.8 | 8.6 |
| | $d3, C10000$ | 99.51(100) | 13.9 | 99.51(100) | 1.8 | 7.6 |
| | $\gamma1, C10$ | 99.63(100) | 6.2 | 99.63(100) | 1.8 | 3.4 |
| | $\gamma1, C10000$ | 99.63(100) | 2.1 | 99.63(100) | 2.0 | 1.1 |
| Blood cell | $d3, C10$ | 91.77(95.12) | 344 | 91.77(95.12) | 268 | 1.3 |
| | $d3, C10000$ | 92.19(99.19) | 6481 | 92.23(99.19) | 1180 | 5.5 |
| | $\gamma1, C10$ | 91.00(93.00) | 300 | 91.00(93.00) | 219 | 1.4 |
| | $\gamma1, C10000$ | 91.90(99.13) | 8760 | 91.87(99.16) | 1136 | 7.7 |
| Thyroid | $d3, C10$ | 95.74(96.77) | 5498 | 95.74(96.77) | 4294 | 1.3 |
| | $d3, C10000$ | 97.20(99.47) | 3204 | 97.20(99.47) | 749 | 4.3 |
| | $\gamma1, C10$ | 95.01(95.55) | 3202 | 95.01(95.55) | 2365 | 1.4 |
| | $\gamma1, C10000$ | 97.43(99.50) | 8891 | 97.43(99.50) | 1323 | 6.7 |
| Hiragana-50 | $d3, C10$ | 98.61(100) | 21031 | 98.59(100) | 748 | 28.1 |
| | $d3, C10000$ | 92.75(94.36) | 20467 | 98.59(100) | 764 | 26.8 |
| | $\gamma1, C10$ | 98.24(100) | 537 | 98.24(100) | 261 | 2.1 |
| | $\gamma1, C10000$ | 98.24(100) | 463 | 98.24(100) | 249 | 1.9 |
| Hiragana-13 | $d3, C10$ | 99.10(99.87) | 10612 | 99.88(99.15) | 927 | 11.4 |
| | $d3, C10000$ | 95.75(96.73) | 26179 | 98.96(100) | 976 | 26.8 |
| | $\gamma1, C10$ | 98.86(99.16) | 2713 | 98.84(99.15) | 743 | 3.7 |
| | $\gamma1, C10000$ | 92.29(100) | 22555 | 99.28(100) | 917 | 24.6 |

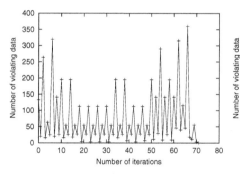
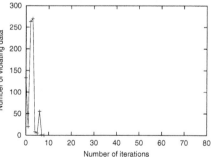

**Fig. 2.** The number of violations during training for the original method

**Fig. 3.** The number of violations during training for the improved method

## 5   Conclusions

In this paper, we formulated the decomposition technique for the LP-SVM and proposed resolving the infinite loop that occurs during training. Furthermore, we proposed an improved working set selection strategy to speed up training.

In the decomposition techniques for LP-SVMs, we select the working set using the complementarity conditions, but unlike the original SVMs this often leads to an infinite loop. When an infinite loop is detected, we resolve the infinite loop by adding all the data in the infinite loop to the working set. And to speed up training, we check if the number of the violating data is increased. If so, we prohibit the important data from going out of the working set.

Using the benchmark data sets, we showed that we can speed up training by the decomposition techniques and that the improved decomposition technique can train an LP-SVM faster than the original decomposition technique.

# References

1. E. Osuna, R. Freund, and F. Girosi, "An improved training algorithm for support vector machines," *Proc. NNSP 97*, pp. 276–285, 1997.
2. V. Vapnik, *The Nature of Statistical Learning Theory*, Springer, 1995.
3. V. Vapnik, *Statistical Learning Theory*, John Wiley & Sons, 1998.
4. C.-J. Lin, "On the convergence of the decomposition method for support vector machines," *IEEE Trans. Neural Networks*, Vol. 12, No. 6, pp. 1288–1298, 2001.
5. S. S. Keerthi and E. G. Gilbert, "Convergence of a generalized SMO algorithm for SVM classifier design," *Machine Learning*, Vol. 46, pp. 351–360, 2002.
6. K. P. Bennett, "Combining support vector and mathematical programming methods for classification," In B. Schölkopf et al., Eds., *Advances in Kernel Methods: Support Vector Learning*, pp. 307–326, MIT Press, 1999.
7. S. Abe, *Support Vector Machines for Pattern Classification*, Springer, 2005.
8. B. Schölkopf and A. J. Smola, *Learning with Kernels: Support Vector Machines, Regularization, Optimization, and Beyond*, MIT Press, 2002.
9. T. Yamada, "lp.c,", http://www.nda.ac.jp/~yamada/programs/lp.c.
10. R. J. Vanderbei, *Linear Programming*, Kluwer Academic Publishers, 2nd Ed., 2001.
11. V. Chavátal, *Linear Programming*, W. H. Freeman and Company, 1983.
12. H. Takenaga et al., "Input layer optimization of neural networks by sensitivity analysis and its application to recognition of numerals," *Electrical Engineering in Japan*, Vol. 111, No. 4, pp. 130–138, 1991.
13. A. Hashizume, J. Motoike, and R. Yabe, "Fully automated blood cell differential system and its application," *Proc. IUPAC 3rd International Congress on Automation and New Technology in the Clinical Laboratory*, pp. 297–302, 1988.
14. S. M. Weiss and I. Kapouleas, "An empirical comparison of pattern recognition, neural nets, and machine learning classification methods," *Proc. IJCAI*, pp. 781–787, 1989.
15. M.-S. Lan, H. Takenaga, and S. Abe, "Character recognition using fuzzy rules extracted from data," *Proc. 3rd IEEE International Conference on Fuzzy Systems*, Vol. 1, pp. 415–420, 1994.
16. S. Abe, *Pattern Classification: Neuro-Fuzzy Methods and Their Comparison*, Springer, 2001.

# Multiple Classifier Systems for Embedded String Patterns

Barbara Spillmann, Michel Neuhaus, and Horst Bunke

Institute of Computer Science and Applied Mathematics, University of Bern,
Neubrückstrasse 10, CH-3012 Bern, Switzerland

**Abstract.** Multiple classifier systems are a well proven and tested in-
strument for enhancing the recognition accuracy in statistical pattern
recognition problems. However, there has been reported only little work
on combining classifiers in structural pattern recognition. In this paper
we describe a method for embedding strings into real vector spaces based
on prototype selection, in order to gain several vectorial descriptions of
the string data. We present methods for combining multiple classifiers
trained on various vectorial data representations. As base classifiers we
use nearest neighbor methods and support vector machine. In our experiments we demonstrate that this approach can be used to significantly
improve the classification accuracy of string patterns.

## 1 Introduction

Building multiple classifier systems (MCSs) has been a topic of intensive research
for many years [1,2]. The goal is to outperform the classification accuracy of a set
of individual classifiers by combining them in an appropriate way. That is, one
aims at creating a set of classifiers with a large diversity such that the weakness
and errors of one classifier are compensated by other classifiers. A large number
of methods for producing multiple classifier systems have been proposed and the
success of these methods has been impressively demonstrated [3,4,5,6,7].

However, almost all papers in the field of multiple classifier systems have
concentrated on vectorial pattern representations. Almost no work using structural data, such as strings or graphs, has been reported in the literature [8,9,10].
Using a structural representation of patterns rather than feature vectors has
some advantages and has been proven to be a powerful means for many applications [11,12,13,14]. In the current paper we focus on pattern representations
in terms of strings, i.e. sequences of symbols. To perform recognition tasks, one
needs to define a distance measure, which is, in case of strings, usually the edit
distance [15]. String edit distance allows one to implement nearest neighbor classifiers. Consequently, building multiple classifier systems is normally restricted
to the creation of an ensemble of $k$-nearest-neighbor classifiers ($k$NN).

In this paper, we present a multiple classifier approach applicable to string
patterns. The key idea is to use the transformation method proposed in [16,17]
for embedding strings into dissimilarity spaces by means of prototype selection.
This method has also been used in [18]. It is a general approach that is suitable

F. Schwenker and S. Marinai (Eds.): ANNPR 2006, LNAI 4087, pp. 177–187, 2006.
© Springer-Verlag Berlin Heidelberg 2006

to make the whole spectrum of classifiers known from statistical pattern recognition available to string representations. It has been shown that the classification accuracy of strings can be significantly increased by applying such an embedding and by classifying the vectorial data gained from this procedure. In this paper we go one step further. As each concrete transformation from the string to the vectorial domain depends on various parameters, it is straightforward to generate several such embeddings by varying these parameters. Then the vectorial representations obtained from different embeddings are utilized to build a classifier ensemble.

This paper is organized as follows. Section 2 gives an overview of the embedding mechanism of strings into vector spaces. In Section 3, the architecture of our multiple classifier systems is described, including the creation of the classifier ensembles. Experimental results of the method, applied to handwritten digits, are discussed in Section 4. Finally, in Section 5 some conclusions are drawn.

## 2   From the String Domain to the Vector Space

Let $A$ be a finite alphabet of symbols and $A^*$ be the set of all strings over $A$. Furthermore, let $\epsilon$ denote the empty symbol. A string can be modified by edit operations: The replacement of a symbol $a \in A$ by $b \in A$ is called a substitution, and if $a = \epsilon$ or $b = \epsilon$ we term it an insertion or deletion, respectively. In order to measure the dissimilarity of strings, a cost $c$ is assigned to each edit operation. Given a sequence $S = e_1, \ldots, e_n$ of edit operations, its cost is defined as $c(S) = \sum_{i=1}^{n} c(e_i)$. Considering two strings $x, y \in A^*$ and all sequences of edit operations that transform $x$ into $y$, the edit distance, $d(x, y)$, of $x$ and $y$ is the sequence with minimum cost. The edit distance can be computed by dynamic programming in $O(nm)$ time and space, where $n$ and $m$ are the lengths of the two strings under consideration [15].

With the notation introduced above, a transformation of a string pattern into a vector representation can be defined. The transformation is based on a set of selected strings, the *prototypes*. A string is transformed into a vector by calculating its edit distances to all prototypes, where each resulting distance represents one vector component. More formally, let $\mathcal{X} \subset A^*$ denote a set of string patterns over the alphabet $A$, and $\mathcal{P} = \{p_1, \ldots p_n\} \subset \mathcal{X}$ a set of selected prototypes. For a given string $x \in \mathcal{X}$ a vectorial description of $x$ is defined by the transformation $t_n^{\mathcal{P}}$:

$$t_n^{\mathcal{P}} : \mathcal{X} \to \mathbb{R}^n \text{ with } t_n^{\mathcal{P}}(x) = (d(x, p_1), \ldots, d(x, p_n)) \tag{1}$$

As a consequence, the number of prototypes, $n$, defines the dimensionality of the vector space, $\mathbb{R}^n$.

Obviously, the characteristics of the transformation depend on the size of $\mathcal{P}$ as well as on the patterns selected as prototypes. An algorithm that selects the prototypes $p_i$ $(i = 1, \ldots, n)$ out of $\mathcal{X}$ is called *prototype selection strategy s*. With $s(\mathcal{X}) = \mathcal{P}$ we denote the procedure of building $\mathcal{P}$ out of $\mathcal{X}$ by applying $s$. Examples of different selection strategies, such as the *border prototype selector*, the *center prototype selector*, the *spanning prototype selector* and the *k-medians prototype selector*, have been discussed in [16,18].

In order to make available classifiers from statistical pattern recognition to string classification by means of the transformation procedure introduced above, the transformation $t_n^{\mathcal{P}}$ is applied to each element of a given dataset. After the transformation is accomplished and the whole dataset is embedded into a vector space, one can train any classifier suitable for vector spaces. Experiments with the $k$NN classifier and the support vector machine have been described in [18].

# 3   Multiple Embedding MCS

The idea underlying the construction of our multiple classifier system is to apply different prototype selection strategies. Each individual selection strategy yields a different embedding of the original string data, i.e. a different set of vectors. For each such set of vectors, an individual classifier is constructed. Eventually these individual classifiers are combined in a multiple classifier system.

## 3.1   Triple Embedding MCS

The prototype selection strategies used in this work are the following.

**Spanning Prototype Selector (*s-ps*) [18].** This is a method that selects prototypes, such that they are evenly distributed over the given set of strings. The procedure is the following. The first prototype selected is the set median string, an approximation of the generalized median string [19]. The next prototypes are iteratively determined by selecting the string with largest sum of the edit distances to the previously selected prototypes.

**Random k-Medians Prototype Selector (*rkm-ps*).** This strategy has been applied in [18], where it is referred to as *k-median prototype selector*. It performs a k-medians clustering and defines the resulting cluster centers to be the prototypes. An important point is that the initial cluster centers are chosen randomly. Thus, the algorithm is non-deterministic.

**Spanning k-Medians Prototype Selector (*skm-ps*).** This method is a deterministic variant of the *rkm-ps*. The initial cluster centers are not chosen randomly, but as specified by the *s-ps* method. That is, the prototype selection according to the *s-ps* method is improved with respect of the k-medians algorithm's clustering properties.

One of the base classifiers applied in this work is the $k$NN classifier (with Minkowski metric). By applying any of the three strategies *s-ps*, *rkm-ps* and *skm-ps* we can transform a dataset of string patterns into a vector space. Formally, we denote a set of string patterns by $\mathcal{X} = \{x_1, \ldots, x_N\}$ and sets of prototypes by $\mathcal{P}_{s\text{-}ps}, \mathcal{P}_{rkm\text{-}ps}, \mathcal{P}_{skm\text{-}ps} \in \mathcal{X}$, where the indices indicate the selection strategy used for their construction. We use parameters $n_{k\mathrm{NN}_{s\text{-}ps}}$, $n_{k\mathrm{NN}_{rkm\text{-}ps}}$ and $n_{k\mathrm{NN}_{skm\text{-}ps}}$ to refer to the number of prototypes, and define the following three transformation functions:

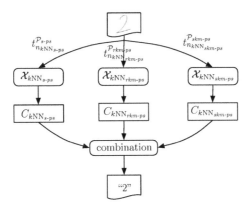

**Fig. 1.** Example classification of a handwritten digit with the *triple embedding MCS* and the $kNN$ classifier as base classifier (*TE-MCS, kNN*)

$$t_{n_{kNN_{s\text{-}ps}}}^{\mathcal{P}_{s\text{-}ps}} \quad : \mathcal{X} \to \mathbb{R}^{n_{kNN_{s\text{-}ps}}}$$

$$t_{n_{kNN_{rkm\text{-}ps}}}^{\mathcal{P}_{rkm\text{-}ps}} \quad : \mathcal{X} \to \mathbb{R}^{n_{kNN_{rkm\text{-}ps}}} \qquad (2)$$

$$t_{n_{kNN_{skm\text{-}ps}}}^{\mathcal{P}_{skm\text{-}ps}} \quad : \mathcal{X} \to \mathbb{R}^{n_{kNN_{skm\text{-}ps}}}$$

By applying the transformations (2) to the whole dataset $\mathcal{X}$ we get three vectorial representations of $\mathcal{X}$, denoted by $\mathcal{X}_{kNN_{s\text{-}ps}}$, $\mathcal{X}_{kNN_{rkm\text{-}ps}}$ and $\mathcal{X}_{kNN_{skm\text{-}ps}}$, respectively. For each of these three sets a specific classifier of the $k$-nearest-neighbor type, denoted by $C_{kNN_{s\text{-}ps}}$, $C_{kNN_{rkm\text{-}ps}}$ and $C_{kNN_{skm\text{-}ps}}$, is constructed. When classifying a pattern $x_i \in \mathcal{X}$, each classifier produces a class prediction. Given an unknown input pattern $x_i$, the combination of the three classifiers' outputs results in the final prediction of the system, $c_{kNN(x_i)}$. We call this setup *triple embedding MCS for the kNN classifier (TE-MCS, kNN)*. Fig. 1 gives an illustration of this setup with an example of a handwritten digit "2" to be recognized.

We can now analogously build a *triple embedding MCS* using as base classifier a support vector machine (SVM) with radial basis function as kernel function. The SVM [20,21] is a classifier for statistical data that makes use of a kernel function to transform vector data into higher-dimensional feature spaces. The key idea is to find a separating hyperplane in the feature space with a maximal margin between the classes. This is an optimization problem usually solved by quadratic programming. For this classifier type we define the transformation functions:

$$t_{n_{\text{SVM-R}_{s\text{-}ps}}}^{\mathcal{P}_{s\text{-}ps}} \quad : \mathcal{X} \to \mathbb{R}^{n_{\text{SVM-R}_{s\text{-}ps}}}$$

$$t_{n_{\text{SVM-R}_{rkm\text{-}ps}}}^{\mathcal{P}_{rkm\text{-}ps}} \quad : \mathcal{X} \to \mathbb{R}^{n_{\text{SVM-R}_{rkm\text{-}ps}}} \qquad (3)$$

$$t_{n_{\text{SVM-R}_{rkm\text{-}ps}}}^{\mathcal{P}_{skm\text{-}ps}} \quad : \mathcal{X} \to \mathbb{R}^{n_{\text{SVM-R}_{rkm\text{-}ps}}}$$

We get another three embeddings into vector spaces $\mathcal{X}_{\text{SVM-R}_{s\text{-}ps}}$, $\mathcal{X}_{\text{SVM-R}_{rkm\text{-}ps}}$ and $\mathcal{X}_{\text{SVM-R}_{skm\text{-}ps}}$. Using these embeddings, an ensemble of three SVM classifiers with radial basis function, $C_{\text{SVM-R}_{s\text{-}ps}}$, $C_{\text{SVM-R}_{rkm\text{-}ps}}$ and $C_{\text{SVM-R}_{skm\text{-}ps}}$, are trained. This ensemble yields output $c_{\text{SVM-R}(x_i)}$ for an input pattern $x_i \in \mathcal{X}$. We call this setup *triple embedding MCS for the SVM with radial basis function (TE-MCS, SVM-R)*.

The third setup of that type is the support vector machine with linear kernel function as base classifier. We define the transformations:

$$t^{\mathcal{P}_{s\text{-}ps}}_{n_{\text{SVM-L}_{s\text{-}ps}}} : \mathcal{X} \rightarrow \mathbb{R}^{n_{\text{SVM-L}_{s\text{-}ps}}}$$

$$t^{\mathcal{P}_{rkm\text{-}ps}}_{n_{\text{SVM-L}_{rkm\text{-}ps}}} : \mathcal{X} \rightarrow \mathbb{R}^{n_{\text{SVM-L}_{rkm\text{-}ps}}} \qquad (4)$$

$$t^{\mathcal{P}_{skm\text{-}ps}}_{n_{\text{SVM-L}_{skm\text{-}ps}}} : \mathcal{X} \rightarrow \mathbb{R}^{n_{\text{SVM-L}_{skm\text{-}ps}}}$$

and denote the transformed datasets by $\mathcal{X}_{\text{SVM-L}_{s\text{-}ps}}$, $\mathcal{X}_{\text{SVM-L}_{rkm\text{-}ps}}$ and $\mathcal{X}_{\text{SVM-L}_{skm\text{-}ps}}$. The classifiers to be trained are called $C_{\text{SVM-L}_{s\text{-}ps}}$, $C_{\text{SVM-L}_{rkm\text{-}ps}}$ and $C_{\text{SVM-L}_{skm\text{-}ps}}$, and the resulting class prediction for a string $x_i \in \mathcal{X}$ is abbreviated with $c_{\text{SVM-L}(x_i)}$. This MCS is referred to as *triple embedding MCS for the SVM with linear kernel function (TE-MCS, SVM-L)*.

### 3.2   Hierarchical Multiple Embedding MCS

In the previous section, three MCSs have been presented that use different string embeddings to generate ensembles. However, the classifier ensembles are always of the same type. Now, we want to make use of the possibility of applying different classifier types, i.e. we define an MCS that aggregates the $k$NN, the SVM with radial basis function, and the SVM with linear kernel function. The idea is to build a hierarchical system that consists of the three *triple embedding MCS* described in Section 3.1. In order to do so we simply combine the class predictions, $c_{k\text{NN}(x_i)}$, $c_{\text{SVM-R}(x_i)}$ and $c_{\text{SVM-L}(x_i)}$, of the three *TE-MCS*. Obviously, this MCS uses a total of nine different embeddings into vector spaces. Let's call this setup *hierarchical multiple embedding MCS (HME-MCS)*. Fig. 2 illustrates the recognition of a string pattern using an *HME-MCS*.

## 4   Experimental Results

In this section we provide experimental results for the *triple embedding MCSs* and the *hierarchical multiple embedding MCS* introduced in Section 3. For our experiments we use the *Pendigits* database described in [22] (original, unnormalized version). The original version consists of 10,992 instances of handwritten digits labeled with one of the ten class names "0" to "9", where 7,494 digits are used for training and 3,498 for testing (see Fig. 3). Each digit is originally given as a sequence of two-dimensional points. Certainly, in case of handwritten digits

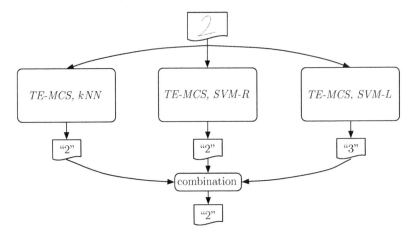

**Fig. 2.** Example classification of a handwritten digit with the *hierarchical multiple embedding MCS (HME-MCS)*

it might also be useful to directly extract features instead of extracting a suitable string representation. However, as we want to demonstrate the feasibility and the possible power of our multiple classifier approach, the *Pendigits* dataset can be regarded as an exemplary representative for any set of string patterns.

To obtain a suitable string representation, each digit curve is approximated by a sequence of vector segments of fixed length $l$, such that each start and end point lies on the original curve. An optimal value of $l$ is determined on a validation set (see below) by performing a $k$-nearest-neighbor classification with the edit distance as a distance measure. Given the sequence of vector segments as a string representation, the substitution costs are defined as the absolute value of the vector difference to the power of $q_v$, where $q_v$ is an arbitrary positive real number. As deletion and insertion costs we take the arithmetic mean of the extremal values (0 and $(2l)^{q_v}$) of the substitution costs, which is $2^{q_v-1}l^{q_v}$. This cost function is referred to as *vector cost function*. Another way of defining a string representation is to consider the sequence of angles between pairs of successive vector segments. The costs assigned to the edit operations are constantly set to $0 \leq q_a \leq \frac{\pi}{2}$ in case of angle insertions and deletions, and for substitutions the costs are given by the absolute difference between the angles. We call this cost function *angle cost function*. Notice that also the values of the cost function parameters $q_v$ and $q_a$ are optimized on the validation set.

Our experimental evaluation consist of six independent runs, where three of them use a vector-based string representation, and the other three use an angle-based one. We use three different splits into training, test and validation set. The first split, referred to as **pen1**, follows the original division into training and test set, where one fifth of the training set is used for validation. The second and third split, **pen2** and **pen3**, are further setups, where the size of each set is approximately the same, but different partitions have been used. The validation set is used for the purpose of optimizing the following parameters:

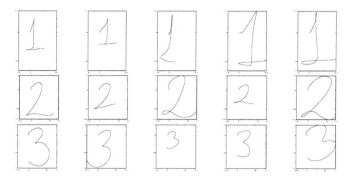

**Fig. 3.** Example patterns of the *Pendigits* dataset with the class labels "1", "2" and "3"

- **String representation parameters** $q_v$, $q_a$, and $l$. To find appropriate values of these parameters we perform a k-nearest-neighbor classification in the string domain and use the edit distance with either the *angle cost function* or the *vector cost function*. Once these parameters are optimized, they are kept unchanged for the rest of the experiment.
- **Dimensionality parameters** $n_{c_s}$, where $c \in \{kNN, SVM\text{-}R, SVM\text{-}L\}$ and $s \in \{s\text{-}ps, rkm\text{-}ps, skm\text{-}ps\}$. They determine the dimensionality of the vector spaces. Practically, we transform the validation set to various vector spaces with the dimensions 50, 100, 150, 200, 300, 400, 500, 800, 1000. In case of the *angle cost function*, also the values 1500 and 2000 are evaluated. The optimized values are determined by the classifier in the vector space. Once optimal values are found, the transformations $t_{n_{c_s}}^{\mathcal{P}_s}$ are applied, i.e. the whole dataset, including the elements of the training and test set, are embedded into vector spaces.
- **Classifier parameters** for the $kNN$ classifier and the support vector machines. For each vectorial representation $\mathcal{X}_{c_s}$ a classifier $C_{c_s}$ is trained on the validation set. For example, in case of the $kNN$ this includes the number of nearest neighbors $k$ and a Minkowski metric parameter.
- **Combination rule.** Normally, in a multiple classifier system, each participating classifier casts one vote, that is, each one chooses the most plausible class. Afterwards these votes have to be combined. There has been much of research on combining decision results in past years [23]. In this work, the classifiers' results are combined by the following three methods.

The *plurality voting* method decides for the class which reaches the most votes among the involved classifiers [24]. It is a simple voting mechanism that only counts the occurrence of each class label output by a classifier. A similar voting method is the *runoff voting* where the voting process is performed in two steps [25]. First, each classifier votes for its most plausible class. The two candidates with the highest number of votes get another chance, and each classifier can vote for one of those two in a second round. The one with the most votes among the two wins the voting. A method different from the

**Table 1.** Recognition rates for the *triple embedding MCSs* and the *hierarchical multiple embedding MCS* using the *angle cost function*, where sequences of angles are used for the string representation. The labels **pen1**, **pen2** and **pen3** denote three different splits of the data into training, test and validation set.

|                       | pen1     | pen2     | pen3     |
|-----------------------|----------|----------|----------|
| *k*NN string domain   | 88.56    | 92.48    | 92.71    |
| *TE-MCS* with *k*NN   | **90.62**| 92.96    | 91.86    |
| *TE-MCS* with SVM-R   | **94.77**| **96.24**| **95.59**|
| *TE-MCS* with SVM-L   | **93.85**| **95.23**| **95.33**|
| *HME-MCS*             | **94.68**| **96.48**| **95.86**|

**Table 2.** Recognition rates for the *triple embedding MCSs* and the *hierarchical multiple embedding MCS* using the *vector cost function*, where sequences of vectors are used for the string representation. The labels **pen1**, **pen2** and **pen3** refer to the same splits of the data into training, test and validation set as in Tab. 1.

|                       | pen1     | pen2     | pen3     |
|-----------------------|----------|----------|----------|
| *k*NN string domain   | 97.48    | 99.33    | 99.33    |
| *TE-MCS* with *k*NN   | 97.57    | 99.36    | 99.01    |
| *TE-MCS* with SVM-R   | **98.20**| **99.55**| **99.55**|
| *TE-MCS* with SVM-L   | 97.74    | **99.60**| 99.33    |
| *HME-MCS*             | **98.31**| **99.68**| **99.57**|

two methods mentioned above is the *Borda count* [26,27]. It belongs to the category of ranking methods, and is based on a complete preference ranking from all classifiers over all classes. For each class the mean rank is computed. Then the top ranked class is declared the winner of the voting.

The validation set is used to determine the best voting strategy among these three methods. The method with highest performance on the validation set is then selected to classify the test set.

The training set is used to select the set of prototypes $\mathcal{P}$ from, i.e. the set of prototypes $\mathcal{P}$ is always a subset of the training set. And of course, it is also used for the training of the classifiers. In case of the $k$NN classifier, the nearest neighbors are selected from the whole training set, while for the SVM the support vectors are chosen from the training set.

The final results are produced on the test set. In Tab. 1 the results on the test set for the string representation with *angle cost function* are listed. Tab. 2 shows the results for the case of *vector cost function*. The first row shows the recognition results achieved with a $k$NN classifier in the original string domain, with optimized cost function parameters $q_v$, $q_a$ and $l$. These three classification results shown in the first row are used as reference values for the classification in the vector domain and are meant to be outperformed by the multiple classifier systems presented in this paper. In rows 2 to 4, the results of the *triple embedding MCSs* with the base classifiers $k$NN, SVM-R, and SVM-L are listed. The results for the *hierarchical multiple embedding MCS* can be found in row 5.

Recognition rates printed in bold face refer to a statistically significant improvement compared to the string classification (row 1) at a significance level of 0.95. Note that the evaluation of each single classifier used for our multiple classifier systems has been presented in [18], where also the detailed classification results can be found.

The first point to notice is that 15 out of 18 experiments for the *triple embedding MCS* clearly outperform the classification in the string domain. There are only two setups, all based on the **pen3** split, where the the $k$NN classifier in the string domain performs better.

All *HME-MCS* have statistically significant better recognition rates than the string domain classification. And in 5 of 6 cases, they outperform all three *TE-MCS* from which they are built. Only in the **pen1** setup with *angle cost functions*, the recognition rate of the *HME-MCS* is slightly below the *TE-MCS* with the SVM-R base classifier. In all the other cases, the experiments with the *HME-MCS* provide the best results. In contrast to the *TE-MCSs* the *HME-MCS* consists of fundamentally different classifiers. Whereas the *TE-MCS* are based on an ensemble of the same classifier type, the *HME-MCS* provides a combination of $k$NN and support vector machine classification. We conclude that the embedding of string patterns into vector spaces using prototype selection allows one to build classifiers of essential diversity. By combining their results the traditional nearest-neighbor string classification can be significantly improved.

In [28], several MCS approaches have been tested on the same data. The methods *bagging, boosting, random subspace, random tree B, random forest-lg, random forest-1* and *random forest-2* were investigated by applying a 10-fold cross-validation. The ensembles were built using nine sets, the remaining set was used for testing, and the *Borda count* method applied for combination. The best result, 99.30, was achieved with the random subspace method. However, due to differences in the test procedure one has to be careful comparing these numbers to the results in Tab. 1 and 2. Yet we can state that two of three *HME-MCS* tests and five of nine *TE-MCS* tests with *vector cost function* outnumber the 99.30% correct recognition rate of the *random subspaces* method reported in [28].

## 5   Conclusions

In the present paper we propose a method for creating multiple classifier systems for string patterns. We apply a transformation procedure to embed strings into real vector spaces based on prototype selection. By selecting and applying three different selection strategies we gain vectorial representations for the string data. Given various vector space embeddings, $k$NN classifiers with Minkowski metric and SVM classifiers with radial basis function and linear kernel function are trained and combined. In a number of experiments we show that especially the combination of different classifier types leads to significantly better classification results than a nearest neighbor classification in the original string domain. This shows that our method can be an effective means to improve string classification. In the future, we would like to investigate further combinations of various selection strategies which might allow us to even improve the current methodology.

## Acknowledgements

M. Neuhaus has been supported by the Swiss National Science Foundation NCCR program *Interactive Multimodal Information Management (IM)2* in the Individual Project *Multimedia Information Access and Content Protection.*

## References

1. Kuncheva, L.I.: Combining Pattern Classifiers: Methods and Algorithms. Wiley-Interscience (2004)
2. Oza, N., Polikar, R., Kittler, J., Roli, F., eds.: Multiple Classifier Systems. Volume 3541 of LNCS., Seaside, CA, USA, Springer (2005)
3. Kittler, J., Roli, F., eds.: Multiple Classifier Systems. Number 1857 in LNCS, Cagliari, Italy, Springer (2000)
4. Kittler, J., Roli, F., eds.: Multiple Classifier Systems. Volume 2096 of LNCS., Cambridge, UK, Springer (2001)
5. Roli, F., Kitler, J., eds.: Multiple Classifier Systems. Volume 2364 of LNCS., Cagliar, Italy, Springer (2002)
6. Windeatt, T., ed.: Multiple Classifier Systems. Volume 2709 of LNCS., Guildford, UK, Springer (2003)
7. Roli, F., Kittler, J., Windeatt, T., eds.: Multiple Classifier Systems. Volume 3077 of LNCS., Cagliari, Italy, Springer (2004)
8. Schenker, A., Bunke, H., Last, M., Kandel, A.: Building graph-based classifier ensembles by random node selection. In: 5th International Workshop on Multiple Classifier Systems. Volume 3077 of LNCS., Springer (2004) 214–222
9. Neuhaus, M., Bunke, H.: Graph-based multiple classifier systems – a data level fusion approach. In: Proc. 13th Int. Conf. on Image Analysis and Processing. LNCS 3617, Springer (2005) 479–486
10. Marcialis, G.L., Roli, F., Serrau, A.: Fusion of statistical and structural fingerprint classifiers. In Kittler, J., Nixon, M.S., eds.: Audio-and Video-Based Biometrie Person Authentication, 4th International Conference. Volume 2688 of LNCS., Guildford, UK, Springer (2003) 310–317
11. Cha, S.H., Shin, Y.C., Srihari, S.N.: Approximate stroke sequence matching algorithm for character recognition and analysis. In: 5th International Conference on Document Analysis and Recognition. (1999) 53–56
12. Bunke, H., Bühler, U.: Applications of approximate string matching to 2D shape recognition. Pattern Recognition **26** (1993) 1797–1812
13. Chen, S.W., Tung, S.T., Fang, C.Y., Cheng, S., Jain, A.K.: Extended attributed string matching for shape recognition. Computer Vision and Image Understanding **70** (1998) 36–50
14. Durbin, R., Eddy, S.R., Krogh, A., Mitchison, G.: Biological sequence analysis. Cambridge University Press, Cambridge, UK (1998)
15. Wagner, R.A., Fischer, M.J.: The string-to-string correction problem. Journal of the ACM **21** (1974) 168–173

16. Pekalska, E., Duin, R.P., Paclík, P.: Prototype selection for dissimilarity-based classifiers. Pattern Recognition **39** (2006) 189–208
17. Pekalska, E., Duin, R.P.W.: The Dissimilarity Representation for Pattern Recognition, Foundations and Applications. Volume 64 of Machine Perception Artificial Intelligence. World Scientific (2005)
18. Spillmann, B., Neuhaus, M., Bunke, H., Pekalska, E., Duin, R.P.: Transforming strings to vector spaces using prototype selection. submitted (2006)
19. Kohonen, T.: Median strings. Pattern Recognition Letters **3** (1985) 309–313
20. Vapnik, V.: The Nature of Statistical Learning Theory. 2nd edn. Springer-Verlag (2000) ISBN: 0-387-98780-0.
21. Vapnik, V.: Statistical Learning Theory. Wiley-Interscience (1998) ISBN: 0-471-03003-1.
22. Alpaydin, E., Alimoglu, F.: Department of Computer Engineering, Bogaziçi University, 80815 Istanbul Turkey (1998) `ftp://ftp.ics.uci.edu/pub/mlearn/databases/pendigits`.
23. Xu, L., Krzyzak, A., Suen, C.Y.: Methods of combining multiple classifiers and their applications to handwriting recognition. IEEE Transactions on Systems, Man, and Cybernetics **22** (1992) 418–435
24. Day, W.: Consensus methods as tools for data analysis. In Bock, H., ed.: classification and related methods for data analysis, Elsevier Sciencce Publishers B.V. (North Holland) (1988) 317–324
25. van Erp, M., Vuurpijl, L., Schomaker, L.: An overview and comparison of voting methods for pattern recognition. In: 8th International Workshop on Frontiers in Handwriting Recognition. (2002)
26. de Borda, J.C.: Memoire sur les elections au scrutin. Histoire de l'Academie Royale des Sciences, Paris (1781)
27. Ho, T.K., Hull, J.J., Srihari, S.N.: Decision combination in multiple classifier systems. IEEE Transactions on Pattern Analysis and Machine Intelligence **16** (1994) 66–75
28. Banfield, R.E., Hall, L.O., Bowyer, K.W., Bhadoria, D., Kegelmeyer, W.P., Eschrich, S.: A comparison of ensemble creation techniques. In Roli, F., Kittler, J., Windeatt, T., eds.: The Fifth International Conference on Multiple Classifier Systems, Cagliari, Italy. Volume 3077 of LNCS., Cagliari, Italy, Springer (2004) 223–232

# Multiple Neural Networks for Facial Feature Localization in Orientation-Free Face Images

Lionel Prevost, Rachid Belaroussi, and Maurice Milgram

Université Pierre et Marie Curie-Paris 6, EA2385 PRC
BC252 4, Place Jussieu, F-75005 France
{lionel.prevost, rachid.belaroussi, maurice.milgram}@upmc.fr

**Abstract.** We present in this paper a new facial feature localizer. It uses a kind of auto-associative neural network trained to localize specific facial features (like eyes and mouth corners) in orientation-free faces. One possible extension is presented where several specialized detectors are trained to deal with each face orientation. To select the best localization hypothesis, we combine radiometric and probabilistic information. The method is quite fast and accurate. The mean localization error (estimated on more than 700 test images) is lower than 9%.

## 1 Introduction

Automatic facial feature detection is becoming a very important task in applications such as model-based video coding, facial image animation, face recognition, facial emotion recognition, visual speech understanding, and intelligent human-computer interaction. Many face recognition systems are based on facial features, such as eyes, nose and mouth, and their spatial relationship, called the constituted approach [3]. Many feature detection methods have been developed in the last decade, but a wide majority concentrates on eye detection. The existing methods can be divided into several categories. A first classification is based on the acquisition device: active infrared-based approaches [13] and passive image-based approaches. Another one depends on the processed images: pre-focused images where rough feature regions have already been located or cluttered images where face detection is proceeded before feature detection. A third category is based on the detection algorithm: image-based approach using one or several low-level detectors to find specific properties (such as edge, colour, symmetry…) [7, 10, 11], statistical appearance-based approach [12], active appearance models [4], deformable templates [15]…

We present in this paper a neural-based facial feature localizer able to deal with orientation-free face images. As we already developed in our lab a face localizer [1], we assume that face has been already roughly localized in a cluttered image. The system uses a kind of auto-associative neural network trained to output a feature map, which maxima correspond to facial feature position.

The communication is organized as follows. In section 2, we describe the database used in the experiments. Section 3 is devoted to the hybrid auto-associative network used to localize facial features. In section 4, we study experimentally this orientation-free localizer and propose an alternate method where several networks are trained to

F. Schwenker and S. Marinai (Eds.): ANNPR 2006, LNAI 4087, pp. 188–197, 2006.
© Springer-Verlag Berlin Heidelberg 2006

deal with specific face pose, in order to increase the system accuracy. Concluding remarks and future works are discussed in section 6.

## 2   Database and Pre-processings

We collected in our lab a face database. It contains images of 40 people with various ages, genders and ethnicities. For each person, we took 36 images (resolution 100x100 pixels) with several facial orientations, expressions and "accessories" like beard or glasses (Fig. 9). In order to increase the number of data, we computed each mirroring image. This procedure results in a 2750 example dataset.

We clicked manually four facial features, respectively left eye (1st feature), right eye (2nd feature), left mouth corner (3rd feature) and right mouth corner (4th feature) to create one feature map $F$ for each face image. This feature map had the size of the face image and its pixels have the following value (where $x_{iT}$ and $y_{iT}$ denote the true feature coordinates):

- At the feature location: $F(x_{iT}, y_{iT}) = +1$
- Anywhere else: $F(i,j) = -1$

To normalize input images (Fig. 1), we performed histogram equalization. To normalize feature maps, we convolved these images with a 3x3 gaussian filter, which results in smoothing feature maps. Several sub-sampling were tested to reduce the data dimension and, thus the number of parameters to be trained.

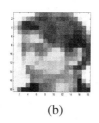
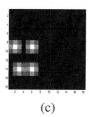

|        (a)        |        (b)        |        (c)        |

**Fig. 1.** Normalization process: original image (a), sub-sampled input image (b), sub-sampled and smoothed feature map (c)

Facial feature are not randomly organized (except in Picasso's paintings perhaps). So, we can get anthropomorphic information about their spatial organization by analyzing feature map. Assuming the feature coordinates joint density distribution is gaussian, we can evaluate its parameters (means and covariance matrix) by using *Maximum a Posteriori* estimator. Assuming this density is monovariate, this estimation can be done on the whole dataset and leads to orientation-free parameters. To take into account the face orientation, we assume that feature density distribution is a mixture of gaussians, one for each face orientation. In this latter case, we estimate parameters on a given cluster. To perform self-supervised orientation clustering, we assumed there existed a unique relationship between 2D facial feature location and 3D face pose. So, knowing the facial feature localization allowed predicting the face orientation. We used a simple K-means algorithm [2] with euclidean distance to get the best center of each subset. Then, we estimated parameters for each subset. We applied this procedure considering up to six face orientations. As can be seen (Fig. 2), the clustering had roughly separated the whole database in subsets, each one corresponding to a certain orientation.

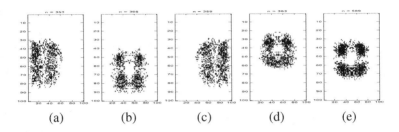

**Fig. 2.** Facial feature position for five clusters: left-sided (a), frontal down (b), right-sided (c), frontal up (d), frontal (e)

## 3   Hybrid Diabolos Networks

The Diabolos network is an auto-associative neural network. It is a completely connected two-layered perceptron. The input and output layers have the same side as the desired output is equal to the input. So, the network is trained to reconstruct an output identical to its input. It implements a specialized compression (quite similar to non-linear principal component analysis) as its hidden layer has much less units than input or output does. This network was successfully used for compression [5], handwritten character recognition [14], and face detection [1, 8]. In this latter application, the network is used to modelize the "face-class" and trained to reconstruct face images. So a non-face image should be badly compressed and the reconstruction error would be higher than for a face image. Here, we do not want to reconstruct a specific pattern class (the "face-class" for example) but to localize specific features within these patterns (eyes and/or mouth corners in the face case). In other words, we want to associate an image of face (input) with a facial feature map (output). So, we used as desired output, the normalized images containing the feature positions described in §2.

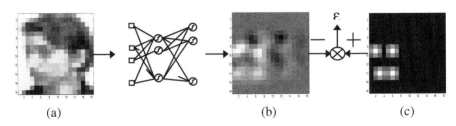

**Fig. 3.** Training process: input image (a) feeds the network. The mean squared error $\varepsilon$ between network output(b) and feature map (c) is used as the cost function.

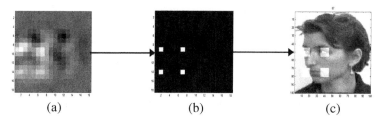

|     |     |     |
| --- | --- | --- |
| (a) | (b) | (c) |

**Fig. 4.** Decision process: network produces the output image (a) where local maxima are detected (b) and back-projected onto the original image(c)

The network is trained using the back-propagation algorithm with adaptive momentum. The cost function is the mean squared error between network output and desired output (Fig. 3). Training parameters (number of epochs, hidden layer size) are tuned by exhaustive research. Once trained, the network is able to localize facial feature on unknown test images. The feature positions can directly be inferred by simply searching the maxima in the output image and back-projected onto the original image (Fig. 4). Let $(x_{iD}, y_{iD})$ be the coordinates of these detected features.

## 4  Experimental Results

To evaluate the localization accuracy, we compute for each image the normalized error i.e the mean euclidean distance $d$ between the detected feature position and the true feature position normalized with respect to the inter-ocular distance.

### 4.1  Orientation-Free Localizer

First, we trained a single neural network to localize facial feature on the whole database and perform orientation-free localization. We divided the whole dataset into two sets: training set (three fourth) and test (one fourth). Several experiments were made with different training and test sets.

In the first experiment, we tested the localizer sensitivity to feature number and position. We dispatched the same people in both training and test sets with slightly different orientations. Then, we trained several localizers. The first one (SFL) consisted of four single feature localizers; each one specialized on one facial feature. The second (DFL) used two double feature localizers and each localizer dealt with a couple of features. Finally, (QFL) was a quadruple feature localizer (Fig. 3 & 4). Table 1 summarizes results in term of mean normalized error. These results are very interesting: the mean normalized error decreases as the number of feature to localize increases. This was quite predictable as the localizer associates a facial feature map with a face image. The more structured the feature map is, the more reliable the association will be. Note that when training an under-dimensioned QFL localizer (with a small number of hidden cells), this always outputs the same map that is the mean feature map whatever the input image is. Owing to these conclusions, we decided to make a thorough study on the QFL localizer. We can summarize its localization results on the test set (Fig 5.a) as follows: 35% of the images have a normalized error lower than 0.05 (5%), 85% of the images have a normalized error lower than 0.1 (10%) and the mean normalized error is 0.096. We can validate localization hypothesis by computing the log-likelihood of the detected features coordinates $(x_{iD}, y_{iD})$. We tuned a threshold on the training set to reject up to 10% of the poorest localization. This decreases the mean normalized error to 0.065.

**Table 1.** Mean normalized error of the single (SFL), double (DFL) and quadruple (QFL) feature localizers on the test set

| Localizer | Mean normalized error |
|-----------|----------------------|
| SFL | 0.163 |
| DFL | 0.133 |
| QFL | 0.096 |

In the second experiment, we tested the QFL localizer sensitivity to identity. We dispatched different people in the training and test sets and trained a quadruple feature localizer. Compared to the first experiment, localization results (Fig. 5.b) are quite disappointing though predictable. Mean normalized errors on the training set are nearly the same for both experiments while they are very different on the test set showing that identity influences greatly the localizer accuracy. Only 15% of the images have a normalized error lower than 0.05 (5%), 60% of the images have a normalized error lower than 0.1 (10%) and the mean normalized error is 0.138.

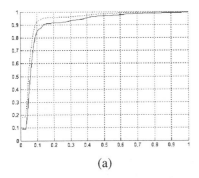
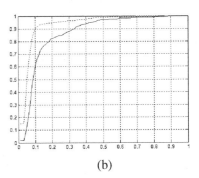

(a)                                        (b)

**Fig. 5.** Ratio of face images versus normalized error on training (dotted) and test (solid) databases. Sensitivity analysis: face orientation (a) and identity (b).

### 4.2 Multiple Localizer

**Training.** To improve the localizer accuracy, we decided to use several localizers; each one specialized on a given orientation. The clustering procedure described in §2 could separate the initial dataset into several subsets corresponding to a given face pose. Given $N$ the number of considered orientations, the corresponding multiple localizer consists in $N$ networks. So, for an input image, we have now $N$ output images and $N$ localization hypothesis corresponding to the four local maxima of each output image (Fig. 6). To compare the accuracy of the multiple localizers, we compute the normalized error for each hypothesis and apply the WTA (Winner Takes All) criterion to select the best one. We have considered up to $N=6$ orientations. As can be seen (Fig. 7) the mean normalized error decreases continuously on both training and test sets when $N$ increases. Such results are quite logical: as the number of specialized networks increases, the range of face orientations each network has to deal with decreases. The association process between face image and feature map becomes easier and the normalized error decreases.

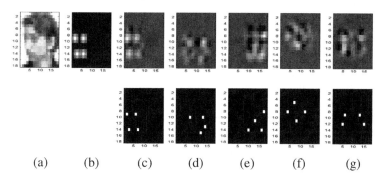

(a)     (b)     (c)     (d)     (e)     (f)     (g)

**Fig. 6.** Multiple localizers: Input image (a), target image (b), output image for the five networks and localization hypothesis (c to g)

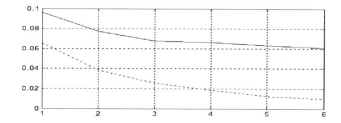

**Fig. 7.** Mean normalized error on the training (dotted) and test (solid) sets versus number of orientations considered

**Decision.** Latter result gave us a lower bound for localization error as it was produced by using the true feature position. As this information is not available, we have to find other criteria to select the best hypothesis.

Visual inspection of the networks output drives us to define a radiometric criterion (RC). As can be seen (Fig. 6), the best hypothesis corresponds to an output image $O$ closed to the feature map, in terms of pixel intensities. This is an advantage of multiple auto-associative networks. As they are trained to localize features for a specific face pose, they perform well on this given orientation and poorly on the others leading to "noisy" outputs. So we define an "ideal" output image $I$ as follows:

- At each maximum position: $I(x_{iD}, y_{iD}) = O(x_{iD}, y_{iD})$
- Anywhere else: $I(i,j) = median(O)$

Then, we compute the distance between the ideal output $I$ and the real output $O$. We get a set of $N$ distances $D_j$ for the $N$ output maps and use the WTA criterion to select the best one.

Another probabilistic criterion (PC) is obvious: the log-likelihood of each hypothesis. Given the coordinates $(x_{iD}, y_{iD})$ of the detected features and the coordinate joint probability distribution for each face orientation, we can compute a set of $N$ likelihoods $L_j$ for the $N$ hypothesis and use the WTA criterion to select the best one. As for the orientation-free localizer, we can reject a poor hypothesis while considering its likelihood (PCR criterion).

Finally, in order to get the best of these radiometric and probabilistic information, we can combine the two criteria. We normalized the distance vector $D = \{D_1, ..., D_N\}$ and the likelihood vector $L = \{L_1, ..., L_N\}$ on $[0;1]$ and use the sum rule [9] to combine them. Note that we experimented several normalization processes and combination operators (weighted sum, neural combination ...) leading to quite similar results.

**Table 2.** Mean normalized error of the multiple localizer using radiometric (RC) criterion, probabilistic (PC) criterion and their combination on the test set

| Criterion | Mean normalized error | |
|---|---|---|
| | N=3 | N=5 |
| RC | 0.088 | 0.089 |
| PC | 0.121 | 0.146 |
| PCR | 0.055 | 0.058 |
| Combination | 0.091 | **0.082** |

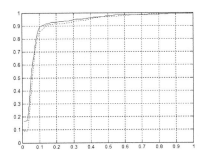

**Fig. 8.** Normalized localization error on the test set: orientation-free localizer (dotted) and multiple localizer combining five specialized networks (solid)

Table 2 summarizes the results for the two criteria and their combination, focusing on two multiple localizers respectively combining three and five specialized networks. The RC criterion outperforms slightly the orientation-free localizer (mean normalized error: 0.096). We can explain the poor results of the PC criterion by reminding the main drawback of auto-associative networks. As these latter are specialized on a specific face pose, they always produce an output that is close to the mean

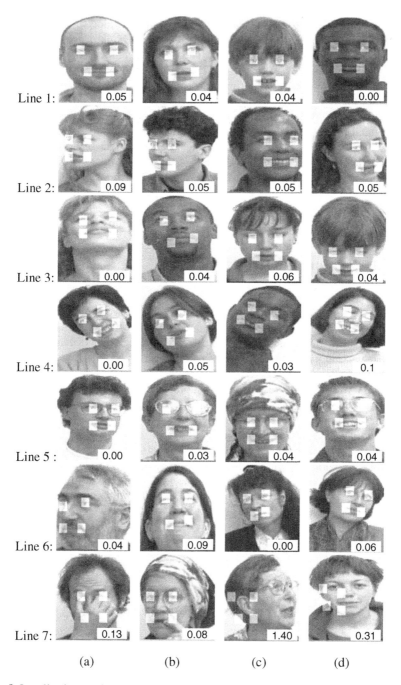

Line 1:   0.05          0.04          0.04          0.00

Line 2:   0.09          0.05          0.05          0.05

Line 3:   0.00          0.04          0.06          0.04

Line 4:   0.00          0.05          0.03          0.1

Line 5 :   0.00          0.03          0.04          0.04

Line 6:   0.04          0.09          0.00          0.06

Line 7:   0.13          0.08          1.40          0.31

(a)          (b)          (c)          (d)

**Fig. 9.** Localization results on some test images. The normalized error is indicated bellow.

feature map of this face pose. This leads to high likelihood value whatever be the face image. Meanwhile, the PCR criterion is quite accurate. The information combination outperforms the orientation-free localizer. The higher accuracy happens when using five specialized networks. We can summarize the multiple localizer results on the test set (Fig. 8) as follows: 50% of the images have a normalized error lower than 0.05 (5%), 90% of the images have a normalized error lower than 0.1 (10%) and the mean normalized error is 0.082. Finally, we present some localization results on test images (Fig. 9): frontal faces (1st line), left-sided and right-sided faces (2nd line), up-sided and down-sided faces (3rd line) and tilted faces (4th line). Localizer sensitivities to glasses (5th line), scale (6th line) and partial occlusions (7th line) are shown. The association procedure makes the system less sensitive to partial occlusions and noise: e.g. if one feature is not visible, its position is inferred by the positions of other visible features. Two localization errors are presented (7th line). Note that, in both cases, an accurate localization hypothesis was found but the combination method failed to select it.

## 5   Conclusions and Future Works

We have presented a novel algorithm for the detection of facial features in a pre-focused face image. It is based on a particular neural network trained to associate a feature map with a face image. We studied thoroughly the single, orientation-free localizer and show that its accuracy increases with the number of features to detect. We proposed an alternate method where several specialized networks were trained to deal with specific face pose. The best localization hypothesis is then selected by com-bining radiometric and probabilistic information. This multiple localizer is more accu-rate than the orientation-free localizer: the mean normalized error decreases from 9.6% to 8.2%. Note that the whole system is quite fast: more than 14 images/second (on a Pentium IV 2.8 Ghz with MathLab).

Training the system on a larger dataset will validate all these results and should in-crease the localization accuracy in two ways. First, we hope it will reduce the sensi-tivity to identity. Secondly, it will increase the generalization ability in the multiple networks case and, by the way, the whole accuracy. To deal with such generalization problems, classical methods like bootstrapping and shared weight networks [6] are under study.

We have to evaluate the accuracy of the complete localizer, by cascading the face localizer [1], with the facial feature localizer. Finally, the cascade should be extended to perform coarse-to-fine localization and deal with finer facial feature (like eye cor-ners or iris for example).

## References

[1] Belaroussi, R., Prevost, L., Milgram, M., Classifier combination for face localization in color images. International Conference on Image Analysis and Processing, Lecture Notes in Computer Sciences, Vol. 3617, (2005), 1043-1050

[2] Bishop, C. M., Neural Networks for Pattern Recognition. Oxford University Press, (1995)

[3] Chellappa, R., Wilson, C.L., Sirohey, S.: Human and machine recognition of faces: a sur-vey, Proceedings of IEEE, Vol. 83, no. 5, (1995), 705-740

[4] Cristinacce, D., Cootes., T.: A comparison of shape constrained facial feature detectors, International Conference on Automatic Face and Gesture Recognition, (2004), 375-380

[5] DeMers, D., Cottrell, G.: Non-linear dimensionality reduction. Neural Information Processing Systems 5, (1993) 580–587hould

[6] Duffner, S., Garcia, C., A Connexionist Approach for Robust and Precise Facial Feature Detection in Complex Scenes, IEEE International Symposium on Image and Signal Processing and Analysis, (2005), 316-321

[7] Feng, G.C., Yuen P.C.: Multi-cues eye detection on gray intensity image, Pattern Recognition Vol. 34, (2001), 1033-1046

[8] Féraud, R., Bernier, O., Viallet, J., Collobert, M.: A fast and accurate face detector based on neural networks, IEEE Transactions on Pattern Analysis and Machine Intelligence, Vol. 23, no. 1, (2002) 42-53

[9] Fumera, G.; Roli, F.;A theoretical and experimental analysis of linear combiners for multiple classifier systems, IEEE Transactions on Pattern Analysis and Machine Intelligence, Vol. 27, no. 6, (2005), 942-956

[10] Ioannou, S., Wallace, M., Karpouzis, K., Raouzaiou, A., Kollias S.: Combination of Multiple Extraction Algorithms in the Detection of Facial Features, International Conference on Image Processing, (2005),

[11] Milgram, M., Belaroussi, R., Prevost L.: Multi-stage combination of geometric and colorimetric detectors for eyes localization, International Conference on Image Analysis and Processing), Lecture Notes in Computer Sciences, Vol. 3617, (2005), 1010-1017

[12] Moghaddam, B. Pentland, A.: Probabilistic visual learning for object representation, IEEE Transactions on Pattern Analysis and Machine Intelligence, Vol. 19, no. 7, (1997), 696-710

[13] Peng P., Chen, L., Ruan, S., Kukharev, G.: A Robust and Efficient Algorithm for Eye Detection on Gray Intensity Face. International Conference on Advances in Pattern Recognition, Lecture Notes in Computer Sciences, Vol. 3687, (2005), 302-308

[14] Schwenk, H., Milgram, M.: Transformation invariant auto-association with application to handwritten character recognition. Neural Information Processing Systems 7, (1995) 991-998

[15] Yuille, A., Hallinan, P., Cohen, D.: Feature extraction from faces using deformable templates. International Journal of Computer Vision, Vol. 8, no. 2, (1992), 99-111

# Hierarchical Neural Networks Utilising Dempster-Shafer Evidence Theory

Rebecca Fay, Friedhelm Schwenker, Christian Thiel, and Günther Palm

University of Ulm
Department of Neural Information Processing
D-89069 Ulm, Germany
{rebecca.fay, friedhelm.schwenker, christian.thiel@uni-ulm.de,
guenther.palm}@uni-ulm.de

**Abstract.** Hierarchical neural networks show many benefits when employed for classification problems even when only simple methods analogous to decision trees are used to retrieve the classification result. More complex ways of evaluating the hierarchy output that take into account the complete information the hierarchy provides yield improved classification results. Due to the hierarchical output space decomposition that is inherent to hierarchical neural networks the usage of Dempster-Shafer evidence theory suggests itself as it allows for the representation of evidence at different levels of abstraction. Moreover, it provides the possibility to differentiate between uncertainty and ignorance. The proposed approach has been evaluated using three different data sets and showed consistently improved classification results compared to the simple decision-tree-like retrieval method.

## 1   Introduction

Hierarchical neural networks have proven suitable for pattern recognition and show many benefits when applied to classification problems of various kind [1][2][3][4][5]. Simple evaluation strategies like retrieving the accumulated classification result in a decision-tree-like manner yield good classification results. Despite all the advantages this simple method features, such as rather short classification time and availability of intermediate results, a major disadvantage is the missing ability to correct misclassifications that occur at higher levels of the hierarchy. Hence it would be beneficial not only to take a single path within the hierarchy into account but to consider all classifiers of the hierarchy.

Due to the inherent characteristics of the hierarchy there are several constraints such a comprehensive evaluation approach should meet. The classifier hierarchy naturally provides a hierarchical class grouping, i.e. the individual classifiers provide results for not necessarily single classes but sets of classes. Thus the evaluation method should provide means of dealing with information provided at different levels of abstraction without enforcing to assign information at a more detailed level than is justified. Moreover, attributed to the fact, that not all classifiers within the hierarchy provide information about all classes, but only

F. Schwenker and S. Marinai (Eds.): ANNPR 2006, LNAI 4087, pp. 198–209, 2006.
© Springer-Verlag Berlin Heidelberg 2006

deal with a specific subset of classes, there must be a possibility to state that a given sample belongs to an unknown class. Therefore it is necessary that the eligible approach offers a possibility to represent lack of knowledge and doubt.

Taking this into consideration the Dempster-Shafer evidence theory seems to be applicable as it fulfills the above mentioned constraints.

## 2   Method

In the following hierarchical neural networks are introduced. This includes the generation of the classifier hierarchies as well as the training of the hierarchy. Furthermore, two methods for hierarchy evaluation are presented: a simple decision-tree-like method and a more complex method based on Dempster-Shafer evidence theory. The proposed evidence theoretic approach only concerns the hierarchy evaluation. The hierarchy generation and training is the same for both methods.

### 2.1   Dempster-Shafer Evidence Theory

Dempster-Shafer evidence theory [6][7] is a mathematical theory of evidence and plausibility reasoning. It provides means of representing and combining measures of evidence. Major advantages of this theory are the ability to discriminate between ignorance and uncertainty, the ability to easily represent evidence at different levels of abstraction and the possibility to combine evidence from different sources. In the following the basic concepts of the Dempster-Shafer evidence theory are briefly explained.

Let $\Omega$ be a finite set of $q$ mutually exclusive atomic hypotheses $\Omega = \{\theta_1, ..., \theta_q\}$ called the *frame of discernment* representing the universe of discourse and let $2^{\Omega}$ denote the power set of $\Omega$.

A *basic probability assignment* or *mass function* $m$ over a frame of discernment $\Omega$ is a function $m : 2^{\Omega} \mapsto [0,1]$ that satisfies the following two conditions:

$$m(\emptyset) = 0 \text{ and } \sum_{A \subseteq \Omega} m(A) = 1 \tag{1}$$

The mass $m(A)$ specifies the belief in hypothesis $A$ which does not need to be atomic, but can be a set of atomic hypothesis. In that case $m(A)$ reflects ignorance as it is not possible to further subdivide the belief in $A$ among the subsets of $A$. Thus the mass $m(A)$ specifies the degree of belief that is assigned to exactly the set $A \subseteq \Omega$ and not to any subset of $A$.

With $m$ being a basic probability assignment the *belief function* $Bel : 2^{\Omega} \mapsto [0,1]$ is defined as follows:

$$Bel(A) = \sum_{B : B \subseteq A} m(B) \tag{2}$$

If $m$ is a basic probability assignment the *plausibility function* $Pl : 2^{\Omega} \mapsto [0,1]$ is defined as:

$$Pl(A) = \sum_{B : A \cap B \neq \emptyset} m(B) \tag{3}$$

Two basic probability assignments $m_1$ and $m_2$ from two independent sources can be combined via Dempster's combination rule, the so called *orthogonal sum* $m_{1,2} = m_1 \oplus m_2$ which is defined as:

$$m_{1,2}(C) = K^{-1} \sum_{A,B:A\cap B=C} m_1(A) \cdot m_2(B), \forall C \neq \emptyset \qquad (4)$$

where $K$ is a measure for the conflict between the two sources. The conflict $K$ is defined as:

$$K = 1 - \sum_{A,B:A\cap B=\emptyset} m_1(A) \cdot m_2(B) = \sum_{A,B:A\cap B\neq\emptyset} m_1(A) \cdot m_2(B) \qquad (5)$$

The orthogonal sum $m_1 \oplus m_2$ does only exists if $K \neq 0$ and the result $m_{1,2}$ is then a basic probability assignment. Otherwise the two sources are said to be totally contradictory.

Within the transferable belief model [8] positive masses can be assigned to the empty set $\emptyset$ entailing unnormalised belief functions [9]:

$$m_{1,2}(C) = \sum_{A,B:A\cap B=C} m_1(A) \cdot m_2(B), \forall C \subseteq \Omega \qquad (6)$$

A high value for the mass of the empty set $\emptyset$ indicates a high conflict between the sources.

## 2.2  Hierarchical Neural Networks

Hierarchial neural networks consist of serval simple neural networks that are hierarchically organised. Thus the nodes within the hierarchy represent individual neural classifiers.

The basic idea of hierarchical neural networks is the hierarchical decomposition of a complex classification problem into several less complex ones. This yields hierarchical class groupings splitting the decision process into multiple steps exploiting rough to fine classification. The hierarchy emerges from recursive partitioning of the original set of classes $C$ into several disjoint subsets $C_i$ until the subsets consisting of single classes result. $C_i$ is the subset of classes to be classified by node $i$, where $i$ is a recursively composed index reflecting the path from the root node to node $i$. The subset $C_i$ of node $i$ is decomposed into $s_i$ disjoint subsets $C_{i,j}$, where $C_{i,j} \subset C_i$, $C_i = \cup_{j=0}^{s_i-1} C_{i,j}$ and $C_{i,j} \cap C_{i,k} = \emptyset$, $j \neq k$. The total set of classes $C_0 = C$ is assigned to the root node. Consequently nodes at higher levels of the hierarchy classify between larger subsets of classes whereas nodes at the lowest level discriminate between single classes. This divide-and-conquer strategy yields several simple classifiers, that are more easily manageable, instead of one extensive classifier. These simple classifiers can be amended much more easily to the decomposed simple classification tasks than one classifier could be adapted to the original complex classification task. Furthermore different feature types $X_i$ are used within the hierarchy. For each classification task the feature type that allows for the best discrimination is chosen. An example of such a hierarchy is shown in figure 1.

**Hierarchy Generation.** The hierarchy is generated by unsupervised $k$-means clustering. In order to decompose the set of classes $C_i$ assigned to one node $i$ into $s_i$ disjoint subsets a $k$-means clustering is performed with all data points $\{x^\mu \in X_i | t^\mu \in C_i\}$ belonging to these classes. Depending on the distribution of the classes across the $k$-means clusters $s_i$ disjoint subsets $C_{i,j}$ are formed. One successor node $j$ corresponds to each subset. For each successor node $j$ again a $k$-means clustering is performed to further decompose the corresponding subset $C_{i,j}$. The $k$-means clustering is performed for each feature type. The different clusterings are evaluated and the clusterings which group data according to their class labels are preferred. Since the $k$-means algorithm depends on the initialisation of the clusters, $k$-means clustering is performed several times per feature type. In this study the number of $k$-means clustering runs per feature type was 10.

The number of clusters $k$ must be at least the number of successor nodes or the number of subsets $s$ respectively but can also exceed this number. If the number of clusters is higher than the number of successor nodes, several clusters are grouped together so that the number of groups equals the number of successor nodes. All possible groupings are evaluated. In the following all equations only refer to clusterings for reasons of simplicity, i.e. the number of clusters $k$ equals the number of successor nodes $s$. A valuation function is used to rate the clusterings or groupings respectively. The valuation function prefers clusterings that group data according to their class labels. Clusterings where data is uniformly distributed across clusters notwithstanding their class labels receive low ratings. Furthermore clusterings are preferred which evenly divide the classes. Thus the valuation function rewards unambiguity regarding the class affiliation of the data assigned to a prototype as well as uniform distribution regarding the number of data points assigned to each prototype.

The valuation function $V(p)$ consists of two terms regulated by a scaling parameter $\lambda > 0$. The first term $E(p)$ calculates the entropy of the distribution of each class across the different clusters. This accounts for unambiguous distribution of the data considering the corresponding classes. The term $E(p)$ becomes minimal if it is ensured for all classes that all data belonging to one class is indeed assigned to one cluster. It becomes maximal if all data belonging to one class is uniformly distributed across all clusters. The second term $D(p)$ computes the deviation from the uniform distribution. This term becomes minimal if each cluster is assigned the same number of data points. This allows for the even division of the classes into subsets. During the hierarchy generation phase we are looking for clusterings that minimise the valuation function $V(p)$. The influence of the respective term is regulated by the scaling parameter $\lambda$. Both terms are normalised so that they return values in the interval $[0, 1]$. The valuation function $V(p)$ is given by

$$V(p) = \frac{1}{l \log_2(k)} E(p) + \lambda \frac{1}{l(k-1)} D(p) \to \min \qquad (7)$$

where $E(p) = -\sum_{i=1}^{l} \sum_{j=1}^{k} p_i^j \log_2(p_i^j)$ and $D(p) = \sum_{j=1}^{k} |\sum_{i=1}^{l} p_i^j - \frac{l}{k}|$ with $p_i^j = \frac{|X_i \cap Z_j|}{|X_i|}$ denoting the rate of patterns from class $i$, that belong to cluster

$j$. Here $X_i = \{x_\mu | \mu = 1, ..., M; t^\mu = i\} \subseteq X$ is the set of data points that belong to class $i$, $R_j = \{x \in \mathbb{R}^d | j = \text{argmin}_{i=1,...,k} \|x - z_i\|\}$ denotes the Voronoi cell defined by cluster $j$ and $Z_j = R_j \cap X$ is the set of data points that were assigned to cluster $j$. The center of cluster $i$ is $z_i$. The best clustering, i.e. the one that minimises the valuation function $V(p)$, is chosen and used for determining the division of the set of classes into subsets. Moreover this also determines which feature type will be used for the corresponding classifier. So each classifier within the hierarchy can potentially use its own feature type. To identify which classes will be added to which subset the distribution of the data across the clusters is considered. The division in subsets $C_j$ is carried out by maximum detection. The set of classes belonging to subset $C_j$ is defined as $C_j = \{i \in C | j = \text{argmax}\{q_{i,1}, ..., q_{i,k}\}\}$ where $q_{i,j} = \frac{|X_i \cap Z_j|}{|Z_j|}$ denotes the rate of class $i$ in cluster $j$. For each class it is determined to which cluster $j^*$ the majority of data points belonging to this class were associated. The class label will then be added to the corresponding subset $C_{j^*}$.

To generate the hierarchy at first the set of all classes is assigned to the root node. Starting with a clustering on the complete data set the set of classes is divided into subsets. Each subset is assigned to a successor node of the root node. Now the decomposition of the subsets is continued until no further decomposition is possible or until the decomposition does not lead to a new division. An example of a classification hierarchy is shown in figure 1.

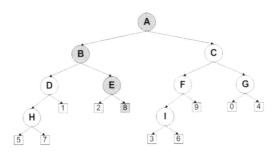

**Fig. 1.** Classifier hierarchy generated for the classification of 10 classes. Each node within the hierarchy represents a neural network which is used as a classifier. The end nodes represent classes. To each node a feature type and a set of classes are assigned. The corresponding neural network uses the assigned feature type to discriminate between the assigned classes. The highlighted path (in grey) shows the nodes activated during the classification of a sample that is classified as class 8.

**Training and Classification.** The hierarchy is trained by separately training the individual classifiers with the data $\{x^\mu \in X_i | t^\mu \in C_i\}$ that belong to the subsets of classes assigned to each classifier. For the training the respective feature type $X_i$ identified during the hierarchy generation phase is used. The data will be relabelled so that all data points of the classes belonging to one subset $C_{i,j}$ have the same label $j$, i.e. $\tilde{t}^\mu = j, x^\mu \in X_i, t^\mu \in C_{i,j}$. The number of input neurons of the single classifiers is defined by the dimension $d_i$ of the respective feature type $X_i$ assigned to the corresponding node $i$. The number of output nodes equals the number of successor nodes $s_i$. The classifiers are trained using supervised learning algorithms. The classifiers within the hierarchy can be trained independently, i.e. all classifiers can be trained in parallel.

Within the hierarchy different types of classifiers can be used. Examples of classifiers would be radial basis function networks, linear vector quantisation classifiers [5] or support vector machines [4]. We chose RBF networks as classifiers. They were trained with a three phase learning algorithm [10].

One way to obtain the classification result is similar to the retrieval process in a decision tree. Starting with the root node the respective feature vector of the object to be classified is presented to the trained classifier. By means of the classification output the next classifier to categorise the data point is determined, i.e. the classifier $j^*$ corresponding to the highest output value $o(j^*)$ is chosen such that $j^* = argmax_{j=1..s_i}(o(j))$. Thus a path through the hierarchy from the root node to an end node is obtained which not only represents the class of the object but also the subsets of classes to which the object most likely belongs. This means that the data point is not presented to all classifiers within the hierarchy and the hierarchical decomposition of the classification problem yields additional intermediate information.

If only intermediate results are of interest it is not necessary to evaluate the complete path. In order to solve a task it might be sufficient to know whether the object to be recognised belongs to a set of classes and the knowledge of the specific category of the object might not add any value. If the task for example is to grasp a cup, it is not necessary to distinguish between red and green cups. Moreover, when looking for a specific object it might in some cases not be necessary to retrieve the final classification result if a decision at a higher level of the hierarchy already excludes this object.

### 2.3 Utilising Dempster-Shafer Evidence Theory for Hierarchy Evaluation

In order to apply Dempster-Shafer theory for the evaluation of the classifier hierarchy it is at first necessary to derive basic probability assignments $m_j$ from the outputs of the individual classifiers within the hierarchy. Not all neural classifiers produce output that satisfies the conditions for probability assignments (equation 1). In these cases a transformation of the outputs is necessary. The output of fuzzy $k$-nearest neighbour classifiers $\Xi_i(x)$ fulfils the conditions for basic probability assignments as the class memberships satisfy the conditions $\Xi_i(x) \in [0,1]$ and $\sum_{i=1}^{l} \Xi_i(x) = 1$ whereas the output of radial basis function networks $z_i(x)$ does not necessarily do so. To enforce the fulfillment of the condition $z_i(x) \in [0,1]$ a ramp function $\Theta(z_i(x)) = \begin{cases} 0, x < 0 \\ x, 0 \le x \ge 1 \\ 1, x > 1 \end{cases}$ is applied to the classifier output setting all negative values to zero and all values greater than one to one. This is justified insofar as only a negligible number of output values violate this condition. In order to account for ignorance which is represents by low classifier outputs the difference of the sum of the output values to one is assigned to $\Omega$. If the sum of the classifier outputs is equal to or greater than one nothing is assigned to $\Omega$. In this case the output is then normalised to sum up to one. Hence in either case the condition $\sum_{i=1}^{l} m_j(i) = 1$ is satisfied. These transformations are applied if necessary to the outputs of all classifiers and then the resulting basic probability assignments $m_j$ of all classifiers are combined using the orthogonal sum without normalisation (equation 6).

According to the hierarchy structure each classifier provides evidence for the specific subsets of $\Omega$ between which the classifier discriminates and for $\Omega$. In case of ignorance strong evidence is assigned to $\Omega$.

Furthermore, a discounting technique is used propagating the classifier responses at higher levels of the hierarchy down. Thus classifier responses along pathes that at a higher level contain a classifier that assigned low responses are weakened strongly whereas pathes below classifiers with strong output are hardly weakened. The discounting is realised by successively multiplying the classifier responses with the classifier output of the respective predecessor node. Hence the root node is not discounted. The discounting accounts for the fact that within the hierarchy there are a not negligible number of classifier that have to provide results for samples belonging to classes they have not been trained with. Hence low classifier responses, as would be desired, cannot be guaranteed in that cases. The discounting thus weakens insular strong responses, which are likely to be caused by a classifier that has been presented a sample of an unknown class. Whereas if only one classifier within a specific path shows a low response but all other classifiers responses are high this leads only to a moderate attenuation. The discounting is applied directly after the transformation of the classifier outputs to basic probability assignments. As a multiplication with the discounting factors $d_i \in [0, 1]$ decreases the basic probability assignments if $d_i < 1$, their sum is then smaller than one $\sum_{j=0}^{s_i-1} d_i m_i(C_{i,j}) < 1$. The difference to one originating from this is then assigned to $\Omega$: $m_i(\Omega) = 1 - \sum_{j=0}^{s_i-1} d_i m_i(C_{i,j})$.

## 3   Results

The proposed approach was evaluated by means of 10 runs of 10-fold cross-validation experiments on three different data sets. The data sets used were the Columbia Object Image Library (COIL20) [11] consisting of 20 objects and 72 images per object, the Letter Recognition Image Data [12] comprising 26 letters and the handwritten STATLOG digits data set [13] containing 10 digits. From the images of the COIL20 data set three different features were extracted: orientation histograms utilising sobel edge detection, orientation histograms utilising canny edge detection and wavelet coefficients.

On all three data sets the Dempster-Shafer evaluation method performed better than the simple decision-tree-like evaluation method. The average classification rates of the evidence theoretic approach are always higher than the average classification rates of the decision tree approach. The precise classification

**Table 1.** Classification rates for the different data sets on the test and training data for the Dempster-Shafer method (DS) and the decision tree method (DT). The evidence theoretic approach outperforms the decision tree approach in all experiments.

| Data Set | Test Data | | Training Data | |
|---|---|---|---|---|
| | DS | DT | DS | DT |
| Letters | $86.74 \pm 0.79\%$ | $85.45 \pm 0.78\%$ | $88.06 \pm 0.36\%$ | $86.88 \pm 0.40\%$ |
| Digits | $94.21 \pm 0.74\%$ | $93.18 \pm 0.79\%$ | $94.50 \pm 0.14\%$ | $93.77 \pm 0.19\%$ |
| COIL20 | $96.88 \pm 1.48\%$ | $94.56 \pm 2.04\%$ | $98.88 \pm 0.23\%$ | $97.74 \pm 0.30\%$ |

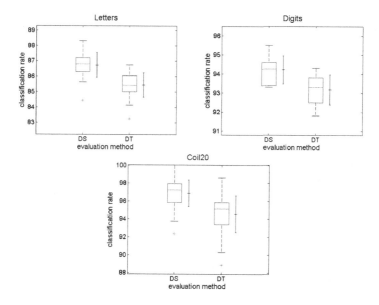

**Fig. 2.** Classification rates for the three data sets (letters, digits, Coil20) on the test data for the evidence based (DS) and the decision-tree-like (DT) approach. The box plots as well as the error bars indicate that Dempster-Shafer methods performs better than the decision tree method on all three data sets.

**Table 2.** Results of the corrected t-test for the different data sets on the test and training data comparing the Dempster-Shafer method and the decision tree method. The table gives the p-values as well as the t-value. The t-test indicates that the evidence theoretic approach outperforms the decision tree approach significantly.

| Data Set | Test Data | | Training Data | |
|---|---|---|---|---|
| | t | p | t | p |
| Letters | 9.2753 | $3.5349e - 10$ | 20.3088 | $1.0835e - 18$ |
| Digits | 4.8025 | $9.7038e - 4$ | 14.5896 | $1.4351e - 7$ |
| COIL20 | 4.7021 | $8.3433e - 6$ | 15.2295 | $1.0837e - 27$ |

rates for the different data sets can be found in table 1. Figure 2 visualises these results by means of box plots and error bars.

A pairwise t-test based on repeated $k$-fold cross validation with a variance correction [14] to compensate the highly violated independence assumption, called corrected repeated $k$-fold cross validation test, implies that the classification results for the evidence theoretic approach are significantly better than the results for the decision-tree-like approach. Table 2 contains the results of the t-test for the different data sets.

## 4    Discussion

The evaluation of the classifier hierarchy by means of Dempster-Shafer evidence theory yields improved classification results compared to the simple decision-tree-like evaluation method. With respect to computation time the decision tree approach outperforms the Dempster-Shafer alternative as for the former only part of the classifiers are evaluated and for the latter all classifiers within the hierarchy are used and additional calculations for transforming the classifier outputs and combining the individual classification results are needed.

Thus in time critical realtime applications an efficient approach would be to first use the simple and faster decision-tree-like method to classify the objects in question. If this method does not yield unambiguous results, the more time consuming Dempster-Shafer method should be used. If time is no critical factor, the usage of the evidence based approach is justified and recommended.

When using the evidence theoretic approach instead of the decision tree approach the advantage of the availability of intermediate classification outputs and the resulting savings of computation time do no longer apply as all classifiers within the hierarchy need to be evaluated. However, the Dempster-Shafer approach provides not only the resulting class but also a measure how likely the presented samples belongs to the specific classes.

A major drawback of the decision-tree-like evaluation method is the fact that there is no possibility to later on correct misclassifications that occur at higher levels of the hierarchy. As the evidence based approach considers all classifiers within the hierarchy a misclassification at higher levels of the hierarchy can be compensated for if the decisions made by the classifiers at the lower levels are correct. The evidence theoretic approach can only compensate misclassifications at higher levels of the hierarchy. If the misclassification takes place at a leaf node, this wrong decision cannot be corrected any more. The evidence theoretic approach can also not compensate for misclassifications where the majority of the classifiers supports the wrong decision.

## 5    Related Work

As the decomposition of problems into simpler sub-problems features advantages such as effectiveness and efficiency in learning and interpretability modular learning has attracted much interest recently. There are various ways of dividing a problem into less complex sub-problems. One possible way is a partitioning of the output space. In [2] a hierarchical decomposition of a multi-class problem into several two-class problems is performed utilising Fisher discriminant analysis in combination with a deterministic annealing process. The grouping of the classes is based on the class distributions resulting in a binary tree architecture. Simple Bayesian classifiers are used to solve the sub-problems. The approach is applied to the problem of categorising landcover using hyperspectral data. Instead of Bayesian classifiers support vector machines are used in [15]. The approach has been evaluated on several pattern recognition problems. An alternative method for the decomposition of the output space is applied in [1]. A max-cut algorithm is successively applied in order to find those class partitions that have a maximal distance. As classifiers support vector machines are used. Another approach for building a hierarchical binary tree classifier architecture is proposed in [3] where a self-organising map is trained in the kernel space where classification by the deployed support vector machines takes place. On the basis of the trained self-organising map the class grouping is determined by identifying the grouping that maximises the inter-group distance while minimising the intra-group variance. In this architecture no disjoint partitioning of the classes is forced, but overlaps are allowed and are shown to improve the performance.

Dempster-Shafer evidence theory has been applied to classifier fusion in numerous applications. In [16] Dempster-Shafer theory was used for multiple classifier fusion. This approach uses prototype-based classifiers and calculates belief functions from distance measures of different classifiers which are then combined utilising Dempster-Shafer evidence theory. As distance measures the inter-class-distances and intra-class-distances were used. Classification rates, misclassification rates and rejection rates were used to derive basic probability assignments in [17]. Dempster's combination rule is applied to combine the evidences. This approach considers an extra class representing unknown classes or ignorance. In [18] a technique closely related to decision templates [19] is used to calculate degrees of belief. The distances between the classifier outputs for the sample to be classified and the mean classifier outputs calculated on the training samples are transformed into basic probability assignments. The so calculated evidences are then combined using the orthogonal sum. This approach has been varied in [20] by using reference outputs adapted to the training data so that the overall mean square error is minimised instead of simply using the mean classifier outputs. In [21] Demspter-Shafer evidence theory is used to combine the normalised outputs of multiple classifiers and to reject samples in case of highly conflicting information. If at all these approaches only exploit the possibility to allocate evidence to non-atomic hypotheses by assigning masses to atomic hypotheses $\theta_i$ and to their not necessarily atomic complement $\overline{\theta_i}$ or to the frame of discernment $\Omega$. The proposed approach utilises this possibility as the classifier hierarchy naturally provides classification results for sets of hypotheses. Expert knowledge about the domain of application is used in [22] to calculate basic probability assignments not only for atomic hypotheses but also for composite hypotheses. Hence this approach is rather specific and less general than the proposed approach.

# 6    Conclusions

The proposed approach of utilising Dempster-Shafer evidence theory for the evaluation of classifier hierarchies has proven functional and shows encouraging results. It yields better classification results than the simple decision-tree-like evaluation strategy, but is more time-consuming. The already good classifications results that are achieved with a simple decision-tree-like evaluation method can be further improved using a more complex evidence based evaluation strategy. The hierarchical class grouping inherent to the classifier hierarchy seems suitable for being utilised within the framework of the Dempster-Shafer evidence theory.

# Acknowledgement

This research has been partially supported by the European Union grant #IST-2001-35282 of the MirrorBot project and by the DFG (German Research Society) grant SCHW 623/3-2.

# References

1. Chen, Y., Crawford, M., Ghosh, J.: Integrating support vector machines in a hierarchical output space decomposition framework. In: IEEE International Geoscience and Remote Sensing Symposium. Volume II. (2004) 949 – 952
2. Kumar, S., Ghosh, J., Crawford, M.: Hierarchical fusion of multiple classifiers for hyperspectral data analysis. International Journal on Pattern Analysis and Applications 5(2) (2002) 210–220
3. Cheong, S., Oh, S., Lee, S.Y.: Support vector machines with binary tree architecture for multi-class classification. Neural Information Processing - Letters and Reviews 2(3) (2004) 47–51
4. Schwenker, F.: Solving multi-class pattern recognition problems with tree structured support vector machines. In Radig, B., Florczyk, S., eds.: Mustererkennung 2001, Springer (2001) 283–290
5. Simon, S., Schwenker, F., Kestler, H.A., Kraetzschmar, G.K., Palm, G.: Hierarchical object classification for autonomous mobile robots. In: International Conference on Artificial Neural Networks (ICANN). (2002) 831–836
6. Shafer, G.: A Mathematical Theory of Evidence. University Press, Princeton (1976)
7. Dempster, A.P.: A generalization of bayesian inference. Journal of the Royal Statistical Society B(30) (1968) 205–247
8. Smets, P., Kennes, R.: The transferable belief model. Artificial Intelligence 66(2) (1994) 191–234
9. Smets, P.: The combination of evidence in the transferable belief model. IEEE Transactions on Pattern Analysis and Machine Learning 12(5) (1990) 447–458
10. Schwenker, F., Kestler, H.A., Palm, G.: Three learning phases for radial-basis-function networks. Neural Networks 14 (2001) 439–458
11. Nene, S.A., Nayar, S.K., Murase, H.: Columbia object image library (coil-20). Technical Report Technical Report CUCS-005-96, Columbia University (1996)

12. Frey, P.W., Slate, D.J.: Letter recognition using holland-style adaptive classifiers. Machine Learning **6**(2) (1991) 161–182
13. Kressel, U.H.G.: The impact of the learning-set size in handwritten-digit recognition. In: Proceedings of the International Confernece on Artificial Neural Networks, ICANN 1991, Elsevier Science Publishers B.V. (1991) 1685–1689
14. Bouckaert, R.R., Eibe, F.: Evaluating the replicability of significance tests for comparing learning algorithms. In: Proceedings of the 8th Pacific-Asia Conference on Knowledge Discovery and Data Mining, PAKDD 2004. Volume 3056 of LNAI., Springer (2004) 3–12
15. Rajan, S., Ghosh, J.: An empirical comparison of hierarchical vs. two-level approaches to multiclass problems. In: Multiple Classifier Systems, Proceedings of the 5th International Workshop. Volume 3077 of LNCS., Springer (2004) 283–292
16. Mandler, E., Schürmann, J.: Combining the classification results of independent classifiers based on the dempaster/shafer theory of evidence. In: Pattern Recognition and Artificial Intelligence PRAI. (1988) 381–393
17. Xu, L., Krzyzak, A., Suen, C.Y.: Methods of combining multiple classifiers and their application to handwriting recognition. IEEE Transaction on Systems, Man and Cybernetics **22**(3) (1992) 418–435
18. Rogova, G.: Combining the results of several neural network classifiers. Neural Networks **7**(5) (1994) 777–781
19. Kuncheva, L.I., Bezdek, J.C., Duin, R.P.W.: Decision templates for multiple classifier fusion: An experimental comparison. Pattern Recognition **34**(2) (2001) 299–314
20. Al-Ani, A.: A new technique for combining multiple classifiers using the dempster-shafer theory of evidence. Journal of Artificial Intelligence Research **17** (2002) 333–361
21. Thiel, C., Schwenker, F., Palm, G.: Using dempster-shafer theory in mcf systems to reject samples. In: Proceedings of the 6th International Workshop on Multiple Classifier Systems, MCS 2005. Volume 3541 of LNCS., Springer (2005) 118–127
22. Milisavljevic, N., Bloch, I.: Sensor fusion in anti-personnel mine detection using a two-level belief function model. IEEE Transactions on Systems, Man and Cybernetics - Part C: Applications and Reviews **33**(2) (2003) 269–283

# Combining MF Networks: A Comparison Among Statistical Methods and Stacked Generalization

Joaquín Torres-Sospedra, Carlos Hernández-Espinosa,
and Mercedes Fernández-Redondo

Departamento de Ingenieria y Ciencia de los Computadores, Universitat Jaume I,
Avda. Sos Baynat s/n, C.P. 12071, Castellon, Spain
{jtorres, espinosa, redondo}@icc.uji.es

**Abstract.** The two key factors to design an ensemble of neural networks are how to train the individual networks and how to combine the different outputs to get a single output. In this paper we focus on the combination module. We have proposed two methods based on *Stacked Generalization* as the combination module of an ensemble of neural networks. In this paper we have performed a comparison among the two versions of *Stacked Generalization* and six statistical combination methods in order to get the best combination method. We have used the mean increase of performance and the mean percentage or error reduction for the comparison. The results show that the methods based on *Stacked Generalization* are better than classical combiners.

## 1 Introduction

The most important property of a neural network is its generalization capability. The ability to correctly respond to inputs which were not used in the training set.

It is clear from the bibliography that the use of an ensemble of neural networks (figure 1) increases the generalization capability, [1,2], for the case of *Multilayer Feedforward* (MF) and other classifiers. The two key factors to design an ensemble are how to train the individual networks and how to combine them.

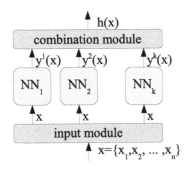

**Fig. 1.** The basic diagram of an Ensemble of Neural Networks

F. Schwenker and S. Marinai (Eds.): ANNPR 2006, LNAI 4087, pp. 210–220, 2006.

Among the methods of training the individual networks there are an important number of alternatives. Our research group has performed a comparison among methods of building ensembles which shows that the *Simple ensemble* method provides a reasonable performance with a lower computational cost [3,4].

Moreover, our research group has performed another comparison among combination methods of ensembles which shows that the *Output Average* is the simpler method but it is one of the best combination methods [5,5].

In this paper, we present some results of two versions of *Stacked Generalization* and we compare them with six *classic* combination methods. We have built ensembles of 3, 9, 20 and 40 networks with *Simple Ensemble* on six databases from the *UCI repository* to test the performance of the combination methods.

The methods are described in 2. The results we have obtained on these six databases are in subsection 3.2. We have also calculated general measurements of the combination methods to compare them, these results appear in subsetion 3.3.

## 2 Theory

In this section, firstly we briefly review the methods of combination that we have used in our experiments in subsections 2.1-2.6. Finally we describe two new methods based on *Stacked Generalization* in subsections 2.7 and 2.8.

### 2.1 Output Average

This approach simply averages the individual classifier outputs across the different classifiers.

$$\overline{y}_{class}(x) = \frac{1}{k} \cdot \sum_{net=1}^{k} y_{class}^{net}(x) \tag{1}$$

The output yielding the maximum of the averaged values is chosen as the correct class.

$$h_{average}(x) = \arg \max_{class=1,...,q} \overline{y}_{class}(x) \tag{2}$$

Where $q$ is the number of classes, $k$ is the number of networks in the ensemble.

### 2.2 Majority Vote

Each classifier provides a vote to a class, given by the highest output. The correct class is the one most often voted by the classifiers.

$$vote_{class}^{net}(x) = \begin{array}{ll} 1 & \text{if } h^{net}(x) = d(x) \\ 0 & \text{otherwhise} \end{array} \tag{3}$$

$$h_{voting}(x) = \arg \max_{class=1,...,q} \left( \sum_{net=1,...,k} vote_{class}^{net}(x) \right) \tag{4}$$

## 2.3   Winner Takes All

In this method, the class with overall maximum output across all classifier and outputs is selected as the correct class.

$$\overline{y}_{class}(x) = \max_{net=1,\dots,k} y_{class}^{net}(x) \tag{5}$$

$$h_{wta}(x) = \arg \max_{class=1,\dots,q} \overline{y}_{class}(x) \tag{6}$$

## 2.4   Borda Count

For any class $c$, the Borda count is the sum of the number of classes ranked below $c$ by each classifier. The Borda count for class $class$ is:

$$Borda_{class}(x) = \sum_{net=1}^{k} Borda_{class}^{net}(x) \tag{7}$$

Where $Borda_{class}^{net}(x)$ is the number of classes ranked below the class $class$ by the $net$-th classifier. The final hipothesys is given by the class yielding the highest Borda count.

$$h_{borda}(x) = \arg \max_{class=1,\dots,q} B_{class}(x) \tag{8}$$

## 2.5   Bayesian Combination

This combination method is based on the belief value, the class with maximum belief value is selected as the correct class. According to [6] this value is the conditional probability that the pattern $x$ belongs to class $i$, it can be approximated by:

$$Belief_{class}(x) = \frac{\prod_{net=1}^{k} p(x \in class | h(y^{net}) = j)}{\sum_{i=1}^{q} \prod_{net=1}^{k} p(x \in i | h(y^{net}) = j)} \tag{9}$$

$$h_{bayesian}(x) = \arg \max_{class=1,\dots,q} Belief_{class}(x) \tag{10}$$

Where the conditional probability that sample x actually belongs to class $i$, given that classifier $k$ assign it to class $j$ can be estimated from the values of the confusion matrix [7].

$$p(x \in i | class(y^{net}) = j) = \frac{c_{i,j}^{net}}{\sum_{m=1}^{q} c_{m,j}^{net}} \tag{11}$$

## 2.6   Dinamically Averaged Networks

It is proposed in reference [8]. It is a weighted output average which introduces weights to the outputs of the different networks prior to averaging. The weights values are derived from the network output of the pattern we are classifying.

$$\overline{y}_{class}(x) = \sum_{net=1}^{k} w_{class}^{net} \cdot y_{class}^{net}(x) \tag{12}$$

Where the weights are calculated by:

$$w_{class}^{net}(x) = \frac{C_{class}^{net}(x)}{\sum_{i=1}^{k} C_{class}^{k}(x)} \tag{13}$$

$$C_{class}^{net}(x) = \begin{cases} y_{class}^{net}(x) & \text{if } y_{class}^{net}(x) \geq 0.5 \\ 1 - y_{class}^{net}(x) & \text{otherwise} \end{cases} \tag{14}$$

$$h_{dan}(x) = \arg \max_{class=1,\ldots,q} \overline{y}_{class}(x) \tag{15}$$

### 2.7   Stacked Generalization

*Stacked Generalization* was introduced by Wolpert [9]. The combination method we propose in this paper is based on the idea of *Stacked Generalization* and it consist on training a neural network to combine the output vectors provided by the networks of the ensemble. The neural network used for combination is called *Combination network*, the networks of the ensemble are also known as *expert networks*. In Figure 2 we can see a diagram of the *Stacked Generalization*.

### 2.8   Stacked Generalization Plus

The use of the original pattern input vector is the difference between *Stacked Generalization* and *Stacked Generalization Plus*. The outputs of the expert networks on patterns from training set and the original pattern input vector are used to train the combination network. In Figure 3 we can see a diagram of the *Stacked Generalization Plus*.

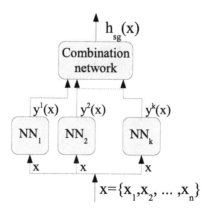

**Fig. 2.** Stacked Generalization diagram

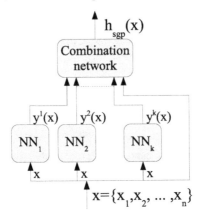

**Fig. 3.** Stacked Generalization Plus diagram

# 3    Experimental Testing

In this section we describe the experimental setup and the datasets we have used in our experiments. Finally, we show and compare the results we have obtained with the combination methods on the different datasets.

## 3.1    Datasets

We have used six different classification problems from the *UCI repository of machine learning databases* [10] to test the performance of methods. The databases we have used are:

**Arrhythmia Database** (aritm)
The aim is to distinguish between the presence and absence of cardiac arrhythmia and to classify it in one of the 16 groups. This dataset contains 443 instances, 277 attributes and 3 classes.

**Glass Identification Database** (glas)
The aim of the dataset is to determinate if the glass analysed was a type of 'float' glass or not for Forensic Science. This dataset contains 2311 instances, 34 attributes and 2 classes.

**Ionosphere Database** (ionos)
Classification of radar returns from the ionosphere. This dataset contains 351 instances, 34 attributes and 2 classes.

**The Monk's Problems 1** (mok1)
Artificial problem with binary inputs. This datasets contain 432 instances, 6 attributes and 2 classes.

**The Monk's Problems 2** (mok2)
Artificial problem with binary inputs. This datasets contain 432 instances, 6 attributes and 2 classes.

**Vowel Database** (vowel)

There is no description about it in the repository. This dataset contains 990 instances, 11 attributes and 11 classes.

Table 1 shows the training parameters (Step, Momentum, Number of Hidde Units and Number of iterations) we have used to train the combination networks for *Stacked Generalization*. Table 2 shows the training parameters for *Stacked Generalization Plus*. Finally, Table 3 shows the training parameters and the performance of expert networks.

All these values has been determined by trial and error.

### 3.2   Results

In this subsection we present the experimental results. Table 4 shows the results we have obtained with ensembles of 3 networks. Tables 5, 6, 7 show the results we have obtained for ensembles of 9, 20 and 40 networks respectively.

### 3.3   Interpretations of Results

Comparing tables 4-7 we can see that both methods based on *Stacked Generalization* are more accurate than the classical methods.

**Table 1.** MF training parameters for Gating Network (Stacked)

| Database | Networks | Hidden | Step | Momentum | Iterations |
|----------|----------|--------|------|----------|------------|
|          | 3        | 0.01   | 0.05 | 3        | 10000      |
| aritm    | 9        | 0.01   | 0.05 | 20       | 500        |
|          | 20       | 0.01   | 0.05 | 1        | 100        |
|          | 40       | 0.01   | 0.05 | 5        | 100        |
|          | 3        | 0.01   | 0.05 | 3        | 10000      |
| glas     | 9        | 0.01   | 0.05 | 3        | 10000      |
|          | 20       | 0.01   | 0.05 | 5        | 10000      |
|          | 40       | 0.01   | 0.05 | 5        | 10000      |
|          | 3        | 0.01   | 0.05 | 7        | 10000      |
| ionos    | 9        | 0.01   | 0.05 | 1        | 10000      |
|          | 20       | 0.01   | 0.05 | 5        | 10000      |
|          | 40       | 0.01   | 0.05 | 5        | 10000      |
|          | 3        | 0.01   | 0.05 | 1        | 10000      |
| mok1     | 9        | 0.01   | 0.05 | 1        | 10000      |
|          | 20       | 0.01   | 0.05 | 1        | 10000      |
|          | 40       | 0.01   | 0.05 | 1        | 10000      |
|          | 3        | 0.01   | 0.05 | 15       | 100        |
| mok2     | 9        | 0.01   | 0.05 | 5        | 100        |
|          | 20       | 0.01   | 0.05 | 5        | 250        |
|          | 40       | 0.01   | 0.05 | 25       | 250        |
|          | 3        | 0.01   | 0.05 | 19       | 10000      |
| vowel    | 9        | 0.01   | 0.05 | 6        | 7500       |
|          | 20       | 0.01   | 0.05 | 20       | 500        |
|          | 40       | 0.01   | 0.05 | 10       | 5000       |

We have calculated the increase of performance of *Stacked Generalization* and *Stacked Generalization Plus* with respect to *Output Average* to see more clearly if *Stacked* combination methods performs better. A positive value of the increase of performance means that the performance is better. A negative value means that the performance of the method on the dataset is worse. The results appear in tables 8 and 9.

Comparing the results showed in tables 8-9 we can see that the improvement in performance using our method depends on the database and the number of networks used

**Table 2.** MF training parameters for Gating Network (Stacked Plus)

| Database | Networks | Hidden | Step | Momentum | Iterations |
|----------|----------|--------|------|----------|------------|
| aritm | 3 | 0.01 | 0.05 | 4 | 2500 |
| | 9 | 0.01 | 0.05 | 6 | 1500 |
| | 20 | 0.01 | 0.05 | 17 | 1500 |
| | 40 | 0.01 | 0.05 | 5 | 1500 |
| glas | 3 | 0.01 | 0.05 | 5 | 10000 |
| | 9 | 0.01 | 0.05 | 4 | 10000 |
| | 20 | 0.01 | 0.05 | 15 | 10000 |
| | 40 | 0.01 | 0.05 | 15 | 10000 |
| ionos | 3 | 0.01 | 0.05 | 1 | 10000 |
| | 9 | 0.01 | 0.05 | 1 | 10000 |
| | 20 | 0.01 | 0.05 | 4 | 10000 |
| | 40 | 0.01 | 0.05 | 5 | 10000 |
| mok1 | 3 | 0.01 | 0.05 | 5 | 10000 |
| | 9 | 0.01 | 0.05 | 5 | 10000 |
| | 20 | 0.01 | 0.05 | 5 | 10000 |
| | 40 | 0.01 | 0.05 | 5 | 10000 |
| mok2 | 3 | 0.01 | 0.05 | 4 | 2500 |
| | 9 | 0.01 | 0.05 | 5 | 250 |
| | 20 | 0.01 | 0.05 | 5 | 250 |
| | 40 | 0.01 | 0.05 | 1 | 250 |
| vowel | 3 | 0.01 | 0.05 | 30 | 2500 |
| | 9 | 0.01 | 0.05 | 13 | 5000 |
| | 20 | 0.01 | 0.05 | 10 | 2500 |
| | 40 | 0.01 | 0.05 | 7 | 5000 |

**Table 3.** MF training parameters for Expert Networks

| Database | Hidden | Iterations | Step | Momentum | Performance |
|----------|--------|------------|------|----------|-------------|
| aritm | 9 | 2500 | 0.1 | 0.05 | $75.6 \pm 0.7$ |
| glas | 3 | 4000 | 0.1 | 0.05 | $78.5 \pm 0.9$ |
| ionos | 8 | 5000 | 0.1 | 0.05 | $87.9 \pm 0.7$ |
| mok1 | 6 | 3000 | 0.1 | 0.05 | $74.3 \pm 1.1$ |
| mok2 | 20 | 7000 | 0.1 | 0.05 | $65.9 \pm 0.5$ |
| vowel | 15 | 4000 | 0.2 | 0.2 | $83.4 \pm 0.6$ |

in the ensemble. We can see that, in general the methods based on *Stacked Generalization* are better than *Output Average*.

We have also calculated the percentage of error reduction (PER) of the ensembles with respect to a single network to get a general value for the comparison among all the methods we have studied. We have used equation 16 to calculate its value.

$$PER = 100 \cdot \frac{Error_{singlenetwork} - Error_{ensemble}}{Error_{singlenetwork}} \qquad (16)$$

**Table 4.** Results for the ensemble of three networks

|          | aritm        | glas         | ionos        | mok1         | mok2         | Vowel        |
|----------|--------------|--------------|--------------|--------------|--------------|--------------|
| Average  | $73.5 \pm 1.1$ | $94 \pm 0.8$ | $91.1 \pm 1.1$ | $98.3 \pm 0.9$ | $88 \pm 2.5$ | $88 \pm 0.9$ |
| Vote     | $73.1 \pm 1$ | $93.6 \pm 0.9$ | $91.3 \pm 1$ | $98.3 \pm 0.9$ | $88 \pm 2.2$ | $86.9 \pm 0.9$ |
| WTA      | $73.6 \pm 1$ | $94 \pm 0.6$ | $91.1 \pm 1.1$ | $98.1 \pm 1$ | $88 \pm 2.4$ | $86.7 \pm 0.8$ |
| Borda    | $73.1 \pm 1$ | $94.4 \pm 0.9$ | $91.3 \pm 1$ | $98.3 \pm 0.9$ | $88 \pm 2.2$ | $85.9 \pm 1$ |
| Bayesian | $73.6 \pm 0.9$ | $94.2 \pm 1$ | $91.4 \pm 1.1$ | $98.4 \pm 0.9$ | $88.8 \pm 2.4$ | $86.4 \pm 1$ |
| DAN      | $73.2 \pm 1.1$ | $92.8 \pm 1.6$ | $90 \pm 1.2$ | $97.1 \pm 1$ | $87 \pm 2.2$ | $84.6 \pm 1.2$ |
| Stacked  | $75.4 \pm 1.4$ | $95.2 \pm 0.9$ | $92 \pm 0.8$ | $98.4 \pm 0.9$ | $88.8 \pm 2.3$ | $89.4 \pm 0.8$ |
| Stacked + | $74.4 \pm 1.4$ | $95.6 \pm 0.9$ | $92 \pm 0.9$ | $99.8 \pm 0.3$ | $88.5 \pm 2.5$ | $89.8 \pm 0.8$ |

**Table 5.** Results for the ensemble of nine networks

|          | aritm        | glas         | ionos        | mok1         | mok2         | Vowel        |
|----------|--------------|--------------|--------------|--------------|--------------|--------------|
| Average  | $73.8 \pm 1.1$ | $94 \pm 0.7$ | $90.3 \pm 1.1$ | $98.8 \pm 0.8$ | $90.8 \pm 1.8$ | $88 \pm 0.9$ |
| Vote     | $73.3 \pm 0.9$ | $93.2 \pm 0.8$ | $90.6 \pm 1.2$ | $98.3 \pm 0.9$ | $90.3 \pm 1.8$ | $88 \pm 0.9$ |
| WTA      | $73.3 \pm 1.1$ | $93.8 \pm 0.6$ | $90.9 \pm 1.3$ | $99.5 \pm 0.5$ | $90 \pm 1.2$ | $88 \pm 0.9$ |
| Borda    | $73.3 \pm 0.9$ | $94.2 \pm 0.7$ | $90.6 \pm 1.2$ | $98.3 \pm 0.9$ | $90.3 \pm 1.8$ | $88 \pm 0.9$ |
| Bayesian | $73.6 \pm 0.9$ | $92.2 \pm 0.9$ | $93.1 \pm 1.4$ | $99.8 \pm 0.3$ | $89.6 \pm 1.7$ | $88 \pm 0.9$ |
| DAN      | $73.6 \pm 1$ | $92.8 \pm 1.1$ | $90 \pm 1.1$ | $98.8 \pm 0.9$ | $86.8 \pm 2.8$ | $88 \pm 0.9$ |
| Stacked  | $75.1 \pm 1.2$ | $96 \pm 0.7$ | $92.9 \pm 1$ | $99.8 \pm 0.3$ | $92.1 \pm 1.2$ | $88 \pm 0.9$ |
| Stacked + | $73.6 \pm 1.7$ | $95.6 \pm 0.8$ | $92.7 \pm 1$ | $100 \pm 0$ | $91.9 \pm 1.3$ | $92.3 \pm 0.6$ |

**Table 6.** Results for the ensemble of twenty networks

|          | aritm        | glas         | ionos        | mok1         | mok2         | Vowel        |
|----------|--------------|--------------|--------------|--------------|--------------|--------------|
| Average  | $73.8 \pm 1$ | $94 \pm 0.7$ | $90.4 \pm 1$ | $98.3 \pm 0.9$ | $91.1 \pm 1.1$ | $91.4 \pm 0.8$ |
| Vote     | $73.3 \pm 1$ | $93.4 \pm 0.9$ | $90 \pm 1.2$ | $98.1 \pm 1$ | $90.4 \pm 1.8$ | $90.6 \pm 0.6$ |
| WTA      | $73.1 \pm 1.2$ | $94.4 \pm 0.7$ | $91.3 \pm 1.1$ | $100 \pm 0$ | $90 \pm 1.1$ | $89.7 \pm 0.7$ |
| Borda    | $73.3 \pm 1$ | $94.4 \pm 0.8$ | $90 \pm 1.2$ | $98.1 \pm 1$ | $90.4 \pm 1.8$ | $88 \pm 0.9$ |
| Bayesian | $73.8 \pm 1$ | $90.6 \pm 0.9$ | $93.1 \pm 1.4$ | $100 \pm 0$ | $89.9 \pm 1.6$ | $74.9 \pm 1$ |
| DAN      | $72.8 \pm 1.2$ | $94.2 \pm 1.2$ | $89.6 \pm 1.1$ | $97.6 \pm 1$ | $86.6 \pm 2.1$ | $85.3 \pm 1.1$ |
| Stacked  | $73.8 \pm 1.3$ | $96.6 \pm 0.8$ | $92.7 \pm 1.1$ | $100 \pm 0$ | $91.5 \pm 1.1$ | $93.3 \pm 0.6$ |
| Stacked + | $74.7 \pm 1.1$ | $96.6 \pm 0.8$ | $92.9 \pm 1.2$ | $100 \pm 0$ | $91.5 \pm 1.1$ | $93.3 \pm 0.7$ |

**Table 7.** Results for the ensemble of forty networks

|            | aritm        | glas         | ionos        | mok1         | mok2         | Vowel        |
|------------|--------------|--------------|--------------|--------------|--------------|--------------|
| Average    | $73.8 \pm 1.1$ | $94.2 \pm 0.6$ | $90.3 \pm 1$   | $98.3 \pm 0.9$ | $91.1 \pm 1.2$ | $92.2 \pm 0.7$ |
| Vote       | $73.5 \pm 1$   | $94 \pm 0.8$   | $90.1 \pm 1.2$ | $98.3 \pm 0.9$ | $91 \pm 1.6$   | $90.5 \pm 0.7$ |
| WTA        | $73.1 \pm 1.2$ | $93.8 \pm 0.9$ | $91.6 \pm 1.1$ | $99.6 \pm 0.4$ | $90 \pm 1.6$   | $89.5 \pm 0.7$ |
| Borda      | $73.5 \pm 1$   | $94.4 \pm 0.8$ | $90.1 \pm 1.2$ | $98.3 \pm 0.9$ | $91 \pm 1.6$   | $88.7 \pm 0.8$ |
| Bayesian   | $74.1 \pm 1.1$ | $90.2 \pm 0.9$ | $93.4 \pm 1.4$ | $100 \pm 0$    | $90.3 \pm 1.5$ | $67.7 \pm 1.3$ |
| DAN        | $73.2 \pm 1$   | $93.2 \pm 0.9$ | $89 \pm 1.2$   | $98.8 \pm 0.8$ | $86.4 \pm 2.8$ | $84.3 \pm 1.2$ |
| Stacked    | $73.9 \pm 1.4$ | $95.8 \pm 0.6$ | $92.4 \pm 1$   | $100 \pm 0$    | $92.4 \pm 1.2$ | $94.2 \pm 0.8$ |
| Stacked +  | $74.5 \pm 1.3$ | $96.6 \pm 0.8$ | $92.4 \pm 1.2$ | $100 \pm 0$    | $91.4 \pm 1.2$ | $94.1 \pm 0.7$ |

**Table 8.** *Stacked Generalization* increase of performance with respect to *Average*

| Database | 3 Nets | 9 Nets | 20 Nets | 40 Nets |
|----------|--------|--------|---------|---------|
| aritm    | 1.95   | 1.27   | 0       | 0.11    |
| glas     | 1.2    | 2      | 2.6     | 1.6     |
| ionos    | 0.85   | 2.56   | 2.27    | 2.14    |
| mok1     | 0.12   | 1      | 1.75    | 1.75    |
| mok2     | 0.75   | 1.38   | 0.37    | 1.25    |
| vowel    | 1.41   | 1.36   | 1.92    | 2.02    |

**Table 9.** *Stacked Generalization Plus* increase of performance with respect to *Output Average*

| Database | 3 Nets | 9 Nets | 20 Nets | 40 Nets |
|----------|--------|--------|---------|---------|
| aritm    | 0.92   | −0.24  | 0.91    | 0.68    |
| glas     | 1.6    | 1.6    | 2.6     | 2.4     |
| ionos    | 0.85   | 2.41   | 2.42    | 2.14    |
| mok1     | 1.5    | 1.25   | 1.75    | 1.75    |
| mok2     | 0.5    | 1.13   | 0.37    | 0.25    |
| vowel    | 1.81   | 1.36   | 1.92    | 1.92    |

The PER value ranges from 0%, where there is no improvement by the use of a particular ensemble method with respect to a single network, to 100%. A negative value means that the performance of the ensemble is worse.

Furthermore, we have calculated the increase of performance with respect to *Single Network* (Table 10) and the mean PER (Table 11) across all databases for each method to get a global measurement.

According to these global measurement *Stacked Generalization* methods are the best performing methods. The highest difference between *Stacked Generalizacion* and *Output Average* is in the 40-network ensemble where the mean $PER$ increase is 9.54%. Although, *Stacked Generalization Plus* is slitghly better than *Stacked Generalization* there are some cases where the second method is better.

**Table 10.** Mean increase of performance across all databases with respect to Single Network

| Method | 3 Nets | 9 Nets | 20 Nets | 40 Nets |
|---|---|---|---|---|
| Average | 11.2 | 12.15 | 12.23 | 12.38 |
| Vote | 10.91 | 11.6 | 11.7 | 11.95 |
| WTA | 10.98 | 12.03 | 12.14 | 11.99 |
| Borda | 10.88 | 11.42 | 11.44 | 11.72 |
| Bayesian | 11.18 | 10.85 | 9.45 | 8.35 |
| DAN | 9.85 | 10.34 | 10.07 | 9.88 |
| Stacked | 12.25 | 13.75 | 13.72 | 13.86 |
| Stacked Plus | 12.4 | 13.41 | 13.9 | 13.9 |

**Table 11.** Mean performance of error reduction across all databases

| Method | 3 Nets | 9 Nets | 20 Nets | 40 Nets |
|---|---|---|---|---|
| Average | 49.17 | 49.66 | 50.16 | 50.94 |
| Vote | 46.94 | 47.18 | 47.55 | 48.57 |
| WTA | 48.41 | 49.43 | 50.05 | 49.52 |
| Borda | 45.68 | 45.87 | 45.73 | 47.05 |
| Bayesian | 38.19 | 43.61 | 35.21 | 28.52 |
| DAN | 39.35 | 41.05 | 39.65 | 38.09 |
| Stacked | 56.78 | 58.3 | 58.56 | 58.98 |
| Stcaked+ | 56.91 | 56.8 | 59.4 | 59.4 |

## 4    Conclusions

In the present paper we have analysed six classical combination methods and we have proposed two methods based on *Stacked Generalization*. We have used ensembles of 3, 9, 20 and 40 networks previously trained with *Simple Ensemble* on six databases from the *UCI Repository* to cover a wide spectrum of the number of networks in the classification system.

The results showed that the improvement by the use of *Stacked Generalization* depends on the database. Moreover, we have calculated the mean increase of performance and the mean percentage of error reduction across all databases with respect to a *Single Network* in order to get global measurements to compare the combination methods we have studied. According to the results of these global measurements *Stacked Generalization* methods perform better than the classical combination methods studied in this paper. In general, *Stacked Generalization* is the best performing combination method for ensembles of 9 networks and *Stacked Generalization Plus* is the best performing combination method for ensembles of 3, 20 and 40 networks.

We can conclude that the use of a *Combination Network* in the module combination of an ensemble increases the generalization capability of the ensemble.

## Acknowlegments

This research was supported by project *P1·1B2004-03* of Universitat Jaume I - Bancaja in Castellón de la Plana, Spain.

# References

1. Tumer, K., Ghosh, J.: Error correlation and error reduction in ensemble classifiers. Connection Science **8**(3-4) (1996) 385–403
2. Raviv, Y., Intratorr, N.: Bootstrapping with noise: An effective regularization technique. Connection Science, Special issue on Combining Estimators **8** (1996) 356–372
3. Hernandez-Espinosa, C., Fernandez-Redondo, M., Torres-Sospedra, J.: Ensembles of multilayer feedforward for classification problems. In: Neural Information Processing, ICONIP 2004. Volume 3316 of Lecture Notes in Computer Science. (2005) 744–749
4. Hernandez-Espinosa, C., Torres-Sospedra, J., Fernandez-Redondo, M.: New experiments on ensembles of multilayer feedforward for classification problems. In: Proceedings of International Conference on Neural Networks, IJCNN 2005, Montreal, Canada. (2005) 1120–1124
5. Torres-Sospedra, J., Fernandez-Redondo, M., Hernandez-Espinosa, C.: A research on combination methods for ensembles of multilayer feedforward. In: Proceedings of International Conference on Neural Networks, IJCNN 2005, Montreal, Canada. (2005) 1125–1130
6. Xu, L., Krzyzak, A., Suen, C.: Methods of combining multiple classifiers and their applications to handwriting recognition. IEEE Transactions on Systems, Man, and Cybernetics **22**(3) (1992) 418–435
7. Verikas, A., Lipnickas, A., Malmqvist, K., Bacauskiene, M., Gelzinis, A.: Soft combination of neural classifiers: A comparative study. Pattern Recognition Letters **20**(4) (1999) 429–444
8. Jimenez, D., Walsh, N.: Dynamically weighted ensemble neural networks for classification. In: IEEE World Congress on Computational Intelligence. Volume 1. (1998) 753–756
9. Wolpert, D.H.: Stacked generalization. Neural Networks **5**(6) (1994) 1289–1301
10. Newman, D.J., Hettich, S., Blake, C.L., Merz, C.J.: UCI repository of machine learning databases (1998)
11. Freund, Y., Schapire, R.E.: Experiments with a new boosting algorithm. In: International Conference on Machine Learning. (1996) 148–156
12. Breiman, L.: Arcing classifiers. The Annals of Statistics **26**(3) (1998) 801–849
13. Kuncheva, L., Whitaker, C.J.: Using diversity with three variants of boosting: Aggressive. In: Proceedings International Workshop on Multiple Classifier Systems , Calgiari, Italy, June 2002. Springer. Volume 2364 of Lecture Notes in Computer Science., Springer (2002)

# Object Detection and Feature Base Learning with Sparse Convolutional Neural Networks

Alexander R.T. Gepperth

Institute for Neural Dynamics Universitätsstraße 150,
44780 Bochum, Germany
alexander.gepperth@neuroinformatik.rub.de
http://www.neuroinformatik.rub.de/thbio

**Abstract.** A new convolutional neural network model termed *sparse convolutional neural network* (SCNN) is presented and its usefulness for real-time object detection in gray-valued, monocular video sequences is demonstrated. SCNNs are trained on "raw" gray values and are intended to perform feature selection as a part of regular neural network training. For this purpose, the learning rule is extended by an unsupervised component which performs a local nonlinear principal components analysis: in this way, meaningful and diverse properties can be computed from local image patches. The SCNN model can be used to train classifiers for different object classes which share a common first layer, i.e., a common preprocessing. This is of advantage since the information needs only to be calculated once for all classifiers. It is further demonstrated how SCNNs can be implemented by successive convolutions of the input image: scanning an image for objects at all possible locations is shown to be possible in real-time using this technique.

## 1  Introduction

In many real-world classification tasks there is a need for classifiers that can learn from examples, such as neural networks (NNs) or support vector machines. Typically, the performance of such classifiers depends strongly on a suitable preprocessing of the input, but it is far from clear what characterizes an optimal preprocessing or if there even exists an optimal solution. Sometimes it is required that the dimensionality of the input should be reduced as far as possible, whereas another objective is to make preprocessing invariant to certain transformations of the input (typically translation, rotation and scaling are investigated in this context). The process of choosing an appropriate preprocessing is referred to as *feature selection*. In addition to constraints on error rates, processing time is usually bounded from above, too, especially in computer vision. Therefore, not only the accuracy of classifiers is important but also their execution speed.

Convolutional neural networks (CNNs) [7] were proposed to address all of these issues. They are specialized instances of multilayer perceptrons (MLPs) and thus essentially feed-forward NNs. Due to their connectivity, CNNs can be implemented by successive convolutions of an input image, permitting very high

F. Schwenker and S. Marinai (Eds.): ANNPR 2006, LNAI 4087, pp. 221–232, 2006.

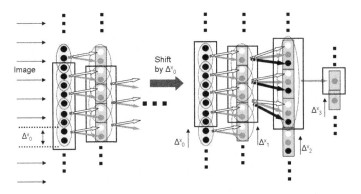

**Fig. 1.** Sketch of the SCNN network model (cross-section, y-dimension not shown). Receptive fields are drawn in by dotted ellipses, cells in the hidden layers are separated by black lines. Input filters connecting neurons to their receptive fields are shown as arrows in different shades of gray which match the shade of the destination neuron they project to. Arrows of the same shade of gray represent *equivalent* input filters, see text for details. In addition, the *step sizes* $\Delta_i^x$ are shown: they give the number of neurons by which the SCNN (indicated by large black boxes) samples its layers, i.e., the input image for $i = 0$, when performing whole-image searches. The effect of spatial sampling, i.e., shifting the classifier in layer 0, is shown on the right-hand side.

execution speed (see [1,11] for recent applications of CNNs). CNNs operating on unprocessed image data essentially *learn* a preprocessing transform, thus integrating feature selection into the training process.

In this article, a new convolutional neural network architecture termed *sparse convolutional neural network* (SCNN) is presented and its possibilities for object detection are explored. Since SCNNs can be implemented using consecutive convolutions, whole-image search at multiple scales is possible in real-time on standard present-day computer hardware. Furthermore, the SCNN model is intended to perform feature selection from unprocessed image data: a hybrid supervised-unsupervised learning algorithm is described which computes meaningful and diverse features by the interplay of local nonlinear PCA and error minimization. Lastly, an algorithm for learning a common image representation that is shared by several SCNN object classifiers is described. The advantage of different classifiers using the same preprocessing is that preprocessing needs only to be performed once per image when performing whole-image searches.

## 2    Sparse Convolutional Neural Network Classifiers

Like the original proposal [7] they are derived from, SCNNs are feed-forward neural networks with local receptive fields (see fig. 1). However, the connection structure in SCNNs has been considerably modified as compared to [7]. The proposed model is simpler and can —once trained— be tested using existing software for simulating multilayer perceptrons. Furthermore, the issue of obtaining meaningful and diverse features is addressed using a direct approach. The original CNN model attempts to achieve this by connecting hidden layers only to certain (not all) succeeding layers, which has been experimentally shown to lead to dissimilar feature maps. It is unknown, though, what effect the global network structure has on this mechanism and how many experimental trials are necessary for this mechanism to work. In the SCNN model (see fig. 1), feature complexity and diversity are enforced by additional unsupervised terms in the learning algorithm. They cause outputs of different feature maps at the same image location to be (nonlinearly) decorrelated and to have extremal variance in a way very similar to nonlinear principal components analysis [4]. Employed principles are gradient-based variance maximization of neuron outputs, decorrelation and weight vector normalization. The SCNN model has an input layer of fixed dimension, one or more hidden layers, and an output layer containing a single element. Each layer receives input from one other layer (the preceding one) and projects to a single layer (the succeeding one, see also fig. 1).

## 2.1   Network Model

Since SCNNs are specialized instances of MLPs, the network structure is discussed without reference to the implementation as successive convolutions. Constraints arising from this implementation are discussed at the end of this section.

**Connectivity.** A layer $l = 0, \ldots, l^{\max}$, having dimensions $L_l^x \times L_l^y$ is composed of identical *cells* of neurons of dimension $C_l^x \times C_l^y$. Thus, a neuron can be assigned coordinates $\boldsymbol{n} = (l, \boldsymbol{c}, \boldsymbol{i})$, where $\boldsymbol{c}$ denotes the two-dimensional index of the cell within layer l, and $\boldsymbol{i}$ the neuron's coordinate within its cell. Within one cell, each neuron is connected to the same rectangular patch of neurons in layer $l-1$ which is termed a neuron's *receptive field* (RF). Receptive fields in layer $l-1$ can overlap in x- and y-direction by $O_{l-1}^x \times O_{l-1}^y$. The set of all weights connecting a neuron to its RF is denoted *input filter*. Since it is in one-to-one correspondence to a RF, it can naturally be arranged in a rectangular scheme with dimensionality $I_{l-1}^x \times I_{l-1}^y$ which is identical to that of the RF. Connection strengths are denoted by $w_{\boldsymbol{n}\prime\boldsymbol{n}}$ where $\boldsymbol{n}$ specifies the coordinates of the destination neuron and $\boldsymbol{n}\prime$ those of the source neuron. Please refer to fig. 1 for a visualization. Each neuron (except for those in the input layer) is connected by a trainable weight to a bias neuron whose activation is constant (here: 1.0).

**Constraints.** The first set of constraints comes from the geometrical consistency of the SCNN. Trivially, given a layer $l$, $L_l^x, L_l^y$ must be integer multiples of $C_l^x, C_l^y$. Furthermore, the number of input filters in layer $l-1$ must be identical to the number of cells in layer $l$. Thus, we get two conditions

$$L_l^{x,y} = kC_l^{x,y}, \; k \in \mathbb{N}^+ \tag{1}$$

$$\frac{L_l^{x,y}}{C_l^{x,y}} = \frac{L_{l-1}^{x,y} - I_{l-1}^{x,y}}{I_{l-1}^{x,y} - O_{l-1}^{x,y}} \tag{2}$$

As in the CNN model, a weight-sharing constraint enters via the requirement that neurons within a layer $l$, having the same within-cell coordinates $i$ but being connected to different RFs, must have identical input filters. It is this constraint which allows to implement a network run by a series of convolutions. In contrast, each neuron in one cell is allowed to be connected to the common RF by different filters than the other neurons in that cell. Effectively, the size of one cell, $C_l^x \times C_l^y$, specifies the number of convolution filters necessary for the simulation of each layer, whereas the size of receptive fields (equal to input filter size $I_{l-1}^x \times I_{l-1}^y$) determines the dimensions of the convolution filters. For each layer $l$, sets of weights that are required to be identical by the weight-sharing property are called *equivalent*. Obviously it is desirable to obtain a trained SCNN which requires as few convolution filters as possible while maintaining high classification accuracy.

A further constraint comes from the implementation that is used for whole-image search (see section 3) although it is not necessary for the simulation of the SCNN model per se: it requires that step sizes $\Delta_l^x$, $\Delta_l^y$ in layer $l$ (i.e., the differences between the size of input filters projecting to layer $l+1$ and their overlap) must be integer multiples of that layer's cell sizes. Thus it is ensured that the classifier starts and ends at cell boundaries in all layers if it is shifted in the input image by $\Delta_0^{x/y}$, see also fig. 1. In precise terms:

$$\Delta_l^{x,y} \equiv I_l^{x,y} - O_l^{x,y} = kC_l^{x,y}, \ k \in \mathbb{N}. \tag{3}$$

**Activation Functions.** The activity $A_n$ of a neuron is calculated from the activities of its RF and the weight values in its input filter as $A_n = \sigma(\sum_{n' \in \text{RF}} A_{n'} w_{nn'})$ using the sigmoidal activation function $\sigma(x) = \frac{x}{1+|x|}$.

## 2.2   Learning in SCNNs

Initially, all weights are initialized to small random values between -0.01 and 0.01 (see [8] for a motivation of this initialization). Then, a weight-sharing step is performed: for each layer $l$, the average of each set of equivalent weights is computed. Subsequently, all equivalent weights within layer $l$ are set to their previously computed average value. In this way, all equivalent weights have identical values at the start of training. During each learning step or *epoch*, all weights of the SCNN are treated as if they were independent. An improved variant of the well-known Rprop learning algorithm (IRprop+, see [5]) is applied to the SCNN using dataset $D_{\text{train}}$ for 80 epochs. After each epoch, the weight-sharing condition is enforced as described before. Note that weight-sharing is enforced separately for the bias weights of each layer.

The mean squared error (MSE) is calculated as $E_{\text{MSE}}(D) = \frac{1}{|D|} \sum_{p=0}^{|D|} (A_p^{out} - c_p)^2$ using a dataset $D$. It uses the class label $c_p$ of pattern $p$ and the activation $A_p^{out}$ of the CNN's output neuron in response to pattern $p$. The learning rule for each weight is composed of the usual MSE-minimizing term plus an additional unsupervised term. The additional term is a nonlinear version of Oja's rule [4]:

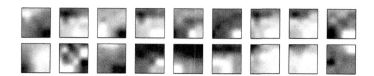

**Fig. 2.** Layer 0 input filters of an SCNN trained on cars (see section 5.1). Shown are filters obtained by different learning rules: MSE gradient (upper row) and hybrid learning rule described in the text (lower row). Many filters in the upper row are almost identical whereas, in the lower row, such redundancy does not occur.

$$\Delta w_{n\prime n} = \gamma A_n (A_{n\prime} \sigma(\sigma^{-1}(A_n)) - A_n w_{n\prime n} - \sum_{j \in \text{cell}(n), j < n} A_j w_{n\prime j} \qquad (4)$$

where $\gamma$ is a small positive constant and the sum on the right-hand side of the equation runs over all neurons in the same cell as $n$ whose within-cell coordinates are component-wise smaller than those of $n$.

During training, model selection is performed using $E_{\text{MSE}}(D_{\text{val}})$ alone. When evaluating the performance of a trained network, the classification error $CE(D_{\text{test}})$ is used. It is defined as $CE(D) = 1 - \frac{1}{|D|} \sum_{p=0}^{|D|} \theta(A_p^{out} - \tau)$, where $\theta$ denotes the step function and $\tau$ a threshold assigned to each NN (always taken to be 0).

A few comments on the chosen learning algorithm are in order: local nonlinear principal components analysis is performed within each receptive field, but modified by the MSE gradient. The unsupervised part of the learning rule performs decorrelation of all neurons within a cell and tends to input filters with an euclidean norm of 1.0. It is an extension of the algorithm given in [2] where only orthonormalization was performed (not by gradient descent but operating directly on the weights). Due to unsupervised learning, neurons within a cell capture a part of their input whose variance is maximally large. Furthermore, the neurons' input filters tend to orthogonality, i.e., diversity (see fig. 2).

For weights connecting to the output neuron, the unsupervised term is not considered because it interferes too much with minimizing the MSE.

## 3   A Convolutional Architecture for Whole-Image Search

The neural network architecture described in the previous sections is particularly suited, due to the weight-sharing constraint, for fast implementation by means of convolution filters (see, e.g., [6] for an introduction). However, it is possible to achieve far greater speed gains when considering *whole-image search*, i.e., the application of a fixed-size classifier at every conceivable position within an image, possibly at several scales. In this context, CNN architectures like the SCNN model have the tremendous advantage that convolutions for overlapping classifiers need only be computed once. This can be understood by considering that input filters in the SCNN do not depend on their spatial position within a

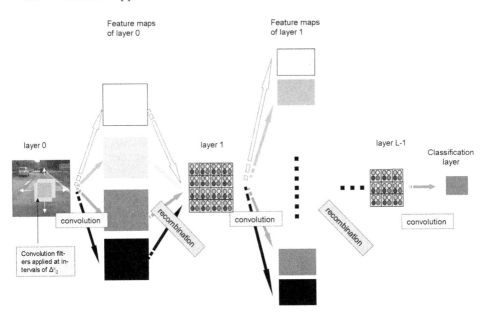

**Fig. 3.** Sketch of the SCNN architecture for whole-image searches. SCNN model. The input layer consists of the whole image, and successive layers are correspondingly enlarged. Input filters of the SCNN translate into convolution filters: convolution results of a layer with its input filters are called *feature maps*. The recombination of feature maps into the next layer is defined by the connectivity of the SCNN. Identical shades of gray of hidden layer neurons and feature maps indicate this. Instead of converging to a single output neuron, the SCNN now converges to a layer where each neuron represents the output of one SCNN classifier. The number of input filters (i.e., feature maps), hidden layer neurons and similar SCNN parameters are examples.

layer due to weight-sharing. By inference, the whole image needs to be convolved *only once* with all input filters in order to produce a classification result at each position within an image. Please see fig. 3 for details of the convolutional architecture and fig. 1 for details on whole-image search. Furthermore, since the input image is usually subsampled by the input filters of the first network layer (always the case when $\Delta_0^x \geq 2$, see fig. 1), only the convolutions with these input filters contribute significantly to the total processing time. The whole-image classification problem then reduces to filtering with a limited number of (usually nonseparable) filters; if real-time performance is desired, the mask size should be small (typically, sizes of 5, 7 or 9 are chosen).

The SCNN model presented here belongs to the class of convolutional neural networks which were originally proposed in [7]. A crucial difference is that no implicit subsampling of feature maps is performed, whereas in [7], feature maps are successively filtered and subsampled until they converge onto one neuron, the output of which is combined with similar neurons to form a classification output. In the SCNN model, subsampling is performed if the step sizes in one layer are chosen larger than 1, but the choice of subsampling filters is not defined a priori

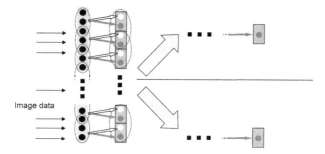

**Fig. 4.** Exemplary SCNN architecture for feature base learning. The horizontal line indicates that the processing streams converging onto the two (or more) output neurons do not have any connections in common.

(i.e., Gaussian smoothing) but learned by the network, too. It should be stressed here that subsampling *is* possible in the SCNN model, but at this point it seems more practical to let the SCNN *learn* the downsampling filters as well. A second difference is that feature maps are recombined into layers in the SCNN model after each convolution, whereas in [7], feature map outputs are recombined only in the last layer of the network. Recombination after each convolution inflicts a small computational cost, but it can be expected that it results in more reliable detection of conjunction features similar to the object detection architectures of [9,12]. Lastly, there exists a direct mechanism of enforcing diversity among the learned features of the SCNN, which guarantees without the need for additional experiments that informative and non-redundant features are learned which, in addition, capture a significant part of the input's local variance (by the local PCA property).

## 4  Feature Base Learning

An interesting application is motivated by the observation made in the previous section that the computational load is biggest during the simulation of the first layer. If two networks had identical processing in that layer, they could be used simultaneously for whole-image search while the convolutions of the input image would only need to be computed once. Stated in different terms, it would be interesting to find out if there is a *common feature base* for two or more object classes, i.e., a preprocessing of the input which is suited for representing all of the object classes under consideration. Therefore, it is investigated if and how a common feature base for $N$ object classes can be learned only from available examples. It is tested by experiment whether it is possible to achieve classification rates comparable to separately trained classifiers. In the formalism of SCNNs, there exists a straightforward approach: $N$ networks are trained independently from each other using methods given in section 2.2, but after each iteration of the learning algorithm, a weight-sharing constraint is enforced between the filters in the input layers of all networks.[1] An alternative interpretation is a single network which converges onto N output neurons by non-interfering processing streams from a common first hidden layer. Please see fig. 4 for a visualization. Model selection is performed using the sum $\sum_{i=0}^{N} E_{\text{MSE}}^i(D_{\text{val}}^i)$ of the mean squared errors of each individual classifier on its validation dataset $D_{\text{val}}^i$.

## 5    Experiments

Two types of experiments are conducted: the speed of the system is (empirically, not theoretically) determined using selected SCNN topologies, and tests of topology-dependent classification performance are conducted. The latter task is performed off-line using data from real-world classification tasks. (see fig. 5).

### 5.1    Classification Tasks and Training Data Generation

Most experiments described here are based on the problem of car classification in real-world video traffic scenes (see, e.g., [3]). For a few experiments, the problem of traffic sign classification is considered in addition. However, this problem is not a present focus of investigations, therefore training data are much less rigorously selected and tested, and results may not be very generalizable.

Object classifiers are trained to distinguish objects from background. Training data are generated by marking rectangular regions of interest (ROIs) that contain objects. Objects are enclosed as tightly as possible. Negative examples are also created manually, although their choice is more ambiguous. Some representative training examples for cars and traffic signs are shown in fig. 5.

Due to the fact that whole-image searches usually sample the image at step sizes $\Delta_0^{x/y} > 1$, the classification must be invariant to certain transformations (especially small translations and rescalings). This requirement is encoded into the training examples. Let us define some notation: a *training example* consists of a *class label* and a *region of interest* (ROI) within a specified image. The ROI either does or does not enclose an object: to indicate this, the class label is set to 1 for an object and to -1 otherwise. A *training dataset D* contains $N$ examples. Before using a dataset for training, a defined number of transformations is applied to the ROI of each example, creating the *transform dataset $D^{\text{tr}}$*.

First of all, the transformations to be applied must be specified as well as the degree of invariance which the classification should have with respect to these transformations. Let us assume that each transformation $f_t^\alpha, t \in [0, \dots, T-1]$ : $D \mapsto D^{\text{tr}}$ can be continuously parametrized by a single parameter $\alpha$, and that a total of $T$ different transformations exists. Let $f_t^{\alpha=0}$ denote the identity transform. Then a limit $\alpha_t^{max} > 0$ must be specified, stating the range of parameters $I_t = [-\alpha_t^{max} \dots \alpha_t^{max}]$ in which classification invariance should hold. Further assuming that all transforms commute (fulfilled for translation, rotation and scaling in two dimensions), we obtain a map

---

[1] Note that the dimensions of the input layers need not be identical, only the dimensions of the input filters in the input layer.

**Fig. 5.** Positive and shared negative examples for the car/traffic sign object classes

$$\tau : D \mapsto D^{\mathrm{tr}}; r \mapsto (f_1^{\alpha_1} \circ \cdots \circ f_T^{\alpha_T})(r), \alpha_k \in I_k, r \in D.$$

that is applied a defined number of times to each example in $D$. From the results, the transform dataset is created: it is therefore larger than the original dataset of examples. In the implementation presented here, a certain invariance to scaling and translation is required. Translation is modelled by two transformations, one for horizontal and one for vertical translations. The parameters $\alpha_x$ and $\alpha_y$ of both transformations are interpreted as the percentage of an ROI's width or height by which it should be shifted. The single scaling transform enlarges or reduces an ROI's width and height by a factor of $\alpha_{sc}$ while ensuring that the center of the ROI stays constant. In addition, it is required for the map $\tau$ that each transformation result must completely contain the original example.

$D^{\mathrm{tr}}$ is generated from labeled data by applying $\tau$ 9 times per example and uniformly drawing from the parameter intervals $I_{x,y}$, $I_{sc}$ defined by $\alpha_{sc}^{max} = \sqrt{2}, \alpha_{x,y}^{max} = 10$. From the transform dataset, three disjunct datasets $D_{\mathrm{train}}$, $D_{\mathrm{val}}$ and $D_{\mathrm{test}}$ are created which contain 2000 examples each, half of them positive. The image content within the ROIs is up- or downsampled to a fixed size of 25x25 pixels. Whenever necessary, appropriate smoothing and bicubic interpolation are performed. For later experiments, three additional car datasets are created from $D^{\mathrm{tr}}$ where each ROI is shifted by 50% of its width to the left. The idea behind this classification task is to make detection more robust by checking if the "left-shifted" object classifier indeed finds half a car at the left of a detected car.

## 5.2   Off-Line Classification Performance of Single SCNNs

Due to the weight-sharing constraint (see section 2.2), the number of free parameters in an SCNN is greatly reduced. The choice of an appropriate topology is therefore crucial since the number of free parameters in the network depends directly on it. Since the correct choice of NN topology for a given classification task is still, in general, an unsolved problem, a number of experiments was conducted to identify suitable topologies. The search space can be reduced by the requirement that small input filters should be used in the input layer, as well as by the architectural constraints (1), (2) and (3) which SCNNs must obey.

In each experiment, a certain SCNN topology is trained 6 times using a different random seed each time, and the best classification result $\mathrm{CE}(D_{\mathrm{test}})$ is

**Table 1.** Best classification errors of various SCNN topologies for cars (C), cars shifted left (L) and traffic signs (TS) (errors are given in percent). Cells and layers are quadratic so only one dimension of their sizes is given. In row 0, the result for two fully connected reference networks of MLP type is given. SCNNs 1-5 demonstrate the effects of varying input filter sizes and numbers. Notable is the improvement when allowing 4x4 input filters as in SCNN 5. Rows 6 and 7 give results for the feature base learning (using topology 4, see text) of two and three object classes. For comparison, the last row shows the results of the SNoW-architecture [10] using the Winnow update rule.

| Nr. | dimensions | filter size | nr.filters | conn. | free param. | $min_{\exp}\mathrm{CE}(D_{\text{test}})$ |
|-----|-----------|-------------|-----------|-------|-------------|-----------|
| 0 | 25-5-1 | (25) | - | 15650 | 15650 | 5.5 (C), 5.4 (L), 6.7(TS) |
| 1 | 25-9-1 | 21-9-x | 3-1-x | 36162 | 4050 | 6.8 |
| 2 | 25-18-1 | 9-18-x | 2-1-x | 26568 | 648 | 7.8 |
| 3 | 25-30-1 | 7-30-x | 3-1-x | 45000 | 1341 | 6.7 |
| 4 | 25-22-1 | 5-22-x | 2-1-x | 12584 | 584 | 6.8(C),5.8(L),11.4(TS) |
| 5 | 25-44-1 | 5-44-x | 4-1-x | 50336 | 2336 | 6.3 |
| 6 | feature base learning using SCNN 4 | | | | | 7.3(C),5.9 (L), 10.9 (TS) |
| 7 | feature base learning using SCNN 4 | | | | | 6.5(C),11.0 (TS) |
| 8 | SNoW, std. parameters, 50 cycles | | | | | 13.6 |

taken to be a measure of that topology's learning capacity. As a baseline, a fully connected NN with one hidden layer is identically trained on the car and traffic sign classification problems. Table 1 gives an overview over representative SCNN topologies as well as the fully connected reference networks. When considering SCNNs with one hidden layer, two ways to improve classification results were identified: increasing the size, or alternatively the number of input filters in the input layer. Obviously, both operations lead to a larger number of free parameters. The best topology found in this way has filter sizes of 5x5 pixels in the input layer, yet it is not quite compatible with real-time requirements since it requires 16 convolutions of the input image in the input layer alone. It uses 80000 connections, although the actual number of free parameters is $2384^2$. Classification performance is only slightly worse than that of the reference network despite the fact that the number of free parameters is much lower.[3] If real-time capability is desired, SCNN 4 is the topology to choose. Although using a much smaller number of connections and free parameters than topology 5, it achieves only slightly worse classification performance. Please see section 5.4 for speed measurements.

For unknown reasons, the inclusion of more hidden layers did not improve performance. Many-layered topologies were constructed by adding new layers onto well-performing SCNNs with one hidden layer. Notable was much slower overall learning convergence. It is therefore conceivable that training was not conducted sufficiently long. More research will have to be applied in order to shed light on this particular point.

---

[2] Note that it is the number of free parameters which determines the speed of whole-image classification.

[3] It was also shown that SCNN performance is slightly superior to that of an MLP with identical connectivity as well as an SCNN using supervised learning only.

## 5.3    Feature Base Learning Results

SCNN topology 4 given in table 1 is used for learning a common feature base for cars and traffic signs. It is not the best-performing topology that was found but comes very close to it; what is more, it allows real-time operation. Training is performed using the algorithm given in section 4. Results are given in table 1. It is evident that classification results are comparable to those of classifiers trained separately on their respective tasks. Observe that the feature base result for traffic signs has to be compared to traffic sign results of topology 4 in table 1, not to the reference network performance: the goal was to show that the performance of the individual classifiers can be reproduced by feature base learning. When choosing SCNN topologies with larger input filters, the performance of the reference network can be approached for traffic signs, too.

## 5.4    Online Performance

All tests were conducted using a 1.86Mhz Centrino processor. Images had a size of 360x288 pixels; convolutions were implemented in C++, and no use was made of the capabilities of the graphics hardware. Classification was performed at three spatial scales for each frame, where each scaled image was obtained by smoothing with a size-5 binomial filter and downsampling by a factor of 2. The best-performing SCNN topology 5 given in table 1 allows a frame rate of 7 frames per second (fps), whereas SCNN 4 allows 22 fps at the price of slightly inferior classification performance. When using three classifiers of topology 4 sharing a common preprocessing, a speed of 19 fps is attainable.

# 6    Discussion

The SCNN model is interesting in several respects: on the one hand, it demonstrates a successful combination of supervised and unsupervised learning rules; on the other hand, it offers very interesting possibilities for practical applications. Due to its real-time capability and the ability to search images simultaneously for several object classes using using feature base learning, it is suited for applications where scene analysis is performed, which usually consists of the recognition of more than one type of object. The driving idea behind the SCNN model was to reduce the need for "manual" feature design. With SCNNs, *some* prior knowledge must still be provided in the form of the network topology: if it is known that, for example, that features of a certain size are characteristic of an object class, the input filters should be chosen accordingly. In many cases, input filter and step sizes are constrained by real-time requirements; once input filter and step sizes are fixed, the SCNN topology constraints are sufficient for removing most of the remaining ambiguities. As with all NNs, the correct choice of topology is an unsolved problem, although in practice one can simply take the SCNN with the largest number of parameters that is compatible with application constraints. As has been demonstrated, increasing the number of free parameters tends to improve classification performance.

The issue of extending SCNN topology successfully to more than one hidden layer is a current research topic: SCNNs with two or more hidden layers may be much more powerful in capturing local combination features; furthermore, it is intuitive that feature base learning can profit greatly from such topologies. The SCNN model itself could also be extended; in particular, shortcut connections which bypass one or more layers, and subsampling layers (as in LeCun's original proposal) suggest themselves. From a theoretical point of view, a detailed examination of the interplay between the supervised and unsupervised terms in the learning rule would be interesting; the relation of learned SCNN input filters to independent components seems to be worth investigating. Last not least, it is intended to use SCNN classifiers (possibly in conjunction with other modules) to build robust and fast object detection systems that reliably work in practice[4].

# References

1. C. Garcia and M. Delakis. Convolutional face finder: A neural architecture for fast and robust face detection. *IEEE Transactions on Pattern Analysis and Machine Intelligence*, 26(11):1408–1423, November 2004.
2. A. Gepperth. Visual object classification by sparse convolutional networks. In *Proceedings of the European Symposium on Artificial Neural Networks (ESANN) 2006*. d-side publications, 2006. accepted.
3. A. Gepperth, J. Edelbrunner, and T. Bücher. Real-time detection of cars in video sequences. In *Proceedings of the IEEE Intelligent Vehicles Symposium*, 2005.
4. A. Hyvärinen. Fast and robust fixed-point algorithms for independent component analysis. *IEEE Transactions on Neural Networks*, 10:626–634, 1999.
5. C. Igel and M. Hüsken. Empirical evaluation of the improved Rprop learning algorithm. *Neurocomputing*, 50(C):105–123, 2003.
6. B. Jähne. *Digital image processing*. Springer-Verlag, 1999.
7. Y. LeCun, L. Bottou, Y. Bengio, and P. Haffner. Gradient-based learning applied to document recognition. *Proc. IEEE*, 86(11):2278–2324, 1998.
8. R. D. Reed and R. J. Marks II. *Neural Smithing*. MIT Press, 1999.
9. M. Riesenhuber and T. Poggio. Hierarchical models of object recognition in cortex. *Nature Neuroscience*, 2(11):1019–1025, 1999.
10. D. Roth. The SNoW learning architecture. Technical Report UIUCDCS-R-99-2101, UIUC Computer Science Department, May 1999.
11. M. Szarvas, A. Yoshizawa, M. Yamamoto, and J. Ogata. Pedestrian detection using convolutional neural networks. In *Proceedings of the IEEE Symposium on Intelligent Vehicles*, pages 224–229, 2005.
12. H. Wersing and E. Körner. Unsupervised learning of combination features for hierarchical recognition models. In *Proceedings of the ICANN*, 2002.

---

[4] Training data as well as the C++ source code for simulating and training SCNNs are available under *http://www.neuroinformatik.rub.de/thbio/group/vision*.

# Visual Classification of Images by Learning Geometric Appearances Through Boosting

Martin Antenreiter, Christian Savu-Krohn, and Peter Auer

Chair of Information Technology (CiT)
University of Leoben, Austria

**Abstract.** We present a multiclass classification system for gray value images through boosting. The feature selection is done using the LPBoost algorithm which selects suitable features of adequate type. In our experiments we use up to nine different kinds of feature types simultaneously. Furthermore, a greedy search strategy within the weak learner is used to find simple geometric relations between selected features from previous boosting rounds. The final hypothesis can also consist of more than one geometric model for an object class. Finally, we provide a weight optimization method for combining the learned one-vs-one classifiers for the multiclass classification. We tested our approach on a publicly available data set and compared our results to other state-of-the-art approaches, such as the "bag of keypoints" method.

## 1 Introduction

Image recognition and categorization are interesting vision problems. There exist many approaches for solving specific problems (e.g. for face recognition). The task becomes more difficult if the goal is to develop an algorithm which is independent from the target object class. A state-of-the-art approach to overcome this problem is to use the "bag of keypoints" idea (see [5]). This method calculates a feature histogram for every image in the data set. Its main advantage is, that standard learning algorithms like SVMs [12,19], which need a fixed dimensional input vector, can be used to construct a classifier. On the other hand, feature histograms cannot exploit geometric relationships between the features contained in an image, although this might be discriminative information.

There exist various methods for incorporating such relationships between parts using statistical models. Early work in this direction was done by Burl et al. [2] for the recognition of planar object classes. There, important parts are selected by previously learned detectors, and afterwards a shape model is learned from the detector locations. This approach was later improved by using a soft-detection strategy in [3]. The two problems; detecting features, and building a shape model from the detection, are solved simultaneously. Furthermore, unsupervised scale-invariant learning of parts and shape models has been done in [7], where an entropy-based feature detector from Kadir [13] has been used to select the important parts from an image.

F. Schwenker and S. Marinai (Eds.): ANNPR 2006, LNAI 4087, pp. 233–243, 2006.

Recently, graph-based models called "$k$-fans" were introduced [4]. The structure of the graph, and therefore the representational power of the shape model is controlled by the parameter $k$. There exist well defined algorithms to solve the learning and detection problems for models with $k$-fan graphs. In general, methods like [2,3,4,7] force the user to predefine a fixed number of parts considered for learning. This quantity is usually determined in a second run by trial and error. In contrast, we show how the correct number of parts as well as the geometric complexity for the model can be estimated during learning with a boosting algorithm.

Previous work from Opelt et al. [17,16] and Fussenegger et al. [9] have shown that image categorization using AdaBoost [8] is a powerful method. Particularly, they have used AdaBoost to select discriminative features to learn a classifier against a background class. This work extends their methods in several directions. First, it is not always clear beforehand which feature types are advisable for learning a certain class. Therefore, we use nine different feature types simultaneously, and leave it up to the learning algorithm to determine the useful types. To reduce computational efforts we cluster each feature type using k-means. Secondly, we use LPBoost [1,6] as the learning algorithm which is advantageous compared to AdaBoost, since LPBoost can handle noisy data well. Our third contribution is a procedure for incorporating geometric relations between features into the weak learner of the boosting algorithm. Finally, we address the multiclass classification problem and provide a weight optimization method for one-vs-one classifiers using Support Vector Machines (SVMs) [12,19]. We conclude with the evaluation and the results obtained on the Xerox image data set [5], which is publicly available at ftp://ftp.xrce.xerox.com/pub/ftp-ipc/. There, we also compare our results with those reported in the literature.

## 2   Classification of Images Through Boosting

In this Section we will present our method for learning a one-vs-one classifier. We will describe our feature extraction method as well as our preprocessing steps. Afterwards, we will give a short overview of the learning algorithm, and introduce an extension of the weak learner in order to manage geometric relations.

### 2.1   Feature Extraction

We use the scale invariant Harris-Laplace detector [15] to obtain regions of interest. From every region we extract four different feature types: scale invariant feature transforms (SIFTs) [14], sub-sampled grayvalues (see [17]), basic moments and moment invariants [11]. In addition to these descriptors, we use the segmentation method and the features of Fussenegger et al. [9]. For some feature types, we also normalize illumination by homomorphic filtering (see e.g. [10], Chap. 4.4.3). Furthermore, all features are normalized by whitening. Additionally, we obtain another feature type by reducing the SIFT-features to their 40 largest components using PCA, which accounts for their sparseness. Altogether, we use

**Table 1.** Feature types with preprocessing steps

| $\phi$ | feature type | intensity normal. | whitening | $m_\phi$ | $k_\phi$ |
|---|---|---|---|---|---|
| 1 | subsampled grayvalues | | x | 854 376 | 1 848 |
| 2 | | x | x | 854 376 | 1 848 |
| 3 | basic moments | | x | 852 755 | 1 846 |
| 4 | | x | x | 854 376 | 1 848 |
| 5 | moment invariants [11] | | x | 854 360 | 1 848 |
| 6 | | x | x | 854 313 | 1 848 |
| 7 | SIFTS [14] | | x | 809 063 | 1 798 |
| 8 | | | PCA 40 | 809 063 | 1 798 |
| 9 | segments [9] | | x | 690 070 | 1 661 |

nine different types of features $\phi$. In a second preprocessing step, we cluster the different features by k-means using $k_\phi = \lfloor 2\sqrt{m_\phi} \rfloor$ centers with a random initialization from the data, where $m_\phi$ denotes the number of features per type extracted from the database. Table 1 shows an overview of the calculated features.

## 2.2 LPBoost

We use a boosting approach since those algorithms are able to select important features from a large feature set. Instead of the common AdaBoost, we use LPBoost as the learning algorithm. One reason is that LPBoost has a well defined stopping criterion; learning is stopped if no further weak hypothesis will improve the value of the objective function for the current combination of weak hypotheses. Furthermore, AdaBoost is a hard margin classifier and therefore might overfit noisy data, whereas LPBoost is a soft margin classifier and handles noisy data well. The linear optimization problem in its primal formulation is:

$$
\begin{aligned}
\max_{\rho,a,\xi} \quad & \rho - D\sum_{n=1}^{m} \xi_i \\
\text{s.t.} \quad & y_i \sum_{t=1}^{T} \alpha_t h_t(x_n) + \xi_i \geq \rho \quad i = 1,\dots,m \\
& \sum_{t=1}^{T} \alpha_t = 1 \qquad\qquad \alpha_t \geq 0 \\
& \xi_i \geq 0 \qquad\qquad\quad i = 1,\dots,m
\end{aligned} \tag{1}
$$

and its dual is given by:

$$
\begin{aligned}
\min_{\beta,w} \quad & \beta \\
\text{s.t.} \quad & \sum_{i=1}^{m} y_i w_i h_t(x_i) \leq \beta \quad t = 1,\dots,T \\
& \sum_{i=1}^{m} w_i = 1 \qquad\qquad 0 \leq w_i \leq D
\end{aligned} \tag{2}
$$

Thus, the final decision function is simply:

$$
f(x_i) = sign\left( \sum_{t=1}^{T} \alpha_t h_t(x_i) \right) \in \{+1, -1\} \tag{3}
$$

Note that the parameter $D$ must be chosen carefully depending on the data set. An interpretation of the parameter and additional information can be found in Bennett et al. [1], Demiriz et al. [6] and Rätsch et al. [18].

## 2.3   Weak Learner

The weak learner is called in every boosting round and selects a hypothesis $h^*$ from the hypothesis space $\mathcal{H}$ which fulfills equation

$$\max_{h \in \mathcal{H}} \left( \sum_{i=1}^{m} h(x_i) y_i w_i \right) = \sum_{i=1}^{m} h^*(x_i) y_i w_i. \tag{4}$$

We implemented three different weak learners. The first and simplest one selects a reference feature of type $\phi$ with an optimal threshold according to the current boosting weights $\mathbf{w_t}$. The second and third weak learners search for geometric relations between distinctive features. Note computational complexity is twofold when building geometric relations based on relative position of the features and their number.

Since a full search over all possible geometric directions is a computationally time consuming process, we use rather simple geometric relations. More precisely, our geometric primitives use four geometric directions (up, down, left, right) relating up to three reference features. If an object category requires a geometric relation consisting of more than three features, our search algorithms build hierarchies of such geometric primitives modeled as trees. These relations are denoted as 'relations A' throughout this paper. Furthermore, we build more complex geometric relations to distinguish between more directions, i.e. we divide our primitives into eight sections and denote those as 'relations B'. Note that our geometric relations are invariant to translation and scale but not to rotation.

To speed up computation, our weak learners use a greedy search strategy to find geometric relations [Fig. 1]. In particular, we combine the previous hypotheses only with the selected hypothesis $h^*$ that has just one reference feature (see Fig. 1, Step 2a). This is reasonable due to (4). There might exist a better feature for a combined hypothesis $h_{and}$, but it would require a search through all features for every previous hypothesis to determine it. Nevertheless, we tested this search

---

1. Select a hypothesis $h^*$ using equation (4) and current boosting weights $\mathbf{w_t}$.
2. For all previously generated hypotheses $h_p$, $p = 1, \ldots, t-1$ do:
   (a) Create a hypothesis with a logical AND using the current simple weak hypothesis $\rightarrow h_{and} = h^*$ AND $h_p$.
   (b) The hypothesis $h_{and}$ is used for the geometric relations search. The two sub hypotheses from $h_{and}$ are applied on every image yielding two point sets. We seek a common geometric relation between these sets, yielding a geometric hypothesis $h_{geom}$.
3. The weak hypothesis finder compares the performance of the simple weak hypothesis $h^*$ and the geometric hypothesis $h_{geom}$ and outputs the hypothesis with the best performance.

**Fig. 1.** Greedy search strategy for the weak learner

strategy on a subset of the data. We create an optimal hypothesis $h_{and}$ for every previous hypothesis $h_p$ by selecting an additional hypothesis $h_{opt}$ with a reference feature, such that the hypothesis $h_{and}$ achieves the least possible weighted error. Since this approach gives comparable results at higher computational cost, we use the faster greedy strategy proposed [Fig. 1].

Within every boosting iteration, the weak learner either builds a simple or geometric hypothesis. During the incremental construction of the geometric hypotheses, various geometric sub hypotheses are generated. If such a sub hypothesis is useful with respect to the training set, LPBoost incorporates it into the final decision function by assigning a positive weight $\alpha_t$ to it; otherwise $\alpha_t$ will be set to zero. Hence, the final classifier can contain more than one geometric hypothesis per object. In consequence we do not have to flip input images to guarantee that the objects always face the same way (e.g. motorbikes, airplanes), but rather to ensure that there are sufficient examples for all the important orientations in the data set.

## 3    Multiclass Image Classification

Within our experiments for multiclass classification, we noticed low performance using one-vs-all and hierarchic classifiers. Considering the object categories of this database, it is likely that the extracted features are shared within different classes. Actually, Csurka et al. [5] do achieve good results learning feature histograms with a one-vs-all strategy. Nevertheless, feature histograms cannot exploit geometric relationships between the features contained in an image, although this might be discriminative information. Hence, we chose a one-vs-one strategy and combine our individual classifiers by a voting scheme.

Simple voting methods like majority voting using hard labels, not only ignore available information about the different degrees of confidence in the different classifiers, but also the classifier's confidence in its own prediction. Hence, a weighted voting scheme incorporating such information seems more reasonable.

An appropriate way to measure a classifier's confidence in its prediction is the signed distance

$$\delta(x_i) = \sum_{t=1}^{T} \alpha_t h_t(x_i), \tag{5}$$

with $\delta(x_i) \in [-1, 1]$, of a data point $x_i$ to the decision boundary. In this case, a great magnitude of $\delta(x_i)$ reflects high confidence in a prediction. Thus, for an $r$-class problem upon $m$ images $x_i$ ($i = 1, ..., m$), we denote the predictions of the $r \cdot (r - 1)$ different classifiers by

$$\mathbf{c}_i = (\delta_{1,2}(x_i), \delta_{2,1}(x_i), ..., \delta_{r-1,r}(x_i), \delta_{r,r-1}(x_i))^T$$
$$\in [-1, 1]^{r \cdot (r-1)} \tag{6}$$

Addressing the overall confidence in each classifier w.r.t. a certain class $l$, we try to find optimal weights $\mathbf{w}_l \in \mathbb{R}^{1 \times r \cdot (r-1)}$ with $l = 1, ..., r$ and some $\mathbf{b} \in \mathbb{R}^r$ such that the overall vote

$$l = \arg\max_{l'} \mathbf{w}_{l'} \cdot \mathbf{c}_i + b_{l'} \tag{7}$$

corresponds to the true class.

Hence, we formulate the following quadratic problem which gives a linear SVM:

$$\min \quad \| (\mathbf{w}_1, ..., \mathbf{w}_r) \|^2 + C \cdot \sum_i \xi_i$$

$$\begin{aligned}
s.t. \quad & \mathbf{w}_l \cdot \mathbf{c}_i + b_l \geq 1 - \xi_i, & l = class(x_i) \\
& -\mathbf{w}_l \cdot \mathbf{c}_i - b_l \geq 1 - \xi_i, & \forall l : l \neq class(x_i) \\
& \xi_i \geq 0 & i = 1, \dots, m, \\
& & l = 1, \dots, r
\end{aligned} \tag{8}$$

where, similar to (1), the amount of slackness over all predictions $\mathbf{c}_i$ is controlled by the parameter $C$.

## 4   Evaluation and Results

For our experiments we used the Xerox database consisting of 1774 real-world images from seven different categories. The categories are faces (790), buildings (150), trees (150), cars (201), phones (216), bikes (125) and books (142). The numbers in brackets indicate the number of images per category.

**Table 2.** Accuracy upon 10-fold cross-validation

| voting | geometry | parameter | mean | (std) |
|---|---|---|---|---|
| majority voting | none | – | 64.25 | (3.21) |
| majority voting | relations A | – | 74.78 | (2.92) |
| majority voting | relations B | – | 75.08 | (2.51) |
| [5] | – | – | 85 | n/a |
| SVM | none | $C = 0.2583$ | 90.60 | (2.06) |
| SVM | relations A | $C = 0.7622$ | 90.90 | (2.16) |
| SVM | relations B | $C = 0.1666$ | **91.28** | (2.28) |

Due to time restrictions we used a 50-50-split of the data in order to optimize the parameters of the learning algorithms, i.e. $D$ for LPBoost, and $C$ for the SVM. In every case, we apply a simple iterative search using nested intervals to obtain reliable estimates. Thus we are able to select the value yielding the lowest test error on the corresponding 50-50 split of the data. Finally, we fix those parameters, and conduct a stratified 10-fold cross-validation on the database [Tab. 2 - 3]. Note each one-vs-one classifier is learned over a reduced training and test set, including only the instances of the class combination. Fixing those hypotheses, we calculate their predictions over the instances from all classes and perform the weighted voting scheme proposed. For the SVM, we use SVMlight [12][1], where we also tried nonlinear kernels but omit their use on since those kernels performed poorer than the linear one.

---

[1] Available at http://svmlight.joachims.org/

**Table 3. (top)** Confusion matrix upon 10-fold cross validation using SVM and the more complex geometry 'relations B'. The true classes are denoted in the top row. **(bottom)** Histogram of the feature types $\phi$ selected by each one-vs-one classifier upon the 50-50-split for the non-geometric case. Thus, a column denotes different background classes. - lower-right: overall selection upon the 50-50-split for the non-geometric case.

| $\rightarrow$ | faces | buildings | trees | cars | phones | bikes | books |
|---|---|---|---|---|---|---|---|
| faces | 98.9873 | 0.6667 | 1.3333 | 8.4762 | 2.6455 | 0 | 0.7143 |
| bldgs | 0 | 70.6667 | 8.0000 | 0 | 0 | 2.8431 | 8.9286 |
| trees | 0 | 10.0000 | 87.3333 | 0 | 0 | 0.8333 | 1.4286 |
| cars | 0.5063 | 0 | 0.6667 | 84.0952 | 9.4180 | 0 | 0 |
| phones | 0.5063 | 0 | 0 | 7.4286 | 87.9365 | 0 | 0 |
| bikes | 0 | 2.6667 | 2.6667 | 0 | 0 | 94.6569 | 2.1429 |
| books | 0 | 16.0000 | 0 | 0 | 0 | 1.6667 | 86.7857 |

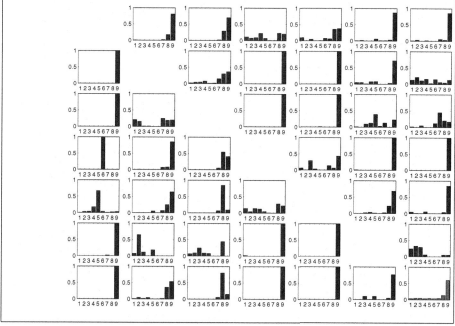

Furthermore, we analyzed the actual feature selection by the total weight assigned by LPBoost to the weak hypotheses of a certain feature type $\phi$ (3). Using the optimal parameters for the 50-50-split, it turned out that most one-vs-one classifiers select segments along with SIFTs (PCA40) for the non-geometric (basic) case [Tab. 3]. As shown in Table 3, we observed a strong correlation between the test error of a one-vs-one classifier and the number of different feature types within it's final hypothesis. If two categories are hard to classify, the

(a)          (b)          (c)

(d)          (e)          (f)

(g)          (h)          (i)

(j)      (k)      (l)      (m)

**Fig. 2.** Example images with voting location of selected weak hypotheses are taken from various one-vs-one classifiers. [Fig. 2(a) - 2(f)] are used for learning buildings against trees. Only the most important hypothesis and its matching feature locations are drawn. [Fig. 2(a) - 2(c)] show correctly classified examples, [Fig. 2(d) - 2(f)] show misclassified examples. [Fig. 2(g) - 2(i)] show three correct classified images using a geometric hypothesis learned from buildings vs books. [Fig. 2(j) - 2(m)] show examples for the geometric hypothesis for the class of faces and a simple hypothesis for phones.

learning algorithm will use more different feature types. This demonstrates the intrinsic flexibility of our method when dealing with difficult class combinations.

Figure 2 shows exemplary images along with weak hypotheses, used by the corresponding one-vs-one classifiers. All of them were taken from a single fold during cross-validation. In case of buildings vs. trees, our method selects only one simple SIFT (PCA40) feature for classification. The weak hypothesis is triggered particularly at window corners [Fig. 2(a) - 2(c)]. Figures 2(d) - 2(e) show false detections of that classifier. Both images belong to the class of trees since those are in the foreground. Although the buildings are in the background, our classifier detects the window corners, visible through and around the tree, and is still able to predict the building. On the other way around, Figure 2(f) gets misclassified as tree because there are no such corners visible. These examples show the difficulties in building an unambiguous database, and confirm the quality of our classifiers.

In that line of argument, one would expect that such a simple feature would be insufficient to distinguish buildings from books, since window corners are similar to those of books. Indeed, the weak hypothesis of highest weight is a geometric relation between two features. One feature represents a window corner and the other triggers on green fields. The second best weak hypothesis uses three features, and votes in the case where there is a hedgerow in front of a building [Fig. 2(g) - 2(i)]. This is reasonable considering that the class book only contains books on bookshelves or desktops, but no plants. Figures 2(j) and 2(k) belong to the class faces. The geometric hypothesis selected votes on triangle configurations of an ear, the hair line and the collar. Figures 2(l) and 2(m) show a weak hypothesis for the class of phones.

## 5  Conclusions and Outlook

In this paper we use a new method for learning geometric relations between features for image categorization through boosting. Our algorithm selects the important feature types, estimates the need of geometric models and learns such models if necessary. A final hypothesis can consist of several geometric hypotheses, that solves the multi-modal appearance problem of objects. We do not have to flip images, such that the target object always faces the same direction. We address the multiclass classification problem with a method for combining one-vs-one classifiers.

We found that learning without geometry already gives good performance, and that slight improvements are achieved by moving from simple to more complex geometric relations. An evaluation of the geometric hypotheses reveals that it is hard to find a relation with more than three features. Simple hypotheses using a single feature and pairwise relations dominate the final solution, which might be due to the rather small cardinality of some classes.

In the future, the framework may be extended with a detector stage. Also other types of geometric primitives within the weak learner are possible and should be tried out.

**Acknowledgments.** This work was supported by the European project LAVA (IST-2001-34405) and by the FSP/JRP Cognitive Vision of the Austrian Science Funds (FWF-JRP S9104-N04 SP4). This work was also supported in part by the IST program of the European Community, under the PASCAL Network of Excellence, IST-2002-506778. This publication only reflects the authors' views.

# References

1. Kristin P. Bennett, Ayhan Demiriz, and John Shawe-Taylor. A column generation algorithm for boosting. In *Proc. 17th International Conf. on Machine Learning*, pages 65–72. Morgan Kaufmann, San Francisco, CA, 2000.
2. M.C. Burl, T.K. Leung, and P. Perona. Recognition of planar object classes. In *Proceedings of the 1996 Conference on Computer Vision and Pattern Recognition (CVPR '96)*, pages 223–230. IEEE Computer Society, 1996.
3. Michael C. Burl, Markus Weber, and Pietro Perona. A probabilistic approach to object recognition using local photometry and global geometry. In *ECCV '98: Proceedings of the 5th European Conference on Computer Vision-Volume II*, volume 1407, pages 628–641. Springer-Verlag, 1998.
4. David Crandall, Pedro F. Felzenszwalb, and Daniel P. Huttenlocher. Spatial priors for part-based recognition using statistical models. In *CVPR (1)*, pages 10–17. IEEE Computer Society, 2005.
5. Gabriela Csurka, Cedric Bray, Christopher Dance, and Lixin Fan. Visual categorization with bags of keypoints. In *European Conference on Computer Vision, ECCV'04*, Prague, Czech Republic, May 2004.
6. Ayhan Demiriz, Kristin P. Bennett, and John Shawe-Taylor. Linear programming boosting via column generation. *Machine Learning*, 46(1-3):225–254, 2002.
7. R. Fergus, P. Perona, and A. Zisserman. Object class recognition by unsupervised scale-invariant learning. In *Proceedings of the IEEE Conference on Computer Vision and Pattern Recognition*, 2003.
8. Yoav Freund and Robert E. Schapire. A decision-theoretic generalization of on-line learning and an application to boosting. In *European Conference on Computational Learning Theory*, pages 23–37, 1995.
9. Michael Fussenegger, Andreas Opelt, Axel Pinz, and Peter Auer. Object recognition using segmentation for feature detection. In *ICPR (3)*, pages 41–44, 2004.
10. R. Gonzalez and R. Woods. *Digital Image Processing*. Addision-Wesley Publishing Company, Inc., 1992.
11. Luc J. Van Gool, Theo Moons, and Dorin Ungureanu. Affine/photometric invariants for planar intensity patterns. In *ECCV '96: Proceedings of the 4th European Conference on Computer Vision-Volume I*, pages 642–651. Springer-Verlag, 1996.
12. Thorsten Joachims. Making large-scale support vector machine learning practical. In *Advances in kernel methods: support vector learning*, pages 169–184. MIT Press, Cambridge, MA, USA, 1999.
13. Timor Kadir and Michael Brady. Saliency, scale and image description. *International Journal of Computer Vision*, 45(2):83–105, 2001.
14. D.G. Lowe. Object recognition from local scale-invariant features. In *Seventh International Conference on Computer Vision*, pages 1150–1157, 1999.
15. K. Mikolajczyk and C. Schmid. Indexing based on scale invariant interest points. In *International Conference on Computer Vision*, pages 525–531, 2001.

16. Andreas Opelt, Michael Fussenegger, Axel Pinz, and Peter Auer. Weak hypotheses and boosting for generic object detection and recognition. In *Proc. of the 8th European Conference on Computer Vision (ECCV)*, volume 2, pages 71–84, 2004.

17. Andreas Opelt, Michael Fussenegger, Axel Pinz, and Peter Auer. Generic object recognition with boosting. *IEEE Transactions on Pattern Analysis and Machine Intelligence*, 28(3):416–431, March 2006.

18. G. Rätsch, B. Schölkopf, A. Smola, K.-R. Müller, T. Onoda, and S. Mika. ν-Arc: Ensemble learning in the presence of outliers. In D.A. Cohn M.S. Kearns, S.A. Solla, editor, *Advances in Neural Information Processing Systems 12*. MIT Press, 2000.

19. Vladimir Vapnik. *The nature of statistical learning theory*. Springer, New York, 1995.

# An Eye Detection System
# Based on Neural Autoassociators

Monica Bianchini and Lorenzo Sarti

Dipartimento di Ingegneria dell'Informazione
Università degli Studi di Siena
Via Roma 56 — 53100 Siena, Italy

**Abstract.** Automatic eye tracking is a challenging task, with numerous applications in biometrics, security, intelligent human–computer interfaces, and driver's sleepiness detection systems. Eye localization and extraction is, therefore, the first step to the solution of such problems. In this paper, we present a new method, based on neural autoassociators, to solve the problem of detecting eyes from a facial image. A subset of the AR Database, collecting individuals both with or without glasses and with open or closed eyes, has been used for experiments and benchmarking. Preliminary experimental results are very promising and demonstrate the efficiency of the proposed eye localization system.

## 1 Introduction

Human face detection is often the first step in numerous applications, such as video surveillance, human–computer interface [1], face recognition, and image database management. Moreover, facial feature extraction, especially with frontal images, has a wide range of usage in automated face modelling, facial expression recognition, face animation, feature–based face recognition, and driver's sleepiness detection [2]. The problem of detecting human eyes has attracted a considerable interest in computer vision society. Many efforts have been addressed to capture the essential physical and emotional information from eyes. In intelligent vehicle systems, eye gaze and the motion of eye pupil provide important information for fatigue analysis [3]. In face detection and recognition systems, eyes can provide the richest identity information [4].

Many different approaches are reported in literature to address the problem of eye detection, based on some observations that could be made on the peculiarities of the "object" to be detected. For instance, since the pupils generally appear darker w.r.t. the surrounding regions, some algorithms search for local gray minima [5]. Techniques such as contrast enhancement and intensity thresholding are involved, in order to extract the dark regions. In [6], the eye regions are located based on an a priori knowledge on the facial feature arrangement (the hair region has the largest area in the binary image, the eyes are situated below the eyebrows, etc.). However, such algorithms are highly sensitive to the thresholding method used, as well as to the lighting conditions, i.e. the gray level information would be helpful in detecting several eye candidates, but it

F. Schwenker and S. Marinai (Eds.): ANNPR 2006, LNAI 4087, pp. 244–252, 2006.

may not be sufficient to filter out different facial features, such as eyebrows, which also appear as dark patches. Alternatively, an artificial template could be built, according to the rough shape of the eye and the eyebrow, such that the correlation coefficient between the template and the eye image can be calculated [7,8]. Hough transform was also employed [9], which implies a preliminary robust edge detection procedure. Finally, more recently, attention has been payed to Gabor wavelets techniques [10], where Gabor wavelet–based linear filters are used for eye corner detection, and non–linear (Gaussian) filters are used for iris detection. All the above mentioned methods belong to the class of feature–based approaches, whereas image–based techniques, like Principal Component Analysis (PCA), have also been applied [11]. Despite these efforts, robust, accurate, and non–intrusive eye detection and tracking remains largely an unsolved issue. The challenges result from eye closure, eye occlusion, variability in scale and face orientation, and different lighting conditions.

In this manuscript, when we refer to the eyes, we are considering not only the iris, but rather the collection of contours forming the pupil, iris, eyelids, eyelashes, eyebrows and the shading around the eye orbit. This general eye region is a larger and more dominant structure as a whole than its individual subcomponents. Therefore, it is more stable and easier to detect. Although the process of including the surrounding region improves robustness, it reduces accuracy since the contours of the eyebrows and eye orbit shading may have a center that does not coincide with the pupil's center.

The method proposed consists of three fundamental steps. First, a preprocessing phase, based on the application of the Sobel filters, is carried out on color images, in order to extract the principal contours [12]; then observing that the eyes exhibit strong transitions, because of the iris and the white part of the eye, the projections of horizontal and vertical transitions are evaluated [13]. Finally, both the projections are used to train two specialized neural autoassociators.

The paper is organized as follows. In the following section, the feature extraction method is described, whereas Section 3 briefly sketches some salient properties of the neural autoassociators used for detecting the eyes. In Section 4, preliminary but promising results are reported, whereas Section 5 collects some conclusions.

## 2    Feature Extraction

The proposed eye detection technique is based on neural autoassociators and on gradient features extracted from the images. The eyes possess strong horizontal and vertical edges [14], therefore the exploitation of gradient features is particularly suited to represent the image content.

In order to determine the gradient transitions, both the Sobel operators [12] are applied to the input image to determine vertical and horizontal edges. Then, the horizontal and vertical projections are computed summing the rows and the columns of the filtered image, respectively (see Fig. 1).

In [13], a thresholding technique is proposed to analyze the projections and to localize the eyes. Unfortunately, this method can fail when the image presents

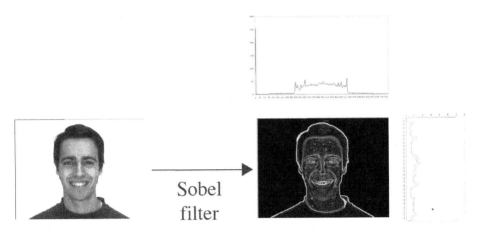

**Fig. 1.** The image is processed using the Sobel operators, then the horizontal and vertical projections are extracted

sharp gradient transitions, for instance, for open mouth faces or in presence of glasses. To overcome such problems, the method proposed in this paper employs two neural autoassociators (one for each projection). For the sake of simplicity, the procedure will be described w.r.t. the horizontal projections, since, as a matter of fact, the vertical projections are managed in the same way.

The horizontal projections are scanned from the top to the bottom of the input image, using a moving window. Initially, the window position corresponds to the top of the image and then it moves down pixel by pixel. For each window position, a vector of integer features, that collects both the window position and the values of the projections that lie behind the window, is created. Therefore, each input vector is an $n + 2$ array of integers, $\mathbf{x} = (a, b, x_1, x_2, \ldots, x_n)$, where $n$ is the window dimension in rows, $a$ and $b$ represent the indexes of the rows that delimit the window, and each $x_i$ counts the number of white pixels in the $i$–th row inside the window. In order to train the neural autoassociator, a target, that assesses if the window position corresponds to the eye area or to a part of it, is associated to each feature vector. A target equal to 1 corresponds to a feature vector that represents a part of the eye area, while a value equal to 0 is associated to the feature vectors that do not belong to the eye area, i.e. if the window intersects the eye area but it is not completely included, then the associated target is posed to 0. Obviously, the window width must be smaller than the eye area, in order to have a set of vectors corresponding to such area. Moreover, the target association is performed knowing the position of the eyes in the training images (the associated ground–truth information is needed).

In order to train the neural autoassociators, a set of training images must be chosen. For each image, two sets of feature vectors, corresponding to horizontal and vertical projections, are extracted and the relative targets are associated. Thus, the autoassociator which deals with the horizontal projections is specialized to locate the vertical position of the eyes, while the other one performs the horizontal localization.

An eye localization system can exploit the trained autoassociators as follows:

- The system is fed with an input image, on which the Sobel operators are applied to compute the gradient transitions, and hence to determine the horizontal and vertical projections;
- Using the moving window technique, two sets of feature vectors are extracted, considering both the horizontal and the vertical projections;
- Each neural autoassociator processes its set of feature vectors and predicts, for each vector, if the associated window position corresponds to a part of the eye area;
- Finally, adjacent window positions predicted as eye locations are merged together to determine the bounding boxes that correspond to the eyes.

The localization system is able to determine the correct position of the eyes if the input and the training images meet the following constraints. First, we need to process facial images, depicted in foreground. Then, persons must appear in a frontal view and only a small inclination of each face is allowed. Finally, each image must possess an uniform background. Nevertheless, the last constraint can be overcome by integrating the system with a preprocessing module for face localization. In fact, face localization allows to reduce the noise represented by the background. Many methods proposed in the past exploit skin–color filters to localize faces. As a matter of fact, the human skin colors range in a relative small region, independently of the particular color space chosen to represent the images [15]. Unfortunately, the performances of skin–color filters deeply depend on the light conditions and on the ethnic group of the depicted persons. In order to overcome such limitations, appearance–based methods, able to infer face models using machine learning techniques, are preferable [16,17].

# 3  Eye Detection Using Autoassociators

Autoassociators are a special kind of neural networks which, by learning to reproduce a given set of patterns, grasp the underlying concept that is useful for pattern classification. The number of inputs and outputs in autoassociators corresponds to the dimension of the input space, whereas a smaller number of units forms the hidden layer. Each autoassociator is trained to reconstruct an input $\mathbf{x}$ at the output $\mathbf{t}$, and its parameters are optimized to minimize the Euclidean distance $||\mathbf{x} - \mathbf{t}||^2$. To achieve an accurate reconstruction, the autoassociator is implicitly forced to discover an appropriate nonlinear mapping of the original input space into a smaller space that captures the properties of the underlying distribution.

Autoassociators are generally used as one–class learning machines. In other words, each network corresponds to a particular category and, during training, it receives only the samples within the category. An important consequence is that the network will learn to accurately reproduce positive samples (those in the corresponding class), producing a prototype for that class. Thus, autoassociators

provide an alternative approach to concept learning. In particular, the higher
the reproduction quality for an input pattern, the more likely it belongs to the
category for which the autoassociator is constructed. Moreover, the specialization
of each autoassociator to a particular class may be reinforced by training each
network also on negative examples and forcing the prototype to be as far as
possible from patterns outside the proper class.

In this paper we use two autoassociators, one for each set of projections, with
sigmoid hidden neurons and linear output units. In [18], such architectures are
proved to realize a sort of clustering in the input space. Moreover, an end–of–
learning condition was stated, assessing that, at the end of the learning process,
an equality relation holds between the output correlation matrix $\mathbf{X}_2'\mathbf{X}_2$ and the
input/output correlation matrix $\mathbf{X}_2'\mathbf{X}_0$, with $\mathbf{X}_0$ and $\mathbf{X}_2$ collecting (by row)
all the training examples and the related outputs, respectively. From the geo-
metrical point of view, such an equality may be interpreted as a loss of energy
spent in the association process, which is higher when the autoassociator is not
able to perfectly reproduce the presented target at the output (i.e. the hidden
compressed representation is not sufficient to hold all the information needed to
reconstruct the pattern).

The standard Backpropagation algorithm, with adaptive learning rate, was
used for training, based on two different error functions related to patterns belonging or not to the class represented by the autoassociator. In fact, for positive
patterns the quadratic error is minimized, whereas the error function for negative
examples is based on the inverse distance:

$$E_p = \sum_{t \in C} ||\mathbf{X}_2(t) - \mathbf{X}_0(t)||^2,$$

$$E_n = \sum_{t \notin C} \frac{1}{||\mathbf{X}_2(t) - \mathbf{X}_0(t)||^2 + \varepsilon},$$

where $\varepsilon$, which can be chosen proportional to the machine precision, was introduced for guaranteeing numerical stability. The connection weights are then

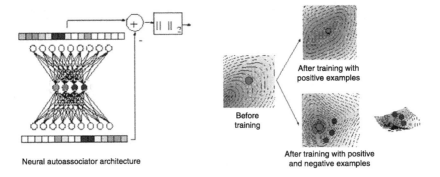

Neural autoassociator architecture

Before training

After training with positive examples

After training with positive and negative examples

**Fig. 2.** Changes on the error surface due to training with positive or positive/negative
patterns

updated based on the joint contributions of $E_p$ and $E_n$. The effects of the introduction of negative examples in the training set consist in focusing the autoassociator on the class is devoted to represent, so that it creates a prototype for that class which is as far as possible from examples belonging to other classes (see Fig. 2). Finally, an *ad hoc* threshold must be chosen to establish whether each pattern belongs or not to a particular class, i.e. is properly represented by the prototype produced by the corresponding autoassociator. Such a threshold could assume different values for different classes, due to the distribution of the input patterns, and is generally computed via a trial–and–error procedure.

## 4   Experimental Results

In order to evaluate the effectiveness of the proposed technique, some experiments were carried out using a subset of the AR Database [19]. This dataset collects 4000 color images corresponding to 126 individuals (70 men and 56 women). The images represent frontal view faces with different facial expressions, illumination conditions, and occlusions, obtained with sunglasses or scarfs (see Figure 3).

**Fig. 3.** Samples of images from the AR database

Our subset collects 210 images randomly chosen from the original database (faces occluded by sunglasses were excluded). The images were subsequently divided into two sets that collect the same number of images: the training and the test sets. Each image was represented as described in Section 2. The reported results are referred to a window width equal to 10 rows/columns of pixels, for horizontal and vertical projections. However, the performances of the system are not particularly affected by this parameter when the window dimension is smaller than the average eye width (height). For each image, 566 vectors represent the horizontal projections, and 758 vectors describe the vertical projections. The percentage of negative examples (vectors extracted using a window position that corresponds to the eye location) is equal, on average, to 2.47% and to

**Table 1.** Equal error rates obtained by the localization system, varying the number of hidden units. The classification thresholds are reported in brackets.

| Architecture | Horizontal projections | Vertical projections |
|---|---|---|
| 6 hidden | 90.02% (0.135) | 91.04 (0.68) % |
| 7 hidden | 90.85% (0.21) | 91.84% (0.73) |
| 8 hidden | 90.05% (0.115) | 88.23% (0.735) |

**Table 2.** Effects of the classification threshold choice. The results were obtained using a neural autoassociator with 7 hidden units.

| Horizontal projections | | |
|---|---|---|
| Classification threshold | Non eye area Accuracy | Eye area Accuracy | Global Accuracy |
| 0.2 | 90.54% | 91.22% | 90.55% |
| 0.15 | 88.91% | 94.62% | 89.05% |
| 0.1 | 86.42% | 97.48% | 86.7% |
| Vertical projections | | |
| Classification threshold | Non eye area Accuracy | Eye area Accuracy | Global Accuracy |
| 0.65 | 90.32% | 92.32% | 90.55% |
| 0.6 | 89.15% | 93.84% | 89.7% |
| 0.55 | 87.93% | 94.99% | 88.75% |

11.61% considering the horizontal and vertical projections, respectively. Several training runs were performed to determine the best autoassociator architectures. The obtained results are summarized in the following tables. Table 1 reports the equal error rates of the neural autoassociators, varying the number of hidden units. The equal error rate is defined as the accuracy of the system when the number of errors in the two classes is equal. Practically, the sensitivity of the system can be chosen varying the classification threshold. When decreasing the classification thresholds, the neural autoassociators increase their ability to localize the eyes. In Table 2, the accuracy rates obtained varying the classification thresholds are reported, showing that the decrease of such parameters does not drastically deteriorate the performances of the whole system, whereas the percentage of negative examples correctly autoassociated (i.e. the percentage of eye localizations) grows significantly. In fact, in eye detection systems, a high recall is generally preferable w.r.t. a high precision and, thus, the choice of a threshold smaller than that able to obtain the equal error rate should be advisable.

## 5   Conclusions

In this paper, an eye localization system is proposed, based on autoassociators, which are trained on horizontal and vertical projections obtained by color images after the application of the Sobel operators. The preliminary experimentation, carried out on a subset of the AR Database, shows very promising results, allowing a best global accuracy of 91.84% for vertical projections, with a recall on the negative examples (i.e. those identifying the eye area) of 95%, whereas 90.85% and 97.48% are the best accuracy and recall for horizontal localization, respectively. It is a matter of future work varying the dimension of the window used for scanning the images, both horizontally and vertically, and trying to collect more informative features (like the area and/or an approximation of the shape of the projections) into the vectors used to train the autoassociators.

# References

1. D. Ward and D. McKay, "Fast hands–free writing by gaze direction," *Nature*, vol. 418, no. 6900, p. 838, 2002.
2. M. Eriksson and N. Papanikotopoulos, "Eye tracking for detection of driver fatigue," in *Proceedings of IEEE Int. Conf. on Intelligent Transportation Systems*, pp. 314–319, IEEE, 1997.
3. Q. Ji and X. Yang, "Real–time eye, gaze, and face pose tracking for monitoring driver vigilance," *Real–Time Imaging*, vol. 8, no. 5, pp. 357–377, 2002.
4. R.-L. Hsu, M. Abdel-Mottaleb, and A. K. Jain, "Face detection in color images," *IEEE Transactions on Pattern Analysis and Machine Intelligence*, vol. 24, no. 5, pp. 696–706, 2002.
5. M. Rizon and T. Kawaguchi, "Automatic eye detection using intensity and edge information," in *Proceedings IEEE TENCON*, vol. 2, pp. 415–420, IEEE, 2000.
6. L. Zhang and P. Lenders, "Knowledge–based eye detection for human face recognition," in *Proceedings of the 4^{th} Int. Conf. on Knowledge–based Intelligent Systems & Allied Technologies*, pp. 117–120, IEEE, 2000.
7. M. Betke and W. Mullay, "Preliminary investigation of real–time monitoring of a driver in city traffic," in *Proceedings of IEEE Intelligent Vehicles Symposium*, IEEE, 2000.
8. S. A. Suandi, S. Enokida, and T. Ejima, "An extended template matching technique for tracking eyes and mouth in real–time," in *Proceedings of Visualization, Imaging and Image Processing*, pp. 586–591, 2003.
9. T. Kawaguchi, D. Hidaka, and M. Rizon, "Detection of eyes from human faces by Hough transform and separability filter," in *Proceedings of Int. Conf. on Image Processing*, pp. 49–52, 2000.
10. S. Sirohey and A. Rosenfeld, "Eye detection in a face image using linear and nonlinear filters," *Pattern Recognition*, vol. 34, pp. 1367–1391, 2001.
11. M. Turk and A. Pentland, "Face recognition using eigenfaces," in *Proceedings IEEE Int. Conf. on Computer Vision and Pattern Recognition*, pp. 586–591, IEEE, 1991.
12. R. Gonzalez and R. Woods, *Digital Image Processing*. Addison Wesley, 1992.
13. X. Deng, C.-H. Chang, and E. Brandle, "A new method for eye extraction from facial image," in *Proceedings of IEEE DELTA*, IEEE, 2004.
14. D. Maio and D. Maltoni, "Real–time face location on gray–scale static images," *Pattern Recognition*, vol. 33, pp. 1525–1539, 2000.
15. J. Yang, W. Lu, and A. Waibel, "Skin–color modeling and adaptation," in *Proceedings of ACCV'98*, vol. 2, pp. 687–694, 1998.
16. M. Bianchini, M. Maggini, L. Sarti, and F. Scarselli, "Recursive neural networks learn to localize faces," *Pattern Recognition Letters*, vol. 26, pp. 1885–1895, 2005.

17. A. Carleson, C. Cumby, J. Rosen, and D. Roth, "The SNoW learning architecture," Tech. Rep. UIUCDCS–R–99–2101, University of Illinois at Urbana–Campaign Computer Science Department, 1999.

18. M. Bianchini, P. Frasconi, and M. Gori, "Learning in multilayered networks used as autoassociators," *IEEE Transactions on Neural Networks*, vol. 6, no. 2, pp. 512–515, 1995.

19. A. Martinez and R. Benavente, "The AR face database," Tech. Rep. 24, CVC Technical Report, 1998.

# Orientation Histograms for Face Recognition

Friedhelm Schwenker, Andreas Sachs, Günther Palm, and Hans A. Kestler

University of Ulm
Department of Neural Information Processing
D-89069 Ulm
`firstname.lastname@uni-ulm.de`

**Abstract.** In this paper we present a method to recognize human faces based on histograms of local orientation. Orientation histograms were used as input feature vectors for a k-nearest neigbour classifier. We present a method to calculate orientation histograms of $n \times n$ subimages partitioning the 2D-camera image with the segmented face. Numerical experiments have been made utilizing the Olivetti Research Laboratory (ORL) database containing 400 images of 40 subjects. Remarkable recognition rates of 98% to 99% were achieved with this extremely simple approach.

**Keywords:** Orientation histograms, Face recognition.

## 1   Introduction

Recognizing people in daily life is typically an effortless and unconscious task. The ease with which humans process such visual data leads to an underestimation of the complexity of this data processing. The identification of a human face poses several tests for any visual classifier system, for instance the high degree of similarity between faces from different persons, the influence to which lighting conditions can alter the 2D camara image of the face, or the large number of different views from which a face can be seen. In addition, there are many other influences on the facial appearance which may change from day to day, such as aging or makeup. For a robust real-life face recognition system all these problems have to be taken into account. In general a real world face recognition task requires the combination of at least three different pattern recognition tasks:

1. Tracking individuals moving around in the room
2. Detection and localization their faces
3. Recognition of the segmented faces

We concentrate on the third problem—recognizing faces of individuals. Over the last ten years, face recognition has become a special application area of computer vision, see for instance [13] for a survey. Sophisticated commercial systems perform face detection, image registration, and image recognition in real time. Many methods have been proposed for face recognition [13]. Basically they can be divided into template matching based systems and geometrical local

F. Schwenker and S. Marinai (Eds.): ANNPR 2006, LNAI 4087, pp. 253–259, 2006.

feature based systems. Typically, these systems perform the recognition task in two steps. First extracting characteristic features utilizing adaptive filters from the segmented camera image, and second classifying the feature vectors through a trainable classifier [6, 11].

In this paper we propose a method to recognize human faces based on histograms of local orientation. These, so-called orientation histograms are then used as input feature vectors for a nearest neigbour classifier. Orientation histograms of images are very simple and fast to compute, so that real-time versions of this technique may be implemented. We present a method to calculate orientation histograms of $n \times n$ subimages of the camera image. Histogram techniques, particularly orientation histogramms, have successfully been applied to different visual 3D object recognition problems such as gesture recognition [12, 10, 7], and optical character recognition [9, 2].

Numerical experiments are made with the Olivetti Research Laboratory (ORL) database containing 400 images ofsubjects.

The paper is organized as follows: In Section 2 the ORL database is described. The orientation histogram technique is introduced in Section 3, the numerical experiments are presented in Section 4. Conclusions are given in Section 5.

## 2   Dataset

For the numerical evaluation the ORL database from the Olivetti Research Laboratory has been used. This database is available free of charge (see URL http://www.cl.cam.ac.uk/Research/DTG/attarchive/facedatabase.html). Images of 40 distinct subjects with 10 recordings per person were taken. For a subsample of this database (one image per person) see Figure 1.

**Fig. 1.** A subsample of 40 images from the Olivetti Research Laboratory database. For each subject a single image is shown. The whole database consists of 10 images for each person. The images are gray scale images (8 bit) with a resolution of $92 \times 112$ pixels.

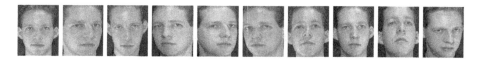

**Fig. 2.** Ten camera images taken from the same person showing the image variation within a class

The images show a variety of variations in facial expression (open/closed eyes) and facial details (glasses/no glasses). All these images were taken in front of a dark homogeneous background with the subjects in an up-right, frontal position. Images are grayscale images (8-bit) with a resolution of $92 \times 112$ pixel (see, [8] for further details on this database). To show the variation a subsample of 10 images taken from the same individual is given in Figure 2.

## 3   Calculation of Orientation Histograms

We now consider the problem of extracting orientation histogram features from camera images. Orientation histograms were introduced by Roth and Freeman to the literature of visual based pattern recognition by their use for hand gesture recognition [12]. In this paper we propose to calculate orientation histograms on subimages. In the first step of this approach the whole image is divided into $n \times n$ sub-images, in Figure 3 the situation of a $2 \times 2$ partitioning with non-overlapping sub-images is illustrated.

For each of these $n^2$ sub-image the orientation histogram of $m$ different directions (range: $0 - 2\pi$, dark/light edges) is calculated [12] from the gray valued image. The orientation histograms of all sub-images are concatenated into the

**A**                                **B**                                **C**

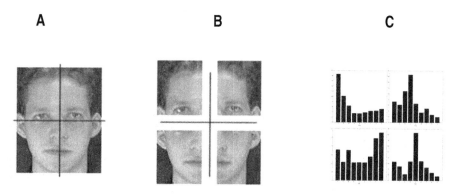

**Fig. 3.** Feature extraction process: The given camera image (A) is divided into overlapping or non-overlapping subimages (B). Then the orientation histograms within each of the $n^2$ subimages are calculated (C). The orientation of dark/light edges are quantized into a predefined number of $m$ bins. The feature extraction procedure leads to feature vectors consisting of $mn^2$ entries. These feature vectors serve as inputs into the classifier.

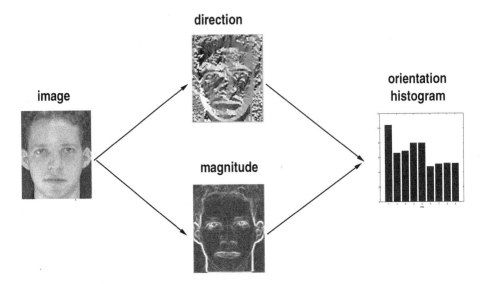

**Fig. 4.** Calculation of the orientation histogram (here with $m = 10$ bins) of a gray scaled camera image. Local orientations are calculated and cummulated into the histogram. Entries in the histogram are determined through counting the number of angles falling into the respective bin.

characterizing feature vector which is the input to a classifier, e.g. a k-nearest-neighbour classifier, artificial neural network based classifier, or decision tree.

For the calculation of the orientation histogram the gradient of an image $f(x, y)$ at location $(x, y)$ is given through the two dimensional vector

$$\begin{pmatrix} G_x \\ G_y \end{pmatrix} = \begin{pmatrix} \frac{\partial f}{\partial x} \\ \frac{\partial f}{\partial y} \end{pmatrix} \approx \begin{pmatrix} f * S_x \\ f * S_y \end{pmatrix}$$

(here $*$ denotes the convolution operation). Gradient directions $(S_x, S_y)$ were then calculated through $3 \times 3$ Sobel operators. The gradient directions are calculated with respect to the $x$-axis:

$$\alpha(x, y) = \text{atan2}\,(f * S_y, f * S_x)$$

The *atan2* function corresponds to the *atan* but additionally uses the sign of the arguments to determine the quadrant of the result [4, 5]. The $m$ bins of the histogram all have equal size $2\pi/m$. The histogram values are calculated by counting the number of angles falling into the respective bin. Histograms are normalized to the size of their sub-images. Figure 4 gives an overview.

## 4   Numerical Experiments

Our goal in this paper is not to develop elaborated machine learning techniques but to evaluate a feature extraction method for face recognition. Therefore, the nearest neighbour classifier has been used in our numerical evaluation which is the most elegant and most simple classifier [1].

Because we have to deal with a rather limited data set we utilized the cross-validation method [3] to evaluate the proposed feature extraction methods. In the $k$-fold cross-validation testing procedure the data set is divided into $k$ disjoint subsets without considering image class. Then the 1-NN-classifier is determined $k$ times, each time using a version of the data set omitting exactly one of the $k$ subsets. The omitted subset is then used to test the 1-NN-classifier. Finally the achieved classification results are averaged over all $r$ classifier tests (generating the partitions randomly for each test). In Tables 1, 2, 3, and 4 the

**Table 1.** Recognition rates for the orientation histogram method calculated on the whole camera image, i.e. $n = 1$. Results are shown for orientation quantization of $m = 4, 8, 16, 32, 64$ bins per circle $[0, 2\pi)$. Means and standard deviation are given for 20 runs of ten-fold cross-validation experiments for the ORL database.

| $m = 4$ | $m = 8$ | $m = 16$ | $m = 32$ | $m = 64$ |
|---|---|---|---|---|
| 0.479 (0.012) | 0.847 (0.010) | 0.929 (0.005) | 0.950 (0.005) | 0.940 (0.006) |

**Table 2.** Classification accuracies of the orientation histogram method calculated on the ORL database. Means and standard deviation are given for 20 runs of ten-fold crossvalidation experiments.

| | $m = 8$ | $m = 16$ | $m = 32$ |
|---|---|---|---|
| $2 \times 2$ | 0.979 (0.004) | 0.985 (0.004) | 0.982 (0.005) |
| $3 \times 3$ | 0.976 (0.004) | 0.984 (0.003) | 0.983 (0.002) |

**Table 3.** Recognition rates for the orientation histogram method with $2 \times 2$ and $3 \times 3$ subimages. The overlap between neighbouring subimages was $o = 0.25$. Means and standard deviations calculated for 20 runs of a 10-fold crossvalidation experiment on the ORL database.

| | $m = 8$ | $m = 16$ | $m = 32$ |
|---|---|---|---|
| $2 \times 2$ | 0.971 (0.005) | 0.974 (0.006) | 0.976 (0.006) |
| $3 \times 3$ | 0.980 (0.005) | 0.985 (0.003) | 0.987 (0.002) |

**Table 4.** Recognition rates for the orientation histogram method with $2 \times 2$ and $3 \times 3$ subimages. The overlap between neighbouring subimages was $o = 0.5$. Means and standard deviations calculated for 20 runs of a 10-fold crossvalidation experiment on the ORL database.

| | $m = 8$ | $m = 16$ | $m = 32$ |
|---|---|---|---|
| $2 \times 2$ | 0.964 (0.007) | 0.968 (0.004) | 0.974 (0.006) |
| $3 \times 3$ | 0.979 (0.004) | 0.990 (0.004) | 0.983 (0.006) |

calculated means of the $r = 20$ *ten*-fold cross-validation testings on the ORL database are given.

In the first series of experiments the orientation hiostograms have been determinted from the whole camera image for a quantization of $m = 4, 8, 16, 32, 64$ bins, see Figure 4. At the first sight, the recognition rate increases with increasing number of orientation bins. We found a maximal recognition rate of 95% for a resolution of $m = 32$ bins.

The second series of experiments is to investigate the influence of the sub-image partitioning. Images were divided into $n \times n$ non-overlaping subimages, again with different quantization levels for orientation. Results of our numerical experiments for the sub-image approach dividing the image into $n \times n$ sub-images with $n = 2, 3$ and with o resolution in the range for $m = 8$ to $m = 32$ histogram bins are given in Table 2. The accuracy for each parameter combination is $> 97\,\%$ this significantly higher as for the basic approach. In the next step overlapping sub-images were considered and results for two different degrees of overlap, $o = 0.25$ and $o = 0.5$, are presented in Table 3 and 4, $o = \alpha$ stands for the overlap of neigbouring sub-images. We found approximately the same recognition rates as for non-overlapping sub-images, but at least for some parameter combinations the performance was slightly improved, and we achieved the best result (error rate 1%) for $3 \times 3$ sub-images with a resolution of $m = 16$ orientation histogram bins and an overlap degree of $o = 1/2$.

## 5   Conclusion

In this paper we have applied the very simple method of orientation histograms to the problem of face recognition. For camera images of human faces the histograms of local orientations were calculated on $n \times n$ subimages. These extracted feature vectors were then concatenated and used as the input vectors of nearest neighbour classifiers. Remarkable recognition rates of 98% to 99% were achieved with this extremely simple approach and compare very well to the 3.8% error rate reported by Lawrence et.al. [8] on the same data. They used more complex classifiers based on convolution neural networks with features derived from the whole image rather then the sub-image approach we applied. This lets us conclude that image pre-processing and feature extraction are extremely important in face recognition and that our method of orientation histograms of sub-images seems feasible in this setting.

## References

1. Richard O. Duda, Peter E. Hart, and David G. Stork. *Pattern Classification*. John Wiley & Sons, New York, 2001.
2. H. Fujisawa and C.-L. Liu. Directional pattern matching for character recognition revisited. In *Proc. of the 7th ICDAR*, pages 794–798, 2003.
3. K. Fukunaga. *Introduction to Statistical Pattern Recognition*. Academic Press, 1991.

4. P. Haberäcker. *Practical Handbook of Image Processing for Scientific Applications.* Hanser-Verlag, 1995.
5. B. Jähne. *Practical Handbook of Image Processing for Scientific Applications.* CRC Press, 1997.
6. K. Jonsson, J. Kittler, Y. Li, and J. Matas. Support vector machines for face authentication. In T. Pridmore and D. Elliman, editors, *Proceedings of the BMVC'99*, pages 543– 553, 1999.
7. H.A. Kestler, S. Simon, A. Baune, F. Schwenker, and G. Palm. Object Classification Using Simple, Colour Based Visual Attention and a Hierarchical Neural Network for Neuro–Symbolic Integration. In W. Burgard, T. Christaller, and A.B. Cremers, editors, *KI–99: Advances in Artificial Intelligence*, pages 267–279. Springer Verlag, 1999.
8. Steve Lawrence, C. Lee Giles, A. C. Tsoi, and A. D. Back. Face recognition: A convolutional neural network approach. *IEEE Transactions on Neural Networks*, 8(1):98–113, 1997.
9. C.-L. Liu, K. Nakashima, H. Sako, and H. Fujisawa. Handwritten digit recognition: benchmarking of state-of-the-art techniques. *Pattern Recognition*, 36(10):2271– 2285, 2003.
10. B. Mel. Seemore: Combining colour, shape, and texture histogramming in a neurally-inspired approach to visual object recognition. *Neural Computation*, 9:777–804, 1997.
11. C. Nakajima, M. Pontil, B. Heisele, and T. Poggio. People recognition in image sequences by supervised learning. Technical report 1633/CBCL Memo No.133, MIT AI, 2000.
12. M. Roth and W.T. Freeman. Orientation histograms for hand gesture recognition. Technical Report 94-03, Mitsubishi Electric Research Laboratorys, Cambridge Research Center, 1995.
13. W. Zhao, R. Chellappa, P.J. Phillips, and A. Rosenfeld. Face recognition: a literature survey. *ACM Computing Surveys*, 35(4):399–458, 2003.

# An Empirical Comparison of Feature Reduction Methods in the Context of Microarray Data Classification

Hans A. Kestler[1,2] and Christoph Müssel[2]

[1] Department of Neural Information Processing, University of Ulm,
89069 Ulm, Germany
hans.kestler@uni-ulm.de

[2] Department of Internal Medicine I, University Hospital Ulm,
Robert-Koch-Str. 8, 89081 Ulm, Germany
christoph.muessel@uni-ulm.de

**Abstract.** The differentiation between cancerous and benign processes in the body often poses a difficult diagnostic problem in the clinical setting while being of major importance for the treatment of patients. Measuring the expression of a large number of genes with DNA microarrays may serve this purpose. While the expression level of several thousands of genes can be measured in a single experiment, only a few dozens of experiments are normally carried out, leading to data sets of very high dimensionality and low cardinality. In this situation, feature reduction techniques capable of reducing the dimensionality of data are essential for building predictive tools based on classification.

*Methods and Data:* We compare the popular feature selection and classification method PAM (Tibshirani et al.) to several other methods. Feature reduction and feature ranking methods, such as Random Projection, Random Feature Selection, Area under the ROC curve and PCA are applied. We employ these together with the classification component of PAM, Linear Discriminant Analysis (LDA), a Nearest Prototype (NP) classifier and linear support vector machines (SVMs). We apply these methods to three publicly available linearly separable gene expression data sets of varying cardinality and dimensionality.

*Results and Conclusions:* In our experiments with the gene expression data we could not discover a clearly superior algorithm, instead most surprisingly we found that feature reduction using random projections or selections performed often equally well.

## 1 Background

The differentiation between cancerous and benign (non-cancerous) processes in the body often poses a difficult diagnostic problem in the clinical setting while being of major importance for the treatment of patients. Since cancer development is thought to be caused by the accumulation of complex genetic alterations in the affected cells and tissues, the differentiation of cancerous vs. non-cancerous

F. Schwenker and S. Marinai (Eds.): ANNPR 2006, LNAI 4087, pp. 260–273, 2006.

clinical samples is an important application –together with feature reduction methods– for the interpretation of DNA array data. Gene expression data have two dimensions, genes on one side, and measurements on the other side. While the expression level of several thousands of genes can be measured in a single experiment, only a few dozens of experiments are normally carried out, leading to data sets of very high dimensionality and low cardinality. In this situation, feature reduction techniques capable of reducing the dimensionality of data are essential for building predictive tools based on classification. It is thought that only a small fraction of the features are needed for classification, while most of the features are not only irrelevant, but may even disturb the classification. This poses the problem of reducing the feature set. The feature reduction methods can be divided into two classes: Transformation methods, which project the original feature space into a lower-dimensional space, and feature selection methods, which choose a subset of the original features. The former have the advantage of not throwing away any features completely, whereas the latter provide results that can be interpreted more easily. One popular feature selection method is the use of shrunken centroids proposed by Tibshirani et al. [1, 2], which is also known as Prediction Analysis for Microarrays (PAM).

We compare the popular feature selection and classification method PAM [1,2] to several other methods. Feature reduction and feature ranking procedures, such as Random Projection, Random Feature Selection, Area under the ROC curve and PCA are applied [3, 4, 5]. We employ these together with the classification component of PAM, Linear Discriminant Analysis (LDA), a Nearest Prototype (NP) classifier and linear support vector machines (SVMs) [4, 6].

## 2   Methods

This section consists of a brief description of the used feature reduction and classification methods (for details see the cited references and any standard text such as Duda&Hart or Webb [4,5]), and the employed gene expression data sets and testing procedures.

### 2.1   Feature Reduction Methods

**Prediction Analysis for Microarrays** (PAM) was described by Tibshirani et al. in [1, 2]. The PAM algorithm performs both feature reduction and classification. PAM chooses class representatives (prototypes, centroids) for every feature and moves (shrinks) them towards the overall centroid (not taking into account any class information) of that particular feature using a fixed threshold value. Whenever a class centroid has zero distance to the feature centroid, it does not play a role in the classification any more and can be discarded. If all class centroids in a feature have been discarded, the feature itself is removed. PAM uses exactly one representative vector per class. The components of the representatives are the centroids of the class samples in each feature.

With samples $j = 1, \ldots, n$, classes $1, \ldots, K$ and $i = 1, \ldots, p$ features/genes, the initial $i$th component of the centroid of class $k$ is $\overline{x}_{ik} = \sum_{j \in C_k} \frac{x_{ij}}{n_k}$, where

$C_k$ are the indices of the samples in class $k$. The $i$th component of the overall centroid of feature $i$ is $\bar{x}_i = \sum_{j=1}^{n} \frac{x_{ij}}{n}$.

The standardized distance between the class centroid and the overall centroid in feature $i$ is

$$d_{ik} = \frac{\bar{x}_{ik} - \bar{x}_i}{m_k \cdot (s_i + s_0)}$$

where

$$s_i^2 = \frac{1}{n-K} \sum_k \sum_{j \in C_k} (x_{ij} - \bar{x}_{ik})^2,$$

and $s_0 = \text{median}\{s_i\}$.

In [1], $m_k$ was defined as $m_k = \sqrt{1/n_k + 1/n}$. However, the PAM implementation provided in the *pamr* package [7] defines it as $m_k = \sqrt{1/n_k - 1/n}$. The second definition was used in the experiments.

The shrunken centroid is

$$\bar{x}'_{ik} = \bar{x} + m_k(s_i + s_0)d'_{ik}$$

where

$$d'_{ik} = \text{sign}(d_{ik})(|d_{ik}| - \Delta)_+$$

($t_+ = t$ if $t > 0$ and zero otherwise)

This means that all centroids whose distances to the overall centroid of the feature are less than $\Delta$ will be the same as the overall centroid and can therefore be eliminated. Tibshirani et al. [1, 2] propose using a sequence of numbers as threshold values $\Delta$ and finding the best one by a 10-fold cross-validation on the training data. We used this unmodified version of PAM in the nested cross-validation tests, but employed a different method for the cross-validation runs with fixed numbers of features:

In fact, choosing arbitrary sequential threshold values $\Delta$ is an inaccurate method, as all possible thresholds can be calculated. The choice of the threshold values should have an impact on the number of remaining centroids, and consequently the set of reasonable thresholds consists of the $d_{ik}$s. Instead of the sequential threshold procedure, we used those pre-calculated threshold values. In addition, it is necessary for our experiments to fix the number of remaining features in order to be comparable to other feature reduction methods. Therefore, we did not choose the best threshold using a cross-validation, but utilized the threshold that leaves exactly $p'$ features:

1. Calculate $\max_k |d_{ik}|$ for each feature $i$
2. Sort these thresholds in descending order
3. Pick the $(p'+1)$th threshold

The PAM classification rule is described in Sect. 2.2.

**Random Feature Selection** (RF) simply chooses a specified number of features at random. Let $I$ be the set of feature indices $\{1, \ldots, p\}$. Then $I' \subset I$ is a random sample of $p'$ indices drawn from $I$ uniformly and without replacement, where $p'$ is the desired number of reduced features. If we let $D$ be the $p \times s$ matrix containing the data (with $p$ being the original number of dimensions), the feature reduction is performed by picking all rows of $D$ with indices $i \in I'$. Random Feature Selection is very simple, but the usefulness of the selected features is not evaluated and features are randomly discarded that may contain important information. It serves as a baseline for comparing the algorithms.

**A Random Projection** (RP) is a transformation with a matrix $R$ whose entries $r$ are chosen from a distribution that is symmetric about the origin. The idea of Random Projections is based on a lemma due to Johnson and Lindenstrauss [8]. The lemma basically states that any set of $n$ points in $\mathbf{R}^d$ can be projected into $\mathbf{R}^k, k \geq O(\epsilon^{-2} \log n)$ so that all distances are preserved up to a factor of $1 \pm \epsilon$. Vempala [3] further describes the distributions that can be used for generating the matrix entries. For the experiment, $p'$ vectors $R_i$ of length $p$ were chosen from the standard normal distribution $N(0,1)$, where $p$ is the original number of features and $p'$ is the desired number of reduced features. If we let $R$ be the $p \times p'$ matrix whose columns are the vectors $R_1 \ldots R_{p'}$ and $D$ the $p \times s$ matrix containing the data (with $s$ being the number of samples), the projection is $D' = R^T \cdot D$.

**Principal Component Analysis** (PCA) is a linear transformation that aligns the first axis (the principal component) of the coordinate system along the greatest variance. Formally, given a $p \times s$ data matrix $D$ (where $p$ is the number of features and $s$ is the number of samples), we use PCA for dimensionality reduction to $p'$ features, i.e. the eigenvectors of the covariance matrix are sorted in decreasing order and we use the first $p'$ eigenvectors.

**The Area Under the ROC Curve** can be a measure of classification quality of a feature in the two class scenario. A ROC curve has the 1-specificity on the horizontal axis and the sensitivity on the vertical axis. It visualizes the possibilities of separating the classes and allows to adjust the misclassification rates for both classes separately. The area under the ROC curve (AUC) is a measurement of discrimination. The closer it approaches 1, the better is the feature suitable for classification. Feature reduction is done by using only first $p'$ features after sorting them in decreasing order according to the AUC.

## 2.2   Classifiers

**The PAM Classifier** described in [1] has the following discriminant function:

$$\delta_k^{\mathrm{PAM}}(x^*) = \sum_{i=1}^{p} \frac{(x_i^* - \overline{x}_{ik}')^2}{(s_i + s_0)^2} - 2 \cdot \log \pi_k,$$

where $\pi_k$ is the prior probability of class $k$.

The classification rule is

$$C^{\mathrm{PAM}}(x^*) = l \text{ where } \delta_l^{\mathrm{PAM}}(x^*) = \min_k \{\delta_k^{\mathrm{PAM}}(x^*)\}$$

However, the *pamr* package [7] uses a different classifier. The *pamr* discriminant function for a sample $x^*$ is

$$\delta_k^{\mathrm{PAMR}}(x^*) = \sum_{i=1}^{p} d'_{ik} \cdot m_k \cdot \left(\frac{x_i^* - \overline{x}_i}{s_0 + s_i} - \frac{1}{2} \cdot d'_{ik} \cdot m_k\right) + \log \pi_k$$

and the classification rule is

$$C^{\mathrm{PAMR}}(x^*) = l \text{ where } \delta_l^{\mathrm{PAMR}}(x^*) = \max_k \{\delta_k^{\mathrm{PAMR}}(x^*)\}$$

To distinguish between the classifier described in the paper and the classifier employed in *pamr*, we call the former the **PAM classifier** and the latter the **PAMR classifier**.

**The Nearest Prototype (NP) Classifier** (also called nearest mean classifier [9]) assigns a sample to the class whose prototype (one prototype per class) has the smallest Euclidian distance to the sample. The discriminant function for a sample $x^*$ is: $\delta_k^{\mathrm{NP}}(x^*) = \|x^* - \overline{x}_k\|_2$, where $\overline{x}_k$ is the prototype of class $k$.

The classification rule is then: $C^{\mathrm{NP}}(x^*) = l$ where $\delta_l^{\mathrm{NP}}(x^*) = \min_k\{\delta_k^{\mathrm{NP}}(x^*)\}$.

**Linear Discriminant Analysis (LDA)** calculates a hyperplane in feature space. A quadratic discriminant function for a sample $x^*$ is

$$\delta_k^{\mathrm{QDA}}(x^*) = (x^* - \overline{x}_k)^T \cdot S^{-1} \cdot (x^* - \overline{x}_k) - 2 \cdot \log \pi_k,$$

where $\overline{x}_k$ is a vector of centroids of class $k$ in the features, $S$ is the pooled estimate of the within-class covariance matrix and $\pi_k$ is the prior probability of class $k$. This generally hyperquadratic decision surface is reduced to a hyperplane through our additional assumption of equal covariance matrices.

**Support Vector Machines (SVMs)** are learning machines that can be applied to classification problems. By solving a constrained quadratic optimization problem they can find a hyperplane that linearly separates a data set [10, 6]. Here, we use only the linear kernel.

### 2.3   Data Sets

**The Golub Data Set** contains leukemia microarray data with originally 6817 genes, 72 samples (47 ALL and 25 AML) and 2 classes. It was first analyzed by Golub et al. [11]. The preprocessing described by Dudoit et al. [12] was applied, reducing the number of features to 3051.

**The Khan Data Set** of small round blue cell tumors was analyzed by Khan et al. [13] and also by Tibshirani et al. in [1]. It consists of 63 samples (SRBCT classes: 23 EWS, 20 RMS, 12 NB, 8 NHL cases) with 2308 features in 4 classes.

**The Diagnostic Chip Data Set** of pancreatic tumors contains 62 samples (37 PaCa and 25 Pitis/Norm) with originally 558 features that were reduced to

169 genes and 2 classes [14]. The genes of this data set are known to be indicative for cancer diseases.

## 2.4   Testing Methods

Two different kinds of experiments were performed.

**Predefined Feature Number.** For comparing the feature reduction methods by the number of remaining features, the number of remaining features was fixed to values $p' = 5, 10, \ldots, 100$. This requires a special treatment of the PAM thresholds (see Sect. 2.1).

We tested each classifier separately on all feature reduction methods. SVMs were only applied on PCA feature reduction. With SVMs and ROC curves being suitable only for 2-class-problems (in the present configuration, i.e. we did not extend these methods to problem with more than two classes), we did not apply them to the Khan data set. In addition, the SVM and the NP classifiers were tested on the original (unreduced) feature sets.

The following testing methods were applied:

- Reclassification, that is, classification of the training data
- Leave-one-out, i. e. training the classifiers with all but one samples and classifying the remaining sample. This was repeated for all samples and the errors were added.
- $10 \times 5$-fold cross-validation: The samples were divided into 5 random groups. Each of the groups was left out once in training and used for classification. The errors were added. The procedure was repeated 10 times and the average error of the 10 runs was calculated.
- $10 \times 10$-fold cross-validation with 10 random groups.

**Nested Cross-Vaildation for Feature Number Determination.** For comparing the feature reduction methods by their optimal number of features, we applied a **nested 10-fold cross-validation**. This means a $10 \times 5$-fold cross-validation and a $10 \times 10$-fold cross-validation were performed, and the optimal number of features was chosen in each fold of this outer cross-validation by a nested $1 \times 10$-fold cross-validation on the training data of the current fold. This is the method proposed by Tibshirani et al. [1] for the PAM threshold selection. As this method cannot be applied reasonably on random methods, it was only performed on PAM, PCA and ROC feature reduction.

- For PAM, 30 sequential threshold values (the default thresholds chosen by the *pamr* package) were cross-validated and the threshold value that lead to the minimum number of errors at the first level and the minimum number of remaining features at the second level was used.
- For the other feature reduction methods, reductions to $p' = 5, 10, \ldots, 100$ features were cross-validated and the transformation that yielded the minimum number of errors at the minimum number of features was chosen.

# 3   Results

## 3.1   Experiments with Fixed Numbers of Features

The testing methods vary in their estimation of generalization error. While re-classification is usually an overly optimistic estimation of generalization error, different types of cross-validation give different hints regarding the match of classifier to data. We performed three types of cross-validation, namely leave-one-out, 10-fold and 5-fold cross-validation. For lack of space we show only the 5-fold cross-validation results in this section, they exhibit the highest error rates. Complete simulation results are given in the supplementary information available at http://www.informatik.uni-ulm.de/ni/mitarbeiter/HKestler/featred/.

**Golub Data Set**

On the Golub data set all classifiers perform reasonably good with average error rates below 10/72 in a 5-fold cross-validation (see Figure 1). With the PAM and PAMR classifiers, the ROC feature reduction and PAM bring the best results in the cross-validations. In the 5-fold cross-validation, both PAM and PAMR start with 5.3 errors for 5 features and finally produce 3.0 errors with 80 features. None of the classifiers achieves an error of zero.

With the NP classifier, PCA is substantially better than other feature reduction methods for up to 55 features, yielding an average error of 1.8 cases or less in the 5-fold cross-validation. PCA error rates rise when the number of features increases. Starting with 70 features, Random Projection achieves comparable results to PAM with NP, leading to error rates mostly below 4.0/72. RP+NP even outperforms PAM+PAMR and PAM+PAM sometimes on feature numbers above 70. This result is surprising, but shows that Random Projection preserves distances quite well and works well with distance-based classifiers. With the LDA classifier, PCA feature reduction also brings good results, with error rates below 2.5/72 in the 5-fold cross-validation, while all other feature reduction methods produce even more errors with an increasing number of features. PCA and LDA also return constant zero error rates in reclassification, with 15 features and more. The SVM classifier yields the overall minimum error of 1.6/72 at 35 features with the PCA feature reduction in the 5-fold cross-validation, but error rates raise quickly with more features. Random Projection is always slightly better than Random Feature Selection and approaches or sometimes even beats PAM as the number of features rises.

**Khan Data Set**

Compared to the Golub data, the Khan data set is harder to classify and needs more features for correct classification. With a low number of features, PCA always performs best on Khan (see Figure 2). Here again, it shows that LDA and PCA go together well, leading to an average of 1 error in the 5-fold cross-validation with only 15 features. With more than 40 features, the PAM feature reduction performs better than PCA, which gets worse. Yet, PAM achieves less

**10 x 5–fold cross–validation on Golub dataset**

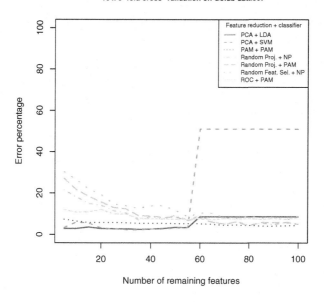

| | 5 | 10 | 15 | 20 | 25 | 30 | 35 | 40 | 45 | 50 | 55 | 60 | 65 | 70 | 75 | 80 | 85 | 90 | 95 | 100 |
|---|---|---|---|---|---|---|---|---|---|---|---|---|---|---|---|---|---|---|---|---|
| PCA + LDA | 2.9 | 2.9 | 3.6 | 2.9 | 2.8 | 2.8 | 2.5 | 2.6 | 2.9 | 3.5 | 3.3 | 8.6 | 8.6 | 8.6 | 8.6 | 8.6 | 8.6 | 8.6 | 8.6 | 8.6 |
| PCA + SVM | 3.3 | 6.0 | 5.6 | 3.2 | 2.8 | 2.4 | 2.2 | 2.6 | 2.6 | 3.2 | 3.3 | 51.0 | 51.0 | 51.0 | 51.0 | 51.0 | 51.0 | 51.0 | 51.0 | 51.0 |
| PAM + PAM | 7.4 | 6.5 | 5.8 | 5.8 | 5.8 | 5.7 | 5.4 | 5.4 | 5.4 | 5.3 | 5.3 | 5.3 | 5.0 | 4.6 | 4.7 | 4.4 | 4.2 | 4.2 | 4.3 | 4.4 |
| Random Proj. + NP | 21.5 | 18.1 | 15.0 | 14.2 | 11.5 | 10.4 | 7.1 | 8.6 | 7.4 | 9.3 | 6.9 | 9.2 | 6.4 | 4.9 | 6.4 | 4.6 | 5.6 | 4.9 | 6.0 | 5.1 |
| Random Proj. + PAM | 27.2 | 21.7 | 18.5 | 15.7 | 13.1 | 12.4 | 9.2 | 8.9 | 8.2 | 8.5 | 6.8 | 7.9 | 6.0 | 5.1 | 6.3 | 4.3 | 5.8 | 5.8 | 5.8 | 5.0 |
| Random Feat. Sel. + NP | 30.4 | 26.5 | 21.9 | 19.3 | 14.7 | 13.9 | 12.6 | 13.9 | 13.9 | 11.7 | 8.6 | 10.4 | 10.3 | 8.1 | 7.8 | 8.9 | 7.9 | 8.5 | 7.1 | 8.9 |
| ROC + PAM | 11.9 | 10.8 | 11.0 | 12.1 | 10.0 | 9.9 | 7.9 | 7.6 | 7.6 | 7.4 | 7.2 | 7.9 | 7.2 | 7.8 | 7.6 | 7.8 | 7.4 | 7.8 | 7.5 | 8.2 |

**Fig. 1.** Golub data set: Error rates of the five-fold cross-validation. Random Projection performs surprisingly well with higher numbers of features. Shown are the error rates for the combinations: ROC+PAM, RF+NP, RP+PAM, RP+NP, PAM+PAM, PCA+SVM, PCA+LDA.

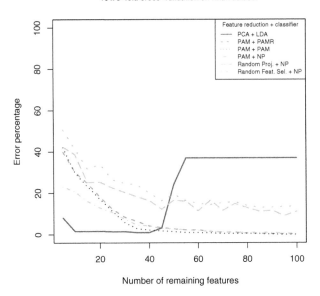

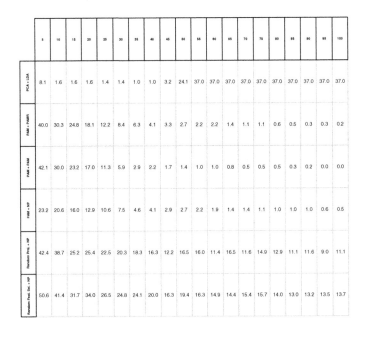

**Fig. 2.** Khan data set: Error rates of the five-fold cross-validation. PCA and LDA perform well with a small number of features, NP outperforms the PAM classifiers with less than 30 features. Shown are the error rates for the combinations: RF+NP, RP+NP, PAM+NP, PAM+PAM, PAM+PAMR, PCA+LDA.

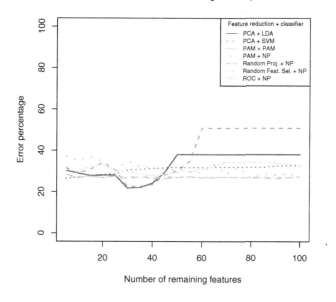

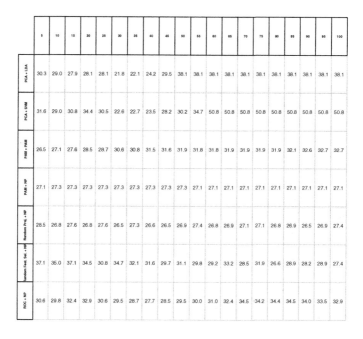

**Fig. 3.** Diagnostic Chip data: Error rates of the five-fold cross-validation. No feature reduction and classifier combination produces acceptable results. Shown are the error rates for the combinations: ROC+PAM, RF+NP, RP+PAM, RP+NP, PAM+PAM, PCA+SVM, PCA+LDA.

than 1 error at 65 features with the PAMR classifier and at 50 features with the PAM classifier. The PAMR and PAM classifiers show similar behaviours, with PAM being slightly better than PAMR in most cases. NP shows analogue characteristics, but yields error rates below those of PAMR and PAM with less than 30 features. With more than 30 features, PAMR and PAM perform slightly better. As with the Golub data set, Random Projection always performs better than Random Feature Selection. However, it does not reach the PAM classifier with the Khan data set.

**Diagnostic Chip Data Set**

All classifiers achieve the highest error rates on the Diagnostic Chip data set. None of the classifiers achieves an error below 10 (SVM: error rate 10.9/62 on the complete data, no feature reduction, 10×5-fold cv). The best result with feature reduction is achieved by PCA and LDA classification with a minimum average error of 13.5 cases with 30 features (10×5-fold cv) and PCA and SVM with a minimum average error of 14 cases with 30 features (10×5-fold cv), see Figure 3. With the PAM and PAMR classifiers, PAM feature reduction leads to bad results, sometimes even worse than Random Feature Selection. Both classifiers produce exactly the same error rates in the 5-fold cross-validation. PCA, Random Projection and ROC are better. With increasing numbers of features, PCA performs best with an error rate of 16.5 in the 5-fold cross-validation starting with 50 features.

The Nearest Prototype classifier returns almost constant error rates of around 17 errors (min 15) for all numbers of features when being applied on feature sets produced by PCA, Random Projection and PAM. The error rates of the other feature reduction methods with the NP classifier are unstable. Without feature reduction, the average error is 22.6 cases. In contrast to the other data sets, the error rates of Random Projection in the different runs are quite stable, i. e. have a low variance. Those facts indicate that it is hard to find a subset of features that suits significantly better for distance-based classification than the original feature set and that none of the feature reduction methods succeeds in finding one. Consequently, the PAM and the PAMR classifiers, which include distance measurements as well, also mostly return error rates that do not change very much with different numbers of features. Only the PAM feature reduction and ROC show slightly increasing error rates with an increasing number of features.

**3.2   Experiments with Nested Cross-Validations**

**Golub Data Set**

PAM seems not to be able to find a stable number of features on Golub. In the 5-fold cross-validation, it determines an average of 1243.9 features for the minimum error of 3.1/72, with a very high standard deviation of 322.3 features. 10-fold cross-validation produces a similar deviation, but a mean value of 1601.0

features and an error of 3.4/72. In fact, PAM achieved even better results at a much lower number of features in the experiments with fixed numbers of features, i. e., 3.0/72 errors at 85 features in the 5-fold cross-validation and 3.0/72 errors at 90 features in the 10-fold cross-validation. This may be due to the fact that the 30 pre-defined thresholds used by the original PAM cover the whole feature set, while our 20 thresholds in the above experiments lead to 5-100 features and thus have a smaller raster in this area. With PCA, the results are mostly comparable to our previous experiments. LDA achieves a mean error of 3.1/72 at an average of 10.9 features in the 5-fold cross-validation. The best result is achieved by the linear SVM at 16.2 features with an error of 2.7/72. ROC feature reduction only produces average errors of 4.9/72 (linear SVM) and more in the 5-fold cross-validation.

### Khan Data Set

On Khan, PAM produces more stable results, yielding a mean error of 1.4/63 at an average of 52.7 features in the 5-fold cross-validation. Anyway, in the fixed-feature experiments, the error rate grew smaller continuously towards 100 features, so this is still not an optimal value. The standard deviation of the number of features is 7.8, while the PCA standard deviation is less than 2.8, depending on the classifier. PCA again performs well with LDA, producing an error of 1.5/63 at only 14.8 features. The results of the fixed-feature experiments were slightly better. The NP classifier achieves an error of 3.6 at 16.1 features in the 5-fold cross-validation, which is also comparable to the previous experiments.

### Diagnostic Chip Data Set

As already seen in the fixed-feature experiments, the error rates on this data set are high. PAM achieves 17/62 errors at 5.7 features (5-fold cross-validation), which is slightly worse than the previous results (16.4 errors at 5 features). The number of features is comparatively stable with a deviation of 1.4. With PCA, NP achieves similar results with 16.9/62 errors at an average of 5.4 features with a very small standard deviation of 0.84. This time, LDA only yields 18.5/62 errors at 22 features with a standard deviation of 5.1. The error rate is comparable with the error rate of the fixed-feature experiments, but the number of features chosen is not the one that produced a minimum error there. With ROC feature reduction, LDA yields a similar error (18.8/62), but needs only 13 features with a smaller deviation of 1.5. The SVM produces a minimum error of 16.4 with 26.1 features. NP performs worse with an error of 19.9/62 at 26 features with a high standard deviation of 7.9 features.

## 4  Discussion

The experimental results show that especially when classifying with small numbers of features, PAM is not the best choice. In particular, PCA feature reduction in combination with the LDA and SVM classifiers performs excellently with very low-dimensional target feature spaces.

In addition, the optimal number of features returned by PCA in the nested cross-validations was quite stable, indicating that the feature selection remains reliable when changing a few elements in the training set.

However, the factors returned by PCA cannot be interpreted easily in order to determine which features in the original feature space are important for classification. Obviously, both the LDA classifier and the SVM classifier (linear kernel) lead to high classification errors when over-fitted, hence they seem not suitable for a larger number of features. Also the different types of microarrays, e.g. whole genome array vs selected genes, seem to play a major role in the classifier performance (together with the type of tissue). For the Golub and Khan data sets genes (n= 6817) were not specifically selected for discrimination, whereas the genes (n= 558) for the pancreas vs pancreatitis diagnostic chip data were selected according to their known or believed involvement in cancer.

Generally speaking, PAM does not stand out compared to other feature reduction methods. The only data set showing major distances between the error rates of PAM and the baseline algorithms Random Feature Selection and Random Projection is the Khan data set, where there are differences of 10 to 15 in the cross-validations. In the other data sets, the random methods are mostly slightly worse, but sometimes even outperform PAM. The nested cross-validation experiments mostly did not find the number of features that lead to the minimum error in the previous fixed-feature experiments which in itself is not surprising. This may be due to the choice of the feasible threshold values in PAM leading sometimes to zero remaining features or including all features in the decision process which is not desirable (linear separability). In contrast, using all possible thresholds that lead to different feature numbers (in a certain range) might avoid this.

Random Projection was observed to perform better than Random Feature Selection. The good results of Random Projection in combination with the Nearest Prototype classifier underline its capability to preserve distances and show that Random Projection is used most effectively with distance-based classifiers. A possible explanation for this phenomenon is the fact that Random Feature Selection completely discards features by random, while Random Projection projects all features to the lower-dimensional space. Thus, Random Projection may not lose as much information as Random Feature Selection. This may shed a new light on an often used premise which is used in normalization procedures, that only a small fraction of genes is regulated in a gene expression microarray experiment.

## Acknowledgments

We thank André Müller for fruitful discussions. This work is supported by the Stifterverband für die Deutsche Wissenschaft (HAK) and the German Science Foundation, SFB 518, Project C5.

# References

1. Tibshirani, R., Hastie, T., Narasimhan, B., Chu, G.: Diagnosis of multiple cancer types by shrunken centroids of gene expression. PNAS **99** (2002) 6567–6572
2. Tibshirani, R., Hastie, T., Narasimhan, B., Chu, G.: Class Prediction by Nearest Shrunken Centroids, with Applications to DNA Microarrays. Statistical Science **18** (2003) 104 – 117
3. Vempala, S.: The Random Projection Method. DIMACS Series in Discrete Mathematics and Theoretical Computer Science, volume 65 (2004)
4. Duda, R.O., Hart, P., Storck, D.: Pattern classification. Wiley (2001)
5. Webb, A.: Statistical Pattern Recognition. Wiley (2002)
6. Cristianini, N., Shawe-Taylor, J.: An Introduction to Support Vector Machines. Cambridge University Press (2000)
7. Tibshirani, R., Hastie, T., Narasimhan, B., Chu, G.: PAMR package version 1.27, http://www-stat.stanford.edu/~tibs/PAM/Rdist (2005)
8. Johnson, W., Lindenstrauss, J.: Extensions of Lipshitz mapping into Hilbert space. Contemporary Mathematics **26** (1984) 189–206
9. Therrien, C.: Decision estimation and classification. Wiley (1989)
10. Boser, B., Guyon, I., Vapnik, V.: A training algorithm for optimal margin classifiers. In Haussler, D., ed.: Proceedings of the 5th Annual ACM Workshop on Computational Learning Theory, ACM Press (1992) 144–152
11. Golub, T., Slonim, D., Tamayo, P., Huard, C., Gaasenbeek, M., Mesirov, J., Coller, H., Loh, M., Downing, J., Caligiuri, M., Bloomfield, C., Lander, E.: Molecular classification of cancer: class discovery and class prediction by gene expression monitoring. Science **286** (1999) 531 – 536
12. Dudoit, S., Fridlyand, J., Speed, T.: Comparison of discrimination methods for the classification of tumors using gene expression data. Journal of the American Statistical Association **97** (2002) 77 –87
13. Khan, J., Wei, J., Ringner, M., Saal, L., Ladanyi, M., Westermann, F., Berthold, F., Schwab, M., Antonescu, C., Peterson, C., Meltzer, P.: Classification and diagnostic prediction of cancers using gene expression profiling and artificial neural networks. Nature Medicine **7** (2001) 673 – 679
14. Buchholz, M., Kestler, H., Bauer, A., Bock, W., Rau, B., Leder, G., Kratzer, W., Bommer, M., Scarpa, A., Schilling, M., Adler, G., Hoheisel, J., Gress, T.: Specialized DNA arrays for the differentiation of pancreatic tumors. Clin. Cancer Res. **11** (2005) 8048–54

# Unsupervised Feature Selection for Biomarker Identification in Chromatography and Gene Expression Data

Marc Strickert[a], Nese Sreenivasulu[b], Silke Peterek[c], Winfriede Weschke[b], Hans-Peter Mock[c], and Udo Seiffert[a]

[a] Pattern Recognition Group, [b] Gene Expression Group, [c] Applied Biochemistry
Leibniz Institute of Plant Genetics and Crop Plant Research Gatersleben,
{stricker, srinivas, peterek, weschke, mock, seiffert}@ipk-gatersleben.de

**Abstract.** A novel approach to feature selection from unlabeled vector data is presented. It is based on the reconstruction of original data relationships in an auxiliary space with either weighted or omitted features. Feature weighting, on one hand, is related to the return forces of factors in a parametric data similarity measure as response to disturbance of their optimum values. Feature omission, on the other hand, inducing measurable loss of reconstruction quality, is realized in an iterative greedy way. The proposed framework allows to apply custom data similarity measures. Here, adaptive Euclidean distance and adaptive Pearson correlation are considered, the former serving as standard reference, the latter being usefully for intensity data. Results of the different strategies are given for chromatography and gene expression data.

**Keywords:** Feature selection, adaptive similarity measures.

## 1 Introduction

Recently developed metabolomic and genomic measuring technologies share the common property to yield in parallel thousands of metabolites and gene expression values from single probes of a given tissue/plant sample. Tools used for these purposes are mass spectrometry, chromatography, and micro- and macroarrays. In high-throughput approaches the number of probe attributes (metabolites, genes) is usually much higher than the number of probes, which is paradigmatic of the curse of dimensionality. Thus, it is desirable for analysis to consider as many experimental probes as data quality allows. Such desire for maximum information preservation for only few unlabeled data samples excludes the utilization of prototype-based data abstractions like supervised neural gas proposed for labeled data [2]. Principal component analysis PCA, the classical approach to factor analysis of unlabeled data, has got different limitations: the analytic focus is shifted away from the data matrix towards the attribute covariance matrix of which eigenvalues are computed to rate the importance of the axes of principal data directions. These axes, however, are linear combinations of the original data

F. Schwenker and S. Marinai (Eds.): ANNPR 2006, LNAI 4087, pp. 274–285, 2006.

attributes – this situation requires a complex interpretation of the eigenvector entries ('loadings') in order to rate the original data attributes. PCA finally results in the amount of feature contribution to the overall data variance. Both, implicit rotation of the data coordinate system and the restriction to variance, implying the Euclidean data metric for a reasonable interpretation, are circumvented in the following approach. In terms of feature subset selection (FSS) the proposed method will be a filter rather than a wrapper [3]. Custom data similarity measures can be integrated to the framework, and, furthermore, the new reconstruction-based feature selection does not require class labels, which complements other approaches such as proposed in [5]. For the lack of data samples, distribution-based separability criteria and expectation maximization methods for unlabeled data, like FSSEM-TR/ML [1], cannot be properly applied in the present case. In the proposed solution, no external clustering is required for evaluating the changes before and after masking (veiling) subset of features; instead, a built-in filter criterion is used which optimizes the reconstruction quality of the veiled data according to the strategy discussed in the following.

## 2    Unsupervised Feature Selection Based on Maximum Reconstruction Quality

Feature selection and weighting do both refer to the process of characterizing the relevance of components in fixed-dimensional data vectors. Unfortunately, many biological data sets do not possess an absolute reference coordinate system upon which a proper attribute analysis can be grounded: the organic material itself and many external influences affect the measurements, and the obtained data are thus, in a certain degree, situated in empirical domains. For example, in gene expression data, a theoretical lower bound of zero intensity exists, but due to background noise this value is never observed in practice. Subsequent standard operations like the logarithm might further amplify this uncertain domain, especially for near zero intensities. The *ad hoc* definition of absolute data domains can be avoided by dealing with relationships expressed by the data similarity matrix. This requires to choose an appropriate similarity measure. In case of the Euclidean metric, the resulting distance matrix is invariant to data (baseline) shifts and coordinate rotations. Invariance can be realized already at data level by using Pearson correlation which is invariant to vector shifting and scaling. This beneficial property is used as quality criterion for comparing data similarity matrices. Using the above ingredients, feature ranking for data from an observation-driven domain is realized by sensitivity analysis, i.e. by analyzing the effect of measure-specific feature veiling on the quality of reconstruction of the original data relationships. This general approach is sketched in Fig. 1. It is required that the data similarity measure d is chosen in advance, such as Euclidean distance or Pearson correlation in the following. If weighting is considered instead of feature dropping, also a parametric counterpart $d^\lambda$ of d is necessary.

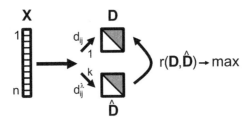

**Fig. 1.** Feature selection by reconstruction quality maximization. Due to symmetry, a number of $n \cdot (n-1)/2$ relationships of data vectors in **X** is once computed with static similarity measure d to yield triangular reference matrix **D** (upper path). Features are dropped or weighted by the $\lambda$-parametrized measure $d^\lambda$ in a $k$-iterative manner (lower path): for greedy selection, those features providing highest correlation between feature-reduced similarity matrix **D** and reference matrix $\mathbf{D}^\lambda$ are further considered important; for parallel selection, the average response to random feature perturbation is calculated.

The parametric Euclidean distance $d_{ij}^\lambda = {}^E d_{ij}^\lambda \in [0;\infty)$ is given by

$$
{}^E d_{ij}^\lambda(\mathbf{x}^i, \mathbf{x}^j) = \sqrt{\sum_{l=1}^{q} \lambda_l \cdot (x_l^i - x_l^j)^2} \, . \tag{1}
$$

Canonic feature weighting is obtained by inserting weight factors to the squared differences – setting $\lambda_l = 1$ for $l = 1 \ldots q$ yields the original Euclidean distance. If just one parameter $\lambda_l$ is zero, the others one, this expresses dropping of feature $l$.

The parametric Pearson correlation $d_{ij}^\lambda = r_{ij}^\lambda \in [-1;1]$ is given by

$$
r_{ij}^\lambda = \frac{\sum_{l=1}^{q} \lambda_l^2 \cdot (x_l^i - \mu_{\mathbf{x}^i}) \cdot (x_l^j - \mu_{\mathbf{x}^j})}{\sqrt{\sum_{l=1}^{q} \lambda_l^2 \cdot (x_l^i - \mu_{\mathbf{x}^i})^2} \cdot \sqrt{\sum_{l=1}^{q} \lambda_l^2 \cdot (x_l^j - \mu_{\mathbf{x}^j})^2}} \, . \tag{2}
$$

Each of the mean-subtracted vector components $(x_l^m - \mu_{\mathbf{x}^m})$ has got its proper relevance factor $\lambda_l$ – again, setting $\lambda_l = 1$ for $l = 1 \ldots q$ yields the original Pearson correlation. Note that, in contrast to Euclidean distance, setting $\lambda_l = 0$, $\lambda_m = 1, m \neq l, m = 1 \ldots q$ is not equivalent to dropping feature $l$, because it still contributes to the vector averages $\mu_{\mathbf{x}^i}$ and $\mu_{\mathbf{x}^j}$. Instead, the feature's induced mean deviation from average is measured.

For feature selection, parameters $\lambda_l$ are searched that provide maximum correlation of parametrized data relationships and original data relationships. Trivial solutions $\lambda_l = C, C > 0, l = 1 \ldots q$ are avoided by construction.

- For dropping, correlation values $r(\mathbf{D}, \mathbf{D}^\lambda)$ are computed for all attributes separately masked. Those with maximum correlation degradation are considered especially important. This attribute can be wiped out and the procedure can be repeated iteratively.
- For weighting, Monte-Carlo sampling around an optimum $\lambda$-vector is performed and the average restoring forces are calculated by a gradient ascent

approach, by analyzing absolute values of gradients pointing into the parameter direction of high correlation values $r(\mathbf{D}, \mathbf{D}^{\lambda})$.

## 2.1 Feature Dropping

Feature relevance can be systematically probed by excluding single attributes from data similarity calculation and testing the impact of that operation on the correlation $r(\mathbf{D}, \mathbf{D}^{\lambda})$. By feature dropping, as a basic assumption, highly important features will induce a larger loss of $r$ than less important ones. Thus, a first approach to relevance rating is the correlation loss resulting from feature dropping. Such a *top-level feature evaluation* can be recursively formulated in a greedy manner. This *iterative feature dropping* approach stores the index and then really excludes the currently most relevant feature from further calculations. It iteratively isolates those attributes that do maximum decorrelate the original similarity matrix $\mathbf{D}$ and the feature-reduced distance matrix $\mathbf{D}_S^{\lambda}$:

$$S(k) = \arg\min_{i} \ r^2(\mathbf{D}, \mathbf{D}^{\lambda}_{S(k-1)\cup i}) \, , \, i \in (1 \ldots T) \backslash S(k-1) \, , k = 1 \ldots T - 1.$$

$S(k)$ is the growing set of index pointers to features which have been isolated until iteration number $k$; by definition $S(0) := \{\}$, and by construction $|S(k)| = k$. $\mathbf{D}^{\lambda}_{S(k-1)\cup i}$ is the similarity matrix that has been calculated by using the data vectors, thereby skipping the features indexed by the set $S(k-1) \cup i$.

The straightforward greedy algorithm does not require further parameters, however, two alternative design criteria need further attention. First, $\mathbf{D}^{\lambda}_{S(k-1)\cup i}$ is correlated with $\mathbf{D}^{\lambda}$, not with $\mathbf{D}^{\lambda}_{S(k-1)}$. The reason is that a drift away from the original data set towards the subsequently reduced data features might occur otherwise, so $\mathbf{D}^{\lambda}$ constitutes a fixed reference. Second, features are iteratively masked out from high relevances to low ones, not the other way round. This way, much of the relation-explaining attributes are already cleared off in the first steps, instead of realizing a culmination towards the crucial data attributes by least-attributes-first exclusion. This is beneficial in large scale applications with thousands of dimensions, because it allows early stopping when the remaining absolute correlation $r^2$ drops below a critical near-zero threshold, or in case of reaching a plateau. These two options – there are certainly many more – and the different results from the alternative greedy feature selection designs are circumvented by parallel feature selection as discussed in the next paragraph.

## 2.2 Feature Weighting

In the following approach, gradients are calculated for rating the data features. Decent perturbations are induced to the parameters $\lambda_l$ of the adaptive similarity measure $d^{\lambda}$, close to the optimum values. The higher, on average, the return forces (gradients) of the disturbed parameters, the more important are the corresponding attributes for restoring maximum correlation $r(\mathbf{D}, \mathbf{D}^{\lambda})$. The proposed method uses several paradigms from artificial neural networks: the perturbation and pattern presentation processes are stochastic, a principle of correlation-maximization is pursued, and parametric similarity measures are optimized – or are at least rated – using gradient dynamic. For the derivatives, an approach is chosen which has been proposed earlier for efficient multi-dimensional scaling [4]. In order to prevent saturation at boundaries of the correlation domain $[-1; 1]$, the widely used Fisher z′-transform with its derivative is utilized:

$$z'(r) = \frac{1}{2} \cdot \log\left(\frac{a+r}{a-r}\right) \quad \Rightarrow \quad \frac{\partial z'(r)}{\partial r} = \frac{a}{a^2 - r^2} .$$

In Fisher's original formulation $a$ is set to 1, but here it is kept variable $a = 1 + \epsilon$ in order to avoid infinitely large values in case of perfect correlation. For example, $a = (1 + \sqrt{401})/20 \approx 1.05$ limits the transformed derivative domain to $[-10; 20/(1+\sqrt{401})]$. Desired gradients for $\lambda_l$ with negative correlation transform result from application of the chain rule to the nested stress function formulation:

$$s = -z' \circ r \circ d^\lambda \circ \boldsymbol{\lambda} \quad \Rightarrow \quad \frac{\partial s}{\partial \lambda_l} = -\sum_{i=1}^{n} \sum_{j=1...n}^{j \neq i} \frac{\partial z'(r)}{\partial r} \cdot \frac{\partial r}{\partial d_{ij}^\lambda} \cdot \frac{\partial d_{ij}^\lambda}{\partial \lambda_l} . \tag{3}$$

Using the abbreviations $r(\mathbf{D}, \mathbf{D}^\lambda) = \mathscr{H}/\sqrt{\mathscr{W} \cdot \mathscr{U}}$ with

$$\begin{aligned}
\mathscr{H} &= \sum_{l=1}^{n} \sum_{m=1}^{n} (d_{lm} - \mu_{\mathbf{D}}) \cdot (d_{lm}^\lambda - \mu_{\mathbf{D}^\lambda}) , \\
\mathscr{W} &= \sum_{l=1}^{n} \sum_{m=1}^{n} (d_{lm} - \mu_{\mathbf{D}})^2 , \\
\mathscr{U} &= \sum_{l=1}^{n} \sum_{m=1}^{n} (d_{lm}^\lambda - \mu_{\mathbf{D}^\lambda})^2 ,
\end{aligned}$$

the derivative of the z′-transformed Pearson correlation is calculated by

$$\frac{\partial z'(r)}{\partial r} \cdot \frac{\partial r}{\partial d_{ij}^\lambda} = \frac{a \cdot \left((d_{ij}^\lambda - \mu_{\mathbf{D}^\lambda}) \cdot \mathscr{H} - (d_{ij} - \mu_{\mathbf{D}}) \cdot \mathscr{U}\right) \cdot \sqrt{\mathscr{W}}}{(\mathscr{H} - a \cdot \sqrt{\mathscr{U} \cdot \mathscr{W}})^2 \cdot \sqrt{\mathscr{U}}} . \tag{4}$$

The term $\mathscr{W}$ needs to be calculated only once, even the mean of the static similarity matrix can be initially removed $d_{lm} \leftarrow (d_{lm} - \mu_{\mathbf{D}})$ in order to save computing operations. Eqn. 3 is evaluated for all features and the absolute values are averaged over a sufficient number of small random perturbations. For better comparison, these averaged gradient responses are rescaled to an upper limit of one representing the most sensitive feature.

Eqn. 4 is generic enough to plug in any differentiable parametric similarity measure. Two interesting choices are the parametric Euclidean distance for data comparisons and an adaptive version of the Pearson correlation that plays an important role in biopattern processing. These measures require derivatives $\partial^E d^\lambda{}_{ij}/\partial\lambda_l$ and $\partial r_{ij}^\lambda/\partial\lambda_l$ as rightmost factors in equation 3, respectively.

**Parametric Euclidean.** The derivative of the parametric Euclidean is easily obtained as:

$$\frac{\partial^E d^\lambda{}_{ij}}{\partial \lambda_l} = \frac{\partial}{\partial \lambda_l} \sqrt{\sum_{m=1}^{q} \lambda_m \cdot (x_m^i - x_m^j)^2} = \frac{(x_l^i - x_l^j)^2}{\sqrt{\sum_{m=1}^{q} \lambda_m \cdot (x_m^i - x_m^j)^2}} = (x_l^i - x_l^j)^2 / {}^E d^\lambda{}_{ij} .$$

**Parametric Pearson Correlation.** For deriving the $\lambda$-weighted correlation $r_{ij}^\lambda$, a focus on component $l$ will be a convenient abbreviation. Similar to the previous matrix correlations, the notation $r_{ij}^\lambda = \mathscr{H}_l / \sqrt{\mathscr{W}_l \cdot \mathscr{U}_l}$ of the correlation term is considered using

$$
\begin{aligned}
\mathscr{H}_l &= \lambda_l^2 \cdot (x_l^i - \mu_{\mathbf{x}^i}) \cdot (x_l^j - \mu_{\mathbf{x}^j}) + \sum_{\substack{u \neq l \\ u=1}}^{q} \lambda_u^2 \cdot (x_u^i - \mu_{\mathbf{x}^i}) \cdot (x_u^j - \mu_{\mathbf{x}^j}), \\
\mathscr{W}_l &= \lambda_l^2 \cdot (x_l^i - \mu_{\mathbf{x}^i})^2 + \sum_{\substack{u \neq l \\ u=1}}^{q} \lambda_u^2 \cdot (x_u^i - \mu_{\mathbf{x}^i})^2, \\
\mathscr{U}_l &= \lambda_l^2 \cdot (x_l^j - \mu_{\mathbf{x}^j})^2 + \sum_{\substack{u \neq l \\ u=1}}^{q} \lambda_u^2 \cdot (x_u^j - \mu_{\mathbf{x}^j})^2.
\end{aligned}
$$

With these isolated subterms, the derivative of interest is

$$
\frac{\partial r_{ij}^\lambda}{\partial \lambda_l} = \frac{\lambda_l \cdot \left( 2(x_l^i - \mu_{\mathbf{x}^i})(x_l^j - \mu_{\mathbf{x}^j}) \cdot \mathscr{W}_l \mathscr{U}_l - \mathscr{H}_l \cdot \left( \mathscr{U}_l \cdot (x_l^i - \mu_{\mathbf{x}^i})^2 + \mathscr{W}_l \cdot (x_l^j - \mu_{\mathbf{x}^j})^2 \right) \right)}{(\mathscr{W}_l \cdot \mathscr{U}_l)^{\frac{3}{2}}}.
$$

Parameters of the feature weighting approach are the gradient delimiter which has been set to $a = 1.01$, the perturbation interval, and the number of iterations for calculating the average response gradients. The interval for random perturbations has been determined by studies on several data sets, including the ones presented in the application section. It has turned out that in case of both parametric Euclidean and Pearson similarity measures, parameters uniformly chosen $\lambda_l \in [0.75; 1.25]$ produce stable results. A number of $k = 1000$ iterations is chosen. Stability has been additionally tested by letting the parameters iteratively adapt according to stochastic descent on s using the calculated gradients: after noise induction, the parameters quickly return to constant values $\lambda_i \approx \lambda_j, \forall i, j$.

## 3  Applications

The presented methods are applied to three data sets of interest: to benchmark data related to absorbance spectra from Infratec Tecator food analyzer, publicly available from statlib data collection at http://lib.stat.cmu.edu/datasets/tecator, (215 samples, 100 dimensions [frequency channels]); to chromatography data from the in-house tomato germplasm database focusing on chemical compound detection at a wavelength of $280 nm$ (19 samples, 3000 dimensions [retention time points]); and to gene expression data from macroarray hybridization experiments of developing endosperm barley tissue at 0–26 days after flowering sampled in steps of two days (two series, 14 samples each, 11786 dimensions [genes]).

**Tecator Benchmark Spectral Data.** The first data set has been included for illustration and reference purposes. It contains 215 food samples analyzed in a near infrared frequency range of $850–1050 nm$ measured with the Tecator Infratec Food and Feed Analyzer. The 100-dimensional spectra, originally used for predicting high and low fat content, are smoothly shaped, as shown for 10 examples in the top left panel of Fig. 2. Looking at the other panels of Fig. 2, several observations are made.

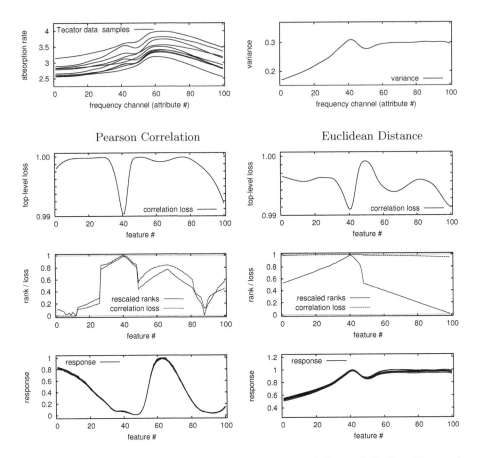

**Fig. 2.** Feature selection for Tecator data set. Top row: left panel displays 10 samples from 100-dimensional spectra; right panel channel variances for entire data set containing 215 samples. Subsequent rows: top-level feature sensitivity measuring the loss of squared correlation with original similarity matrix, $r^2(\mathbf{D}, \mathbf{D}_l^\lambda)$, caused by dropping feature $l$ (low correlation indicates high feature sensitivity); loss of squared correlation and corresponding feature rank caused by iterative dropping of the currently most sensitive feature (multiple application of top-level analysis with recursively reduced feature set); feature weighting based on gradients that point towards optimum state after random parameter perturbations of the adaptive similarity measure (graphs of ten independent runs are overlaid showing high reproducibility). Left column refers to adaptive Pearson correlation, right column to parametric Euclidean distance for the three investigated methods.

Most importantly, pairs of plots in the left column – corresponding to Pearson correlation similarity – and in the right column – displaying results for Euclidean distance – are rather different. Thus, as expected, the choice of data similarity measure has crucial influence on the highly rated features.

Row two for top level loss contains plots of the loss of correlation $r^2(\mathbf{D}, \mathbf{D}_l^\lambda)$ after deletion of attribute $l$. Both plots exhibit a common minimum around feature $l = 41$, pointing out these attributes as highly sensitive for both similarity measures. However, for other attributes just ratings are computed. It is pointed out that, due to data redundancy and the high number of 100 dimensions, the maximum correlation loss for many dropped features is still very close to one.

Row three, showing plots of rank and loss for iterative feature dropping, gives support to the top-ranked features around index 41 of high importance for correlation reconstruction. The loss described by the dotted lines has much higher variability in case of Pearson similarity than in case of Euclidean distance. Subsequent feature ranking is obtained by assigning their ascending sorting indices. These ranks have been divided by the number of dimensions in order to obtain a mapping into the value range of squared correlation. As a consequence of greedy feature selection, large-scale discontinuities appear in the resulting graphs.

Row four with response plots contains smooth non-ranked attribute weights obtained by gradient calculations. Three important properties are observed. First, indices around 41 for Pearson similarity are remarkably insensitive in contrast to the results from the other two approaches. Second, the results of ten independent runs of the gradient method display very high reproducibility. Third, the graphs for Euclidean distance in the bottom right panel are strikingly similar to the simple variance plot in the top right panel – the average squared correlation between the ten response graphs with the variance is $r^2(\text{variance}, \text{Euclidean response}) = 0.991$. This is a key observation. On one hand, this meets the expectation of the role of variance for Euclidean distance as a natural measure of data variability – although the presented approach measures, inversely, the sensitivity of the parametric Euclidean distance. On the other hand, this essential solution for the Euclidean distance induces high confidence in analog results for non-Euclidean case, like those given for the adaptive Pearson similarity. This approach can thus be regarded as generalization of the concept of variance to other types of parametric data similarity measures.

To conclude, quite different feature evaluations are obtained for the different approaches. This points out that feature dropping is structurally different from parametric measure perturbation. The case of correlation measure shows insensitivity to attribute scaling where entire feature dropping produces the highest loss, around index 41. However, in case of masked or weighted Euclidean distance, the special importance of that feature set around index 41 is common sense for all methods.

**Tomato Peel Chromatograms for Chemical Compound Analysis.** High performance liquid chromatography (HPLC) allows recording of high resolution spectra related to compound-specific absorbance rates. Especially the group of health protective flavonoids is of great interest for the evaluation of food crops. Here, a collection of tomato plants is studied at a wavelength of $280nm$ to capture the chemical constituents within the fruit peel. A measuring duration of $50min$ considered with a sampling of $1Hz$, producing values for 3000 retention times per fruit. Biological attention is put on 19 of these chromatograms to find intervals of retention times with characteristic variability in absorption. The integrated values in those intervals are proportional to the abundance of the corresponding chemical compounds. For precise further calculations, the chromatogram have

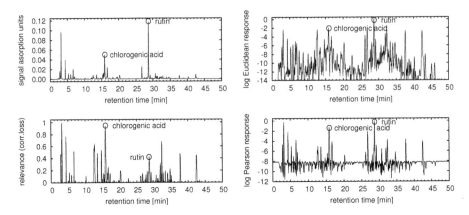

**Fig. 3.** Feature selection for tomato data set. Top left: one exemplary chromatogram from the data set used for feature rating. Bottom left: iterative correlation loss for feature dropping with Pearson similarity. Right: gradient responses for adaptive Euclidean distance (top) and parametric Pearson correlation (bottom). For comparison, two important substances representative for all chromatograms are encircled: chlorogenic acid and rutin.

been baseline-corrected and their peaks have been aligned by the correlation optimized warping method.

Fig. 3 contains results for different feature rating methods applied to the tomato peel chromatograms. The original chromatograms look very peaky if plotted with a condense time axis like in the top right panel; by zooming onto the time axis, however, smoother details become visible. A reason for not using adaptive Euclidean response is shown in the top right panel: two time intervals can be identified, $[10; 20]$ and $[25; 35]$, which intermediately drift to higher relevance values just because of a higher overall variability in these domains. A very good correspondence of Euclidean response and variance is supported by a high squared correlation value of $r^2$(log variance, log Euclidean response) $= 0.976$.

The strongly oscillating plot for feature variance is complemented by the Pearson correlation response, as shown in the lower left panel. A straight baseline is identified at a value of about -8, and the peaks provide much clear candidates of interesting retention times. For the present high-dimensional data set with few data points, iterative feature dropping for Pearson similarity yields very similar results, as given in the bottom left panel of Fig. 3. As a matter of fact, correlation-based chromatogram comparison usually has more biological impact than in Euclidean manner. This is already supported at the level of chromatogram peak alignment where correlation-optimized warping yields most accepted curve alignments. The Pearson correlation response in the lower left panel points out retention times that are in high agreement with biological knowledge. Moreover, the clear baseline can be used to define a threshold above which time intervals might be automatically integrated for further analysis.

**Barley Endosperm Gene Expression Data.** Discovery of sequential processes involved in tissue differentiation are available from gene expression data. The search for key identity genes specific for observed tissue differentiation is a valuable desire. Micro- and macroarray technology allows parallel recording of the abundance of thousands of gene expression intensities. The identification of key regulators from such a usually long list of expression values is a particularly challenging task. Here, log-normalized expression values for 11786 genes from in-house macroarray hybridization experiments are analyzed. Two independent series of experiments are available concerning the development of endosperm barley tissue at 0–26 days after flowering, sampled in steps of two days.

Analytic focus has been put on correlation-based feature identification. This overcomes limitations of Euclidean distance approaches that emphasize genes which are mainly related to high variance. Two lists of top-rated 25 genes out of 11786 are computed, one by feature dropping and the other by response

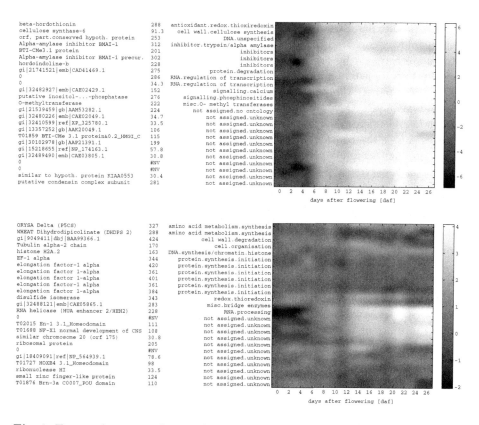

**Fig. 4.** Temporal gene regulation of top 25 genes in endosperm barley tissue. Upper panel: results from feature dropping. Bottom panel: results from gradient response analysis. Both panels are related to the Pearson similarity measure. Gene profiles have been ordered by a combination of one-dimensional self-organizing map and functional annotation. Shades of gray denote normalized gene expression intensities according to the reference bar. Text columns contain Blast description, Blast score, and functional category of genes.

gradients. Thereby, the two independent series of gene expression experiments are processed separately, their gene ranks are summed up, and the highest 25 sums of ranks are considered top candidate genes. Rank summation has been regarded as a valid operation after confirming that the squared correlation of the ranks of all genes is greater than 0.9. In order to compare results of feature dropping and response gradients, the temporal gene regulation profiles associated with the top-rated genes are plotted in Fig. 4.

In summary, feature evaluation based on Pearson correlation yields quite different results for feature dropping and gradient response analysis. The group of genes obtained by feature dropping (upper panel) exhibits common patterns of strong up-regulation. Among the top-rated 25 genes detected by feature dropping, most of them are found to be endosperm-specific and exclusively detected in *triticeae* species. In other words, the feature of up-regulation is considered important for characterizing the data set, which is a reasonable finding for the temporally related experiments. Nonetheless, this very prominent regulation characteristic could be captured by standard clustering techniques. Qualitatively new patterns are revealed by gradient response analysis (lower panel). Intermediate regulations are shown in addition to the group of moderately up-regulated genes (Fig. 4, lower panel). Thus, again, variability alone does not take too much influence on gene selection. Interestingly, most detected genes that are expressed during late endosperm development are connected to protein synthesis initiation processes. These are considered to have an important functional role during the peak of product accumulation.

## 4    Conclusions

A new approach to unsupervised feature selection has been proposed. Its basic principle is the detection of features that maximum decorrelate original and feature-masked data relationships. These features are supposed to be most critical for faithful relationship reconstruction. The considered data relationships are defined by appropriate data similarity measures, such as the presented Euclidean distance and Pearson correlation. Sensitivity is obtained as response to feature dropping or as gradient-based reaction to small perturbations in parametric formulations of the utilized similarity measure. Both ways measure correlation loss, but, by construction, they are structurally different. As has been demonstrated in the experiments, gradient-based response analysis can be regarded as for measure-specific counterpart of variance. This canonic interpretation, its computational advantage over greedy feature dropping, and the parallel feature probing makes response analysis the preferred feature selection method. Whichever technology is chosen, reasonable automatic feature rating essentially helps to pre-structure the data, to get different views and to formulate hypotheses about the data sets, like for the three examined high-dimensional data sets. In unsupervised scenarios the data-driven, method-intrinsic dynamic fully determines the outcome; therefore, since unsupervised methods optimize different goals, objective quality criteria are missing in comparisons, and the results must be judged by a combination of subjectiveness and additional knowledge. In future studies, further potential of the proposed methods will be assessed in close cooperation with biological experts and their additional background knowledge.

*Acknowledgement.* The work is supported by BMBF grant FKZ 0313115, GABI-SEED-II.

# References

1. J. Dy and C. Brodley. Feature selection for unsupervised learning. *Journal of Machine Learning Research*, 5:845–889, 2004.
2. B. Hammer, M. Strickert, and T. Villmann. Supervised neural gas with general similarity measure. *Neural Processing Letters*, 21(1):21–44, 2005.
3. N. Søndberg-Madsen, C. Thomsen, and J. Pena. Unsupervised feature subset selection. In *Proceedings on the Workshop on Probabilistic Graphical Models for Classification*, pages 71–82, 2003.
4. M. Strickert, S. Teichmann, N. Sreenivasulu, and U. Seiffert. High-Throughput Multi-Dimensional Scaling (HiT-MDS) for cDNA-array expression data. In W. Duch et al., editor, *Artificial Neural Networks: Biological Inspirations, Part I, LNCS 3696*, pages 625–634. Springer, 2005.
5. L. Yu and H. Liu. Feature selection for high-dimensional data: A fast correlation-based filter solution. In *Proceedings of the 20th International Conference on Machine Leaning (ICML-03)*, pages 856–863, 2003.

# Learning and Feature Selection Using the Set Covering Machine with Data-Dependent Rays on Gene Expression Profiles

Hans A. Kestler[1,2], Wolfgang Lindner[3], and André Müller[2]

[1] Neural Information Processing, University of Ulm, 89069 Ulm
hans.kestler@uni-ulm.de
[2] Internal Medicine I, University Hospital Ulm, Robert-Koch-Str. 8, 89081 Ulm
lindner@informatik.uni-ulm.de
[3] Theoretical Computer Science, University of Ulm, 89069 Ulm, Germany
andre.mueller@uniklinik-ulm.de

**Abstract.** Microarray technologies are increasingly being used in biological and medical sciences for high throughput analyses of genetic information on the genome, transcriptome and proteome levels. The differentiation between cancerous and benign processes in the body often poses a difficult diagnostic problem in the clinical setting while being of major importance for the treatment of patients. In this situation, feature reduction techniques capable of reducing the dimensionality of data are essential for building predictive tools based on classification. We extend the set covering machine of Marchand and Shawe-Taylor to data dependent rays in order to achieve a feature reduction and direct interpretation of the found conjunctions of intervals on individual genes. We give bounds for the generalization error as a function of the amount of data compression and the number of training errors achieved during training. In experiments with artificial data and a real world data set of gene expression profiles from the pancreas we show the utility of the approach and its applicability to microarray data classification.

## 1 Background

Microarray technologies are increasingly being used in biological and medical sciences for high throughput analyses of genetic information on the genome, transcriptome, and proteome levels. Gene-expression microarrays permit the estimation of mRNA concentrations for a large number of genes in parallel. These types of analysis generate vast amounts of data, often in the form of large lists of genes differentially expressed between different sample sets being insufficient for class prediction purposes. One challenge involves finding biologically meaningful subgroups of genes that are congruently expressed in multiple experiments (e.g. cell lines under different conditions or tissues from different disease states). Especially the differentiation between cancerous and benign processes in the body often poses a difficult diagnostic problem in the clinical setting while being of major importance for the treatment of patients. In this situation techniques

F. Schwenker and S. Marinai (Eds.): ANNPR 2006, LNAI 4087, pp. 286–297, 2006.

for generating simple rules on the expression values are of major importance. This usually implies a reduction of the dimensionality of the data either with principal component approaches or with feature selection methods. The latter is clearly more desirable, since these methods retain a direct interpretability if the subsequent classification concept is not too complex.

One of the few learning algorithms which provably performs well in the presence of many irrelevant attributes is the algorithm for learning conjunctions of few Boolean variables due to Haussler [1]. Given a sample of size $m$ whose examples are labeled according to a conjunction with at most $s$ out of $n$ Boolean variables, the algorithm finds a consistent conjunction with at most $s \log m$ variables in polynomial time in $n$ and $m$. By a standard Occam's Razor bound based on the cardinality of the hypothesis class it follows that a sample size $m$ which is linear in $s$ but only logarithmic in the dimension $n$ suffices to guarantee a small generalization error with high confidence. This means that the algorithm performs well even when the dimension $n$ is exponential in the sample size $m$, provided that sample is labeled by a conjunction which depends only on very few attributes.

The set covering machine (SCM) of Marchand and Shawe-Taylor [2] is a generalization of the algorithm of Haussler where the Boolean variables are replaced by a set of *features*, where each feature is a Boolean-valued function on the example space. In general, the example space may be an arbitrary subset of $\mathbb{R}^n$, each feature may depend on all of the $n$ attributes, and the set of features used by the SCM may depend on the given sample. The algorithm of Haussler is then used to find a conjunction of few features which makes only few errors on the sample to allow a trade-off between accuracy and complexity. Marchand and Shawe-Taylor further consider the specific set of so-called data-dependent balls as features and bound the generalization error of the corresponding SCM in terms of the amount of data compression the SCM achieves during training. The bound is obtained by a technique first used by Littlestone and Warmuth [3]. Subsequently, Marchand et al. [4] consider data-dependent half-spaces as an alternative to data-dependent balls.

In [5], Marchand and Shah consider rays as features and an algorithm similar to the SCM to classify gene expression data. Rays are simple threshold functions which depend on a single attribute. The algorithm is guided by a PAC-Bayesian style analysis of the generalization error as initiated by McAllester [6]. This approach amounts to specify a prior distribution $P$ on the set of conjunctions of rays. Then the error bound applies to the Bayesian classifier which is the weighted majority vote over all binary hypothesis and where the weight corresponds to the posterior distribution $Q$ induced by the prior distribution $P$ and the given sample $S$. The resulting algorithm attains good theoretical and experimental results on high-dimensional gene expression data. However, the Bayesian classifier can no longer be expressed as a simple conjunction of rays and this might significantly aggravate the interpretation of the classifier in the clinical setting.

In this paper we use the SCM with *data-dependent rays* as features. The resulting classifier is then a simple conjunction of a small number of rays. We give bounds on the generalization error based on both an analysis of the VC dimension of the (data-independent) hypotheses space as well as on the amount of data compression the SCM achieves during training. Finally we apply the proposed algorithm to gene expression data with the task of distinguishing between malignant and inflammatory tumors of the pancreas.

## 2    The Set Covering Machine with Rays as Features

In order to describe the SCM of Marchand and Shawe-Taylor [2] we will briefly review the algorithm for learning conjunctions with few Boolean variables of Haussler [1]. Suppose that we are given a sample $S$ of examples from the Boolean hypercube $X = \{0,1\}^n$ where the examples are labeled according to some conjunction with at most $r$ variables. Let $P$ and $N$ denote the subsets of all positive and negative examples from $S$, respectively. We say that a variable $x_j$ is *consistent* with a labeled example $(\mathbf{x}, y)$ if the $j$-th coordinate of $\mathbf{x}$ coincides with its label $y$. The aim is to find a conjunction which is consistent with $S$ and posses as few variables as possible.

The algorithm is based on the observation that a conjunction

$$\bigwedge_{x_j \in R} x_j$$

is consistent with the sample $S$ if and only if the set of variables $R$ possess the following two properties.

1. Every variable $x_j \in R$ is consistent with each positive example $\mathbf{x} \in P$.
2. For every negative example $\mathbf{x} \in N$ there is at least one variable $x_j \in R$ which is consistent with $\mathbf{x}$.

These two properties can be equivalently expressed in terms of the collections of sets $R_j$ and $Q_j$, where $R_j$ is the set of all positive examples $\mathbf{x} \in P$ such that the variable $x_j$ is not consistent with $\mathbf{x}$, and $Q_j$ is the set of all negative examples $\mathbf{x} \in N$ such that the variable $x_j$ is consistent with $\mathbf{x}$ ($R$ is a set of variables, whereas $R_j$ and $Q_j$ are sets of examples). Then the first property is equivalent to the fact that $R_j = \emptyset$ for all $x_j \in R$, and the second property is equivalent to saying that the union of sets $Q_j$ for $x_j \in R$ *covers* the sets $N$ in the sense that $\bigcup_{x_j \in R} Q_j = N$.

The algorithm of finding such a set of variables can be described by the following two steps:

1. Find a set of variables that is consistent with all positive examples
2. Cover this set with as few subsets of variables, that are consistent with the negative examples.

The task of finding the *smallest* such set $R$ can be easily transformed into an instance of the *Minimal Set Cover Problem*, a well-known NP-complete problem [7] and is thus intractable. There is, however, a simple greedy strategy to efficiently find an approximate solution. Here we successively select the variables

$x_k$ for which $R_k = \emptyset$ and $|Q_k|$ is maximal and thus $Q_k$ covers as many negative examples as possible. After the selection of $x_k$ for inclusion in $R$ we discard $Q_k$ from all $Q_j$ and repeat this process with the remaining variables until there is no negative example left to cover. It is not hard to see that after at most $r \log m$ selected variables we have found a cover of $N$ and thus the resulting conjunction is consistent with $S$. Note that the size of the conjunction is only by the factor $\log m$ larger than the optimal solution of size $r$. Furthermore, the running time is polynomial in $n$ and $m$. For a more detailed description of the algorithm we refer to [8].

Now let us turn to the SCM algorithm. In contrast to the Boolean setting we are now given a sample $S$ of labeled examples from an example space $X$ which may be any subset of the $n$-dimensional real space $\mathrm{R}^n$. The Boolean variables are replaced by a set of *features* $H$, where each feature $h_j \in H$ is an arbitrary Boolean-valued function on $X$. The set of features $H$ is assumed to be finite but may depend on the sample $S$. The collections $R_j$ and $Q_j$ are defined analogously. That is, $R_j$ is the subset of positive examples from $P$ that are misclassified by $h_j$, and $Q_j$ is the subset of negative examples from $N$ that are correctly classified by $h_j$. The aim is now to find a small subset of features $R \subseteq H$ such that the conjunction

$$h(\mathbf{x}) = \bigwedge_{h_j \in R} h_j(\mathbf{x})$$

is consistent with $S$. This will be done in a greedy manner similarly as above.

In order to allow a trade-off between accuracy and complexity we are given additionally a *early stopping* value $s$ and a *penalty* parameter $p$. Rather than solely based on the the cardinality $|Q_j|$ under the constraint that $R_j = \emptyset$ as above, now the greedy strategy selects the features $h_j$ according to their *usefulness*

$$U_j = |Q_j| - p|R_j| \ .$$

Furthermore, the SCM algorithm stops as soon as the number of selected features reaches the value of $s$. Thus, the parameter $s$ bounds the number of selected features, and the parameter $p$ controls the fraction of errors on the positive examples among all errors on $S$. Note that when $p$ and $s$ are both set to $\infty$, then the SCM algorithm corresponds precisely to Haussler's algorithm in the Boolean setting where $H$ is just the set of variables $x_j$ for $j = 1, \ldots, n$. A more formal description of the algorithm can be found in Figure 1.

## 2.1   VC Dimension

We first consider the SCM with *data-independent* rays as its set of features and bound the generalization error of the corresponding SCM in terms of the VC dimension of its hypotheses space (cf. [9]). A *ray* over the example space $X = \mathrm{R}^n$ is a simple threshold function of the form

$$h_j^t(\mathbf{x}) = \begin{cases} 1 & \text{if } (\mathbf{x})_j \geq t \\ 0 & \text{otherwise} \end{cases}$$

**Algorithm** SCM($S, H, s, p$)

1. Initially set $P \leftarrow \{\mathbf{x} \mid (x, 1) \in S\}$, $N \leftarrow \{\mathbf{x} \mid (x, 0) \in S\}$ and $R \leftarrow \emptyset$.
2. For each $h_j \in H$ let $Q_j = \{\mathbf{x} \in N \mid h_j(\mathbf{x}) = 0\}$ and $R_j = \{\mathbf{x} \in P \mid h_j(\mathbf{x}) = 0\}$.
3. Select the feature $h_k \in H$ with largest usefulness $U_k = |Q_k| - p|R_k|$. If $Q_k = \emptyset$ then goto step 7.
4. Set $R \leftarrow R \cup \{h_k\}$.
5. For each $h_j \in H$ set $Q_j \leftarrow Q_j \setminus Q_k$ and $R_j \leftarrow R_j \setminus R_k$.
6. If $\bigcup_{h_j \in R} Q_j = N$ or $|R| = s$ then go to step 7. Else go to step 3.
7. Return $h = \bigwedge_{h_j \in R} h_j$

**Fig. 1.** The SCM Algorithm

where $(\mathbf{x})_j$ denotes the $j$-th coordinate of the vector $x \in X$ and $t$ is a real-valued threshold. The only constraint we impose on the set of rays when used as the set of features of a SCM is that the thresholds are taken form a finite set of values and consequently also the corresponding set of all rays over $X = \mathrm{R}^n$ is finite.

We now bound the VC dimension of the hypotheses space of all conjunctions over a bounded number of rays (with no constraint on the number of admissible thresholds) as follows.

**Theorem 1.** *Let $H_n^r$ denote the hypotheses space of all conjunctions of at most $r$ rays over the example space $X = \mathrm{R}^n$. Then,*

$$r \log \left(\frac{n}{r}\right) \le \mathrm{VCdim}(H_n^r) \le 2r \log \left(\frac{n}{r}\right) + 6r \ .$$

It is well-known that the generalization error $\mathrm{err}_D(h)$ of hypothesis $h$ produced by a learning algorithm can be bounded in terms of the VC dimension of its hypotheses space [10,9]. Recall that the generalization error $\mathrm{err}_D(h)$ is the probability that $h(\mathbf{x}) \ne y$ for some labeled example $(\mathbf{x}, y)$ drawn according to $D$. We want to bound the generalization error in terms of the number of features $r$ and the number of errors $k$ of the hypothesis $h$ produced by the SCM with rays as its set of features. Note that both $r$ and $k$ are quantities which may depend on $S$. For this reason we use the following bound of [11]. Let $H_1 \subseteq H_2 \subseteq \cdots \subseteq H_M$ be a nested sequence of hypotheses classes such that $\mathrm{VCdim}(H_i) = d_i$ for $i = 1, \ldots, M$, let $D$ be any probability distribution on $X \times \{0, 1\}$, and let $S$ be a random sample of $m$ labeled examples drawn independently according to $D$. Then with probability $1 - \delta$, if a learning algorithm finds a hypothesis $h \in H_i$ which makes $k$ errors on the training set $S$, then the generalization error $\mathrm{err}_D(h)$ is at most

$$\frac{2k}{m} + \frac{4}{m} \left( d_i \log \left(\frac{2em}{d_i}\right) + \log \left(\frac{4M(m+1)}{\delta}\right) \right)$$

provided that $d \le m$. Applying Theorem 1 we get the following bound for the SCM with rays as its set of features.

**Corollary 1.** *Let $D$ be any probability distribution on $X \times \{0, 1\}$, and and let $S$ be a random sample of $m$ labeled examples drawn independently according to $D$.*

*Suppose that the SCM algorithm with any finite set of rays as its set of features on the sample $S$ produces a hypothesis $h = \bigwedge_{h_j^t \in R} h_j^t$ with $|R| = r$ and such that $h$ makes $k$ errors on $S$. Then with probability $1 - \delta$ the generalization error $\mathrm{err}_D(h)$ is at most*

$$\frac{2k}{m} + \frac{4}{m}\left(\left(2r\log\left(\frac{n}{r}\right) + 6r\right)\log\left(\frac{2em}{r\log(n/r)}\right) + \log\left(\frac{4n(m+1)}{\delta}\right)\right)$$

*provided that $r \le \frac{m}{2\log n + 6}$.*

## 2.2   Sample Compression

Bounds on the generalization error based on the VC dimension are generally rather pessimistic. Better bounds can sometimes be achieved by considering the amount of data compression a learning algorithm achieves during training. For this purpose we consider *data-dependent* rays as features for the SCM algorithm. That is, for a given sample

$$S = ((\mathbf{x}_1, y_1), \ldots, (\mathbf{x}_m, y_m))$$

with examples from $X = \mathbb{R}^n$, each feature $h_j^i \in H$ has the form

$$h_j^i(\mathbf{x}) = \begin{cases} 1 & \text{if } (\mathbf{x})_j \ge (\mathbf{x}_i)_j \\ 0 & \text{otherwise} \end{cases}$$

for some position $j \in \{1, \ldots, n\}$ and some index $i \in \{1, \ldots, m\}$ of a positive example $\mathbf{x}_i \in P$. Recall that $(\mathbf{x})_j$ denotes the $j$-th coordinate of any vector $x \in X$. Thus, the final hypothesis has the form

$$h = \bigwedge_{h_j^i \in R} h_j^i \ .$$

Let us now see how the corresponding SCM algorithm can be regarded as a compression scheme for the sample $S$. Let $A$ denote the SCM algorithm with data-dependent rays as its set of features and with parameters $s$ and $p$. Then $A$ can be decomposed into a *compression* function $f$ and a *reconstruction* function $g$ as follows. The function $f$ maps the sample $S$ to the *compression set* $S_I$ and an additional set of positions $J$, where $I = \{i \mid h_j^i \in R\}$ and $J = \{j \mid h_j^i \in R\}$ and $S_I$ denotes the subsequence of $S$ which consists only of those positive examples $\mathbf{x}_i \in P$ with indices $i \in I$. The reconstruction function $g$ takes $S_I$ and $J$ as inputs and returns the hypothesis

$$g(S_I, J) = \bigwedge_{j \in J} h_j^{t_j}$$

where the threshold $t_j$ of each ray $h_j^{t_j}$ is defined as $t_j = \min\{(\mathbf{x})_j \mid \mathbf{x} \in S_I\}$.

When $A$ is run with penalty $p = \infty$, then each feature $h_j^i$ selected by $A$ is consistent with all positive examples $\mathbf{x} \in P$. This means that for each $h_j^i \in R$ we have $\mathbf{x}_i \in S_I$ and $(\mathbf{x})_j \geq (\mathbf{x}_i)_j$ for all $\mathbf{x} \in S_I$ and, hence, $(\mathbf{x}_i)_j = \min\{(\mathbf{x})_j \mid x \in S_I\}$. It follows that the reconstructed hypothesis $g(S_I, J)$ coincides with the hypothesis $h$ produced by $A$ and thus $A(S) = g(f(S))$. Note that if $h$ makes no errors on $S$ then the labels of all examples from $S$ can be determined solely from the compression set $S_I$ and from the additional information $J$. In this sense $A$ indeed can be regarded as a compression scheme for $S$.

When $A$ is run with penalty $p < \infty$, then a selected feature $h_j^i$ might be inconsistent with some positive examples $x \in S_I$. For this reason we slightly modify the SCM algorithm $A$ by considering a feature $h_j^i$ for inclusion in the current set $R$ only if $(\mathbf{x}_i)_j \leq (\mathbf{x})_j$ for all examples $\mathbf{x}$ in the current compression set $S_I$. This modification implies that all features $h_j^i$ in the final set $R$ satisfy $\mathbf{x}_i \in S_I$ and $(\mathbf{x})_j \geq (\mathbf{x}_i)_j$ for all $\mathbf{x} \in S_I$ as in the case of $p = \infty$ above. Thus for the modified algorithm $A$ we have $A(S) = g(f(S))$ also in the case $p < \infty$.

By using similar arguments as in [12,2] we can now bound the generalization error in terms of the size of the compression set $S_I$, the number of features used in the hypothesis $h$, and the number of errors $h$ makes on $S$ as follows.

**Theorem 2.** *Let $D$ be a probability distribution on $X \times \{0,1\}$, and let $S$ be a random sample of $m$ labeled examples drawn independently according to $D$. Suppose the SCM algorithm with data-dependent rays as its set of features on the sample $S$ finds a hypothesis $h = \bigwedge_{h_j^i \in R} h_j^i$ which makes $k$ errors on $S$, such that $|I| = d$ and $|J| = r$ for the sets $I = \{i \mid h_j^i \in R\}$ and $J = \{j \mid h_j^i \in R\}$. Then with probability $1 - \delta$ the error $\mathrm{err}_D(h)$ is at most*

$$\varepsilon(d,r,k) = 1 - \exp\left(-\frac{1}{m-d-k}\ln\left(\frac{B(d,r,k)}{\delta(d,r,k)}\right)\right)$$

*where*

$$B(d,r,k) = \binom{m}{d}\binom{n}{r}\binom{m-d}{k}$$

*and*

$$\delta(d,r,k) = \delta\left(\frac{\pi^2}{6}\right)^{-3}((d+1)(r+1)(k+1))^{-2}$$

*Proof.* Let $S = ((\mathbf{x}_1, y_1), \ldots, (\mathbf{x}_m, y_m))$ and let $f$ and $g$ be the compression scheme as described above. Recall that $f(S) = (S_I, J)$ and $g(S_I, J) = h$. Further let $K = \{i \mid h(\mathbf{x}_i) \neq y_i\}$ be the set of $k$ indices of examples $\mathbf{x}_i$ which are misclassified by $h$. Note that the compression set $S_I$ is always correctly classified by $h$ and hence we may assume that the sets $I$ and $K$ are disjoint. We want to bound the probability

$$\Pr_{S \sim D^m}\left(\mathrm{err}_D(h) > \varepsilon(d,r,k)\right)$$

$$= \sum \Pr_{S \sim D^m}\left(\mathrm{err}_D(h) > \varepsilon(d_0, r_0, k_0), I = I_0, J = J_0, K = K_0\right)$$

where the sum is taken over all possible values $0 \leq d_0 \leq m$, $0 \leq r_0 \leq n$ and $0 \leq k_0 \leq m - d_0$, and all possible sets $I_0 \subseteq \{1, \ldots, m\}$, $J_0 \subseteq \{1, \ldots, n\}$ and $K_0 \subseteq \{1, \ldots, m\} \setminus I_0$ with $|I_0| = d_0$, $|J_0| = r_0$ and $|K_0| = k_0$.

To bound the probability of $\mathrm{err}_D(h) > \varepsilon(d_0, r_0, k_0)$ with respect to fixed sets $I = I_0$, $J = J_0$ and $K = K_0$ of cardinalities $d_0$, $r_0$, $k_0$, first observe that $h = g(S_{I_0}, J_0)$ and hence the hypothesis $h$ is fixed as soon as the examples in the subsequence $S_{I_0}$ are drawn. Since the examples in $S$ are drawn independently according to $D$, we may further assume that the $d_0 + k_0$ examples from the subsequences $S_{I_0}$ and $S_{K_0}$ are drawn first. Next the remaining $m - d_0 - k_0$ examples of $S$ are drawn. If $\mathrm{err}_D(h) > \varepsilon$ then the probability that a single example drawn according to $D$ is consistent with $h$ is less than $1 - \varepsilon$. It follows that

$$\Pr_{S \sim D^m} \left( \mathrm{err}_D(h) > \varepsilon(d_0, r_0, k_0), I = I_0, J = J_0, K = K_0 \right)$$

$$< (1 - \varepsilon(d_0, r_0, k_0))^{m - d_0 - k_0} = \frac{\delta(d_0, r_0, k_0)}{B(d_0, r_0, k_0)}$$

Note that $B(d_0, r_0, k_0)$ is just the number of possible ways to choose the sets $I_0$, $J_0$ and $K_0$ of cardinalities $d_0$, $r_0$ and $k_0$. Hence, by summing up over all possible $d_0$, $r_0$, $k_0$, $I_0$, $J_0$ and $K_0$ we get

$$\Pr_{S \sim D^m} \left( \mathrm{err}_D(h) > \varepsilon(d, r, k) \right) < \sum \frac{\delta(d_0, r_0, k_0)}{B(d_0, r_0, k_0)} < \delta$$

where for the last inequality we additionally used the fact that $\sum_{i \geq 1} 1/i^2 = \pi^2/6$.

$\square$

The bound of Theorem 2 is 0.27 for a data set with $n = 20$ dimensions $m = 100$ examples, 2 resulting features and 1 error on the training set ($\delta = 0.01$). The PAC bound from Corollary 1 is 7.23 in this case.

## 3    Experimental Results

The hypothesis space consisting of conjunctions of left-open intervals (the quadrant space) is often too restrictive - the concept could lie as well on the right side of a threshold - the union of the left open and the right open quadrant concept space is always used in the following.

### 3.1    Learning Algorithms

The following algorithms were applied to artificial and microarray data.

**SCM.1** Choose $p = \infty$ so that only left- and right-open rays consistent with the positive examples were used. The SCM was trained until no errors on the training set remained ($s = \infty$). The possible ties in step 3. (Figure 1) were recursively broken to generate equivalent solutions (at most 50 distinct solutions were sought).

**SCM.2** As SCM.1 but this time the classifier with the lowest theoretical generalization bound according to Theorem 2 was taken. A run of SCM with
$s = \infty$ defines at step 3. (Figure 1) a sequence of features $i_1, i_2 \ldots i_{s'}$ (in this
order), that are combined by conjunctions, such that the classifiers $(C_k)_1^{s'}$,
$C_k$ including the hypotheses $h_{i_1} \ldots h_{i_k}$, form a sequence of increasing complexity $C_1 \subset C_2 \ldots \subset C_{s'}$. The $C_k$ with the smallest generalization bound
was taken.

**SCM.3** For this classifier $p$ was varied over every fifth value of the set $\{i/j \mid i = 1 \ldots m_n, j = 1 \ldots m_p\}$ sorted in ascending order and $p = \infty$. All possible $\leq m$
rays were generated for each feature. The theoretical bound from Theorem
2 was used to select the optimal classifier(s).

**SVM** A support vector machine with linear kernel was used (the support vector implementation from the R [13] package e1071 [14] was called with *ker-
nel="linear"*, *scale=FALSE*.

**1-nn** One-nearest-neighbor with Euclidean distances.

**Cart** Classification tree with pruning (R package rpart [15] with Gini impurity
measure).

### 3.2 Artificial Data

Artificial data was generated with a randomly chosen concept $C$ from the union
of the left-open and right-open quadrant hypothesis space $Q_k \cup Q_k^c$ on the domain $\mathcal{X} = [0,1]^k$ for $k < n$ relevant coordinates for $k = 5$. Once generated the
concept $C$ was held constant and was used to generate $m_p = 50$ positive samples
and $m_n = 50$ negative samples with a uniform distribution of the coordinates in
$C$ and in $C^c$. The remaining $n - k$ coordinates were filled up with uniformly distributed random numbers on $[0,1]^{n-k}$ in order to create $n$-dimensional random
vectors with $k$ relevant and $n - k$ irrelevant features. The number of dimensions
$n$ were varied from $\{20, 100, 200, 3000\}$.

| Data Set / n | SCM.1 ($p = \infty$) | | | | SCM.2 ($p = \infty$) | | | | SCM.3 | | | | | |
|---|---|---|---|---|---|---|---|---|---|---|---|---|---|---|
| | TR | TE | size | num | TR | TE | size | num | TR | TE | size | num | s | p |
| rnd/20 | 0 | 31 | 2 | 1 | 0 | 31 | 2 | 1 | 0 | 31 | 2 | 1 | 2 | 3 |
| rnd/100 | 0 | 55.75 | 3 | 8 | 1 | 43 | 2 | 1 | 1 | 43 | 2 | 1 | 2 | 4 |
| rnd/200 | 0 | 78.42 | 4 | 38 | 2 | 59 | 2 | 1 | 2 | 49.78 | 2 | 9 | 2 | 4 |
| rnd/3000 | 0 | 60.5 | 3 | 4 | 2 | 38 | 2 | 1 | 2 | 20.6 | 2 | 4 | 2 | 4 |

| Data Set / n | 1-nn | | SVM | | cart | |
|---|---|---|---|---|---|---|
| | TR | TE | TR | TE | TR | TE |
| rnd/20 | 0 | 264 | 3 | 139 | 3 | 64 |
| rnd/100 | 0 | 387 | 0 | 245 | 3 | 53 |
| rnd/200 | 0 | 457 | 0 | 318 | 5 | 78 |
| rnd/3000 | 0 | 491 | 0 | 448 | 6 | 43 |

After training the classifiers the generalization error was estimated by applying the trained classifier to an independent test set with 500 positive and 500 negative samples which were chosen i.i.d. from $C$ and $C^c$.

### 3.3 Application to Microarray Data

The described method was applied to a previously published gene expression dataset (see Buchholz et al. [16]) with $n = 169$ features and 62 samples divided into a training set of $m = 42$ ($m_p = 25$ and $m_n = 17$) and a test set of 12 positive and 8 negative samples. The best result on the test set was obtained with the following classifier (Algorithm SCM.1):

| s | $err_{TR}$ | $err_{TE}$ | feature | ray |
|---|---|---|---|---|
| 1 | 4 | 4 | Annexin A2 (ANXA2) | $[0.5505, \infty)$ |
| 2 | 1 | 4 | serine/threonine-protein kinase PLK1 | $[0.1245, \infty)$ |
| 3 | 0 | 3 | Asparagine synthetase (= ts11, a G1 prog protein) | $[0.982, \infty)$ |

For $s > 1$ every preceding feature $s' < s$ is included in the classifier (conjunction).

We have compared the ray learning algorithm with other standard methods on the PaCa data. PaCa training and test set, and $10\times$ 5-fold cross-validation results are given in the table below. For the SCM simulations up to 50 solutions were allowed. Results are given as cases (mean $\pm$ stdev):

| PaCa | TR | TE | features | solutions | CV |
|---|---|---|---|---|---|
| 1-nn | 0 | 2 | | | $14.1 \pm 1.45$ |
| SVM | 0 | 6 | | | $13.8 \pm 2.82$ |
| CART | 2 | 3 | | | $7.9 \pm 1.60$ |
| SCM.1 | 0 | $5.46 \pm 1.04$ | $3 \pm 0$ | 37 | $19.62 \pm 2.76$ |
| SCM.2 | 0 | $7 \pm 0$ | $3 \pm 0$ | 2 | $17.7 \pm 2.46$ |
| SCM.3 | $1 \pm 0$ | $5.25 \pm 0.96$ | $3 \pm 0$ | 4 | $16.15 \pm 2.13$ |

## 4   Discussion and Conclusion

In contrast to the original SCM, which uses data dependent balls, the proposed conjunction of rays allows a direct correspondence to the original feature space leading to concise interpretable hypotheses, which in turn may trigger further biological investigations. It is easy to show that for high-dimensional spaces with a low sample size the probability to find a consistent hypothesis reaches one.

Malignant and inflammatory tumors of the pancreas could be separated with 3 genes (which would be improbable for random data) leading to a low error on the test set. The results on the artificial data indicate a very good performance of the SCM with data dependent rays when there are only a few informative features within a large set of features containing noise. This construction was chosen to resemble the microarray data, as it is assumed that in standard microarray studies the number of genes which are regulated across the different conditions is low in comparison to the total number of genes investigated. The nearest neighbor and the support vector machine attained almost an error rate of 50% on the test sets. It seems that in these cases feature reduction is of greater importance than the complexity of the classifier. Even for the highly selected (for involvement in cancer) gene sets used in the PaCa data the performance is still comparable to SVMs, only CART gave better results here.

Extensions of the scheme could include the optimization of the rays using different utility functions and combination of sets of consistent hypotheses to possibly increase robustness or to consider margins of the rays to break ties of equivalent greedy solutions.

The main advantage of fusing decisions on singular features is the independence of a precise knowledge of their scale. For instance it is still unclear on what scale expression values in microarray experiments are. It is argued that only comparisons of expression values within a gene are reasonable. With our approach we only rely on an ordinal scale. Decision tree algorithms allowing only axis parallel splits behave similar in this aspect, but have an infinite VC dimension and thus possibly generate much more complex decision rules. In contrast our algorithm only generates rules of the form "IF expression for gene A is above 3.4 AND expression for gene B is below 2.5 AND ... THEN the risk of the subject having disease C is increased". These types of rules seem to be much more appropriate for performing diagnosis or differential diagnosis in a clinical setting.

## Acknowledgments

This work is supported by the German Science Foundation, SFB 518, Project C5 (HAK and AM) and the Stifterverband für die Deutsche Wissenschaft (HAK).

## References

1. Haussler, D.: Quantifying inductive bias: AI learning algorithms and Valiant's learning framework. Artificial Intelligence **36** (1988) 177–221
2. Marchand, M., Shawe-Taylor, J.: The set covering machine. Journal of Machine Learning Research **3** (2002) 723–746
3. Littlestone, N., Warmuth, M.: Relating data compression and learnability. Technical report, University of California, Santa Cruz (1986)
4. Marchand, M., Shah, M., Shawe-Taylor, J., Sokolova, M.: The set covering machine with data-dependent half-spaces. In: Proceedings of the Twentieth International Conference on Machine Learning (ICML). (2003) 520–527
5. Marchand, M., Shah, M.: PAC-Bayes Learning of Conjunctions and Classification of Gene-Expression Data. In Saul, L.K., Weiss, Y., Bottou, L., eds.: Advances in Neural Information Processing Systems 17. MIT Press, Cambridge, MA (2005) 881–888

6. McAllester, D.: Some PAC-Bayesian theorems. Machine Learning **37** (1999) 355–363

7. Garey, M., Johnson, D.: Computers and Intractability – A Guide to the Theory of NP-Completeness. Freeman and Company (1979)

8. Kearns, M., Vazirani, U.: An Introduction to Computational Learning Theory. MIT Press (1994)

9. Vapnik, V.: Statistical Learning Theory. Wiley (1998)

10. Blumer, A., Ehrenfeucht, A., Haussler, D., Warmuth, M.K.: Learnability and the Vapnik-Chervonenkis dimension. Journal of the ACM **36** (1989) 929–965

11. Shawe-Taylor, J., Bartlett, P.L., Williamson, R.C., Anthony., M.: Structural risk minimization over data-dependent hierarchies. IEEE Trans. on Information Theory **44** (1998) 1926–1940

12. Floyd, S., Warmuth, M.: Sample compression, learnability, and the Vapnik-Chervonenkis dimension. Machine Learning **21** (1995) 269–304

13. R Development Core Team: R: A Language and Environment for Statistical Computing. R Foundation for Statistical Computing, Vienna, Austria. (2006) ISBN 3-900051-07-0.

14. Dimitriadou, E., Hornik, K., Leisch, F., Meyer, D., Weingessel, A.: e1071: Misc Functions of the Department of Statistics (e1071), TU Wien. (2006) R package version 1.5-13.

15. Therneau, T.M., port by Brian Ripley <ripley@stats.ox.ac.uk>, B.A.R.: rpart: Recursive Partitioning. (2005) R package version 3.1-27.

16. Buchholz, M., Kestler, H.A., Bauer, A., Bock, W., Rau, B., Leder, G., Kratzer, W., Bommer, M., Scarpa, A., Schilling, M., Adler, G., Hoheisel, J., Gress, T.: Specialized DNA arrays for the differentiation of pancreatic tumors. Clin. Cancer Res. **11** (2005) 8048–54

# Author Index

# Lecture Notes in Artificial Intelligence (LNAI)